Abortion Bibliography
for 1976

Abortion Bibliography
for 1976

Compiled by
Mary K. Floyd

Whitston Publishing Company
Troy, New York
1978

PREFACE

ABORTION BIBLIOGRAPHY for 1976 is the sixth annual
list of books and articles surrounding the subject of abortion
in the preceeding year. It appears serially each fall as a
contribution toward documenting in one place as compre-
hensively as possible the literature of one of our central
social issues. It is an attempt at a comprehensive world
bibliography.

Searches in compiling this material have covered the
following sources: APPLIED SCIENCE AND TECHNOLOGY
INDEX; BIBLIOGRAPHIC INDEX; BIOLOGICAL ABSTRACTS;
BRITISH BOOKS IN PRINT; BRITISH HUMANITIES INDEX;
BUSINESS PERIODICALS INDEX; CANADIAN PERIODICAL
INDEX; CATHOLIC PERIODICALS AND LITERATURE INDEX;
CUMULATIVE BOOK INDEX; CURRENT INDEX TO JOURNALS
IN EDUCATION; EDUCATION INDEX; GUIDE TO SOCIAL
SCIENCE AND RELIGION IN PERIODICAL LITERATURE;
HOSPITAL LITERATURE INDEX; HUMAN RESOURCES AB-
STRACTS; HUMANITIES INDEX; INDEX TO LEGAL PERIOD-
ICALS; INDEX MEDICUS; INDEX TO PERIODICAL ARTICLES
RELATED TO LAW; INTERNATIONAL NURSING INDEX;
LIBRARY OF CONGRESS CATALOG: BOOKS: SUBJECTS; THE
NEW YORK TIMES INDEX; NURSING LITERATURE INDEX;
PHILOSOPHERS INDEX; PSYCHOLOGICAL ABSTRACTS;
PUBLIC AFFAIRS INFORMATION SERVICE; READERS GUIDE
TO PERIODICAL LITERATURE; SOCIAL SCIENCES INDEX;
SOCIOLOGICAL ABSTRACTS; SUBJECT GUIDE TO BOOKS IN
PRINT; U.S. SUPERINTENDENT OF DOCUMENTS: MONTHLY
CATALOG OF U.S. GOVERNMENT PUBLICATIONS; WHITA-
KER'S CUMULATIVE BOOK INDEX.

The bibliography is divided into two sections: a title
section in alphabetical order; and a subject section. Thus,

if the researcher does not wish to observe the subject heads of the compiler, he can use the title section exclusively. The 223 subject heads have been allowed to issue from the nature of the material indexed rather than being imposed from Library of Congress subject heads of other standard lists.

Countries are listed alphabetically under subjects: "Abortion: Africa," etc.; with states listed alphabetically under "Abortion: United States:" Arkansas, California, etc.; drugs are listed under the specific drug involved; entries evolving from Biological, Psychological or Sociological Abstracts are so indicated with abstract number cited; and all abstracts of news stories appearing in The New York Times Index include story length indicators: (L) long, (M) medium and (S) short. Editorials, editorial page columns and reviews will not include this indicator. In addition, each Times entry concludes with date, page, column, (e.g., May 1, 1:8 means story was published on May 1, page 1, column 8). Sunday sections, other than the main news section, are identified by Roman numerals following the date (e.g., May 6, IV, 3:4 means the numeral IV indicates the News of the Week in Review section).

The Book section has been expanded to include Government Publications and Monographs.

Commencing with this bibliography the Subject Heading Index has been expanded to include page numbers.

Mary K. Floyd
Troy, New York
October, 1977

LIST OF PERIODICALS

ANA Clinical Sessions
AORN Journal. Association of Operating Room Nurses, Inc.
Acta Anaesthesiologica Scandinavica. Supplement
Acta Europaea Fertilitatis
Acta Medica Scandinavica. Supplement
Acta Morphologica Academia Scientiarum Hungaricae
Acta Obstetrica et Gynaecologica Japonica
Acta Obstetricia et Gynecologica Scandinavica
Acta Obstetricia et Gynecologica Scandinavica. Supplement
Acta Psychiatrica Scandinavica
Adolescence
Akron Law Review
Akusherstvo i Ginekologiia (Moscow)
Akusherstvo i Ginekologiia (Sofia)
America
American Catholic Philosophical Association Proceedings
American Ecclesiastical Review
American Journal of Chinese Medicine
American Journal of Epidemiology
American Journal of Human Genetics
American Journal of Jurisprudence
American Journal of Law and Medicine
American Journal of Medicine
American Journal of Nursing
American Journal of Obstetrics and Gynecology
American Journal of Orthopsychiatry
American Journal of Public Health
American Journal of Roentgenology
American Journal of Veterinary Research
American Medical News
Analysis
Anethesie, Analgesie, Reanimation
Annales d'Anatomie Pathologique
Annales Chirurgiae et Gynaecologiae Fenniae

Annales de Genetique
Annales d'Immunologie
Annales Medico-Psychologiques
Annales Universitatis Mariae Curie-Sklodawska; Sectio D:
  Medicina
Annali di Ostetricia, Ginecologia, Medicina Perinatale
Annali Sclavo
Antibiotics and Chemotherapy
Archiv fur Gynaekologie
Archives of General Psychiatry
Archives of Pathology and Laboratory Medicine
Archives of Surgery
Arkhiv Anatomii Gistologii i Embriologii
Arkhiv Pathologie
Atlantic
The Atlantic Advocate
Australian Journal of Social Issues
Australasian Nurses Journal
Aviation Space and Environmental Medicine

Bangladesh Development Studies
Banner
Beitraege zur Gerichtlichen Medizin
Biology of Reproduction
Biomedicine Express (Paris)
Boston University Law Review
Brigham Young University Law Review
British Journal of Criminology
British Journal of Obstetrics and Gynaecology
British Journal of Preventive and Social Medicine
British Journal of Psychiatry
British Medical Journal
British Veterinary Journal
Bruxelles-Medical
Bulletin of the World Health Organization
Byulleten' Eksperimental'noi Biologii i Meditseny

C.I.C.I.A.M.S. Nouvelles; Bulletin d'Information du Comite
  International Catholique des Infirmieres et Assistantes
  Medico-Sociales
California Law Review

Canadian Forum
Canadian Journal of Comparative Medicine
Canadian Journal of Philosophy
Canadian Journal of Public Health
Canadian Medical Association Journal
Canadian Nurse
Canadian Veterinary Journal
Casopis Lekaru Ceskych
Catalog of Selected Documents in Psychology
Catholic Digest
Catholic Lawyer
Catholic Mind
Ceskoslovenska Gynekologie
Christian Century
Christian Herald
Christian Ministry
Christian Standard
Christianity and Crisis
Christianity Today
Church Herald
Clinical Endocrinology
Clinical Genetics
Columbia Human Rights Law Review
Columbia Journal of Law and Social Problems
Commentary
Commonweal
Comprehensive Therapy
Comptes Rendus Hebdomadaires des Seances de l'Academie
   des Sciences; D: Sciences Naturelles
Congressional Quarterly Weekly Report
Connecticut Medicine
Contemporary Review
Contraception
Cornell Law Review
Cuadernos de Realidades Sociales
Current Psychiatric Therapies

Daily Telegraph
Demográfiá
Demography
Dermatologische Monatsschrift

Deutsche Tieraerztliche Wochenschrift
Developments in Biological Standardization
Dimension
Dimensions in Health Service
Dissertations Abstracts International
Duquesne Law Review

Economist
Editor and Publisher-The Fourth Estate
Editorial Research Reports
Encounter (Christian Theological Seminary)
Endocrinology
Environmental Research
Esquire
ETC
Ethics
Ethics in Science and Medicine
Excerpta Medica
Executive
Experientia

Faith for the Family
Family Health
Family Planning Perspectives
Fel'dsker i Akusherka
Fertility and Sterility
Folia Medica Cracoviensia
Fortschritte du Medizin
Futurist

Geburtshilfe und Frauenheilkunde
Genetika
George Washington Law Review
Germanic Review   '
Ginekologia Polaska
Good Housekeeping
Guardian

Harefuah
Harpers Bazaar
Hastings Center Report

Hawaii Bar Journal
Health Care Dimensions
Health Education Monographs
Health Laboratory Science
Health and Social Service Journal
Health and Social Work
Hofstra Law Review
Hospital Formulary Management
Hospital Practice
Hospital Progress
Hospitals; Journal of the American Hospital Association
Human Genetics
Human Heredity
Humangenetik
The Humanist

Indian Journal of Medical Research
Indiana Law Review
Infirmière Canadienne
Inquire; Journal of Medical Care Organization, Provision
    and Financing
Intellect
International Journal of Fertility
International Journal of Gynaecology and Obstetrics
International Journal of Social Psychiatry
International Journal of Sociology of the Family
International Philosophical Quarterly
International Review of Modern Sociology
International Surgery
Irish Medical Journal

JAMA; Journal of the American Medical Association
JOGN; Journal of Obstetric, Gynecologic and Neonatal Nursing
Jamaican Nurse
Japanese Journal for Midwives
Japanese Journal of Fertility and Sterility
The John Marshall Journal of Practice and Procedure
Journal for the Scientific Study of Religion
Journal of the American Venereal Disease Association
Journal of the American Veterinary Medical Association
Journal of Applied Psychology

Journal of Biosocial Science
Journal of Clinical Pathology
Journal of Clinical Psychology
Journal of Counseling Psychology
Journal of Dairy Science
Journal of Endocrinology
Journal of Family Law
Journal de Genetique Humaine
Journal de Gynecologie, Obstetrique et Biologie de la
   Reproduction
Journal of Health and Social Behavior
Journal of the Indian Medical Association
Journal of Laboratory and Clinical Medicine
Journal of Legal Medicine
Journal of the Medical Association of Georgia
Journal of Medical Ethics
Journal of Medical Genetics
Journal of the Medical Society of New Jersey
Journal of the Mississippi State Medical Association
Journal of Perinatal Medicine
Journal of Political Economy
Journal of Postgraduate Medicine
Journal of Reproduction and Fertility
Journal of Reproduction and Fertility [Supplement]
Journal of Reproductive Medicine
Journal of the Royal College of General Practitioners
Journal of School Health
Journal of Sex Research
Jugoslovenska Ginekologija i Opstetricija
Jurist

Kansas Law Review
Katilolehti
Kentucky Law Journal

Laboratory Animal Science
Laboratory Investigation
Lakartidningen
Lamp
Lancet
Liguorian

Lijecnicki Vjesnik
Lille Medical
Linacre Quarterly
Link
Lutheran

Mademoiselle
Man and Medicine
Management Science: Journal of the Institute of Management
   Sciences
Marriage and Family Living
Maternal-Child Nursing Journal
McCalls
McGill Law Journal
Medecine Interne
Medecine Legale et Dommage Corporel
Medical Clinics of North America
Medical Journal of Australia
Medical Journal of Malaysia
Medical World News
Medicinski Arhiv
Medicinski Pregled
Medico-Legal Bulletin
Medizinische Klinik
Midwife, Health Visitor and Community Nurse
Minerva Ginecologia
Modern Healthcare, Short-Term Care Edition
Momentum
Month
Mount Sinai Journal of Medicine, New York
Ms Magazine
Muenchener Medizinische Wochenschrift

Nation
National Catholic Reporter
National Review
Nature
Nebraska Law Review
Nebraska Medical Journal
Nederlands Tijdschrift voor Geneeskunde
Nephron

New England Journal of Medicine
New England Law Review
New Humanist
New Law Journal
New Republic
New Society
New Statesman
New York State Journal of Medicine
The New York Times
New Zealand Medical Journal
New Zealand Veterinary Journal
Newsweek
Nigerian Nurse
Nordisk Medicin
Nordisk Veterinaer Medicin
North Carolina Law Review
Nova
Nouvelle Presse Medicale
Nursing
Nurings (Jenkintown)
Nursing Digest
Nursing Forum (Auckland)
Nursing Forum; Nurses' Reform Association of New Zealand
Nursing Mirror and Midwives' Journal
Nursing Times
Nursing Update

Observer
Obstetrical and Gynecological Survey
Obstetrics and Gynecology
Oeffentliche Gesundheitswesen
Ohio Northern University Law Review
Ohio State Medical Journal
Oklahoma Law Review
Orvosi Hetilap
Osgoode Hall Law Journal
L'Osservatore Romano
Ottawa Law Review
Our Sunday Visitor
Our Sunday Visitor Magazine

Pacific Sociological Review
Pediatrics
Pediatriia Akusherstvo i Ginekologiia
Perceptual and Motor Skills
Perspectives in Biology and Medicine
Perspectives in Family Planning
Philosophy and Public Affairs
Polski Tygodnik Lekarski
Population Studies
Postgraduate Medical Journal
Praxis
Presbyterian Journal
Primary Care; Clinics in Office Practice
Proceedings of the National Academy of Sciences of the
     United States of America
Professioni Infermieristiche
Prostaglandins
Psychiatric Nursing
Psychiatry
Psychological Reports
Psychology Today
Public Health Reports

Radiologia
Reports on Population-Family Planning
Review of Metaphysics
Revista da Associacao Medica Brasileira
Revista Chilena de Obstetricia y Ginecologia
Revista Enfermagem em Novas Dimensoes
Revista de Medicina de la Universidad de Navarra
Revista de Neuro-Psiquiatria
Revista de Sanidad e Higiene Publica
Revue Medicale de Liege
Revue Roumaine de Medecine; now, Medecine Interne
Rivista Italiana di Ginecologia
Rocky Mountain Medical Journal

Sabouraudia; Journal of the International Society for Human
     and Animal Mycology
Santa Clara Lawyer
Scandinavian Journal of Immunology

School Counselor
Schwestern Revue
Science
Scientific American
Seventeen
Singapore Medical Journal
Social Biology
Social Science Journal
Social Theory and Practice
Society
Sociological Analysis
South African Medical Journal
Southern Medical Journal
Soviet Studies
Spectator
St. Anthony Messenger
St. Mary's Law Journal
Studies in Family Planning
Sunday Times
Supervisor Nurse
Sygeplejersken
Sykepleien

Tablet (London)
Tax Executive
Teratology; Journal of Abnormal Development
Tex Hospitals
Texas Medicine
Theology Today
Therapeutische Umschaw
Theriogenology
Thrombosis Research
Tidsskrfit for den Norske Laegeforening
Tijdschrift voor Diergeneeskunde
Time
Times
Toxicology and Applied Pharmacology
Transfusion
Tsitologiia

U.C.L.A. Law Review

Ugeskrift for Laeger
Union Medicale du Canada
University of Cincinnati Law Review
University of Kansas Law Review
University of Michigan Journal of Law Reform
University of Missouri at Kansas City Law Review
University of Richmond Law Review
University of Toledo Law Review
U.S. Catholic
U.S. News and World Report

Verhandelingen; Koninklÿke Academie voor Geneeskunde
   von Belgie
Veterinariia
Veterinarno-Meditsinski Nauki
Veterinary Record
Viata Medicala; Revista de Informore Profesionala si
   Stüntifica a Codrelor Medii Sanitare
Virginia Law Review
Vital Christianity
Voprosy Okhrany Materinstva i Detstva

Wall Street Journal
Wayne Law Review
West Indian Medical Journal
Western Folklore
Western Humanities Review
Western Ontario Law Review
Western State University Law Review
Who Chronicle
Wiener Klinische Wochenschrift
William and Mary Law Review
Women's Rights Law Reporter
World Health Organization
World Health Organization Technical Report Series
World of Irish Nursing

Zdravookhranenie Rossiiskoi Federatsii
Zeitschrift fur Aerztliche Fortbildung
Zeitschrift fur Allgemeinmedizin; der Landarzt
Zeitschrift fur die Gesamte Hygiene und Ihre Grenzgebiete

Zeitschrift fur Urologie und Nephrologie

Zentralblatt fur Bakteriologie Parasitenkunde, Infektionskrank-
heiten und Hygiene; Erste Abteilung: Originale, Reihe B:
Hygiene, Praeventive Medizin

Zentralblatt fur Gynaekologie

Zentralblatt fuer Veterinaermedizine. Journal of Veterinary
Medicine [B]

SUBJECT HEADING INDEX

Abnormalities	127	Abortion: Puerto Rico	136
Abortion (General)	127	Abortion: Rhodesia	136
Abortion Act	127	Abortion: Scandinavia	136
Abortion: Austria	127	Abortion: Singapore	136
Abortion: Belgium	127	Abortion: Sweden	136
Abortion: Canada	127	Abortion: Taiwan	136
Abortion: Caroline		Abortion: Thailand	137
Islands	129	Abortion: Uganda	137
Abortion: Chile	129	Abortion: United	
Abortion: China	129	Kingdom	137
Abortion: Cuba	129	Abortion: United States	140
Abortion: Czecho-		Arizona	140
slovakia	129	Arkansas	140
Abortion: Denmark	129	California	140
Abortion: Europe	130	Chicago	140
Abortion: Finland	130	Cincinnati	140
Abortion: France	130	Colorado	140
Abortion: Germany	131	Connecticut	140
Abortion: Ghana	131	Florida	141
Abortion: Hungary	131	Georgia	141
Abortion: India	132	Hawaii	141
Abortion: Italy	132	Illinois	141
Abortion: Jamaica	134	Indiana	141
Abortion: Japan	134	Iowa	141
Abortion: Malaysia	134	Louisiana	141
Abortion: Mexico	135	Maryland	141
Abortion: Nether-		Massachusetts	141
lands	135	Michigan	142
Abortion: New		Minnesota	142
Zealand	135	Mississippi	142
Abortion: Nigeria	135	Missouri	142
Abortion: Norway	135	Montana	143
Abortion: Pakistan	135	Nebraska	143
Abortion: Poland	136	New Hampshire	143
Abortion: Portugal	136	New Jersey	143

New York	144	and Insufficiency	153
North Carolina	147	Chlormadinone	153
Oklahoma	147	Clinical Aspects	153
Oregon	147	Clomiphene	154
Pennsylvania	147	College Women	155
Rhode Island	147	Complications	155
South Dakota	147	Contraception	164
Tennessee	147	Criminal Abortion	166
Texas	147		
Vermont	147	Demography	166
Wisconsin	148	Diagnosis	167
Abortion: USSR	148	Diazepam	171
Abortion: Yugoslavia	148	Diethylstilbestrol	171
Adoption	148	Dinoprost Thomethamine	171
Alupent	148	Doxicillin	171
American College of		Drug Therapy	171
Obstetricians and			
Gynecologists	148	E-Aminocaproic Acid	171
American Hospital		Education	171
Association	148	Endotoxin	171
American Public		Estradiol	172
Health Association	148	Ethyl Alcohol	172
Amoglandin	148	Etidocaine	172
Amoxicillin	148	Euthanasia	172
Anesthesia	148		
Antibodies	149	Family Planning	172
Arachidonic Acid	149	Faustan	173
Artificial Abortion	149	Fees & Public	
Aspirin	150	Assistance	173
		Fertility	175
Behavior	150	Fetus	175
Bibliography	150	Flavoxate	177
Birth Control	150	Flumethasone	177
Blood	151		
		Genetics	177
Campaign Issues	152	Gentamicin Garamycin	183
Candidiasis	153	Gestanon	183
Cardiovascular		Gonorrhea	183
System	153	Gynecology	183
Cephalothin	153	Gynesthesin	183
Cervical Incompetence			

Habitual Abortion   183   Orciprenaline   260
Halothane   183   Oxytocin   260
Hemorrhage   189
Heparin   189   Paramedics   261
Hexenal   189   Parsley Extract   261
History   189   Patient Counseling   261
Hormones   190   Pentazocine   261
Hospitals   191   Pharmacists   261
                              Politics   262
Immunity   192   Population   267
Indomethacin   194   Potassium Ampicillin   267
Induced Abortion   194   Pregnancy Interruption   268
Infanticide   227   Progesterone   268
Infection   227   Prostaglandins   268
Isoptin   227   Psychology   281
Isoxsuprine   227   Public Health   284

Law Enforcement   227   Radiologists   285
Laws & Legislation   227   Referral Agencies
Listerosis   255   Services   285
                              Regitine   285
Male Attitudes   256   Religion and Ethics   285
March of Dimes   256   Research   295
Mefenamic Acid   256   Respiratory System   305
Menstruation   256   Rixampicin   305
Mentally Retarded   256   Rivanol   305
Microbiology   256   Rubella   305
Miscarriages   256
Morbidity   257   Sepsis   306
Mortality   257   Septic Abortion and
Mycoplasma   259   Septic Shock   306
                              Sociology and Behavior   308
NAL   259   Sodium Chloride   314
NCCB   259   Sombrevin   314
Napthalene   259   S.P.U.C.   314
Neonatal   259   Spontaneous Abortion   314
Neuraminidase   259   Statistics   319
Nurses   259   Sterility   323
Nursing Homes   260   Sterilization   324
                              Stilbestrol   325
Obstetrics   260   Students   325

Surgical Treatment
  and Management   325
Surveys   327
Symposia   327
Syntocinon   327

Techniques of
  Abortion   327
Tetracycline   334
TH 1165a   334
Therapeutic Abortion 335
Threatened Abortion   340
Toxoplasmas   345
Transplacental
  Hemorrhage   346
Triploidy   346
Tucinal   346

Veterinary Abortions 346

Youth   346

TABLE OF CONTENTS

Preface.   i

List of Periodicals.   iii

Subject Heading Index   xv

Books, Government Publications and Monographs . . .   1

Periodical Literature:
    Title Index   5
    Subject Index.   127

Author Index   349

BOOKS, GOVERNMENT PUBLICATIONS,
AND MONOGRAPHS

Bajema, C. E. ABORTION AND THE MEANING OF
PERSONHOOD. Grand Rapids, Michigan: Baker Book
House, 1976.

Bergström S, ed. REPORT FROM MEETINGS OF THE
PROSTAGLANDIN TASK FORCE STEERING COMMITTEE.
Stockholm, 1973. QV 175 W927r 1972-73.

Columbia University School of Social Work. COUNSELING
IN ABORTION SERVICES: Physician - Nurse - Social
Worker. New York: University Book Service, 1974.

da Paz AC, et al., ed. RECENT ADVANCES IN HUMAN
REPRODUCTION. Amsterdam, Excerpta Medica, 1976.
W3 EX89 no. 370 1974.

Denes, Magda. IN NECESSITY & SORROW: Life & Death
in an Abortion Hospital. New York: Basic Books, Inc.,
Publishers, 1976.

Dennis. ABORTION, BABIES AND CONTRACEPTION:
A.B.C. of Eugenics. Southampton: University of
Southampton, 1975.

Devereux, George A STUDY OF ABORTION IN PRIMITIVE
SOCIETIES, rev. ed. New York: International University
Press, 1976.

DeGiacomo, James, ed. ABORTION: A Question of Values.
(Conscience & Concern Ser : No. 1). Washington, D.C.:

V. H Winston & Sons, Inc. , 1975.

Fallaci, Oriana. LETTER TO A CHILD NEVER BORN.
New York: Simon & Schuster, Inc. , 1976.

Floyd, Mary K. , compiler. ABORTION BIBLIOGRAPHY
FOR 1975. Troy, New York: Whitston Publishing
Company, 1976.

Gaylor, A. N. ABORTION IS A BLESSING. New York:
Psychological Dimensions, Inc. , 1975.

Gebhard, Paul H. , et al. PREGNANCY, BIRTH &
ABORTION. Westport, Connecticut: Greenwood Press,
Inc. , 1976.

Harrison, C. P. IN THE SHADOW OF THE CURETTE.
New York: Vantage, 1976.

Hefnawi F, Segal SJ, ed. ANALYSIS OF INTRAUTERINE
CONTRACEPTION. Amsterdam, North-Holland, 1975.
W3 IN182AI 1974a.

Kahn RH, Lands WE, ed. PROSTAGLANDINS AND CYCLIC
AMP. New York, Academic Press, 1973. QU 90 S991p
1972

Kaplan BA, ed. ANTHROPOLOGICAL STUDIES OF
HUMAN FERTILITY. Detroit, Wayne State Univ Press,
1976. GN 241 S989a 1975

Kazner E, et al. , ed. ULTRASONICS IN MEDICINE.
Amsterdam. Excerpta Medica, 1975. W3 EX89 no. 363
1975.

Kelly S, et al. , ed. BIRTH DEFECTS: risks and consequences. New York, Academic Press, 1976. QS 675
B622 1974.

Kleinman, Ronald L. INDUCED ABORTION. New York:
International Publications Service, 1972.

Kluge, E. H. W. THE PRACTICE OF DEATH. New Haven, Connecticut: Yale University Press, 1976.

Luker, Kristin. TAKING CHANCES: Abortion & the Decision Not to Contracept. Berkeley, California: University of California Press, 1976.

Mace. ABORTION: The Agonising Decision. London: Oliphants, 1973.

Mancari, C. R. ABORTION AND THE BIBLE. New York: Vantage, 1976.

Marchesi F, Cittandini E, ed. FERTILITA E STERILITA. Taormina, Minerva Medica, 1974. WP 570 S679f 1973.

Moghissi KS, Evans TN, ed. REGULATION OF HUMAN FERTILITY. Detroit, Wayne State Univ Press, 1976. W3 HA292 1973r.

Osofsky, H. J. and J. Osofsky. ABORTION EXPERIENCE: Psychological and Medical Impact. New York: Harper & Row, 1974.

Segal SJ, et al., ed. THE REGULATION OF MAMMALIAN REPRODUCTION. Springfield, Ill., Thomas, 1973. W3 F049 no. 8 1973.

Seuyhart, B. A. D. BIOETHICAL DECISION-MAKING. Philadelphia, Pennsylvania: Fortress Press, 1975.

Shepard TH, et al., ed. METHODS FOR DETECTION OF ENVIRONMENTAL AGENTS THAT PRODUCE CONGENITAL DEFECTS. Amsterdam, North-Holland, 1975. QS 675 M592 1974.

SUPPLEMENT ON ABORTION. Statistical Review of England and Wales. London: Population Censuses & Surveys Office, 1971.

Tietze, C. and M. C. Murstein. INDUCED ABORTION:

3

1975 factbook. 2d ed. December, 1975. New York: Population Council, 1975.

United States. Bureau of Epidemiology. Family Planning Evaluation Division. ABORTION SURVEILLANCE, Annual Summary 1972 [with list of references]. Atlanta, Georgia: Center for Disease Control, Health, Education, and Welfare Department, 1974.

United States. Congress. Senate. Committee on the Judiciary. Subcommittee on Constitutional Amendments. ABORTION: hearings before the Subcommittee on Constitutional Amendments of the Committee on the Judiciary, United States Senate, Ninety-third Congress, second session, on S.J. Res. 119 ... and S.J. Res. 130 ... Washington: U.S. Govt. Print. Off., 1974.

--Pt. 2, hearings held April 25-July 24, 1974.

--Pt. 3, hearings held August 21-October 8, 1974.

United States. Congress. Senate. Committee on the Judiciary. Subcommittee on Constitutional Amendments. ABORTION: hearings, pt. 4 before the Subcommittee on Constitutional Amendments of the Committee on the Judiciary, United States Senate, Ninety-fourth Congress, first session on S.J. Res. 6 ... and S.J. Res. 10 and 11, and S.J. 91. Washington: U.S. Govt. Print. Off., 1976.

Visentin, Charles. A MESSAGE TO AN ABORTED BABY KILLED BY THE COWARDICE OF HIS MOTHER & THE VENAL COMPLICITY OF THE ATTENDING PHYSICIAN. Albuquerque, New Mexico: American Classical College Press, 1976.

Vokaer R., et al., ed. REPRODUCTIVE ENDOCRINOLOGY. Oxford, Pergamon Press, 1975. WQ 200 F673r 1973.

Weisheit, Eldon. ABORTION? Resources for Pastoral Counseling. St. Louis, Missouri: Concordia Publishing House, 1976.

4

PERIODICAL LITERATURE

TITLE INDEX

"Abortifacient effect of steroids from Ananas comosus and
their analogues on mice," by A. Pakrashi, et al.
JOURNAL OF REPRODUCTION AND FERTILITY 46
(2):461-462, March, 1976.

"Abortifacient efficiency of 15 (S) 15-methyl-prostaglandin
F2alpha-methyl ester administered vaginally during
early pregnancy," by O. Ylikorkala, et al. PROSTA-
GLANDINS 12(4):609-624, October, 1976.

"Abortifacient effects of Vibrio cholerae exo-enterotoxin
and endotoxin in mice," by G. J. Gasic, et al.
JOURNAL OF REPRODUCTION AND FERTILITY
45(2):315-322, November, 1975.

"Abortion." (editorial). LANCET 2(7980):296, August 7,
1976.

"Abortion." THE NEW YORK TIMES (S), January 27, 12:3,
1976.

"Abortion," (editorial), by W. R. Barclay. JAMA; JOURNAL
OF THE AMERICAN MEDICAL ASSOCIATION 236(4):388,
July 26, 1976.

"Abortion," by J. Margolis. ETHICS 84, 1:51-61, October,
1973. (Socio. Abstrs. 1976, 76I1759)

"Abortion Abuses." THE NEW YORK TIMES (S), May 2, 57:1,

1976.

"Abortion (amendment) bill," (letter), by J. B. Metcalfe.
BRITISH MEDICAL JOURNAL 3(5982):544, August 30,
1975.

"Abortion and cannibalism in squirrel monkeys (Saimiri
sciureus) associated with experimental protein deficiency
during gestation," by S. L. Manocha. LABORATORY
ANIMAL SCIENCE 26(4):649-650, August, 1976.

"Abortion and the concept of a person," by J. English.
CANADIAN JOURNAL OF PHILOSOPHY 5, 233-243,
October, 1975.

"Abortion and the constitution: the need for a life-protective
amendment," by R. A. Destro. CALIFORNIA LAW
REVIEW 63:1250-1351, September, 1975.

"Abortion and contraception information during first period
under new legislation," by K. Sundström. LAKAR-
TIDNINGEN 72(38):3531-3533, September 17, 1975.

"Abortion and fertility control (a brief world review)," by
R. Dutta. JOURNAL OF THE INDIAN MEDICAL
ASSOCIATION 64(11):315-320, June 1, 1975.

"Abortion and inalienable rights in classical liberalism,"
by G. D. Glenn. AMERICAN JOURNAL OF JURIS-
PRUDENCE 20:62-80, 1975.

"Abortion and maternal deaths." (editorial). BRITISH
MEDICAL JOURNAL 2(6027):70, July 10, 1976.

"Abortion and maternal deaths," (letter), by C. Brook.
BRITISH MEDICAL JOURNAL 2(6034):524-525,
August 28, 1976.

"Abortion and maternal deaths," (letter), by C. B.
Goodhart. BRITISH MEDICAL JOURNAL 2(6033):477,
August 21, 1976.

"Abortion and maternal deaths," (letter), by A. M. Smith.
    BRITISH MEDICAL JOURNAL 2(6031):368, August 7,
    1976.

"Abortion and 1976 politics; with editorial comment," by
    R. N. Lynch. AMERICA 134:173, 177-178, March 6,
    1976.

"Abortion and politics," by E. Doerr. HUMANIST 36:42,
    March, 1976.

"Abortion and the right to life," by L. S. Carrier. SOCIAL
    THEORY AND PRACTICE 3:381-401, Fall, 1975.

"Abortion and the sanctity of human life, by B. Brody. A
    review," by P. J. Rossi. AMERICA 133-471, December 27,
    1975.
"Abortion as a problem of medical education," by J.
    Jiménea-Vargas, et al. REVISTA DE MEDICINA DE
    LA UNIVERSIDAD DE NAVARRA 17(3):273-279,
    September, 1973.

"Abortion associated with Hemophilus somnus infection in
    a bovine fetus," by A. A. van Dreumel, et al. CANADIAN
    VETERINARY JOURNAL 16(12):367-370, December, 1975.

"Abortion associated with mixed Leptospira equid herpes-
    virus 1 infection," by W. A. Ellis, et al. VETERINARY
    RECORD 98(11):218-219, March 13, 1976.

"Abortion attitudes among Catholic college students," by
    P. D. Bardis. ADOLESCENCE 10(39):433-441, Fall,
    1975.

"Abortion: the avoidable moral dilemma," by J. M. Humber.
    THE JOURNAL OF VALUE INQUIRY 9, 282-302, Winter,
    1975.

"Abortion Backers on March in Rome." THE NEW YORK
    TIMES (S), April 4, 20:1, 1976.

"Abortion Backers Seek Out Carter." THE NEW YORK
    TIMES (S), September 3, I, 9:4, 1976.

"Abortion because of other the desired fetal sex?" by E.
    Schwinger. BEITRAEGE ZUR GERICHTLICHEN
    MEDIZIN 33:46-48, 1975.

"Abortion: the class religion," by M. J. Sobran, Jr.
    NATIONAL REVIEW 28:28-31, January 23, 1976.

"Abortion conscience and the constitution: an examination
    of federal institutional conscience clauses," by H. F.
    Pilpel. COLUMBIA HUMAN RIGHTS LAW REVIEW
    6:279-350, Fall-Winter, 1975.

"Abortion conscience clauses." COLUMBIA JOURNAL OF
    LAW AND SOCIAL PROBLEMS 11:571-627, Summer,
    1975.

"Abortion Curb Defeated." THE NEW YORK TIMES
    (S), June 29, 14:3, 1976.

"Abortion: the danger of confusing responsibility with
    punishment," by Anne McLaren. TIMES 7, July 9,
    1975.

"The Abortion Debate," by J. A. O'Hare. THE NEW YORK
    TIMES (M), February 8, IV, 15:2, 1976.

"Abortion debate: finding a true pro-life stance," by R. J.
    Westley. AMERICA 134:489-492, June 5, 1976.

"Abortion Debate Heats Up in Italy," by C. Lord. THE NEW
    YORK TIMES (M), August 9, 7:1, 1976.

"The Abortion Decision." (editorial). THE NEW YORK
    TIMES July 3, 20:1, 1976.

"Abortion decision and evolving limits on state intervention,"
    by D. MacDougal, et al. HAWAII BAR JOURNAL 11:51-
    72, Fall, 1974.

"Abortion development in the Scandinavian countries 1965-1974," by P. C. Matthiessen. UGESKRIFT FOR LAEGER 138(6):351-353, February 2, 1976.

"Abortion for the fetus's own sake?" by P. F. Camenisch. HASTINGS CENTER REPORT 54, 38-41, April-June, 1975.

"Abortion: how we won the battle and nearly lost the war," by P. Ashdown-Sharp. NOVA 62-64, October, 1975.

"Abortion: the husband's constitutional rights," by W. D. H. Teo. EHTICS 85:337-342, July, 1975; Reply by L. W. Purdy, 86:247-251, April, 1976.

"Abortion: a hypothesis on the role of ABO blood groups and placental alkaline phosphatase," by E. Bottini. SOCIAL BIOLOGY 22(3):221-228, 1975. (Bio. Abstrs. 1976, 24579)

"Abortion in cows as a probable consequence of mycosis," by B. Sielicka, et al. DERMATOLOGISCHE MONATS-SCHRIFT 162(2):184-185, February, 1976.

"Abortion in India," by R. P. Mohan. SOCIAL SCIENCE 50,3: 141-143, Summer, 1975. (Socio. Abstrs. 1976, 76I2523)

"Abortion in New Zealand. A review," by A. D. Trlin. AUSTRALIAN JOURNAL OF SOCIAL ISSUES 10, 3: 179-196, August, 1975. (Socio. Abstrs. 1976, 76H8920)

"Abortion in 1975: the psychiatric perspective and contraception in adolescence," by P. D. Barglow. JOGN; JOURNAL OF OBSTETRIC, GYNECOLOGIC AND NEONATAL NURSING 5:41-47, January-February, 1976.

"Abortion in 1975: the psychiatric perspective, with a discussion of abortion and contraception in adolescence," by P. D. Barglow. JOGN; JOURNAL OF OBSTETRIC, GYNECOLOGIC AND NEONATAL NURSING 5(1):41-48, January-February, 1976.

"Abortion in sheep and goats in Cyprus caused by Coxiella burneti," by R. W. Crowther, et al. VETERINARY RECORD 99(2):29-30, July 10, 1976.

"Abortion incidence and medical legislation in Scandinavia," by K. Sundström. LAKARTIDNINGEN 73(36):2896, September 1, 1976.

"Abortion increase in Scandinavia in 1975." NORDISK VETERINAER MEDICA 91(4):115, April, 1976.

"Abortion induction using prostaglandin E2," by K. Feishart. ARCHIV FUR GYNAEKOLOGIE 219(1-4):500-501, November 18, 1975.

"Abortion isn't a Catholic issue but an issue for all, Protestant pro-life leaders say," by P. Dubec. OUR SUNDAY VISITOR 64:1, December 21, 1975.

"The abortion issue." (editorial). JOURNAL OF MEDICAL ETHICS 1(3):109-110, September, 1975.

"The Abortion Issue," by T. Wicker. THE NEW YORK TIMES September 10, I, 25:2, 1976.

"The abortion issue; England," by D. Sullivan. TABLET 230:710-711, July 24, 1976.

"Abortion language and logic," by R. A. Hipkiss. ETC 33:207-210, June, 1976.

"Abortion: the last resort," by M. C. Segers. AMERICA 133:456-458, December 27, 1975; Discussion 134: 22, January 17, 1976.

"The abortion law and legal paradox," by J. M. B. Crawford. MONTH 9:97-100, March, 1976.

"Abortion law; unexpectedly cautious [Britain]." ECONOMIST 260:29, July 31, 1976.

"An abortion law update," by A. H. Berstein. HOSPITALS
50(11):90-92, June 1, 1976.

"Abortion law: what for? [Britain]." ECONOMIST 258:34,
February 11, 1976.

"Abortion: let the whole truth be heard," by R. Butt.
TIMES 16, April 24, 1975.

"Abortion liberalization: a worldwide trend," by L. R.
Brown, et al. FUTURIST 10:140-143, June, 1976.

"Abortion: a logical oddity. Postscript," by J. M. B.
Crawford. NEW LAW JOURNAL 126:252-254, 298-299,
March 11-18, 1976.

"Abortion: a lucrative business," by J. Hewitt. FAITH
FOR THE FAMILY 10, November-December, 1975.

"Abortion: Medicaid's unwanted child?" WOMEN's RIGHTS
LAW REPORTER 3:22-27, September, 1975.

"Abortion--the medical facts," by L. Machol, et al.
FAMILY HEALTH 8:42-45 passim, February, 1976.

"Abortion need and services in the United States, 1974-
1975," by E. Weinstock, et al. FAMILY PLANNING
PERSPECTIVES 8(2):58-69, March-April, 1976.

"Abortion needs another look," by J. White. TIMES
12, February 9, 1976.

"Abortion: no middle ground," by M. Greenfield.
NEWSWEEK 87:92, February 16, 1976.

"Abortion--the nurse's feelings," by A. Danon. ANA
CLINICAL SESSIONS Pt. 2 :60-65, 1974.

"Abortion: Perception and contemporary genocide myth:
a comparative study among low-income pregnant Black
and Puerto Rican women," by B. R. Hughes.

DISSERTATION ABSTRACTS INTERNATIONAL 34(6-A): 3542-3543, December, 1973. (Psycho. Abstr. 1976, 4369)

"Abortion: a philosophical analysis," by F. Myrna. FEM STUD 1, 49-63, Fall, 1972.

"Abortion: pinning down the politicians." ECONOMIST 258:404, February 14, 1976.

"Abortion politics," by S. Stencel. EDITORIAL RESEARCH REPORTS 767-784, October 22, 1976.

"Abortion practice: could drugs replace doctors?" by S. Whitehead. NURSING TIMES 72(15):564-565, April 15, 1976.

"Abortion practice in NZ public hospitals." NURSING FORUM (Auckl) 3(4):5-7, November-December, 1975.

"Abortion: privacy and fantasy," by R. M. Cooper. ENCOUNTER (Christian Theological Seminary) 37:181-188, Spring, 1976.

"Abortion: the problems that remain." MCCALLS 103:33-34, March, 1976.

"Abortion, the public morals, and the police power: the ethical function of substantive due process," by M. J. Perry. U.C.L.A. LAW REVIEW 23:689-736, April, 1976.

"Abortion: questions and answers from a Catholic perspective; the Catholic Church's view," by J. Bernardin. L'OSSERVATORE ROMANO 45(449):9 passim, November 4, 1976.

"Abortion recommendations accepted." BRITISH MEDICAL JOURNAL 4(5991):293-294, November 1, 1975.

"Abortion research in Latin America," by S. G. Sainz. STUDIES IN FAMILY PLANNING 7:211-217, August, 1976.

12

"Abortion Revisited," by H. Moody. CHRISTIANITY AND
CRISIS 166, July 21, 1975.

"Abortion: rights and risks," by D. Rice. HARPERS
BAZAAR 109:71 passim, June, 1976.

"Abortion Ruling." THE NEW YORK TIMES (S), October 24,
IV, 6:6, 1976.

"Abortion Ruling is Expected to Affect Restrictive Laws in
at Least 26 States," by S. S. King. THE NEW YORK
TIMES (M), July 2, I, 8:3, 1976.

"Abortion Ruling 'Monumental' to Some, 'Appalling' to
Others," by T. Goldstein. THE NEW YORK TIMES
(M), July 2, I, 9:1, 1976.

"Abortion-seeking women's views on the importance of
social benefits as an alternative to induced abortion,"
by T. Ganes, et al. TIDSSKRIFT FOR DEN NORSKE
LAEGEFORENING 96(13):768-770, May 10, 1976.

"Abortion since 1967," by M. Simms. NEW HUMANIST
91:269-271, February, 1976.

"Abortion Stand by Carter Vexes Catholic Bishops," by
C. Mohr. THE NEW YORK TIMES (M), September 1,
1:5, 1976.

"Abortion: stop shielding the facts with a white coat," by
R. Butt. TIMES 14, May 8, 1975.

"Abortion today," by A. Ruppersberg, Jr. OHIO STATE
MEDICAL JOURNAL 72(3):161-163, March, 1976.

"Abortion: an unresolved issue - are parental consent
statutes unconstitutional?" NEBRASKA LAW REVIEW
55:256-282, 1976.

"Abortion vs manslaughter," (letter), by W. V. Dolan.
ARCHIVES OF SURGERY 111(1):93, January, 1976.

"Abortion: Weighing the decision," by M. Osterhaven. CHRISTIAN HERALD 6, May 30, 1975.

"Abortion: What the trends are," by P. Harrison. NEW SOCIETY 33,669:242-244, July 31, 1975. (Socio. Abstrs. 1976, 76H8900)

"Abortion will be an issue at Protestant conventions." OUR SUNDAY VISITOR 65:2, June 13, 1976.

"Abortion: the woman's choice." ECONOMIST 260:35, July 10, 1976.

"Abortionist's advertisement," by G. Monteiro. WESTERN FOLKLORE 35:74, January, 1976.

"Abortions denied," by L. Lader. NATION 223:38-39, July 17, 1976.

"Abortions-government hospitals Peninsular Malaysia 1960-1972," by J. A. Thambu. MEDICAL JOURNAL OF MALAYSIA 29(4):258-262, June, 1975.

"Abortions in cows caused by Aspergillus fumigatus fresenius I," by S. Venev. VETERINARNO-MEDITSIN-SKI NAUKI 11(9):67-71, 1974.

"Abortions in 1973 in Linköping--contraceptive technics and postoperative complications," by U. Larsson-Cohn. LAKARTIDNINGEN 72(44):4282-4284, October 29, 1975.

"Abortions in Portugal a Complex Controversy," by M. Howe. THE NEW YORK TIMES (M), March 13, 13:6, 1976.

"Abortive action of 20 percent NaCl and alpha F2 prostaglandin solutions administered intra-amniotically in rats," by N. S. Hung, et al. JOURNAL DE GYNECOLOGIE, OBSTETRIQUE ET BIOLOGIE DE LA REPRODUCTION 3(8):1169-1188, December, 1974.

"The abortive effect of halothane," by A. Doenicke, et al.
ANESTHESIE, ANALGESIE, REANIMATION 32(1):41–46,
January–February, 1975.

"Abortive Medicaid." (editorial). THE NEW YORK TIMES
September 17, I, 22:1, 1976.

"Abortogenic activity of antiserum to alpha-foetoprotein,"
by G. L. Mizejewski, et al. NATURE 259(5540)222–
224, January 22, 1976.

"Abruptio placentae complicated by retinal artery
thrombosis," by A. T. Coopland. AMERICAN JOURNAL
OF OBSTETRICS AND GYNECOLOGY 123(8):917–918,
December 15, 1975.

"Abruptio placentae following a negative oxytocin challenge
test," by J. C. Seski, et al. AMERICAN JOURNAL OF
OBSTETRICS AND GYNECOLOGY 125(2):276, May 15,
1976.

"Acquittal of Canadian Physician in Illegal-Abortion Case
Upheld," by R. Trumbull. THE NEW YORK TIMES
(M)January 21, 12:4, 1976.

"The action of antitrophoblastic antibodies on pregnancy: an
experimental study," by P. Morin et al. JOURNAL DE
GYNECOLOGIE OBSTETRIQUE ET BIOLOGIE DE LA
REPRODUCTION 4(3):309–314, 1975. (Bio. Abstrs. 1976,
17021)

"The action of the vaccinia virus upon placenta and fetus in
revaccinated pregnants," by V. Topciu, et al. ZENTRA-
BLATT FUR BAKTERIOLOGIE [Originale, Reihe B]
161(5–6):551–556, March, 1976.

"Active pre-term management of severe osteogenesis im-
perfecta," by J. Swinhoe, et al. ACTA OBSTETRICIA
ET GYNECOLOGICA SCANDINAVICA 55(1):81–83, 1976.
(Bio. Abstrs. 1976, 1152)

15

"Acute coagulation disorders in missed abortion," by R.
Alumna. REVISTA CHILENA DE OBSTETRICIA Y
GINECOLOGIA 38(6):272-285, 1973.

"Acute complications of abortion," by E. Obel. UGESKRIFT
FOR LAEGER 138(6):319-323, February 2, 1976.

"Acute renal failure in the postpartum and post-abortion
periods observed in the maternity department of the
Hôpital Charles Nicolle," by B. Farza, et al. JOURNAL
DE GYNECOLOGIE, OBSTETRIQUE ET BIOLOGIE DE
LA REPRODUCTION 1(5 Suppl 2):443-447, 1972.

"Administrative law - social security - availability of
medicaid funds for elective abortions." WAYNE
LAW REVIEW 22:857-870, March, 1976.

"Adolescent pregnancy and abortion," by D. D. Youngs, et
al. MEDICAL CLINICS OF NORTH AMERICA 59(6):
1419-1427, November, 1975.

"Adrenaline and noradrenaline excretion during an induced
abortion," by M. Bokiniec, et al. ANNALES UNIVER-
SITATIS MARIAE CURIE-SKLODOWSKA; SECTIO D:
MEDICINA 29:151-156, 1974.

"Advances in Planned Parenthood," by R. Wynn. EXCERPTA
MEDICA 10,4:52, 1975. (Bio. Abstrs. 1976, 48468)

"Advances in Planned Parenthood," by R. Wynn. EXCERPTA
MEDICA 11,1:51, 1976. (Bio. Abstrs. 1976, 48469)

"Aetiology of anencephaly and spina bifida." (letter).
BRITISH MEDICAL JOURNAL 1(6007):455-456, February 21, 1976.

"Aetiology of spontaneous abortion. A cytogenetic and
epidemiological study of 288 abortuses and their parents,"
by J. G. Lauritsen. ACTA OBSTETRICIA ET GYNE-
COLOGICA SCANDINAVICA SUPPLEMENT (52):1-29,
1976.

"Albany Changes Bill on Abortion," by R. Smothers. THE
NEW YORK TIMES (M), May 26, 34:3, 1976.

"All Charges Withdrawn in Quebec Abortion Case." THE
NEW YORK TIMES (S), December 11, 9:6, 1976.

"Allied health board on abortion: Patients have to be favored
more than the personnel." LAKARTIDNINGEN 72(51):
5042, December 17, 1975.

"Alpha-fetoprotein during mid-trimester induced abortion,"
(letter), by Y. Beyth, et al. LANCET 2(7937):709,
October 11, 1975.

"Alpha-fetoprotein levels in maternal plasma and amniotic
fluid during prostaglandin-induced mid-trimester
abortions: the relation to fetal distress and death," by
R. H. Ward, et al. BRITISH JOURNAL OF OBSTETRICS
AND GYNAECOLOGY 83(4):299-302, April, 1976.

"Ambulatory anesthesia for induced abortion," by P. P.
Olsen. UGESKRIFT FOR LAEGER 138(30):1814-1817,
July 19, 1976.

"The American birth rate: evidences of a coming rise," by
J. Sklar, et al. SCIENCE 189(4204):693-700, 1975.
(Bio. Abstrs. 1976, 51944)

"Amniocentesis-abortion woes: many who opt to end pregnancy are unhappy about it later." MEDICAL WORLD
NEWS 17:72, July 12, 1976.

"Amniotic fluid removal prior to saline abortion," by A. C.
Mehta, et al. ANNALES CHIRURGIAE ET GYNAE-
COLOGIAE FENNIAE 65(1):68-71, 1976.

"Anaesthetics and abortions," (letter), by D. I. Rushton.
LANCET 2(7977):141, July 17, 1976.

"Analysis of the 1974 Massachusetts abortion statute and a
minor's right to abortion." NEW ENGLAND LAW REVIEW

10:417-454, Spring, 1975.

"Anencephaly: early ultrasonic diagnosis and interruption of pregnancy. Apropos of a case," by R. Chef, et al. JOURNAL DE GYNECOLOGIE, OBSTETRIQUE ET BIOLOGIE DE LA REPRODUCTION 3(1):93-104, January-February, 1974.

"Annual abortion action," by C. Ingham. MS MAGAZINE 4:79, February, 1976.

"Another opinion on abortion." SYGEPLEJERSKEN 75(33): 13-14, August 20, 1975.

"The Antiabortion Bill is Vetoed by Carey," by I. Peterson. THE NEW YORK TIMES (M), June 23, 42:2, 1976.

"Anti-abortion, the bishops and the crusaders," by J. Castelli. AMERICA 134:442-444, May 22, 1976.

"Antiabortion Candidate Sparks Funding Debate," by G. Vecsey. THE NEW YORK TIMES (M), February 9, 32:6, 1976.

"Anti-abortion Unit Calls for Inquiry." THE NEW YORK TIMES (S), July 4, 18:8, 1976.

"The antifeminism of abortion," by R. Kress. MARRIAGE AND FAMILY LIVING 58:2-5, February, 1976.

"Antigenic analysis and immunological studies of the utero-tropic bacterial strains SH6 and O1 isolated from aborted cows," by I. Gelev. VETERINARNO-MEDITSINKI NAUKI 13(4):13-22, 1976.

"Anti-PP1PK (anti-Tja) and habitual abortion," by D. B. Weiss et al. FERTILITY AND STERILITY 26(9):901-903, September, 1975.

"Application of Guttman scale analysis to physicians' attitudes regarding abortion," by M. Koslowsky, et al. JOURNAL OF APPLIED PSYCHOLOGY 61:301-304,

June, 1976.

"Application of radioimmunologic determination of placental
lactogen hormone to the prognosis of spontaneous threatened
abortion," by R. Hechtermans, et al. JOURNAL DE
GYNECOLOGIE, OBSTETRIQUE ET BIOLOGIE DE LA
REPRODUCTION 1(5 Suppl 2):331-334, 1972.

"Application of a radioeceptorassay of human chorionic
gonadotropin in the diagnosis of early abortion," by T.
P. Rosal, et al. FERTILITY AND STERILITY 26(11):
1105-1112, November, 1975.

"Archbishop Bernardin calls Ford stand disappointing, asks
support for the unborn." OUR SUNDAY VISITOR 64:1,
February 15, 1976.

"Archbishop Bernardin open to meeting with Carter."
L'OSSERVATORE ROMANO 32(436):6, August 5, 1976.

"Are progestational agents indicated in threatened abortion?"
NEDERLANDS TIJDSCHRIFT VOOR GENEESKUNDE 119
(48):1904-1905, November 29, 1975.

"Are progestational agents indicated in threatened abortion?"
(letter), by J. Wildschut. NEDERLANDS TIJDSKRIFT
VOOR GENEESKUNDE 120(7):296-297, February 14, 1976.

"Are women becoming endangered species?" by J. Anderson.
OUR SUNDAY VISITOR MAGAZINE 65:1 passim,
October 24, 1976.

"Area differences in the incidence of neural tube defect and
the rate of spontaneous abortion," by J. Fedrick, et al.
BRITISH JOURNAL OF PREVENTIVE AND SOCIAL
MEDICINE 30(1):32-35, March, 1976.

"Artificial abortion: reasons and management," by A. C.
Drogendijk, Jr. NEDERLANDS TIJDSKRIFT VOOR
GENEESKUNDE 120(19):809-814, May, 1976.

"Artificial abortion: reasons and management," by T. A. Eskes. NEDERLANDS TIJDSHRIFT VOOR GENEESKUNDE 120(19):815-816, May, 1976.

"Artificial interruption and female morbidity," by A. Kotásek, et al. CESKOSLOVENSKA GYNEKOLOGIE 41(1):31-33, March, 1976.

"As Carter Moves into Limelight He Becomes Highly Visible and Vunerable," by J. T. Wooten. THE NEW YORK TIMES (M), February 4, 15:1, 1976.

"Asherman's syndrome (Fritsch-Asherman)," by E. G. Waters. JOURNAL OF THE MEDICAL SOCIETY OF NEW JERSEY 73(9):745-747, September, 1976.

"Asherman's syndrome, the Massouras Duck's Foot-IUD (MDF-IUD) and Peacock Hook. Treatment and prevention. pp. 265-272," by H. G. Massouras. In: da Paz AC, et al., ed. Recent advances in human reporduction. Amsterdam, Excerpta Medica, 1976. W3 EX89 no. 370 1974.

"Assembly Revives An Abortion Bill," by L. Brown. THE NEW YORK TIMES (M), June 3, 74:5, 1976.

"Assembly's Abortion Bill Advances, Then Falters," by R. Smothers. THE NEW YORK TIMES (M), May 14, II, 4:7, 1976.

"Association between maternal bleeding during gestation and congenital anomalies in the offspring," by A. Ornay, et al. AMERICAN JOURNAL OF OBSTETRICS AND GYNECOLOGY 124(5):474-478, 1976. (Bio. Abstrs. 1976, 12921)

"Association of pericentric inversion of chromosome 9 and reproductive failure in ten unrealted families," by J. Boué, et al. HUMANGENETIK 30(3):217-224, September 20, 1975.

"Attempt to elucidate the causes of certain complications

following artificial abortion using radioisotopes," by A.
Atanasov, et al. AKUSHERSTVO I GINEKOLOGIIA
(Sofia) 14(5):372-375, 1975.

"Attitude of some elites towards introduction of abortion as a
method of family planning in Bangladesh," by R. H.
Chaudhury. BANGLADESH DEVELOPMENT STUDIES
3:479-494, October, 1975.

"The attitude of women to anticonception after artificial
interruption of gravidity," by D. Fukalová, et al.
CESKOSLOVENSKA GYNEKOLOGIE 40(9):680-681,
November, 1975.

"The Availability of Abortion." THE NEW YORK TIMES
February 29, IV, 7:1, 1976.

"Availability of abortion, sterilization, and other medical
treatment for minor patients," by L. J. Dunn, Jr.
UNIVERSITY OF MISSOURI AT KANSAS CITY LAW
REVIEW 44:1-22, Fall, 1975.

"Bacterial infection in cows associated with abortion,
endometritis and infertility," by I. Gelev. ZENTRAL-
BLATT FUER VETERINAERMEDIZINE. JOURNAL OF
VETERINARY MEDICINE [B] 22(5):372-380, July, 1975.

"Bacteriologic study of aerobes and anaerobes in the vaginal
flora of pregnant women and in incomplete septic abortion,"
by G. Galan, et al. REVISTA CHILENA DE OBSTETRICIA
Y GINECOLOGIA 39(6):238-243, 1974.

"The bad old days: clandestine abortions among the poor in
New York City before liberalization of the abortion law,"
by S. Polgar, et al. FAMILY PLANNING PERSPECTIVES
8(3):125-127, May-June, 1976.

"Balanced homologous translocation t(22q22q) in a
phenotypically normal woman with repeated spontaneous
abortions," by L. M. Farah, et al. HUMANGENETIK

21

28(4):357-360, August 25, 1975.

"Ban all abortions? interviews," by J. L. Bernardin, et al.
U.S. NEWS AND WORLD REPORT 81:27-28, September 27, 1976.

"Ban all abortions? No-- 'We believe in a woman's right
to make her own choice.' (interview)," by Rabbi R. S.
Sternberger. U.S. NEWS AND WORLD REPORT 81:27-
28, September 27, 1976.

"Ban all abortions? Yes-- '1 million lives are destroyed
each year;' interview," by Archbishop J. L. Bernardin.
U.S. NEWS AND WORLD REPORT 81:27-28, September 27, 1976.

"Baptists, in Shift, Ask Members to Seek Antiabortion
'Climate'," by K. A. Briggs. THE NEW YORK TIMES
(M), June 18, I, 11:1, 1976.

"The battle of abortion," by J. Turner. NEW SOCIETY
541-542, March 11, 1976.

"Battle underway on funding of abortions by governments."
OUR SUNDAY VISITOR 65:2, August 8, 1976.

"Behavior of serum magnesium level during abortion," by M.
Cilensek, et al. ZENTRALBLATT FUR GYNAEKOLOGIE
97(19):1176-1178, 1975.

"Behind the day care abortion decision," by D. Loshak.
DAILY TELEGRAPH 13, January 30, 1976.

"Bill Restricting Abortions Passed by Senate in Albany,"
by R. Smothers. THE NEW YORK TIMES (M), March 31,
18:3, 1976.

"Biological and clinical aspects of legal abortion," by G.
Pescetto. ANNALI DI OSTETRICIA, GINECOLOGIA
MEDICINA PERINATALE 96(4):215-227, July-August,
1975.

"Birth Curb Research Asked." THE NEW YORK TIMES
(S), February 29, 42:6, 1976.

"Birth rights," by C. Dix, et al. GUARDIAN 11, February 6, 1975.

"Bishop asks Catholics join Washington March for Life."
OUR SUNDAY VISITOR 64:3, January 18, 1976.

"Bishops encouraged by Ford abortion stand," by R. Casey.
NATIONAL CATHOLIC REPORTER 12:1-2, September 17,
1976.

"Bishops in politics: the big plunge; National conference of
Catholic bishops' Pastoral plan for pro-life activities,"
by P. J. Weber. AMERICA 134:220-223, March 20,
1976.

"Bishops move." ECONOMIST 260:26, September 11, 1976.

"The bishops of Columbia for the defence of life."
L'OSSERVATORE ROMANO 15(419), April 8, 1976.

"Bishops Plan Drive to Ban Abortions." THE NEW YORK
TIMES (S), January 3, 35:4, 1976.

"Bishops' plan for pro-life activities." AMERICA 133:454-
455, December 27, 1975.

"Blood coagulation studies in prostaglandin abortion,"
(proceedings), by R. Lang, et al. ARCHIV FUR
GYNAEKOLOGIE 219(1-4):501-502, November 18, 1975.

"Bovine fetal cerebal absidiomycosis," by W. U. Knudtson,
et al. SABOURAUDIA; JOURNAL OF THE INTERNATIONAL
SOCIETY FOR HUMAN AND ANIMAL MYCOLOGY 13(3):
299-302, 1975. (Bio. Abstrs. 1976, 24575)

"Bovine viral diarrhea virus-induced abortion," by J. W.
Kendrick. THERIOGENOLOGY 5(3):91-93, 1976.
(Bio. Abstrs. 1976, 32438)

"Bronchoconstriction and pulmonary hypertension during abortion induced by 15-ethyl-prostaglandin F2a," by E. K. Weir, et al. AMERICAN JOURNAL OF MEDICINE 60(4):556-562, 1976. (Bio. Abstrs. 1976, 23180)

"Brucella abortus infection in sheep: I. Field case," by W. B. Shaw. BRITISH VETERINARY JOURNAL 132(1):18-27, 1976. (Bio. Abstrs. 1976, 55552)

"Brucella abortus infection in sheep. II. Experimental infection of ewes," by W. B. Shaw. BRITISH VETERINARY JOURNAL 132(2):143-151, March-April, 1976.

"Canada's Top Court Bars Move to Reverse Abortion Acquittal." THE NEW YORK TIMES (M), March 16, 4:5, 1976.

"Canadian Abortion Doctor Wins Third Acquittal." THE NEW YORK TIMES (S), September 19, 7:1, 1976.

"The Canadian abortion law," by P. G. Coffey. CANADIAN MEDICAL ASSOCIATION JOURNAL 115(3):211-216, August 7, 1976.

"The Canadian abortion law," by M. Cohen, et al. CANADIAN MEDICAL ASSOCIATION JOURNAL 114(7): 593, April 3, 1976.

"Canadian Physician, Jailed in Abortion Case, Is Freed." THE NEW YORK TIMES (S), January 27, 2:5, 1976.

"Candidates on the issues: abortion," by E. Bowman, et al. CONGRESSIONAL QUARTERLY WEEKLY REPORT 34:463-466, February 28, 1976.

" 'Cannot be Neutral,' on Abortion Issue, Cardinal Proclaims," by G. Dugan. THE NEW YORK TIMES (S), September 27, 37:6, 1976.

"Cardinal Terence Cooke on the rights of the unborn," by

Card. T. Cooke. L'OSSERVATORE ROMANO 41(445):11-12, October 7, 1976.

"Carey Welcomes Mondale," by L. Charlton. THE NEW YORK TIMES (M) August 26, 23:2, 1976.

"Caring for all the people; respect life program on a parish level," by E. Mowery. LIGUORIAN 64:34-39, November 9, 1976.

"Carter and the Bishops." (editorial). THE NEW YORK TIMES September 2, 30:1, 1976.

"Carter and the Bishops," by K. A. Briggs. THE NEW YORK TIMES (M), September 3, I, 9:1, 1976.

"Carter Campaign Moving to Mollify Catholics After Dispute Over Democratic Party's Abortion Stand," by K. A. Briggs. THE NEW YORK TIMES (M), August 26, 10:1, 1976.

"Carter opposed to abortion but not for an amendment." OUR SUNDAY VISITOR 65:1, August 29, 1976.

"Carter says his abortion stand same as platform's." OUR SUNDAY VISITOR 65:1, August 1, 1976.

"The case for day care abortion," by J. Turner. NEW HUMANIST 91:231-232, January, 1976.

"Case of the lack of effect of anesthetization in the intravenous administration of sombrevin and hexenal," by P. M. Veropotvelian, et al. PEDIATRIIA AKUSHERSTVO I GINEKOLOGIIA (5):62, 1975.

"Case of old uterine perforation after abortus mens II/III," by J. Laube, et al. ZENTRALBLATT FUR GYNAEKOLOGIE 97(22):1378-1379, 1975.

"Case of rhinopneumonia in horses in Kirghizia," by A. V. Mokrousova, et al. VETERINARIIA (2):57,

February, 1976.

"A case of ring 18 chromosome in a sibship with multiple spontaneous abortions," by R. Coco, et al. ANNALES DE GENETIQUE 18(2):135-137, June, 1975.

"A case report: septic midtrimester abortion with an intrauterine device," by T. L. Connolly, et al. NEBRASKA MEDICAL JOURNAL 60(11):435-438, November, 1975.

"Catholic Alternatives center open to counsel on birth control," by J. Buckley. NATIONAL CATHOLIC RE-PORTER 13:6, November 5, 1976.

"Catholic bishops: abortion the issue," by W. F. Willoughby. CHRISTIANITY TODAY 20:35, December 19, 1975.

"Catholic League charges Carter endorsed abortion." OUR SUNDAY VISITOR 65:2, September 19, 1976.

"Catholic political leaders and abortion; a house divided; a look at the record of prominent Catholic national political leaders and their stance on pro-life legislation," by F. Lee. OUR SUNDAY VISITOR MAGAZINE 65:1 passim, August 29, 1976.

"Catholic vote: bishops' move." ECONOMIST 260:26, September 11, 1976.

"Catholics Promise to Oppose Abortion," by G. Dugan. THE NEW YORK TIMES (M), October 4, 10:3, 1976.

"Catholics' use of abortion," by J. J. Leon, et al. SOCIOLOGICAL ANALYSIS 36,2:125-136, Summer, 1975. (Socio. Abstrs. 1976, 76H9195)

"Causes of unwanted pregnancies and reasons for their inter-ruption," by A. Meyer. ZENTRALBLATT FUR GYNAE-KOLOGIE 97(23):1444-1449, 1975.

"The Center for Disease Control." AORN JOURNAL;
ASSOCIATION OF OPERATING ROOM NURSES 24:
333-334 passim, August, 1976.

"Certain immunologic indicators in miscarriage," by M. A.
Omarov, et al. AKUSHERSTVO I GINEKOLOGIIA (Moscow)
(9);61-62, September, 1975.

"Certain indicators of the functional state of fetoplacental
complex in pregnancy complicated by late toxemia and
threatened abortion," by M. I. Anisimova, et al.
VOPROSY OKHRANY MATERINSTVA DETSTVA 19(4):
62-66, April, 1974.

"Certain problems of the pathogenesis, clinical course and
therapy of threatened abortion (to aid the practicing
physician)," by S. M. Bekker, et al. VOPROSY
OKHRANY MATERINSTVA I DETSTVA 20(7):73-79,
July, 1975.

"Cervical diameter after suction termination of pregnancy,"
(letter), by M. M. Black, et al. BRITISH MEDICAL
JOURNAL 1(6014):902, April 10, 1976.

"Cervical diameter after suction termination of pregnancy,"
by F. D. Johnstone, et al. BRITISH MEDICAL JOURNAL
1(6001):68-69, January 10, 1976.

"Cervical dilatation and pregnancy interruption using Rivanol
for intrauterine filling," by I. Máthé, et al. ORVOSI
HETILAP 116(47):2782-2785, November 23, 1975.

"Characteristics of pregnant women who report previous
abortions," by S. Harlap, et al. BULLETIN OF THE
WORLD HEALTH ORGANIZATION 52(2):149-154, 1975.
(Bio. Abstrs. 1976, 16900)

"Childbirth or abortion? - problems of notification," by J.
Augustin. CESKOSLOVENSKA GYNEKOLOGIE 40(10):
728-729, December, 1975.

"Chlamydial abortion in sheep and goats," by Iu. D. Karavaev. VETERINARIIA (6):96-97, June, 1976.

"Chorionic haemangiomata and abruptio placentae. Case report and review," by H. G. Kohler, et al. BRITISH JOURNAL OF OBSTETRICS AND GYNAECOLOGY 83 (8):667-670, August, 1976.

"Chromosomal aberrations and disorders of evolution in repeated spontaneous abortions," by A. Zwinger, et al. CESKOSLOVENSKA GYNEKOLOGIE 41(2):121-126, April, 1976.

"Chromosomal and anatomic studies of pregnancies after discontinuation of steroid contraceptives," by A. Boué, et al. JOUNRAL DE GYNECOLOGIE, OBSTETRIQUE ET BIOLOGIE DE LA REPRODUCTION 2(2):141-154, March, 1973.

"Chromosomal study of 65 couples with spontaneous abortions," by J. L. Taillemite, et al. JOURNAL DE GYNECOLOGIE, OBSTETRIQUE ET BIOLOGIE DE LA REPRODUCTION 5(3):343-349, April-May, 1976.

"Chromosome aberrations as a cause of spontaneous abortion," by J. Kleinebrecht, et al. ZEITSCHRIFT FUR ALLGEMEINMEDIZIN; DU LANDARZT 51(22):974-977, August 10, 1975.

"Chromosome studies in couples with repeated spontaneous abortions," by C. Tsenghi, et al. OBSTETRICS AND GYNECOLOGY 47(4):463-468, 1976. (Bio. Abstrs. 1976 42979)

"Chromosome studies in 500 induced abortions," by M. Yamamoto, et al. HUMANGENETIK 29(1):9-14, August 29, 1975.

"Church in the world: abortion and divorce; a change in attitudes?" by J. Deedy. THEOLOGY TODAY 32: 86-88, April, 1975.

"The Churches and abortion." NEW HUMANIST 92:32-35, May-June, 1976.

"City setting and tolerance toward abortion: an exploratory study of attitudes of coeds," by J. P. Reed, et al. INTERNATIONAL JOURNAL OF SOCIOLOGY OF THE FAMILY 5,1:103-110, Spring, 1975. (Socio. Abstrs. 1976, 7612582)

"Clinical and epizootiological aspects of bovine, caprine, and ovine brucellosis in Greece," by P. A. Karvounaris. DEVELOPMENTS IN BIOLOGICAL STANDARDIZATION 31: 254-264, 1976.

"Clinical aspects and treatment of puerperal and postabortion staphylococcal sepsis," by V. I. Kuznetsova, et al. PEDIATRIIA AKUSHERSTVO I GINEKOLOGIIA :55-58, May-June, 1976.

"Clinical conference: Abortion and sterilization." JOURNAL OF MEDICAL ETHICS 1(1):45-48, April, 1975.

"Clinical experience using intraamniotic prostaglandin F2 alpha for midtrimester abortion in 600 patients," by G. G. Anderson, et al. OBSTETRICS AND GYNECOLOGY 46(5):591-595, November, 1975.

"Clinical observation of the prevention of RH isoimmuni-zation with immunoglobulin anti-D," by S. Hisanaga, et al. ACTA OBSTETRICA ET GYNAECOLOGICA JAPONICA 21(2):97-102, 1974. (Bio. Abstrs. 1976, 14294)

"Clinical observations with a prostaglandin-containing silastic vaginal device for pregnancy termination," by C. H. Hendricks, et al. PROSTAGLANDINS 12 Suppl: 99-122, 1976.

"A clotting defect following pregnancy termination by dilatation and curettage," by R. J. Solyn. INTERNATIONAL SURGERY 61(2):86-87, February, 1976.

"Coagulation changes during second-trimester abortion induced by intra-amniotic prostaglandin E2 and hypertonic solutions," by I. Z. Makenzie, et al. LANCET 2(7944):1066-1069, 1975. (Bio. Abstrs. 1976, 5680)

"Coagulation disorders after hypertonic-saline abortion," (letter), by J. W. ten Cate, et al. LANCET 1(7952): 205, January 24, 1976.

"Coagulation disorders after hypertonic-saline abortion," (letter), by J. R. O'Brien. LANCET 1(7955):367, February 14, 1976.

"Coagulation disorders and abortion using hypertonic solutions," (letter), by I. Craft, et al. LANCET 1(7956):428, February 21, 1976.

"Combination therapy for midtrimester abortion: Laminaria and analogues of prostaglandins," by P. G. Stubblefield, et al. CONTRACEPTION 13(6):723-729, 1976. (Bio. Abstrs. 1976, 39255)

"Comparative effects of hyperosmolar urea administered by intra-amniotic, intravenous, and intraperitoneal routes in rhesus monkeys," by D. A. Blake, et al. AMERICAN JOURNAL OF OBSTETRICS AND GYNECOLOGY 124(3):239-244, 1976. (Bio. Abstrs. 1976, 11034)

"Comparative evaluation of quantitive variation of 5 per cent intra-amniotic saline for mid-trimester abortion," by A. K. Ghosh. JOURNAL OF THE INDIAN MEDICAL ASSOCIATION 64(11):305-306, June 1, 1975.

"Comparative studies on the cytohormonal and cytochemical exponents of estrogens-progesterone activity in the vaginal lining epithelium in women with pregnancy complications. I. Threatened abortion," by J. Dudkiewicz. GINEKOLOGIA POLASKA 46(11):1133-1146, November, 1975.

"Comparative study of the causes of induced abortion and the knowledge of family planning," by M. D. Ramos Netto. REVISTA ENFERMAGEM EM NOVAS DIMENSOES 1(4): 172, September-October, 1975.

"A comparative study of intra-amniotic saline and two prostaglandin F2a dose schedules for midtrimester abortion," by D. A. Edleman, et al. AMERICAN JOURNAL OF OBSTETRICS AND GYNECOLOGY 125(2):188-195, 1976. (Bio. Abstrs. 1976, 39271)

"Comparison of culdoscopic and lararoscopic tubal sterilization," by S. Koetsawany, et al. AMERICAN JOURNAL OF OBSTETRICS AND GYNECOLOGY 124(6):601-606, 1976. (Bio. Abstrs. 1976, 11031)

"Comparison of dexamethasone trimethylacetate and prostaglandin F-2alpha as abortifacients in the cow," (proceedings), by C. A. Sloan. JOURNAL OF REPRODUCTION AND FERTILITY 46(2):529, March, 1976.

"A comparison of four methods for determining prevalence of induced abortion, Taiwan, 1970-1971," by R. V. Rider, et al. AMERICAN JOURNAL OF EPIDEMIOLOGY 103(1):37-50, January, 1976.

"Comparison of intra-amniotic prostaglandin F2 alpha and hypertonic saline for induction of second-trimester abortion." BRITISH MEDICAL JOURNAL 1(6022):1373-1376, June 5, 1976.

"A comparison of metal and plastic cannulae for performing vacuum," by S. S. Moghadam, et al. JOURNAL OF REPRODUCTIVE MEDICINE 17(3):181-187, September, 1976.

"Comparison of the MMPI and Mini-Mult with women who request abortion," by W. F. Gayton, et al. JOURNAL OF CLINICAL PSYCHOLOGY 32(3):648-650, July, 1976.

"A comparison of saline and prostaglandin abortions at the

Medical Center of Central Georgia," by J. R. Harrison, et al. JOURNAL OF THE MEDICAL ASSOCIATION OF GEORGIA 65(2):53-54, February, 1976.

"Competition between spontaneous and induced abortion," by R. G. Potter, et al. DEMOGRAPHY 12:129-141, February, 1975.

"The complexity of compiling abortion statistics," by J. C. Smith. PUBLIC HEALTH REPORTS 90(6):502-503, November-December, 1975.

"Complications after abortion. Hospitalization for early post-abortion morbidity after voluntary abortion," by G. E. Feichter. FORTSCHRITTE DU MEDIZIN 94 (16):965-967, June 3, 1976.

"Complications following ambulatory abortion," by G. Wolters. FORTSCHRITTE DU MEDIZIN 94(27):1473-1475, September 23, 1976.

"Compromise reached on use of federal funds for abortions," by T. P. Southwick. CONGRESSIONAL QUARTERLY WEEKLY REPORT 34:2541, September 18, 1976.

"Compulsory abortion: next challenge to liberated women?" by G. S. Swan. OHIO NORTHERN UNIVERSITY LAW REVIEW 3:152-175, 1975.

"Conceptual problems in our public health demography," by A. A. Curbelo. REVISTA DE SANIDAD E HIGIENE PUBLICA 48(11):1015-1019, November, 1974.

"Concurrent use of prostaglandin F2a and laminaria tents for induction of midtrimester abortion," by J. H. Duenhoelter, et al. OBSTETRICS AND GYNECOLOGY 47(4):469-472, 1976. (Bio. Abstrs. 1976, 33635)

"Conference Vote Ban on Medicaid Funds For Most Abortions," by D. E. Rosenbaum. THE NEW YORK TIMES (M), September 16, 1:3, 1976.

"Confronting objections to an anti-abortion amendment," by
R. Byrn. AMERICA 134:529-534, June 19, 1976.

"Congenital abnormalities and selective abortion," by M. J.
Seller. JOURNAL OF MEDICAL ETHICS 2(3):138-141,
September, 1976.

"Congenital malformations of the central nervous system
in spontaneous abortion," by M. R. Creasy, et al.
JOURNAL OF MEDICAL GENETICS 13(1):9-16, 1976.
(Bio. Abstrs. 1976, 14103)

"Congress Acts on Abortions." (editorial). THE NEW
YORK TIMES (S), September 19, IV, 2:2, 1976.

"Congress Approves Curb on Abortions, But Veto is
Likely," by D. E. Rosenbaum. THE NEW YORK TIMES
(M), September 18, 1:6, 1976.

"Congress Overrides Ford's Veto of Bill of Social Services,"
by R. D. Lyons. THE NEW YORK TIMES (M), October 1,
I, 1:1, 1976.

"Connecticut Loses Suit Over Minor's Abortions." THE
NEW YORK TIMES (S), October 3, 41:1, 1976.

"Connecticut physicians' attitudes toward abortion," by G.
L. Pratt, et al. AMERICAN JOURNAL OF PUBLIC
HEALTH 66:288-290, March, 1976; Reply with rejoinder,
K. Solomon, 66:905-906, September, 1976.

"Conscience clause may be next target of proabortion forces,"
by E. J. Schulte. HOSPITAL PROGRESS 57:19 passim,
August, 1976.

"Conscience of the law," by J. E. Hogan. CAHTOLIC
LAWYER 21:190-196, Summer, 1975.

"Consent question--parental and spousal consent for abortions," by C. D. Davis. TEX HOSPITALS 32:27-30,
September, 1976.

"Consideration on the problem of pregnancy with inter-
occurrency of acute illness in the patient and the so
called therapeutic abortion," by J. E. dos Santos Alves,
et al. REVISTA DA ASSOCIACAO MEDICA BRASILEIRA
22(1):21-28, January, 1976.

"Constitutional law - abortion - parental and spousal consent
requirements violate right to privacy in abortion decision."
KANSAS LAW REVIEW 24:446-462, Winter, 1976.

"Constitutional law - abortion - Utah statute requiring notification of husband by physician upheld." WESTERN
STATE UNIVERSITY LAW REVIEW 3:313-323, Spring,
1976.

"Constitutional law - commercial speech doctrine - a
clarification of the protection afforded advertising under
the first amendment." BRIGHAM YOUNG UNIVERSITY
LAW REVIEW 1975:797-811, 1975.

"Constitutional law - denial of equal protection to patient as
also constituting denial of equal protection to physician."
UNIVERSITY OF TOLEDO LAW REVIEW 7:213-229,
Fall, 1975.

"Constitutional law - first amendment - freedom of speech -
advertising cannot be denied first amendment protection,
absent a showing by the state of a legitimate public
interest justifying its regulation." UNIVERSITY OF
CINCINNATI LAW REVIEW 44:852-859, 1975.

"Constitutional law - first amendment - newspaper advertisement of abortion referral service entitled to first
amendment protection." UNIVERSITY OF RICHMOND
LAW REVIEW 10:427-433, Winter, 1976.

"Constitutional law - first amendment - United States
Supreme Court held that the first amendment protected
an abortion advertisement which conveyed information
of potential interest to an audience, despite its appearance in the form of a paid commercial advertisement."

INDIANA LAW REVIEW 8:890-897, 1975.

"Constitutional law - freedom of the press - prohibition
of abortion referral service advertising held unconstitutional." CORNELL LAW REVIEW 61:640-660, April,
1976.

"Constitutional right of privacy - minor's right to an abortion - statutory requirement of spousal consent, or
parental consent in the case of an unmarried, minor
female, is an unconstitutional deprivation of a woman's
right to determine whether to undergo an abortion."
HOFSTRA LAW REVIEW 4:531-547, Winter, 1976.

"Constitutional validity of abortion legislation: a comparative
note," by H. P. Glenn. MCGILL LAW JOURNAL 21:673-
684, Winter, 1975.

"Consultation for abortion. Experiences and results," by
V. S. Sievers, et al. FORTSCHRITTE DU MEDIZIN
94(2):70-72, January 15, 1976.

"Contraception alone will not allow us to control population,"
by T. Smith. TIMES 12, July 7, 1975.

"Contraception, sterilization and abortion in NZ."
NURSING FORUM (Auckl) 4:6-9, June-July, 1976.

"Contraceptive practice and prevention as alternative to
legitimization of indiscriminate abortion," by I. Vandelli,
et al. ANNALI DI OSTETRICIA, GINECOLOGIA,
MEDICINA PERINATALE 96(4):254-273, July-August,
1975.

"The contribution of hysterosalpinography to the study of
post partum and post abortum menstrual insufficiency,"
by M. Georgian, et al. RADIOLOGIA 14(1):27-34,
1975. (Bio. Abstrs. 1976, 16978)

"Cooke, On Anniversay of Ruling, Scores Court's Abortion
Position," by G. Dugan. THE NEW YORK TIMES

(M), January 23, 20:4, 1976.

"Correlation of the diagnostic value of vaginal cytology and
   estimation of total urinary oestrogens in threatened
   pregnancies," by I. Misinger, et al. CESKOSLOVENSKA
   GYNEKOLOGIE 40(7):512-514, August, 1975.

"Corynebacterium pyogenes-induced abortion," by R. E.
   Smith. THERIOGENOLOGY 5(3):107-109, 1976.
   (Bio. Abstrs. 1976, 26769)

"Counsel for abortion," by J. Turner. GUARDIAN 11,
   August 15, 1975.

"Counselling for abortion," by M. Blair. MIDWIFE,
   HEALTH VISITOR AND COMMUNITY NURSE 11(11):
   355-356, November, 1975.

"Courageous Veto." (editorial). THE NEW YORK TIMES
   June 25, I, 26:2, 1976.

"Court abortion decisions draw strong criticisms." OUR
   SUNDAY VISITOR 65:2, July 18, 1976.

"Court Lifts Medicaid Ban for Voluntary Abortions." THE
   NEW YORK TIMES (S), March 11, 42:6, 1976.

"Created in the image of God: man and abortion," by R.
   Slesinski. LINACRE 43:36-48, February, 1976.

"Criminal abortion using ruta roots (Ruta graveolens L.),"
   by K. Wehr. BEITRAEGE ZUR GERICHTLICHEN
   MEDIZIN 32:126-131, 1974.

"Criminal law: defence: #45-criminal code: charge of performing illegal abortion: whether defence available where
   criminal code procedure not followed: elements of the
   defence: criminal code #'s 45, 251." OTTAWA LAW
   REVIEW 8:59-69, Winter, 1976.

"The culturability of fibroblasts from the skin of abortuses

after intra-amniotic instillation of urea or prostaglandin,"
by K. S. Ju, et al. AMERICAN JOURNAL OF OBSTETRICS
AND GYNECOLOGY 125(8):1155, August 15, 1976.

"Culture Lacking Jerseyans Feel." THE NEW YORK TIMES
(M), March 25, 76:6, 1976.

"The current status of prostaglandins as abortifacients," by
W. E. Brenner. AMERICAL JOURNAL OF OBSTETRICS
AND GYNECOLOGY 123(3):306-328, October 1, 1975.

"Cystine aminopeptidase activity (oxytocinase) in pregnant
guinea pigs: Normal and infected with Campylobacter
fetus," by R. Hrabak, et al. AMERICAN JOURNAL OF
VETERINARY RESEARCH 37(3):343-344, 1976. (Bio.
Abstrs. 1976, 36106)

"Cytogenetic studies in reproductive loss," by R. Schmidt,
et al. JAMA; JOURNAL OF THE AMERICAN MEDICAL
ASSOCIATION 236(40:369-373, 1976. (Bio. Abstrs.
1976, 54722)

"Cytogenetic study of families with habitual abortions," by
G. Vulkova, et al. AKUSHERSTVO I GINEKOLOGIIA
(Moscow) 15(2):111-115, 1976.

"A cytogenetic study of human spontaneous abortions using
banding techniques," by M. R. Creasy, et al. HUMAN
GENETICS 31(2):177-196, February 29, 1976. (Bio.
Abstrs. 1976, 31538)

"Cytogenetics of fetal wastage," by H. J. Kim, et al.
NEW ENGLAND JOURNAL OF MEDICINE 293(17):844-
847, October 23, 1975.

"Dangerous developments on the subject of therapeutic
abortion; Italy's decisions after the Seveso contamination,"
by G. Guzzetti. L'OSSERVATORE ROMANO 39(443):11,
September 23, 1976.

37

"Day-care abortion: facts and fantasies," by C. Tomalin.
HEALTH AND SOCIAL SERVICE JOURNAL 86:353,
February 21, 1976.

"Days of hope," by J. Turner. GUARDIAN 9, November 12,
1975.

"Death Bill." (editorial). THE NEW YORK TIMES May 11,
32:2, 1976.

"Debating abortion: a non-Catholic and a scientist; amend
the constitution," by H. Arkes. WALL STREET JOURNAL
188:26, October 26, 1976.

"Declaration of Permanent Council of Italian Bishops'
Conference; abortion issue." L'OSSERVATORE ROMANO
1(405):9, January 1, 1976.

"Declaration on procured abortion," by J. Hamer.
C.I.C.I.A.M.S. NOUVELLES (2):7-18, 1975.

"The defence of the true and complete values of life," by
A. Vernaschi. L'OSSERVATORE ROMANO 17(421):
8-9, April 22, 1976.

"Defining the 'benefits' to the malformed fetus. Abortion:
for the fetus's own sake?" by P. F. Camenisch.
HASTINGS CENTER REPORT 6(2):38-41, April, 1976.

"Delayed morbidity following prostaglandin-induced abortion,"
by I. Z. Mackenzie, et al. INTERNATIONAL JOURNAL
OF GYNAECOLOGY AND OBSTETRICS 13(5):209-214,
1975. (Bio. Abstrs. 1976, 23175)

"Democrats for Life formed to work for an amendment."
OUR SUNDAY VISITOR 65:2, August 1, 1976.

"Democrats take stand against pro-lifers." OUR SUNDAY
VISITOR 65:1, June 27, 1976.

"The demographic effect of induced abortion," by C. Tietze,

et al. OBSTETRICAL AND GYNECOLOGICAL SURVEY
31(10):699–709, October, 1976.

"Depressed mixed lymphocyte culture reactivity in mothers
with recurrent spontaneous abortion," by J. G. Lauritsen,
et al. AMERICAN JOURNAL OF OBSTETRICS AND
GYNECOLOGY 125(1):35–39, 1976. (Bio. Abstrs. 1976,
34459)

"Detection of anti–HL–A serum antibodies in habitual abortion (possibilities of the use of the leukoagglutination
method) pp. 167–172," by N. S. Cavallaro, et al. In:
Marchesi F, Cittadini E, ed. Fertilità e sterilità.
Taormina, Minerva medica, 1974. WP 570 S679f 1973.

"Detection of anti–Toxoplasma gondii antibodies in subjects
with repeated abortions, perinatal mortality and malformed infants," by A. Castro, et al. ANNALI SCLAVO
18(1):75–81, January–February, 1976.

"Determination of Rh blood group of fetuses in abortions
by suction curettage," by R. M. Greendyke, et al.
TRANSFUSION 16(3):267–269, May–June, 1976.

"The development of instruments to measure attitudes toward
abortion and knowledge of abortion," by S. Snegroff.
JOURNAL OF SCHOOL HEALTH 46(5):273–277, May, 1976.

"The diagnosis and treatment of threatened miscarriage," by
B. Faris. AUSTRALASIAN NURSES JOURNAL 4:7,
October, 1975.

"Diagnosis of Asherman's syndrome (intrauterine synechiae),"
by I. Berta, et al. ZENTRALBLATT FUR GYNAE-
KOLOGIE 98(8):495–503, 1976.

"The diagnosis of early pregnancy failure by sonar," by H.
P. Robinson. BRITISH JOURNAL OF OBSTETRICS
AND GYNAECOLOGY 82(11):849–857, November, 1975.

"Diagnosis, treatment and prognosis of threatened abortion,"

by H. Wilken, et al. ZENTRALBLATT FUR GYNAE-
KOLOGIE 98(19):577-586, 1976.

"Diagnostic and therapeutic studies of abortion caused by
cervix insufficiency based on our case records from 1964
to the present, pp. 173-193," by S. Mangiameli. In:
Marchesi F, Cittadini E, ed. Fertilità e sterilità.
Taormina, Minerva medica, 1974. WP 570 S679f 1973.

"Diagnostic and therapy of the asherman's syndrome," by K.
Poradovský, et al. CESKOSLOVENSKA GYNEKOLOGIE
40(7):502-503, August, 1975.

"Diagnostic examination methods in threatened pregnancy.
Panel discussion." ARCHIV FUR GYNAEKOLOGIE
219(1-4):399 passim, November 18, 1975.

"Diagnostic X-Ray Examination Called No Ground for
Abortion." THE NEW YORK TIMES (M), October 21,
16:1, 1976.

"Dietary urea for dairy cattle: II. Effect of functional
traits," by R. E. Erb, et al. JOURNAL OF DAIRY
SCIENCE 59(4):656-667, 1976. (Bio. Abstrs. 1976,
23478)

"Dilemma." (pictorial). CANADIAN NURSE 72:51-55,
August, 1976.

"Dilemma: therapeutic abortion following amniocentesis,"
by N. L. Rudd, et al. CANADIAN NURSE 72:51-56,
August, 1976.

"Disclosure on abortion," (letter), by P. J. Huntingford.
LANCET 1(7956):434-435, February 21, 1976.

"Discretionary killing," by G. F. Will. NEWSWEEK 88:
96, September 20, 1976.

"Disseminated intravascular coagulation in abruptio
placentae--report of a case," by N. Saito, et al.

ACTA OBSTETRICA ET GYNAECOLOGICA JAPONICA 22(2):113-118, April, 1975.

"Dissent '76; amendment not answer to abortion," by M. Bunson. NATIONAL CATHOLIC REPORTER 12:5, March 26, 1976.

"The distribution within the placenta, myometrium, and decidua of 24Na-labelled hypertonic saline solution following intra-amniotic or extra-amniotic injection," by B. Gustavii. BRITISH JOURNAL OF OBSTETRICS AND GYNAECOLOGY 82(9):734-739, September, 1975.

"Do the medical schools discriminate against anti-abortion applicants?" by E. Diamond. LINACRE 43:29-35, February, 1976.

"Doctor Asks Court to Overturn His Conviction in Fetus Death." THE NEW YORK TIMES (S), April 6, 25:2, 1976.

"Doctor predicts abortion without death in future." OUR SUNDAY VISITOR 64:1, March 7, 1976.

"Doe v. Beal (523 F 2d 611): abortion, Medicaid and equal protection." VIRGINIA LAW REVIEW 62:811-837, May, 1976.

"Doe v. Doe [(Mass) 314 N E 2d 128]: the wife's right to an abortion over her husband's objections." NEW ENGLAND LAW REVIEW 11:205-224, Fall, 1975.

"Dole campaign ad controversy revived [antiabortion ads]." EDITOR AND PUBLISHER-THE FOURTH ESTATE 109:34, September 4, 1976.

"Domestic relations: minors and abortion - the requirement of parental consent." OKLAHOMA LAW REVIEW 29: 145-155, Winter, 1976.

"Draft letter on abortion sent bishops." NATIONAL

CATHOLIC REPORTER 12:14, January 9, 1976.

"Dropsy of the fetal sacs in mares: induced and spontaneous abortion," by M. Vandeplassche, et al. VETERINARY RECORD 99(4):67-69, July 24, 1976.

"Due process and equal protection: constitutional implications of abortion notice and reporting requirements." BOSTON UNIVERSITY LAW REVIEW 56:522-541, May, 1976.

"Dutch Senate, by 7 Votes, Rejects Legal Abortions; Coalition Crisis Allayed." THE NEW YORK TIMES (S), December 15, I, 14:3, 1976.

"Early complications and late sequelae of induced abortion. A review of the literature," by K. G. B. Edström. BULLETIN OF THE WORLD HEALTH ORGANIZATION 52(2):123-139, 1975. (Bio. Abstrs. 1976, 16899)

"Early pregnancy interruption by 15(S) 15 methyl prostaglandin F2a methyl ester," by M. Bygdeman, et al. OBSTETRICS AND GYNECOLOGY 48(2):221-224, 1976. (Bio. Abstrs. 1976, 56848)

"Early pregnancy testing and its relationship to abortion," by C. F. Irwin. JOURNAL OF REPORDUCTION AND FERTILITY [SUPPLEMENT] (23):485-488, October, 1975.

"Early termination of pregnancy: a comparative study of intrauterine prostaglandin F2 alpha and vacuum aspiration," by M. I. Ragab, et al. PROSTAGLANDINS 11(2):261-273, February, 1976.

"Early vacuum aspiration: minimizing procedures to non-pregnant women," by E. R. Miller, et al. FAMILY PLANNING PERSPECTIVES 8(1):33-38, January-February, 1976.

"Economic value of statute reform: the case of liberalized
abortion," by T. A. Deyak, et al. JOURNAL OF
POLITICAL ECONOMY 84:83-99, February, 1976.

"Ectopic pregnancy after postcoital diethylstillbestrol,"
by A. R. Smythe, et al. AMERICAN JOURNAL OF
OBSTETRICS AND GYNECOLOGY 121(2):284-285,
1975. (Bio. Abstrs. 1976, 11530)

"Edelin case rekindles right-to-life hopes," by R. Adams.
FAITH FOR THE FAMILY 9, November-December,
1975.

"Effect of aspirin on bleeding time during elective abortion," by R. Waltman, et al. OBSTETRICS AND
GYNECOLOGY 48(1):108-110, 1976. (Bio. Abstrs.
1976, 58163)

"Effect of climatic-weather conditions on the incidence of
miscarriage," by I. I. Nikberg, et al. VOPROSY
OKHRANY MATERINSTVA I DETSTVA 21(1):28-31,
January, 1976.

"The effect of dilysosomal macrophages on the development
and the outcome of pneumonia induced by the agent of
anzootic abortion of ewes," by V. E. Pigarevskii, et al.
BYULLETEN' EKSPERIMENTAL' NOI BIOLOGII I
MEDITSENY 81(4):440-442, 1976. (Bio. Abstrs. 1976,
55559)

"Effect of the extracts from Aristolochia indica Linn. on
interception in female mice," by A. Pakrashi, et al.
EXPERIENTIA 32(3):394-395, March 15, 1976.

"Effect of large daily doses of ascarlic acid on pregnancy in
guinea pigs, rats and hamsters," by F. R. Alleva, et al.
TOXICOLOGY AND APPLIED PHARMACOLOGY 35(2):
393-395, 1976. (Bio. Abstrs. 1976, 7026)

"The effect of the legalization of abortion on public health
and some of it social concomitants in Hungary," by

M. Miklos. DEMOGRÁFIA 16,1:70-113, 1976. (Socio. Abstrs. 1976, 76I1408)

"The effect of meperidine analgesia on midtrimester abortions induced with intra-amniotic prostaglandin F2a," by L. G. Staurovsky, et al. AMERICAN JOURNAL OF OBSTETRICS AND GYNECOLOGY 125(2):185-187, 1976. (Bio. Abstrs. 1976, 50604)

"Effect of prostaglandin F2 alpha on the neurohypophysis: A histo-chemical study," by U. Singh, et al. ACTA MORPHOLOGICA ACADEMIA SCIENTIARUM HUNGARICAE 23(1):51-57, 1975. (Bio. Abstrs. 1976, 13626)

"Effectiveness of ultrasonic diagnosis in abortion," by W. W. Stein, et al. ARCHIV FUR GYNAEKOLOGIE 219 (1-4):549-550, November 18, 1975.

"Effectiveness of vaccination against Chlamydia abortion in sheep," by W. A. Valder, et al. DEUTSCHE TIERAERZTLICHE WOCHENSCHRIFT 82(6):221-225, 1975.

"The effects of attitude and direction of true-false intersperesed questions on the learning of a prase passage on a controversial topic," by S. S. El-Azzabi. DISSERTATION ABSTRACTS INTERNATIONAL 34(11-A), 7039, May, 1974. (Pscho. Abstrs. 1976, 13140)

"Effects of legal termination and subsequent pregnancy," by R. E. Coles, et al. BRITISH MEDICAL JOURNAL 2(6026):45, July 3, 1976.

"Effects of legal termination on subsequent pregnancy," (letter), by G. Dixon, et al. BRITISH MEDICAL JOURNAL 2(6030):299, July 31, 1976.

"Effects of legal termination on subsequent pregnancy," by J. A. Richardson, et al. BRITISH MEDICAL JOURNAL 1(6021):1303-1304, May 29, 1976.

"The effects of a liberalized abortion law on pregnancy
outcome. pp. 135-137," by J. T. Lanman, et al.
In: Kelly S, et al., ed. Birth defects: risks and consequences. New York, Academic Press, 1976. OS
675 B622 1974.

"Effects of prostaglandin E2 and F2 alpha therapy," by
I. S. Fraser. COMPREHENSIVE THERAPY 2(9):
55-59, September, 1976.

"The effects of selective withdrawal of FSH or LH on
spermatogenesis in the immature rat," by R. H. G.
Madhwa. BIOLOGY OF REPRODUCTION 14(4):489-
494, 1976. (Bio. Abstrs. 1976, 13477)

"Effects of spontaneous abortions on the frequency of
birth of twins," by P. Lazar. COMPES RENDUS
HEBDOMADAIRES DES SEANCES DE L'ACADEMIE
DES SCIENCES; D: SCIENCES NATURELLES 282(3):
243-246, January 12, 1976.

"The efficacy and safety of intramuscularly administered
15(S) 15 methyl prostaglandin E2 methyl ester for
induction of artificial abortion," by W. E. Brenner,
et al. AMERICAN JOURNAL OF OBSTETRICS AND
GYNECOLOGY 123(1):19-29, September 1, 1975.

"The efficacy of intravaginal 15 methyl prostaglandin F2
alpha methyl ester in first and second trimester abortion," by T. F. Dillon, et al. PROSTAGLANDINS
12 Suppl:81-98, 1976.

"Electoencephalographic changes following intraamniotic
prostaglandin F2a administration for therapeutic
abortion," by A. Faden, et al. OBSTETRICS AND
GYNECOLOGY 47(5):607-608, 1976. (Bio. Abstrs.
1976, 27851)

"Ellen McCormack: campaigning for the unborn," by B.
Beckwith. ST. ANTHONY MESSENGER 83:30-36, May,
1976.

"Elimination of spontaneous and chemically induced chromosome aberrations in mice during early embryogenesis," by A. Basler, et al. HUMAN GENETICS 33(2):121-130, July 27, 1976.

"An Emotional Issue's Status in the Courts," by L. Oelsner. THE NEW YORK TIMES (M), March 1, 28:1, 1976.

"The end of the Dalkon shield." (editorial). MEDICAL JOURNAL OF AUSTRALIA 2(14):542, October 4, 1975.

"End of Medicaid for Abortions Feared," by G. Goodman, Jr. THE NEW YORK TIMES (M), February 14, 12:4, 1976.

"Endocrine assessment of threatened abortion," (proceedings), by R. E. Rewell. JOURNAL OF CLINICAL PATHOLOGY 28(9):757, September, 1975.

"Endocrine habitual abortion. pp. 63-76," by C. Montoneri. In: Marchesi F, Cittadini E, ed. Fertilità e sterilità. Taormina, Minerva medica, 1974. WP 570 S679f 1973.

"Endometrial aspiration in fertility control. A report of 500 cases," by R. P. Bendel, et al. AMERICAN JOURNAL OF OBSTETRICS AND GYNECOLOGY 125(3): 328-332, June 1, 1976.

"Endometrial ossification," by C. Hsu. BRITISH JOURNAL OF OBSTETRICS AND GYNAECOLOGY 82(10):836-839, October, 1975.

"The epidemiology of infertility." WHO CHRONICLE 30(6): 229-233, June, 1976.

"Epizootic bovine abortion," by J. W. Kendrick. THERIO-GENOLOGY 5(3):99-101, 1976. (Bio. Abstrs. 1976, 26785)

"Equine rhinopneumonitis virus infection in horses," by R. G. Dijkstra. TIJDSCHRIFT VOOR DIERGENEESKUNDE 100

(17):930-931, September 1, 1975.

"Equine virus abortion," (letter), by J. I. Phillip. VETER-
INARY RECORD 98(14):283, April 3, 1976.

"E.R.A. and Abortion Face Senate Test," by M. Waldron.
THE NEW YORK TIMES (M), December 5, XI, 6:5,
1976.

"Error during abortion--2 physicians got warning."
LAKARTIDNINGEN 73(4):231-232, January 21, 1976.

"Establishment of prognosis in threatened abortion. Value
of the combined use of diagnostic ultrasound and quantitative determination of chorionic gonadotropin hormone,"
by S. Levi, et al. JOURNAL DE GYNECOLOGIE,
OBSTETRIQUE ET BIOLOGIE DE LA REPRODUCTION
2(2):155-160, March, 1973.

"Estrogen content of the amniotic fluid, plasma and placental
tissue during abortion induced by prostaglandin F2 alpha
and 15-methyl-prostaglandin F2 alpha," by V. G. Orlova,
et al. AKUSHERSTVO I GINEKOLOGIE (Moscow) (6):
24-28, June, 1975.

"Ethics in embryo: abortion and the problem of morality in
post-war German literature," by A. F. Keele.
GERMANIC REVIEW 51:229-241, May, 1976.

"Etiopathogenesis of habitual abortion. pp. 3-9," by I.
Panella, et al. In: Marchesi F, Cittadini E, ed.
Fertilità e sterilità. Taormina, Minerva medica, 1974.
WP 570 S679f 1973.

"Eugenic recognition in Canadian law," by B. M. Dickens.
OSGOODE HALL LAW JOURNAL 13:547-577, October,
1975.

"European Communist states turn away from abortion," by
H. Szablya. OUR SUNDAY VISITOR 64:3, January 25,
1976.

47

"Evaluation of abortion techniques: recent and future trends. pp. 164-173," by R. J. Pion, et al. In: Moghissi KS, Evans TN, ed. Regulation of human fertility. Detroit, Wyane State Univ Press, 1976. W3 HA292 1973r.

"Evaluation of the causes of habitual abortion and malformation in children based on cytogenetic examination of parents," by E. Samochowiec, et al. ZENTRALBLATT FUR GYNAEKOLOGIE 97(7):419-425, 1975.

"Evaluation of the chorionic gonadotropin level, determined by the immunological method, in the prognosis of threatened abortion," by C. Croce, et al. MINERVA GINECOLOGIA 28(2):112-117, February, 1976.

"Evaluation of intramuscular 15(S)-15-methyl prostaglandin F2 alpha tromethamine salt for induction of abortion, medications to attenuate side effects, and intracervical laminaria tents," by W. Gruber, et al. FERTILITY AND STERILITY 27(9):1009-1023, September, 1976.

"Evaluation of a preevacuated endometrial suction apparatus in general obstetric-gynecologic practice," by M. J. Padawer, et al. NEW YORK STATE JOURNAL OF MEDICINE 76(6):885-888, June, 1976.

"Evaluation of vaginal delivery systems containing 15[s]15-methyl PGF2alpha methyl ester," by C. H. Spilman, et al. PROSTAGLANDINS 12 Suppl:1-16, 1976.

"Evangelical looks at the abortion phenomenon," by H. O. J. Brown. AMERICA 135:161-164, September 25, 1976.

"Evidence of the Royal College of General Practitioners to the Select Committee of Parilament on the Abortion (Amendment) Bill." JOURNAL OF THE ROYAL COLLEGE OF GENERAL PRACTITIONERS 25(159): 774-776, October, 1975.

"Evidence of serum HPL level for prognosis of threatening abortion," by P. Tykal, et al. ARCHIV FUR

GYNAEKOLOGIE 219(1-4):418-419, November 18, 1975.

"The evolution of ideas about therapeutic interruption of
pregnancy," by M. Monrozies. JOURNAL DE GYNE-
COLOGIE, OBSTETRIQUE ET BIOLOGIE DE LA
REPRODUCTION 4(2):162-175, March, 1975.

"Exemption on Abortion Reported in Italy." THE NEW YORK
TIMES (S), August 3, 2:4, 1976.

"Experience with 276 intra-amniotic prostaglandin F2a
induced midtrimester abortions," by M. S. Golbus, et
al. PROSTAGLANDINS 11(5):841-851, 1976. (Bio.
Abstrs. 1976, 62686)

"Experimental abortions in mice and guinea pigs caused by
Aspergillus fumigatus spores," by S. Venev.
VETERINARNO-MEDITSINSKI NAUKE 13(1):86-93, 1976.

"An experimental study of Salmonella dublin abortion in
cattle," by G. A. Hall, et al. BRITISH VETERINARY
JOURNAL 132(1):60-65, 1976. (Bio. Abstrs. 1976,
55553)

"Experimentally induced bovine abortion with Mycoplasma
agalactiae subsp bovis," by O. H. Stalheim, et al.
AMERICAN JOURNAL OF VETERINARY RESEARCH
37(8):879-883, August, 1976.

"Extra-amniotic 15 (S)-15 methyl PGF2alpha to induce
abortion: a study of three administration schedules," by
I. Z. Mackenzie, et al. PROSTAGLANDINS
12(3):443-453, September, 1976.

"Extra-amniotic mannitol for pregnancy termaintion (preliminary report)," by M. A. Deshmukh, et al. JOURNAL
OF POSTGRADUATE MEDICINE 22(1):23-25, January,
1976.

"Facing a grand jury." AMERICAN JOURNAL OF NURSING

76:398-400, March, 1976.

"Factor analysis of attitudes toward abortion," by B.
Corenblum, et al. PERCEPTUAL AND MOTOR SKILLS
40(2):587-591, April, 1975.

"Facts and evils of free abortion; reprint from Civilta
Cattolica, March 6, 1976," by G. Caprile.
L'OSSERVATORE ROMANO 21(425):5 passim, May 20,
1976.

"Familial C/D translocation t(9;13)(9p23.13q21) in a male
associated with recurrent abortion," by D. Singh-
Kahlon, et al. HUMAN GENETICS 33(3):223-230,
August 30, 1976.

"Fatal case of nivaquine poisoning. Medico-legal and
toxicological study," by H. J. Lazarini, et al.
MEDICINE LEGALE ET DOMMAGE CORPOREL
7(4):332, October-December, 1974.

"Fatal complication of pregnancy interruption (Karman
method)," (letter), by H. Larrieu, et al. NOUVELLE
PRESSE MEDICALE 4(38):2733, November 8, 1975.

"Fatal fulminating diabetes mellitus," by J. F. Jewett.
NEW ENGLAND JOURNAL OF MEDICINE 294(23):
1289-1290, June 3, 1976.

"The fate of the child after threatened abortion," by H.
J. Wallner. JOURNAL OF PERINATAL MEDICINE
2(1):54-60, 1974.

"Federal hospitals to follow Supreme Court abortion rules."
MODERN HEALTHCARE, SHORT-TERM CARE EDITION
5:16b, February, 1976.

"Fertility and fertility problems in some beef herds in
Sweden," by S. Einarsson, et al. NORDISK VETER-
INAER MEDICIN 27(9):411-428, September, 1975.

"Fertility control transition from abortion to contraception in Japan since 1948," by T. Aso. INTERNATIONAL REVIEW OF MODERN SOCIOLOGY 4,1,43-53, Spring, 1974. (Socio. Abstrs. 1976, 76I1520)

"Fertility patterns in female mice following treament with arginine vasotocin or melatonin," by M. K. Vaughan, et al. INTERNATIONAL JOURNAL OF FERTILITY 21(1):65-68, 1976. (Bio. Abstrs. 1976, 30927)

"Fertility problems caused by infectious agents pigs in the Netherlands," by J. P. Akkermans. TIJDSCHRIFT VOOR DIERGENEESKUNDE 100(15):809-820, August 1, 1975.

"Fetal loss and familial chromosome 1 translocations," by J. H. Garrett, et al. CLINICAL GENETICS 8(5):341-348, November, 1975.

"Fetal membranes. Microscopic aspects in abortions and intrauterine deaths with retention," by A. Turcas, et al. JOURNAL DE GYNECOLOGIE, OBSTETRIQUE BIOLOGIE DE LA REPRODUCTION 2(1):23-32, January-February, 1973.

"Fetomaternal transfusion in abortion and pregnancy interruptions and Rh-prevention," by H. Radzuweit, et al. ZENTRALBLATT FUR GYNAEKOLOGIE 97(22):1367-1374, 1975.

"Fetus papyraceus," (letter), by R. P. Balfour. OBSTETRICS AND GYNECOLOGY 47(4):507, April, 1976.

"Fetus papyraceus," by A. Targaszewska, et al. POLSKI TYGODNIK LEKARSKI 30(41):1713-1714, October 13, 1975.

"The fight for life: it's up to you; some practical guidelines to make your voice heard," by M. Bunson. OUR SUNDAY VISITOR MAGAZINE 64:1 passim, May 2, 1976.

"First and repeat abortions: a study of decision-making and delay," by M. B. Bracken, et al. JOURNAL OF BIO-SOCIAL SCIENCE 7,4:473-491, October, 1975. (Socio. Abstrs. 1976, 7612866)

"First experiences with a (15S)-15-methyl prostaglandin F2alpha vaginal device for termination of early first trimester pregnancy with serial sonographic observations," by H. J. Duenhoelter, et al. PROSTAGLANDINS 12 Suppl:135-145, 1976.

"First trimester abortion by vacuum aspiration," by E. Borko, et al. ANNALES CHIRURGIAE ET GYNAE-COLOGIAE FENNIAE 64(5):320-325, 1975.

"Fitting the bill," by J. Cook. GUARDIAN 11, October 21, 1975.

"Focal glomerulonephritis, pregnancy and miscarriage," (letter), by E. Lusvarghi. NEPHRON 16(4):322-323, 1976.

"Foley Pressing Antiabortion Issue," by M. Waldron. THE NEW YORK TIMES (S), May 21, II, 21:1, 1976.

"Ford Abortion Stand Draws Criticism." THE NEW YORK TIMES (M), February 5, 15:1, 1976.

"Ford Says Court 'Went to Far' on Abortion '73," by J. M. Naughton. THE NEW YORK TIMES (M), February 4, 1:3, 1976.

"Foe of Abortion Qualifies for U.S. Aid," by E. Shanahan. THE NEW YORK TIMES (M), February 26, 21:3, 1976.

"Foreign workers and pregnancy interruption," by E. Burckhardt-Tamm, et al. THERAPEUTISCHE UMSCHAW 32(9):577-579, September, 1975.

"Four familial translocations ascertained through spontaneous abortions," by D. H. Carr, et al. HUMAN

GENETICS 31(1):93-96, 1976. (Bio. Abstrs. 1976, 25779

"419,000 Abortions in India." THE NEW YORK TIMES (S), August 21, 18:2, 1976.

"45,XO Turner's syndrome without evidence of mosaicism in a patient with two pregnancies," by J. Philip, et al. ACTA OBSTETRICIA ET GYNECOLOGICA SCANDINAVICA 55(3):283-286, 1976. (Bio. Abstrs. 1976, 54731)

"The frequency and causes of spontaneous abortion following artificial insemination," by A. Campana, et al. GEBURTSHILFE UND FRAUENKEILKUNDE 36(5):421-429, May, 1976.

"French Critize Medical Society," by J. F. Clarity. THE NEW YORK TIMES (M), April 11, 19:1, 1976.

"Functional colpocytology in threatened abortion and internal abortion. pp. 153-5," by N. Marotta, et al. In: Marchesi F, Cittadini E, ed. Fertilità e sterilità. Taormina, Minerva medica, 1974. WP 570 S679f 1973.

"A further chromosome analysis in induced abortions," by M. Yamamoto, et al. HUMAN GENETICS 34(1):69-71, September 10, 1976.

"G. B. Drayson, M.P." NEW HUMANIST 9:287-288, March, 1976.

"Genital cytologic abnormalities in patients having therapeutic abortion," by W. T. Creasman, et al. SOUTHERN MEDICAL JOURNAL 69(2):199-200, February, 1976.

"Genital listeriosis (a case report)," by P. Jagtap, et al. JOURNAL OF POSTGRADUATE MEDICINE 21(3):157-160, July, 1975.

"Genetic analysis of families with reciprocal translocations,"
by I. V. Lur'e, et al. GENETIKA 9(11):159-164,
November, 1973.

"Genetic aspects of habitual abortion. pp. 31-41," by F.
Mollica. In: Marchesi F, Cittadini E, ed. Fertilità
e sterilità. Taormina, Minerva medica, 1974. WP
570 S679f 1973.

"Genetic examination of patients in consultation for sterility
or miscarriage," by M. M. Freund, et al. JOURNAL
DE GENETIQUE HUMAINE 23 Suppl:112-113, October,
1975.

"Give us our daily bread (a feature on aborting abnormal
fetus)," by H. Yeager. CATHOLIC MIND 28, September,
1975.

"Gonorrhea in obstetric patients," by D. E. Jones, et al.
JOURNAL OF THE AMERICAN VENEREAL DISEASE
ASSOCIATION 2(3):30-32, 1976. (Bio. Abstrs. 1976,
28653)

"Gravibinan in the treatment of threatened abortion," by J.
Krzysiek, et al. GINEKOLOGIA POLASKA 47(3):321-
325, March, 1976.

"Grieving and unplanned pregnancy," by M. E. Swigar, et
al. PSYCHIATRY 39:72-80, February, 1976.

"Group Plans to Sue to Bar Any Change in Rules on Abortion,"
by J. Cummings. THE NEW YORK TIMES (S), September 29, 19:5, 1976.

"Guidance prior to abortion," by V. Sele. UGESKRIFT FOR
LAEGER 138(6):379, February 2, 1976.

"Gun or slow poison." TIME 107:61-62, April 19, 1976.

"Habitual abortion and pathology of the seminal fluid.

pp. 195-202," by R. Agostini, et al. In: Marchesi F,
Cittadini E, ed. Fertilità e sterilità. Taormina,
Minerva medica, 1974. WP 570 S679f 1973.

"Habitual abortion: biochemical aspects. pp. 77-90," by L.
Iachello. In: Marchesi F, Cittadini E, ed. Fertilità
e sterilità. Taormina, Minerva medica, 1974. WP
570 S679f 1973.

"Habitual abortion: causes and pathogenetic aspects.
pp. 11-29," by S. di Leo. In: Marchesi F, Cittadini E,
ed. Fertilità e sterilità. Taormina, Minerva medica,
1974. WP 570 S679f 1973.

"Habitual abortion studied in the light of our seminological
knowledge. pp. 203-212," by G. Nicora, et al. In:
Marchesi F, Cittadini E, ed. Fertilità e sterilità.
Taormina, Minerva medica, 1974. WP 570 S679f 1973.

"Haemophilus parahemolyticus associated with abortion in
swine," by R. W. Wilson, et al. CANADIAN VETER-
INARY JOURNAL 17(8):222, August, 1976.

"Hare on abortion," by R. Werner. ANALYSIS 36:177-
181, June, 1976.

"Health Aides and Abortion Groups Assail Proposed
Medicaid Control," by J. Maynard. THE NEW YORK
TIMES (M), September 18, 9:1, 1976.

"Health and human rights," (pictorial), by N. Howard-Jones,
et al. WORLD HEALTH ORGANIZATION :3-31, January,
1976.

"Health care issues," by Sister M. A. A. Zasowska, et al.
HEALTH CARE DIMENSIONS :1-158, Fall, 1974.

"Health personnel organization for professional self-
determination," by B. Brekke. SYKEPLEIEN 61(22):
1145-1147, November 20, 1974.

"HCG, HPL, oestradiol, progesterone and AFP in serum in patients with threatened abortion," by J. Kunz, et al. BRITISH JOURNAL OF OBSTETRICS AND GYNAE-COLOGY 83(8):640-644, August, 1976.

"H.E.W. Funds Bill Stalled in House by Abortion Issue." THE NEW YORK TIMES (S), August 11, 71:4, 1976.

"High Court Affirms Lower Federal Court Ruling." THE NEW YORK TIMES (S), November 30, 31:1, 1976.

"High court again gives approval for abortion in three new decisions." OUR SUNDAY VISITOR 65:1, July 11, 1976.

"High Court Bars Challenge to Hospital Abortion Curb," by L. Olesner. THE NEW YORK TIMES (M), March 2, 1:5, 1976.

"High Court Bars Giving a Husband Veto on Abortion," by L. Oelsner. THE NEW YORK TIMES (M), July 2, I, 1:8, 1976.

"The High Courts' Last Full Week is its Fullest." THE NEW YORK TIMES (S), July 4, IV, 3:1, 1976.

"High court forbids parental, spouse veto over abortions [state laws that require a married woman to get her husband's consent or a minor to have her parent's or guardian's permission to obtain a first-trimester abortion were declared unconstitutional by the U.S. supreme court on July 1, 1976]." FAMILY PLANNING PER-SPECTIVES 8:177-178, July-August, 1976.

"Histological analysis of spontaneous abortions with trisomy 2: first description of an embryo," by J. Kleinebrecht, et al. HUMANGENETIK 29(1):15-22, August 29, 1975.

"Histological studies on hemostasis in abortions in the second and third month of pregnancy: comparison with post partum hemostasis," by R. Slunsky. ARCHIV FUR GYNAEKOLOGIE 220(4):325-338, 1976. (Bio.

Abstrs. 1976, 51867)

"A histologic study of the placentas of patients with saline-
and prostaglandin-induced abortion," by S. Puri.
OBSTETRICS AND GYNECOLOGY 48(2):216-220, 1976.
(Bio. Abstrs. 1976, 56851)

"Historical record explains Bartlett Amendment defeat,"
(letter), by P. G. Driscoll. HOSPITAL PROGRESS
56(11):6, 1975.

"History of the relation between pregnancy and pulmonary
tuberculosis and therapeutic abortion," by T. M.
Caffaratto. MINERVA GINECOLOGIA 28(2):192-201,
February, 1976.

"Hormonal consequences of the therapeutic interruption of
pregnancy by an intraamniotic injection of concentrated
sodium chloride solution. pp. 21-33," by H. de
Watteville, et al. In: Vokaer R, De Bock G, ed.
Reproductive endocrinology. Oxford, Pergamon Press,
1975. WQ 200 F673r 1973.

"Hormonal surveillance in the 1st trimester of pregnancy,"
by E. van Bogaert, et al. BRUXELLES-MEDICAL 55
(2):71-78, February, 1975.

"Hormonal treatment in habitual abortions," by S. Grigorov,
et al. AKUSHERSTVO I GINEKOLOGIIA (Sofia) 14(3):
171-175, 1975.

"Hormone release and abortifacient effectiveness of a
newly developed silastic device containing 15-ME-
PGF2alpha methyl ester in concentrations of 0.5% and
1.0%," by N. H. Lauersen, et al. PROSTAGLANDINS
12 Suppl:63-79, 1976.

"Hospital Sued Over Abortion." THE NEW YORK TIMES
(S), March 18, 45:1, 1976.

"Hospitals - a current analysis of the right to abortions

57

and sterilizations in the Fourth circuit: state action and the church amendment." NORTH CAROLINA LAW REVIEW 54:1307-1316, September, 1976.

"House Panel Hears Abortion Argument." THE NEW YORK TIMES (S), February 6, 36:5, 1976.

"House subcommittee hears wide range of testimony on pro-life amendment." OUR SUNDAY VISITOR 64:2, February 22, 1976.

"House unit hears prelates, legal experts argue for, against abortion amendment." NATIONAL CATHOLIC REPORTER 12:32, April 2, 1976.

"How abortion spread to the Mideast and the Orient," by M. Bunson. OUR SUNDAY VISITOR MAGAZINE 65:1 passim, June 27, 1976.

"How to abort a government." ECONOMIST 259:62, April 10, 1976.

"Human being: the boundaries of the concept," by L. C. Becker. PHILOSOPHY AND PUBLIC AFFAIRS 4:334-359, Summer, 1975.

"Human placental lactogen levels in the serum during early pregnancy," by R. Dudenhausen, et al. JOURNAL OF PERINATAL MEDICINE 2(2):93-100, 1974.

"Human values and biotechnology," by M. A. Seibert, et al. MOMENTUM 7:4-12, February, 1976.

"Humane abortion services: a revolution in human right and the delivery of a medical service," by M. S. Burnhill. MOUNT SINAI JOURNAL OF MEDICINE, NEW YORK 42(5):431-438, September-October, 1975.

"Husband's consent for abortion struck down by U.S. Supreme Court: Missouri." HOSPITALS 50:22, August 1, 1976.

"I was a spy at a Right-to-life convention," by L. Farr.
MS MAGAZINE 4:77-78 passim, February, 1976.

"Ideal family size as an intervening variable between
religion and attitudes towards abortion," by M. Rehzi.
JOURNAL FOR THE SCIENTIFIC STUDY OF RELIGION
14,1:23-27, March, 1975. (Socio. Abstrs. 1976,
76H7964)

"Identification of C trisomies in human abortuses," by J.
Boue, et al. JOURNAL OF MEDICAL GENETICS 12
(3):265-268, 1975. (Bio. Abstrs. 1976, 60541)

"Illegal abortions and the Abortion Act 1967," by P.
Cavadino. BRITISH JOURNAL OF CRIMINOLOGY 16:
63-67, January, 1976.

"Illegal abortions in the united states: 1972-1974," by W.
Cates, Jr., et al. FAMILY PLANNING PERSPECTIVES
8(2):86-92, March-April, 1976.

"I'm here to scrub your tummy; abortion clinic," by M.
Amundson. MS MAGAZINE 4:20, June, 1976.

"Immunologic rejection of chromosomally abnormal
fetuses," by T. Kushnick. PERSPECTIVES IN
BIOLOGY AND MEDICINE 18(2):292-293, Winter, 1975.

"Immunological aspects of habitual abortion. pp. 43-61,"
by N. S. Cavallaro. In: Marchesi F, Cittadini E, ed.
Fertilità e sterilità. Taormina, Minerva medica, 1974.
WP 570 S679f 1973.

"Impact of the abortion decisions upon the father's role," by
J. P. Witherspoon. JURIST 35:32-65, 1975.

"The impact of induced abortions on fertility," by M. Károly.
DEMOGRAFIÁ 13,4:413-420, 1970. (Socio. Abstrs. 1976.
76I0122)

"The impact of liberalized abortion legislation on contra-

59

ceptive practice in Denmark," by R. L. Somers, et al.
STUDIES IN FAMILY PLANNING 7(8):218-223, August,
1976.

"The impact of voluntary abortion on American obstetrics
and gynecology," by D. P. Swartz. MOUNT SINAI
JOURNAL OF MEDICINE, NEW YORK 42(5):468-
478, September-October, 1975.

"Implications of pregnanediol titre pattern on the fate of
threatened abortion," by R. N. Ghosh. JOURNAL OF
THE INDIAN MEDICAL ASSOCIATION 66(1):4-6,
January 1, 1976.

"Importance of Abortion." THE NEW YORK TIMES (S),
February 8, IV, 3:1, 1976.

"In defence of life and love; homily," by Card. G.
Colombo. L'OSSERVATORE ROMANO 20(424):4-5,
May 13, 1976.

"Incidence of abortion and contraception patterns during
1968-1974," by R. L. Somers, et al. UGESKRIFT FOR
LAEGER 138(6):353-355, February 2, 1976.

"Incidence of abortion during treatment with ovulation
inducers. pp. 219-224," by G. Guastella, et al. In:
Marchesi F, Cittadini E, ed. Fertilità e sterilità.
Taormina, Minerva medica, 1974. WP 570 S679f
1973.

"Incidence of infections associated with the intrauterine
contraceptive device in an isolated community," by
P. B. Mead, et al. AMERICAN JOURNAL OF
OBSTETRICS AND GYNECOLOGY 125(1):79-82, 1976.
(Bio. Abstrs. 1976, 34365)

"Incomplete abortions in Accra and Bangkok University
Hospitals 1972-1973," by I. C. Chi, et al. INTER-
NATIONAL JOURNAL OF GYNAECOLOGY AND
OBSTETRICS 13(4):148-161, 1975. (Bio. Abstrs. 1976,

22865)

"An inconvenient fetus." NURSING MIRROR AND MID-
WIVES' JOURNAL 141:76, July 17, 1975.

"Indiana Abortion Rule Voided." THE NEW YORK TIMES
(S), June 17, 36:8, 1976.

"Indications and contraindications for the interruption
in dermatologic diseases," by N. Sönnichsen.
THERAPEUTISCHE UMSCHAW 31(5):301-306, May,
1974.

"Indications of choice for extra-amniotic perfusion of
physiologic serum," by M. Blum, et al. JOURNAL DE
GYNECOLOGIE, OBSTETRIQUE BIOLOGIE DE LA
REPRODUCTION 5(4):577-584, June, 1976.

"Induced abortion," by K. W. Andersen, et al. UGESKRIFT
FOR LAEGER 137(46):2716, November 10, 1975.

"Induced abortion and contraceptive practice: an experience
in Taiwan," by I. H. Su, et al. STUDIES IN FAMILY
PLANNING 7:224-230, August, 1976.

"Induced abortion and the course of the next pregnancy,
labor and puerperium," by H. Zrubek, et al.
GINEKOLOGIA POLASKA 47(1):32-37, January, 1976.

"Induced abortion and secondary infertility," by D.
Trichopoulos, et al. BRITISH JOURNAL OF OBSTE-
TRICS AND GYNAECOLOGY 83(8):645-650, August,
1976.

"Induced abortion: epidemiological aspects," by D. Baird.
JOURNAL OF MEDICAL ETHICS 1(3):122-126,
September, 1975.

"Induced abortion in the 8-9th week of pregnancy with
vaginally administered 15-methyl PGF2alpha methyl
ester," by A. Leader, et al. PROSTAGLANDINS

61

12(4):631-637, October, 1976.

"Induced abortion in Texas," by L. H. Roht, et al. TEXAS
MEDICINE 72(4):84-91, April, 1976.

"Induced abortion, Jewish law and Jewish morality," by
F. Rosner. MAN AND MEDICINE 1:213-224, Spring,
1976.

"Induced abortion-a new major study." JOURNAL OF THE
ROYAL COLLEGE OF GENERAL PRACTITIONERS
26(169):558-559, August, 1976.

"Induced abortion: 1975 factbook," by C. Tietze, et al.
REPORTS ON POPULATION-FAMILY PLANNING
(14):1-75, December, 1975.

"Induced abortions and spontaneous abortions. Psychopathological aspects apropos of a preliminary sample
of 411 requests for pregnancy interruption," by M.
Bourgeois, et al. ANNALES MEDICO-PSYCHOL-
OGIQUES 2(2):339-366, July, 1975.

"Induced legal abortions of juveniles," by M. Farkas, et
al. DEMOGRÁFIA 17,2:236-243, 1974. (Socio.
Abstrs. 1976, 76I1399)

"Induction of abortion by vaginal administration of 15(s)15-
methyl prostaglandin F2alpha methyl ester. A comparison of two delivery systems," by M. Bygdeman,
et al. PROSTAGLANDINS 12 Suppl: 27-51, 1976.

"Induction of abortion in cattle with prostaglandin F2alpha
and oestradiol valerate," by A. Brand, et al.
TIJDESHRIFT VOOR DIERGENEESKUNDE 100(8):432-
435, April 15, 1975.

"Induction of abortion with anti-feto-placental antibody,"
by Y. Amano. CLINICAL ENDOCRINOLOGY 24(7):
625-629, July, 1976.

"Induction of abortion with intra-amniotic or intra-muscular 15(S)-15-methyl-prostaglandin F2alpha," by O. Ylikorkala, et al. PROSTAGLANDINS 10(3): 423-434, September, 1975.

"Induction of midtrimester abortion by serial intravaginal administration of 15(S)-15-methyl-prostaglandin F2 alpha (THAM) suppositories," by N. H. Lauersen, et al. PROSTAGLANDINS 10(6):1037-1045, December, 1975.

"Induction of midtrimester abortion with intraamniotic urea, intravenous oxytocin and laminaria," by I. M. Golditch, et al. JOURNAL OF REPRODUCTIVE MEDICINE 15(6):225-228, December, 1975.

"Induction of second trimester abortion by infusion of intraamniotic hypertonic and extraamniotic physiological saline solution," by M. Blum, et al. GEBURTSHILFE UND FRAUENHEILKUNDE 36(5): 444-447, May, 1976.

"Infectious bovine rhinotracheitis virus: experimental attempts at inducing bovine abortion with a New Zealand isolate," by P. J. Durham, et al. NEW ZEALAND VETERINARY JOURNAL 23(5):93-94, May, 1975.

"Infectious bovine rhinotracheites virus-induced abortion," by C. A. Kirkbride. THERIOGENOLOGY 5(3):94-97, 1976. (Bio. Abstrs. 1976, 26841)

"Influence of abortion-rate in Czechoslovakia on the selected phenomena of reproduction processes," by H. Wynnyczuková, et al. DEMOGRAFIE 17,3:193-204, 1975. (Socio. Abstrs. 1976, 76I0155)

"Influence of abortions and interruptions of pregnancies on subsequent deliveries. I. Course of pregnancy," by P. Knorre. ZENTRALBLATT FUR GYNAEKOLOGIE 98(10):587-590, 1976.

"Influence of abortions and interruptions of pregnancies on subsequent deliveries. II. Course of labor," by P. Knorre. ZENTRALBLATT FUR GYNAEKOLOGIE 98(10):591-594, 1976.

"Influence of abortions and interruptions of pregnancies on subsequent deliveries. III. After-labor-period and puerperium," by P. Knorre. ZENTRALBLATT FUR GYNAEKOLOGIE 98(10):595-599, 1976.

"The influence of aspirin on the course of induced mid-trimester abortion," by J. R. Niebyl, et al. AMERICAN JOURNAL OF OBSTETRICS AND GYNECOLOGY 124(6): 607-610, 1976. (Bio. Abstrs. 1976, 16218)

"The influence of induced abortion on Taiwanese fertility," by J. M. Sullivan, et al. STUDIES IN FAMILY PLANNING 7(8):231-238, August, 1976.

"Inhalation anesthetics--more vinyl chloride?" by T. H. Corbett. ENVIRONMENTAL RESEARCH 9:211-214, June, 1975.

"Inhibitory effect of progesterone on the lactogenic and abortive action of prostaglandin F2alpha," by N. T. Vermouth, et al. JOURNAL OF ENDOCRINOLOGY 66(2):21-29, July, 1975.

"Insertion of the Lippe's loop immediately after abrasio residuorum and interruptio graviditatis," by D. Mishev. AKUSHERSTVO I GINEKOLOGIIA (Sofia) 15(1):49-52, 1976.

"An interdisciplinary course in human sexuality for medical and nursing students," by F. H. Mims. DISSERTATION ABSTRACTS INTERNATIONAL 35(3-A), 1506, September, 1974.

"Interpretative analysis of 50 cases of tocolysis treated with isoxsuprine," by A. Tomassini, et al. MINERVA GINECOLOGIA 27(11):861-873, November, 1975.

"Interruption of pregnancy in the Netherlands." (letter).
ZEITSCHRIFT FUR ALLGEMEINMEDIZIN; DU
LANDARZT 51(10):493-499, April 10, 1975.

"Intra-abdominal bleeding following subcutaneous heparin
application in septic abortion," by D. Susemihl, et al.
GEBURTSHILFE UND FRAUENHEILKUNDE 36(2):126-
127, February, 1976.

"Intra-amniotic administration of 15(S)-15-methyl-
prostaglandin F2alpha for the induction of midtrimester
abortion," by J. R. Dingfelder, et al. AMERICAN
JOURNAL OF OBSTETRICS AND GYNECOLOGY 125
(6):821-826, July 15, 1976.

"Intra-amniotic administration of prostaglandin F2 alpha,
12-methyl-prostaglandin F2 alpha and hypertonic
sodium chloride solution for induction of abortion in
second-trimester pregnancy," by L. S. Persianinov,
et al. ZENTRALBLATT FUR GYNAEKOLOGIE 97(19):
1153-1159, 1975.

"Intra-amniotic instillation of a hypertonic solution via the
cervical canal," by G. Geshev. AKUSHERSTVO I
GINEKOLOGIIA (Sofia) 14(4):275-278, 1975.

"Intra-amniotic urea and prostaglandin F2 alpha for midtrimester abortion: a modified regimen," by R. T.
Burkman, et al. AMERICAN JOURNAL OF OBSTE-
TRICS AND GYNECOLOGY 126(3):328-333, October 1,
1976.

"Intramuscular (15S)-15-methyl prostaglandin F2alpha
for midtrimester and missed abortions," by S. D.
Sharma, et al. OBSTETRICS AND GYNECOLOGY
46(4):468-472, October, 1975.

"Intrauterine adhesions secondary to elective abortion.
Hysteroscopic diagnosis and management," by C. M.
March, et al. OBSTETRICS AND GYNECOLOGY
48(4):422-444, October, 1976.

"Intra-uterine administration of prostaglandin F2alpha for
induction of abortion. pp. 27-30." In: Bergström S, ed.
Report from meetings of the Prostaglandin Task Force
Steering Committee. Stockholm, 1973. QV 175 W927r
1972-1973.

"Intra-uterine administration of prostaglandin F2alpha or
15-methyl PGF2alpha for induction of abortion. Intra-
amniotic method. pp. 79." In: Bergström S, ed.
Report from meetings of the Prostaglandin Task Force
Steering Committee. Stockholm, 1973. QV 175 W927r
1972-1973.

"Intrauterine aspiration in humans in the early fetal period,"
by M. Makkaveeva. ARKHIV PATHOLOGIE 37(12):41-
46, 1975. (Bio. Abstrs. 1976, 36105)

"Intrauterine extra-amniotic 15(s)-15-methyl prostaglandin
F2alpha for induction of early midtrimester abortion,"
by A. G. Shapiro. FERTILITY AND STERILITY 27(9):
1024-1028, September, 1976.

"Intrauterine (extraamniotic) prostaglandins in the management of unsuccessful pregnancy," by A. A. Calder,
et al. JOURNAL OF REPRODUCTIVE MEDICINE
16(5):271-275, May, 1976.

"Intrauterine injection of 15(S)-15-methyl-prostaglandin
F2alpha for termination of early pregnancy in outpatient," by O. Ylikorkala, et al. PROSTAGLANDINS
10(2):333-341, August, 1975.

"The intravenous infusion of prostaglandin F2alpha in the
management of intrauterine death of the fetus," by
N. Moe. ACTA OBSTETRICIA ET GYNECOLOGICA
SCANDINAVICA 55(2):113-114, 1976.

"Invited discussion: the use of induced abortuses for
monitoring. pp. 197-203," by T. Tanimura. In:
Shepard Th et al., ed. Methods for detection of
environmental agents that produce congenital defects.

Amsterdam, North-Holland, 1975. QS 675 M592 1974, 1974.

"The Irish emigrant and the abortion crisis." WORLD OF IRISH NURSING 4(10):1-2, October, 1975.

"Is abortion a Catholic issue?" CHRISTIANITY TODAY 20:29, January 16, 1976.

"Is abortion ever a 'last resort'." AMERICA 140, February 21, 1976.

"Is abortion only a Catholic issue?" by J. Higgins. LIGUORIAN 64:24-28, May, 1976.

"Is the pro-life movement dying at the grass-roots?" by F. Gannon. OUR SUNDAY VISITOR MAGAZINE 65:1 passim, August 8, 1976.

"Isolation and identification of a virus causing abortions and stillbirths in swine: a preliminary communication," by M. Dilovski, et al. VETERINARNO-MEDITSINSKI NAUKI 12(8):52-53, 1975. (Bio. Abstrs. 1976, 29133)

"Isolation of antigen in the diagnosis of enzootic abortion of sheep by use of the complement fixation test," by R. V. Borovik, et al. VETERINARIIA (6):51-53, June, 1975.

"Italian bishops get flack because of anti-Communism." OUR SUNDAY VISITOR 64:2, January 4, 1975.

"Italian Catholic jurists on question of abortion." L'OSSERVATORE ROMANO 14(418):4, April 1, 1976.

"Italian Party Chief, in One-Man Drive, Seeks a National Consensus on Policy," by A. Shuster. THE NEW YORK TIMES (M), April 7, 2:4, 1976.

"Italy Allocates Funds for Gassed Region." THE NEW YORK TIMES (S), August 11, 2:6, 1976.

"Italy in a Political Crisis Over Abortion," by A. Shuster. THE NEW YORK TIMES (M), April 3, 9:4, 1976.

"Italy: our decision, say women." ECONOMIST 257:49, December 13, 1975.

"Italy: stoking hell's fire." ECONOMIST 257:49, December 20, 1975.

"IUD and induced abortion," by S. O. Skouby. UGESKRIFT FOR LAEGER 138(6):339-341, February 2, 1976.

"Jackson Abortion Stand is Disputed by His Wife." THE NEW YORK TIMES (S), March 11, 34:1, 1976.

"James White's bid for reform," by J. White. GUARDIAN 11, July 30, 1976.

"Jimmy Carter and the Catholic Bishops," by W. V. Shannon. THE NEW YORK TIMES September 5, IV, 13:2, 1976.

"Justice Byron White gives dissent on abortion cases," by J. Castelli. OUR SUNDAY VISITOR 65:3, July 18, 1976.

"Justices, Back Tomorrow, to Face Abortion and Death Penalty Issues," by L. Oelsner. THE NEW YORK TIMES (M), October 3, 1:4, 1976.

"Justifying 'wholesale slaughter'," by D. Van De Veer. CANADIAN JOURNAL OF PHILOSOPHY 5,245-258, October, 1975.

"Karyotype of the parents after spontaneous abortion? Translocation 46 XY t(2p-;21q⁄) detected in the husband of a woman who presented with 2 early spontaneous abortions," by D. Rabineau, et al. JOURNAL DE GYNECOLOGIE, OBSTETRIQUE BIOLOGIE DE LA REPRODUCTION 3(2):265-270, March, 1974.

"Karyotypes of spontaneous human abortuses and several

aspects of their phenotypic presentation," by N. M.
Slozina, et al. TSITOLOGIIA 17(8):989-993, August,
1975.

"Karyotyping of in cases of spontaneous abortions," by L.
Wisniewski, et al. GINEKOLOGIA POLASKA 47(1):57-66,
January, 1976.

"Key weapon in flight for life; bishops outline a workable
plan against abortion," by J. Fink. OUR SUNDAY
VISITOR MAGAZINE 64:1 passim, January 25, 1976.

"Kill or cure," by J. Linklater. SPECTATOR 782,
June 28, 1975.

"Killing--mission of the physician? I." by E. Trube-
Becker. MEDIZINISCHE KLINIK 71(18):786-788,
April 30, 1976.

"Kinetic and metabolic studies of 15-methyl-prostaglandin
F2a administered intra-amniotically for induction of
abortion," by K. Green, et al. PROSTAGLANDINS
11(4):699-711, 1976. (Bio. Abstrs. 1976, 50694)

"Kyematopathological studies in cases of late abortion,"
(proceedings), by D. Lüthje, et al. ARCHIV FUR
GYNAEKOLOGIE 219(1-4):285, November 18, 1975.

"Labor induction by intra-amniotic administration of
prostaglandin F 2 alpha," by H. Halle, et al.
ZENTRALBLATT FUR GYNAEKOLOGIE 97(19):1160-
1165, 1975.

"Laboratory diagnosis of Vibrio fetus-induced abortion,"
by J. H. Bryner. THERIOGENOLOGY 5(3):129-138,
1976. (Bio. Abstrs. 1976, 26770)

"Laceration of umbilical artery and abruptio placentae
secondary to amniocentesis," by J. D. James, et al.
OBSTETRICS AND GYNECOLOGY 48(1 Suppl):44S-45S,

July, 1976.

"Lament for one million fetuses," by M. Mulder. BANNER 4, August 15, 1975.

"Laminaria augmentation of intra-amniotic PGF2 for midtrimester pregnancy termination," by P. G. Stubblefield, et al. PROSTAGLANDINS 10(3):413-422, September, 1975.

"Laminaria augmentation of midtrimester pregnancy termination by intramuscular prostaglandin 15 (S)-15-methyl F2 alpha," by J. Robins, et al. JOURNAL OF REPRODUCTIVE MEDICINE 16(6):334-336, June, 1976.

"Laminaria in abortion. Use in 1368 patients in first trimester," by W. M. Hern. ROCKY MOUNTAIN MEDICAL JOURNAL 72(9):390-395, September, 1975.

"A large pericentric inversion of human chromosome 8," by R. Herva, et al. AMERICAN JOURNAL OF HUMAN GENETICS 28(3):208-212, May, 1976.

"Late complications following abortus provocatus," by E. Obel. UGESKRIFT FOR LAEGER 138(6):323-328, February 2, 1976.

"Late therapeutic abortion induced by intra-amniotic injection of a hypertonic saline solution," by R. Wyss, et al. JOURNAL DE GYNECOLOGIE, OBSTETRIQUE BIOLOGIE DE LA REPRODUCTION 3(8):1189-1206, December, 1974.

"Law and life sciences. Abortion and the Supreme Court: round two," by G. J. Annas. HASTINGS CENTER REPORT 6(5):15-17, October, 1976.

"Law birth weight subsequent to induced abortion: a historical prospective study of 948 women in Skopje, Yugoslavia," by C. J. Hogue. AMERICAN JOURNAL OF OBSTETRICS AND GYNECOLOGY 123(7):675-681, 1975. (Bio. Abstrs. 1976, 5154)

"Law for the nurse supervisor," by H. Creighton.
    SUPERVISOR NURSE 6:10-11 passim, April, 1975.

"Lead content of tissues of baby rats born of, and nourished
    by lead-poisoned mothers," by N. P. Singh, et al.
    JOURNAL OF LABORATORY AND CLINICAL MEDICINE
    87(2):273-280, 1976. (Bio. Abstrs. 1976, 23141)

"Legal abortion. Abortion as a form of contraception? A
    prospective study of 608 women applying for abortion,"
    by P. Diederich, et al. UGESKRIFT FOR LAEGER
    138(6):355-359, February 2, 1976.

"Legal abortion and hemostasis. Histological examinations
    and comparison to post partum hemostasis," by R.
    Slunsky. ARCHIV FUR GYNAEKOLOGIE 220(4):325-
    338, April 29, 1976.

"Legal abortion: an appraisal of its health impact," by G. S.
    Berger. INTERNATIONAL JOURNAL OF GYNAECOLOGY
    AND OBSTETRICS 13(4):165-170, 1975. (Bio. Abstrs.
    1976, 22866)

"Legal abortion: a half-decade of experience," by J. Pakter,
    et al. FAMILY PLANNING PERSPECTIVES 7(6):248-
    255, November-December, 1975.

"Legal abortion in the county of Funen in relation to the
    liberalized Danish legislation," by F. H. Nielsen, et al.
    UGESKRIFT FOR LAEGER 138(6):369-375, February 2,
    1976.

"Legal abortion in gynecological departments following free
    access to abortion," by F. Lundvall. UGESKRIFT FOR
    LAEGER 138(6):360-363, February 2, 1976.

"Legal abortion--1000 women. Data concerning contra-
    ception, age and obstetric history," by F. Lundvall.
    UGESKRIFT FOR LAEGER 138(6):363-369, February 2,
    1976.

"Legal abortion. Organizational and medical problems,"
(editorial), by V. Sele. UGESKRIFT FOR LAEGER
138(6):350, February 2, 1976.

"Legal abortion. A prospective study of outpatient legal
abortion in the Municipal hospital in Arhus during a 1
year period," by B.R. Moller, et al. UGESKRIFT
FOR LAEGER 138(6):329-333, February 2, 1976.

"Legal abortion. Review after introduction of outpatient
abortions," by P. C. Davidsen, et al. UGESKRIFT
FOR LAEGER 138(6):375-378, February 2, 1976.

"Legal abortions at the University-Gynecological Clinic
Mannheim during 1971-1974," by W. von Mühlenfels,
et al. FORTSCHRITTE DU MEDIZIN 93(31):1530-
1532, November 6, 1975.

"Legal aspects of menstrual regulation: some preliminary
observations," by L. T. Lee, et al. JOURNAL OF
FAMILY LAW 14:181-221, 1975.

"Legal aspects of some methods of birth-control," by
N. Endre. DEMOGRÁFIA 13,4:355-385, 1970.
(Socio. Abstrs. 1976, 76I0044)

"Legal consequences of the 'right' to abortion," by L. E.
Rozovsky. DIMENSIONS IN HEALTH SERVICE 53(4):
14-15, April, 1976.

"Legal enforcement, moral pluralism and abortion," by
R. De George. AMERICAN CATHOLIC PHILOSOPHICAL
ASSOCIATION PROCEEDINGS 49:171-180, 1975.

"Legal problems related to abortion and menstrual regu-
lation," by A. M. Dourlen-Rollier. COLUMBIA
HUMAN RIGHTS LAW REVIEW 7:120-135, Spring-
Summer, 1975.

"Legal rights of minors to sex-related medical care," by
E. W. Paul. COLUMBIA HUMAN RIGHTS LAW REVIEW

6:357-377, Fall-Winter, 1975.

"Leptospirosis-induced abortion," by C. S. Roberts.
THERIOGENOLOGY 5(3):110-122, 1976. (Bio.
Abstrs. 1976, 26768)

"Let's lower our voices about abortion," by K. Axe.
U.S. CATHOLIC 41:14-15, June, 1976.

"Let's not reject children of chance," by A. Nowlan.
THE ATLANTIC ADVOCATE 66:79, June, 1976.

"A life threatening pregnancy," by E. Moult. MATERNAL-
CHILD NURSING JOURNAL 4(3):207-211, Fall, 1975.

"Life With Uncle," by R. Baker. THE NEW YORK TIMES
(M), March 28, VI, p. 9, 1976.

"Listeria monocytogenes-induced abortion," by R. E.
Smith. THERIOGENOLOGY 5(3):123-127, 1976.
(Bio. Abstrs. 1976, 32339)

"Live birth: a condition precedent to recognition of rights."
HOFSTRA LAW REVIEW 4:805-836, Spring, 1976.

"Long Island Poll," by F. Lynn. THE NEW YORK TIMES
(M), May 2, XXI, 31:1, 1976.

"Low birth weight subsequent to induced abortion. A historical prospective study of 948 women in Skopje, Yugoslavia," by C. J. Hogue. AMERICAN JOURNAL OF
OBSTETRICS AND GYNECOLOGY 123(7):675-681,
December 1, 1975.

"The luteal phase defect," by G. S. Jones. FERTILITY
AND STERILITY 27(4):351-356, April, 1976.

"Luteolytic and abortifacient effects of serial intramuscular
injections of 15(S)-15-methyl-prostaglandin F2alpha in
early pregnancy," by N. H. Lauersen, et al. AMERICAN
JOURNAL OF OBSTETRICS AND GYNECOLOGY 124(4):

425-429, February 15, 1976.

"The MacNeil Report," by J. Hennesee. THE NEW YORK
TIMES (M), April 4, II, 25:1, 1976.

"Magisterial teaching on life issues," by Card. H.
Medeiros. L'OSSERVATORE ROMANO 36(440):4-5,
September 2, 1976.

"Mail on Abortion." THE NEW YORK TIMES (S), July 25,
30:8, 1976.

"Main Street Now: Burgers' 'n Sex," by F. Ferretti. THE
NEW YORK TIMES (M), February 1, XI, 1:1, 1976.

"Management of failed prostaglandin abortions," by N. H.
Lauersen, et al. OBSTETRICS AND GYNECOLOGY
47(4):473-478, 1976. (Bio. Abstrs. 1976, 16203)

"Management of intrauterine fetal demise and missed
abortion using prostaglandin E2 vaginal suppositories,"
by E. M. Southern, et al. OBSTETRICS AND GYNE-
COLOGY 47(5):602-606, 1976. (Bio. Abstrs. 1976,
24567)

"Management of patients at risk for fetal malformation,"
by M. Watt. NURSING MIRROR AND MIDWIVES'
JOURNAL 142:61-63, May 6, 1976.

"Management of spontaneous abortion and fetal death by
extra-amnial administration of a single dose of alpha
prostaglandin 2," by K. Lajos, et al. ORVOSI HETILAP
117(30):1815-1817, July 25, 1976.

"Management of threatened abortion." (editorial).
BRITISH MEDICAL JOURNAL 1(6017):1034, May 1, 1976.

"Management of threatened abortion," (letter), by D. H.
Darwish. BRITISH MEDICAL JOURNAL 1(6022):
1402, June 5, 1976.

"March Against Abortion." THE NEW YORK TIMES (S), January 25, IV, 3:2, 1976.

"Marchers for Life amass in D.C." NATIONAL CATHOLIC REPORTER 12:6, February 6, 1976.

"Marie Stopes Memorial Lecture 1975. The compulsory pregnancy lobby--then and now," by M. Simms. JOURNAL OF THE ROYAL COLLEGE OF GENERAL PRACTITIONERS 25(159):709-719, October, 1975.

"Massachusetts Poll Hints Deep Democrat Rifts," by R. Reinhold. THE NEW YORK TIMES (M), March 4, 18:3, 1976.

"Massive form of Couvelaire's syndrome with preservation of the uterus," by T. Pasanku. MEDICINSKI PREGLED 28(3-4):145-147, 1975.

"Massive invasion of fetal lymphocytes into the mother's blood at induced abortion," by R. Zilliacus, et al. SCANDINAVIAN JOURNAL OF IMMUNOLOGY 4(5-6): 601-605, September, 1975.

"Maternal factors associated with fetal chromosomal anomalies in spontaneous abortions," by E. Alberman, et al. BRITISH JOURNAL OF OBSTETRICS AND GYNAECOLOGY 83(8):621-627, August, 1976.

"Maternal mortality from septic abortions in University Hospital, Kuala Lumpur from March 1968 to February 1974," by K. H. Ng, et al. MEDICAL JOURNAL OF MALAYSIA 30(1):52-54, September, 1975.

"May hospitals prohibit abortions and sterilizations?" by J. A. Turpin. MEDICO-LEGAL BULLETIN 24(9): 1-9, September, 1975.

"Measures Passed by Albany Legislature," by R. Smothers. THE NEW YORK TIMES (M), June 11, II, 4:1, 1976.

"Measurements by ultrasonics of the gestation sac in
threatened abortion," by S. Levi. JOURNAL DE
GYNECOLOGIE, OBSTETRIQUE BIOLOGIE DE LA
REPRODUCTION 5(3):359-365, April-May, 1976.

"Mechanism of action of prostaglandin F2 alpha and its
clinical use in obstetrics," by L. S. Persianinov.
AKUSHERSTVO I GINEKOLOGIIA (Moscow) (6):7-15,
June, 1975.

"Media manipulation promotes world abortion craze,"
by M. Bunson. OUR SUNDAY VISITOR MAGAZINE 65:1
passim, June 20, 1976.

"Medicaid and the abortion right." GEORGE WASHINGTON
LAW REVIEW 44:404-417, March, 1976.

"Medicaid coverage of abortions in New York City: costs
and benefits," by M. Robinson, et al. FAMILY
PLANNING PERSPECTIVES 6, 4:202-208, Fall, 1974.
(Socio. Abstrs. 1976, 76I0425)

"Medicaid Stayed on Abortion Curb," by W. E. Waggoner.
THE NEW YORK TIMES (M), January 17, 56:8, 1976.

"Medical counterindications for pregnancy," by J. C.
Monnier. LILLE MEDICAL 20:242-246, 1975.

"The medical indications of therapeutic abortion yesterday
and today," by D. Stucki, et al. PRAXIS 65(2):49-53,
January 13, 1976.

"Medical interruption of pregnancy in India," by T. Chandy.
MUENCHENER MEDIZINISCHE WOCHENSCHRIFT
117(34):1349-1352, August 22, 1975.

"Medical License Seized from an Abortion Doctor Charged
with Ineptitude." THE NEW YORK TIMES (S), October 26,
36:2, 1976.

"Medical termination of Pregnancy Act, 1971 and the

registered medical practitioners." (letter). JOURNAL OF THE INDIAN MEDICAL ASSOCIATION 65(11):320-321, December 1, 1975.

"The Medical Termination of Pregnancy Act, 1971 and the registered medical practitioners," by J. B. Mukherjee. JOURNAL OF THE INDIAN MEDICAL ASSOCIATION 65(1):13-17, July 1, 1975.

"Medico-social problems following the reform of para 218 - potential and limits of the future practice of abortion," by A. Trojan, et al. OEFFENTLICHE GESUNDHEITSWESEN 37(11):693-699, November, 1975.

"Menstrual induction by the vaginal application of ICI 81008 gel," by A. I. Csapo, et al. PROSTAGLANDINS 12(3):455-461, September, 1976.

"Menstrual induction: its place in clinical practice," by K. R. Irani, et al. OBSTETRICS AND GYNECOLOGY 46(5):596-598, November, 1975.

"Menstrual induction with the PGF2alpha-analogue ICI 81008," by A. I. Csapo, et al. PROSTAGLANDINS 11(1):155-162, January, 1976.

"Menstrual regulation." (editorial). LANCET 1(7966): 947, May 1, 1976.

"Menstrual regulation (a new procedure for fertility control)," by C. S. Dawn, et al. JOURNAL OF THE INDIAN MEDICAL ASSOCIATION 64(11):293-296, June 1, 1975.

"Method of payment--relation to abortion complications," by R. G. Smith, et al. HEALTH AND SOCIAL WORK 1:5-28, May, 1976.

"Methodological observations on research concerning the effects of induced abortions," by R. Andorka, et al. DEMOGRAFIA 17, 1:63-73, 1974. (Socio. Abstrs. 1976,

76I1392)

"Methodology for determining the optimal design of a free standing abortion clinic," by H. S. Gitlow. MANAGEMENT SCIENCE: JOURNAL OF THE INSTITUTE OF MANAGEMENT SCIENCE 22:1289-1298, August, 1976.

"Miscarriage and abortion: I. Induced and spontaneous abortion. Psychopathological aspects in connection with a first sample of 411 requests for interruption of pregnancy," by M. Bourgeois, et al. ANNALES MEDICO-PSYCHOLOGIQUES 2(2):339-366, July, 1975. (Psycho. Abstrs. 1976, 12347)

--II. Voluntary abortion and resistance to contraception," by M. Bourgeois, et al. ANNALES MEDICO-PSYCHOLOGIQUES 2(2):366-377, July, 1975. (Psycho. Abstrs. 1976, 12348)

"Midtrimester abortion induced by serial intramuscular injections of 15(S)-15-methyl-prostaglandin E2 methyl ester," by N. H. Lauersen, et al. AMERICAN JOURNAL OF OBSTETRICS AND GYNECOLOGY 123(7):665-670, December 1, 1975.

"Midtrimester pregnancy termination by intramuscular injection of a 15-methyl analogue of prostaglandin F2 alpha," by J. Robins, et al. AMERICAN JOURNAL OF OBSTETRICS AND GYNECOLOGY 123(6):625-631, November 15, 1975.

"Midtrimester pregnancy termination with prostaglandin E2 vaginal suppositories," by M. Hochman, et al. JOURNAL OF REPRODUCTIVE MEDICINE 16(5): 263-268, May, 1976.

"Midtrimester prostaglandin-induced abortion: gross and light microscopic findings in the placenta," by L. H. Honore. PROSTAGLANDINS 11(6):1019-1032, 1976. (Bio. Abstrs. 1976, 62674)

"Mid-trimester termination." (editorial). BRITISH
MEDICAL JOURNAL 1(6022):1357-1358, June 5, 1976.

"Mid-trimester termination," (letter), by R. V. Clements,
et al. BRITISH MEDICAL JOURNAL 2(6035):587,
September 4, 1976.

"Militancy and the Abortion Fight," by M. D. Dreger.
THE NEW YORK TIMES (M), November 21, XXI, 26:1,
1976.

"Modern use of the laminaria tent," by K. R. Niswander."
MOUNT SINAI JOURNAL OF MEDICINE, NEW YORK
42(5):424-430, September-October, 1975.

"Molecular aspects of defibrination in a Reptilase-treated
case of 'dead fetus syndrome'," by R. Hafter, et al.
THROMBOSIS RESEARCH 7(3):391-399, September,
1975.

"Moral ethics seminar; opening address of medical ethics
seminar in Dublin," by Abp. D. Ryan. L'OSSERVATORE
ROMANO 49(401):9, December 4, 1975.

"Moral rights and abortion," by H. V. McLachian.
CONTEMPORARY REVIEW 228:323-333, June, 1976.

"Moral sentiment in judicial opinions on abortion," by E.
N. Moore. SANTA CLARA LAWYER 15:591-634,
Spring, 1975.

"Mortality and morbidity associated with legal abortions in
Hungary, 1960-1973," by Z. Bognar, et al. AMERICAN
JOURNAL OF PUBLIC HEALTH 66:568-575, June,
1975.

"Morbidity of therapeutic abortion in Auckland," by M. A.
Baird. NEW ZEALAND MEDICAL JOURNAL 83(565):
395-399, June, 1976.

"More on abortion," by S. Fraker, et al. NEWSWEEK

88:15, July 12, 1976.

"The Morgentaler case," (letter), by G. Carruthers. CANADIAN MEDICAL ASSOCIATION JOURNAL 113(9): 818, November 8, 1975.

"Morgentaler freed, new trial ordered," by B. Richardson. HUMANIST 36:50, March, 1976.

"Morphologic and virologic studies of the fetus and placenta in neorickettsial abortion in cattle," by A. Angelov, et al. VETERINARNO-MEDITSINSKI NAUKI 12(7):20-27, 1975.

"Morphological studies on cases of early abortion with special reference to HCG excretion," by M. Hölzl, et al. ARCHIV FUR GYNAEKOLOGIE 219(1-4):550-551, November 18, 1975.

"Most abortions by suction in 10th week or less; typical patient is young, unmarried, white, never-before pregnant." FAMILY PLANNING PERSPECTIVES 8(2):70-72, March-April, 1976.

"The motivation of the physician's behavior in correlation to the legalization of abortion," by G. Thomascheci. BEITRAEGE ZUR GERICHTLICHEN MEDIZIN 33:15-17, 1975.

"Mr. Ford on Abortion." (editorial). THE NEW YORK TIMES February 5, 30:2, 1976.

"Mycoplasmas in humans: significance of Ureaplasma urealyticum," by R. B. Kundsin. HEALTH LABORATORY SCIENCE 13(2):144-151, 1976. (Bio. Abstrs. 1976, 43909)

"Mycotic abortion," by C. Kirkbride. THERIOGENOLOGY 5(3):139-149, 1976. (Bio. Abstrs. 1976, 26804)

"The need for more facts about abortion?" JOURNAL OF

THE ROYAL COLLEGE OF GENERAL PRACTITIONERS
25(153):235-236, April, 1975.

"Neonatal death after induced abortion," by R. Prywes, et
al. HAREFUAH 90(10):453-456, May 16, 1976.

"A new ethical approach to abortion and its implications for
the euthanasia dispute," by R. F. Gardner. JOURNAL
OF MEDICAL ETHICS 1(3):127-131, September, 1975.

"New Hampshire Held Liable On All Welfare Abortions."
THE NEW YORK TIMES (S), January 20, 16:4, 1976.

"New Icelandic abortion law. Abortion on social indications
before the 16th week." NORDISK MEDICIN 90(12):290,
December, 1975.

"New Jersey Briefs: 4 Hospitals Said to Violate Rights."
THE NEW YORK TIMES (S), June 4, II, 21:1, 1976.

"New Jersey Briefs: Medicaid Restrictions Enjoined."
THE NEW YORK TIMES (S), February 3, 67:7, 1976.

"New Jersey Court Rules for Abortion." THE NEW YORK
TIMES November 21, IV, 7:4, 1976.

"The new jurisprudence," by R. M. Bryn. JAMA; JOURNAL
OF THE AMERICAN MEDICAL ASSOCIATION 236(4):359-
360, July 26, 1976.

"A new look at the etiology of cervical incompetence: with
review of seven-year experience at Pennsylvania
Hospital," by U. C. Nwosu. INTERNATIONAL JOURNAL
OF GYNAECOLOGY AND OBSTETRICS 13(5):201-205,
1975. (Bio. Abstrs. 1976, 28723)

"The new morality and abortion," by E. Lio. L'OSSERVA-
TORE ROMANO 5(409):8-9, January 29, 1976.

"New pro-life legislation: patterns and recommendations,"
by J. P. Witherspoon. ST. MARY'S LAW JOURNAL

7:637-697, 1976.

"New Security Measures Will Protect Assembly," by M.
Waldron. THE NEW YORK TIMES (S), April 27, 75:8,
1976.

"New York Times/New Jersey Poll," by J. F. Sullivan.
THE NEW YORK TIMES (L), March 21, XI, 17:2, 1976.

"NFPC says bishops place too much emphasis on abortion."
OUR SUNDAY VISITOR 65:1, September 26, 1976.

"No bargaining about abortion; exhortation of bishops of
Lazio," by Card. U. Poletti. L'OSSERVATORE
ROMANO 45(449):11, November 4, 1976.

"No Chance is Seen of Overriding Carey's Veto of Abortion
Bill," by L. Greenhouse. THE NEW YORK TIMES
(M), June 24, 66:5, 1976.

"No going back," by D. Gould. NEW STATESMAN 132,
January 31, 1975.

"No Process of Law," by A. Lewis. THE NEW YORK
TIMES April 8, 37:1, 1976.

"No retreat on abortion," by J. D. Rockefeller, III.
NEWSWEEK 87:11, June 21, 1976.

"Nonsectarian Hospitals in Jersey Are Ordered to Permit
Abortions," by A. A. Narvaez. THE NEW YORK TIMES
(M), November 18, 1:1, 1976.

"None but the brave?" by D. Gould. NEW STATESMAN
89:774, June 13, 1975.

"Nor piety nor wit: the Supreme Court on abortion," by J. W.
Dellapenna. COLUMBIA HUMAN RIGHTS LAW REVIEW
6:379-413, Fall-Winter, 1974-1975.

"Not much hope House will approve pro-life amendment," by

J. Maher. OUR SUNDAY VISITOR 64:2, February 22, 1976.

"A note on the unborn person," by R. Masiello. LINCARE 43:112-114, May, 1976.

"Nurse's attitudes to termination of pregnancy." NURSING FORUM (Auckl) 2(5):6-7, November-December, 1974.

"Nurses who work to save lives," by I. Curtin. OUR SUNDAY VISITOR MAGAZINE 64:16, January 25, 1976.

"A nursing care study of tracheloplasty on a 25 year old woman," by C. C. Nwaekpe. NIGERIAN NURSE 8(1): 26-28, January-March, 1973.

"Observation of the behavior of aborted women in the days immediately following abortion," by M. Houmont. REVUE MEDICALE DE LIEGE 30(8):261-265, April 15, 1975.

"Obstetric complications after treatment of intrauterine synechiae (Asherman's syndrome)," by R. Jewelewicz, et al. OBSTETRICS AND GYNECOLOGY 47(6):701-705, 1976. (Bio. Abstrs. 1976, 46115)

"Obtaining hyperimmune serum for the diagnosis of enzootic ovine abortion," by R. Kh. Khamadaev, et al. VETERINARIIA (10):36-38, October, 1975.

"Occult manifestations of septic abortion," by J. E. Dewhurst, et al. NURSING MIRROR AND MIDWIVES' JOURNAL 142:62-63, April 29, 1976.

"Occult pregnancy. A pilot study," by S. K. Bloch. OBSTETRICS AND GYNECOLOGY 43(3):365-368, September, 1976.

"Occupation and miscarriage," by W. Helbing. ZEITSCHRIFT FUR DIE GESAMTE HYGIENE UND IHRE

GRENZGEBIETE 21(11):819-821, 1975.

"Of many things; views of Catholic bishops," by J. O'Hare. AMERICA 134:inside cover, January 31, 1976.

"On abortion and right to life," by E. J. Kirsch. AMERICAN JOURNAL OF PUBLIC HEALTH 66(9):906, September, 1976.

"On the bounds of freedom: from the treatment of fetuses to euthanasia," by H. T. Engelhardt, Jr. CONNETICUT MEDICINE 40(1):51-54, 57, January, 1976.

"On Long Island's Mind: Some Surprises in a Poll," by F. Lynn. THE NEW YORK TIMES (L), April 18, XXI, 1:1, 1976.

"On the method of mathematical statistical surveys connected with certain gestation processes," by M. Miklos. DEMOGRÁFIA 17, 2:206-212, 1974. (Socio. Abstrs. 1976, 76I1279)

"On the sociology and social ethics of abortion," by C. Bagley. ETHICS IN SCIENCE AND MEDICINE 3(1):21-32, May, 1976.

"100,000 at 'World' Mass as Catholic Parley Closes." THE NEW YORK TIMES (M), August 9, 1:3, 1976.

"1,703 Persons Queried in Times-CBS Survey." THE NEW YORK TIMES (M), September 10, I, 19:1, 1976.

"Only amendment will save the unborn, professor says." OUR SUNDAY VISITOR 65:3, October 31, 1976.

"Options in the abortion debate," by J. M. Wall. CHRISTIAN CENTURY 93:139-140, February 18, 1976.

"Origin of the extra chromosome in trisomy 16," by J. G. Lauritsen, et al. CLINICAL GENETICS 10(3):156-160, September, 1976.

"Orthodox Church condemns abortion and euthanasia." OUR SUNDAY VISITOR 64:3, December 7, 1975.

"Orthodox Rabbis Rebuke Jews Who Back Permissive Abortion," by I. Spiegel. THE NEW YORK TIMES (M), January 28, 36:2, 1976.

"Our decision, say women." ECONOMIST 257:49, December 13, 1975.

"Our resources for contraceptive advice and legal abortions," by J. Asplund. LAKARTIDNINGEN 72(47): 4609-4610, November 19, 1975.

"Outcome and quality of pregnancies obtained by ovulation inducers in infertile women: apropos of 229 pregnancies in 91 women, of whom 42 were treated for spontaneous abortion and 49 treated for ovarian sterility," by J. Henry-Suchet, et al. JOURNAL DE GYNECOLOGIE, OBSTETRIQUE BIOLOGIE DE LA REPRODUCTION 2(6): 653-672, September, 1973.

"Outcome following therapeutic abortion," by E. C. Payne, et al. ARCHIVES OF GENERAL PSYCHIATRY 33(6): 725-733, June, 1976.

"The outcome of pregnancy in former oral contraceptive users." BRITISH JOURNAL OF OBSTETRICS AND GYNAECOLOGY 83(8):608-616, August, 1976.

"Outpatient legal abortion. 500 operations with paracervical anesthesia," by J. Prest, et al. UGESKRIFT FOR LAEGER 138(6):333-335, February 2, 1976.

"Outpatient legal abortion using a modified Vabra aspirator and paracervical anesthesia," by J. Praest, et al. UGESKRIFT FOR LAEGER 138(6):336-338, February 2, 1976.

"Outpatient postconceptional fertility control with vaginally administered 15(S)-15-methyl-PGF2alpha-methyl ester,"

by M. Bygdeman, et al. AMERICAN JOURNAL OF
OBSTETRICS AND GYNECOLOGY 124(5):495-498,
March 1, 1976.

"Override of fund bill veto leaves abortion ban intact."
NATIONAL CATHOLIC REPORTER 12:14, October 8,
1976.

"Ovine chlamydial abortion in Alberta," by G. A. Chalmers,
et al. CANADIAN VETERINARY JOURNAL 17(3):76-81,
1976.

"Pakistan may allow abortion as part of a new deal for
women," by H. Akhtar. TIMES 6, August 20, 1976.

"Paracervical block with etidocaine for out-patient abortion,"
by G. Willdeck-Lund, et al. ACTA ANAESTHESIOLOGICA
SCANDINAVICA. SUPPLEMENT (60):106-109, 1975.

"Paris Counts 45,085 Abortions in First Year After Change
in Law." THE NEW YORK TIMES (S), November 17,
I, 19:1, 1976.

"Parity of women contracting rubella in pregnancy: Implications with respect to rubella vaccination," by W. C.
Marshall. LANCET 1(7971):1231-1233, 1976.

"Pastoral letter for all bishops calls abortion laws unjust
and immoral; asks for action." OUR SUNDAY VISITOR
MAGAZINE 64:1, January 18, 1976.

"A pastoral plan for pro-life activities." CATHOLIC MIND
74:55-64, March, 1976.

"Pastoral plan for pro-life activities; statement," by Card.
T. Cooke, et al. L'OSSERVATORE ROMANO 1(405):3-4,
January 1, 1976.

"Pathogenicity of T. foetus after various periods of storage,"
by R. V. Kazeev, et al. VETERINARIIA (6):90-93, June,
1975.

"Pathological features of the placenta in fetal death," by A. Ornoy, et al. ARCHIVES OF PATHOLOGY AND LABORATORY MEDICINE 100(7):367-371, 1976. (Bio. Abstrs. 1976, 59485)

"Pathologicoanatomic and histomorphological changes in the fetus in chlamydial abortion in swine," vy A. I. Iatsyshin, et al. VETERINARIIA (4):80-84, April, 1976.

"Pathomorphological changes in an early spontaneous abortus with triploidy (69,XXX)," by V. P. Kulazenko, et al. HUMAN GENETICS 32(2):211-215, 1976. (Bio. Abstrs. 1976, 60586)

"Pathomorphological changes in sheep in experimental enzootic abortion," by Iu. T. Andriishin. VETERINARIIA (8):72-76, August, 1976.

"Pathophysiology of disseminated intravascular coagulation in saline-induced abortion," by R. K. Laros, Jr., et al. OBSTETRICS AND GYNECOLOGY 48(3):353-356, September, 1976.

"Patterns of contraceptive failures: the role of motivation re-examined," by W. Cobliner, et al. JOURNAL OF BIOSOCIAL SCIENCE 7, 3:307-318, July, 1975. (Socio. Abstrs. 1976, 76H9180)

"Pax Romana, Catholic jurists against abortion." L'OSSERVATORE ROMANO 43(447):10, October 21, 1976.

"Perceptions of abortion. The circle of choice: a decision-making process observed in women considering abortions," by G. K. Adams. ANA CLINICAL SESSIONS :47-59, 1974.

"Performing abortions," by M. Denes. COMMENTARY 62:33-37, October, 1976.

"Performing second-trimester abortions. Rationale for

impatient basis," by G. Stroh, et al. NEW YORK STATE
JOURNAL OF MEDICINE 75(12):2168-2171, October,
1975.

"Personal experience with therapeutic abortion in cases of
rubella," by Y. Darbois, et al. JOURNAL DE
GYNECOLOGIE, OBSTETRIQUE ET BIOLOGIE DE
LA REPRODUCTION 3(6):943-954, September, 1974.

"PGE2 as a vaginal abortifacient - diaphragm effect,"
(letter), by S. L. Corson, et al. PROSTAGLANDINS
10(3):543-544, September, 1975.

"Pharmacokinetics of intra-amniotically administered
hyperosmolar urea in rhesus monkeys," by D. A. Blake,
et al. AMERICAN JOURNAL OF OBSTETRICS AND
GYNECOLOGY 124(3):245-250, February 1, 1976.

"Phenotypic expression of lethal chromosomal anomalies in
human abortuses," by J. Bouié, et al. TEROTOLOGY;
JOURNAL OF ABNORMAL DEVELOPMENT 14(1):3-19,
August, 1976.

"Phosphoglucomutase phenotypes and prenatal selection.
Studies of spontaneous and induced abortions," by G.
Beckman, et al. HUMAN HEREDITY 25(3):172-176,
1975.

"Physician's decision-making role in abortion cases," by J.
R. Marcin, et al. JURIST 35:66-76, 1975.

"A pilot study of demographic and psychosocial factors in
medical termination of pregnancy," by R. Goraya, et
al. JOURNAL OF THE INDIAN MEDICAL ASSOCIATION
64(11):309-315, June 1, 1975.

"Pinning down the politicians." ECONOMIST 258:40 passim,
Feburary 14, 1976.

"The placental and fetal response to the intra-amniotic injection of prostaglandin F2alpha in midtrimester abortions,"

by P. Jouppila, et al. BRITISH JOURNAL OF OBSTETRICS AND GYNAECOLOGY 83(4):303-306, April, 1976.

"Placental cultures for cytogenetic assessment in saline-aborted fetuses," by H. A. Gardner, et al. AMERICAN JOURNAL OF OBSTETRICS AND GYNECOLOGY 126(3): 350-352, October 1, 1976.

"A plain woman's guide to abortion," by A. McHardy. GUARDIAN 9, August 5, 1976.

"Planned Parenthood of Cent. Mo. v. Danforth, 96 Sup Ct 2831." (Bicentennial issue). OKLAHOMA LAW REVIEW 29:785-788, Summer, 1976.

"Plasma levels of the methyl ester of 15-methyl PGF2a in connection with intravenous and vaginal administration to the human," by K. Green, et al. PROSTAGLANDINS 11(5):879-892, 1976. (Bio. Abstrs. 1976, 62691)

"Plasma renin activity in abortion," by P. Soveri, et al. ACTA OBSTETRICIA ET GYNECOLOGICA SCANDINA-VICA 55(2):175-177, 1976. (Bio. Abstrs. 1976, 30739)

"Pneumonia associated with Torulopsis glabrata in an aborted bovine feuts," by W. U. Knudtson, et al. SABOURAUDIA; JOURNAL OF THE INTERNATIONAL SOCIETY FOR HUMAN AND ANIMAL MYCOLOGY 14(1): 43-45, March, 1976.

"Poisonous Cloud's Effects Still Baffle Italy's Officials," by S. V. Roberts. THE NEW YORK TIMES (L), August 13, I, 3:1, 1976.

"Political Crisis Plagues Italy," by A. Shuster. THE NEW YORK TIMES (M), April 13, 10:4, 1976.

"Political responsibility and abortion." AMERICA 134:173, March 6, 1976.

"Politics and abortion." COMMONWEAL 103:131-132,

February 27, 1976.

"Politics & abortion," by G. Brandmeyer. COMMONWEAL 103:432-433, July 2, 1976.

"Politics of abortion." NEW STATESMAN 91:275, March 5, 1976.

"Politics of abortion," by J. Armstrong. CHRISTIAN CENTURY 93:215, March 10, 1976.

"Pope Denies View is Outdated." THE NEW YORK TIMES (S), January 22, 32:1, 1976.

"Pope Praises Catholic Education in U.S." THE NEW YORK TIMES (S), June 25, I, 2:4, 1976.

"Population, abortion, birth rates," by J. Kettle. EXECUTIVE 17:47-48, November, 1975.

"Population control in Australia today: contraception, sterilization and abortion," by J. Leeton. MEDICAL JOURNAL OF AUSTRALIA 2(17):682-685, October 25, 1975.

"Porcine abortion caused by Actinobacillus equuli," by R. E. Werdin, et al. JOURNAL OF THE AMERICAN VETERINARY MEDICAL ASSOCIATION 169(7):704-706, October 1, 1976.

"Possible andrological factor as cause of spontaneous abortion," by R. Schoysman. VERHANDELINGEN; KONINKLIJKE ACADEMIE VOOR GENEESKUNDE VON BELGIE 37(2):33-41, 1975.

"The possible deleterious effects of the intramyometrial injection of hypertonic urea," by T. H. Parmley, et al. OBSTETRICS AND GYNECOLOGY 47(2):210-212, February, 1976.

"Possibilities for work organization in the abortion sections

90

of district gynecology departments," by D. Andreev, et al. AKUSHERSTVO I GINEKOLOGIIA (Sofia) 13(6):466-471, 1974.

"Postabortal and postpartum tetanus. A review of 19 cases," by M. J. Bennett. SOUTH AFRICAN MEDICAL JOURNAL 50(13):513-516, March 24, 1976.

"Post-abortal tetanus," by C. Newman, et al. CONNECTICUT MEDICINE 39(12):773-774, December, 1975.

"Postabortion insertion of the intrauterine copper T (TCu 200). pp. 115-8," by K. G. Nygren, et al. In: Hefnawi F, Segal SJ, ed. Analysis of intrauterine contraceptions. Amsterdam, North-Holland, 1975. W3 IN182AI 1974a.

"Postabortion psychiatric illness," by C. M. Donovan, et al. NURSING DIGEST 3:12-16, September-October, 1975; Nursing implications. Addendum, by C. A. Farrar. NURSING DIGEST 3:17, September-October, 1975.

"Postpartum and postabortal ovarian vein thrombophlebitis," by T. R. Allan, et al. OBSTETRICS AND GYNECOLOGY 47(5):525-528, 1976. (Bio. Abstrs. 1976, 24056)

"Post-partum and post-abortum contraception," by B. Fonty, et al. JOURNAL DE GYNECOLOGIE, OBSTETRIQUE ET BIOLOGIE DE LA REPORDUCTION 4(3):395-404, 1975. (Bio. Abstrs. 1976, 22786)

"Postpartum contraception: subsequent pregnancy, delivery, and abortion rates," by J. J. Shulman, et al. FERTILITY AND STERILITY 27(1):97-103, January, 1976.

"Potential anti-fertility plants from Chinese medicine," by Y. C. Kong, et al. AMERICAN JOURNAL OF CHINESE MEDICINE 4(2):105-128, Summer, 1976.

"Potentiality in the abortion discussion," by F. C. Wade. REVIEW OF METAPHYSICS 29:239-255, December, 1975.

"Practical aspects of equine virus abortion in the United Kingdom," by L. B. Jeffcott, et al. VETERINARY RECORD 98(8):153-155, February 21, 1976.

"Preclinical abortion. pp. 125-144," by S. Cianci, et al. In: Marchesi F, Cittadini E, ed. Fertilità e sterilità. Taormina, Minerva Medica, 1974. WP 570 S679f 1973.

"The predictive value of thyroid "test profile" in habitual abortion," by D. Winikoff, et al. BRITISH JOURNAL OF OBSTETRICS AND GYNAECOLOGY 82(9):760-766, September, 1975.

"Pregnancies of Irish residents terminated in England and Wales in 1973," by D. Walsh. IRISH MEDICAL JOURNAL 69(1):16-18, January 17, 1976.

"Pregnancy and abortion in adolescence: a comparative legal survey and proposals for reform," by L. T. Lee, et al. COLUMBIA HUMAN RIGHTS LAW REVIEW 6:307-355, Fall-Winter, 1974-1975.

"Pregnancy and abortion in adolescence. Report of a WHO meeting." WORLD HEALTH ORGANIZATION TECHNICAL REPORT SERIES (583):1-27, 1975.

"Pregnancy counseling and abortion referral for patients in Federally funded family planning programs," by J. I. Rosoff. FAMILY PLANNING PERSPECTIVES 8(1):43-46, January-February, 1976.

"Pregnancy interruption by vacuum aspiration," (letter), by G. Gergely. ORVOSI HETILAP 116(46):2748-2749, November 16, 1975.

"Pregnancy planning/abortion," by C. Tietze. FAMILY PLANNING PERSPECTIVES 7(6):247, November-December, 1975.

"Pregnancy termination in dogs with novel nonhormonal

compounds," by G. Galliani, et al. AMERICAN JOURNAL
OF VETERINARY RESEARCH 37(3):263-268, March, 1976.

"Pregnancy with concurrent acute disease and the so-called
therapeutic abortion," by J. E. Alves, et al. REVISTA
DA ASSOCIACAO MEDICA BRASILEIRA 22(1):21-28,
January, 1976.

"Pregnant stewardess - should she fly?" by P. Scholten.
AVIATION SPACE AND ENVIRONMENTAL MEDICINE
47(1):77-81, 1976. (Bio. Abstrs. 1976, 52518)

"Preliminary trials of vaginal silastic devices containing
(15s)-15 methyl prostaglandin f2 alpha methyl ester for
the induction of menses and for pregnancy termination
summary of brook lodge workshop (January 29, 1976),"
by E. M. Southern. PROSTAGLANDINS 12 Suppl:147-
152, 1976.

"Premarital sexual permissiveness and abortion: standards
of college women," by A. M. Mirande, et al. PACIFIC
SOCIOLOGICAL REVIEW 17, 4:485-503, October, 1974.
(Socio. Abstrs. 1976, 76H8170)

"Premature labor in the Palmanova Hospital in the period
1963-1973," by S. Garofalo, et al. MINERVA GINE-
COLOGIA 28(2):118-123, February, 1976.

"Prenatal diagnosis of trisomy 9," by U. Francke, et al.
HUMANGENETIK 29(3):243-250, 1975. (Bio. Abstrs.
1976, 60536)

"Prenatal genetic diagnosis in 350 amniocenteses," by B. F.
Crandall. OBSTETRICS AND GYNECOLOGY 48(2):158-
162, 1976. (Bio. Abstrs. 1976, 66501)

"Preoperative cervical dilatation by small doses of
prostaglandin F2a," by R. Andriesse, et al. CONTRA-
CEPTION 14(1):93-99, 1976. (Bio. Abstrs. 1976, 50661)

"President Vetoes $56 Billion Bill for Manpower, H.E.W.

Programs," by P. Shabecoff. (M), September 30, 1:4, 1976.

"Prevention and therapy of habitual abortion. pp. 101-124," by P. Spanio, et al. In: Marchesi F, Cittadini E, ed. Feterilità e sterilità. Taormina, Minerva medica, 1974. WP 570 S679f 1973.

"Prevention of Rh hemolytic disease: ten years' clinical experience with Rh immune globulin," by V. J. Freda, et al. NEW ENGLAND JOURNAL OF MEDICINE 292(19):1014-1016, 1975. (Bio. Abstrs. 1976, 14306)

"Prevention of RH immunization in therapeutic abortion," by M. Bulić. LIJECNICKI VJESNIK 98(2):103-104, February, 1976.

"Private Hospitals to Decide Soon Whether to Challenge Abortion Ruling," by A. A. Narvaez. (M), November 19, II, 19:3, 1976.

"The problem of abortion. Viewpoint of the general practitioner," by J. Henrion. REVUE MEDICALE DE LIEGE 30(8):249-253, April 15, 1975.

"The problem of abortion. Viewpoint of a gynecologist," by A. Wery. REVUE MEDICALE DE LIEGE 30(8):253-258, April 15, 1975.

Problem of abortions in the European socialist countries," by V. V. Bodrova. ZDRAVOOKHRANENIE ROSSIISKOI FEDERATSII (5):34-40, May, 1975.

"Problem of causative relation between pregnancy interruption and following premature termination of pregnancy," by R. Voigt, et al. ZENTRALBLATT FUR GYNAEKOLOGIE 97(22):1375-1377, 1975.

"The problem of prognostication in disturbed pregnancies," by E. Picha. WIENER KLINISCHE WOCHENSCHRIFT 87(20):702-704, October 31, 1975.

"Problems of decision making of interruption commissions,"
by D. Fukalová. CESKOSLOVENSKA GYNEKOLOGIE
40(9):669-671, November, 1975.

"Procedures in the termination of pregnancy, 'Mannheim'
proposal - document symbol Paragraph 218/new 76,"
by S. Sievers, et al. FORTSCHRITTE DU MEDIZIN
94(27):1471-1472, September 23, 1976.

"Producing change in attitudes toward abortion," by R. A.
Lewis. THE JOURNAL OF SEX RESEARCH 9, 1:52-
68, 1973. (Socio. Abstrs. 1976, 76I1755)

"The profilactic and therapeutic attitude in abortion," by
C. Tatic, et al. VIATA MEDICALA 23(9):57-60,
September, 1975.

"Progesterone levels in amniotic fluid and maternal plasma
in prostaglandin F2alpha-induced midtrimester abortion,"
by Z. Koren, et al. OBSTETRICS AND GYNECOLOGY
48(4):427 passim, October, 1976.

"Progesterone withdrawal induced by ICI 81008 in pregnant
rats," by D. H. Warnock, et al. PROSTAGLANDINS
10(4):715-724, October, 1975.

"Prognosis in threatened abortion: a comparison between
predictions made by sonar urinary hormone assays and
clinical judgement," by G. B. Duff. BRITISH JOURNAL
OF OBSTETRICS AND GYNAECOLOGY 82(11):858-862,
November, 1975.

"Prognostic and diagnostic value of bidimensional echo-
graphy in threatened abortion," by N. Rodriguez.
REVISTA CHILENA DE OBSTETRICIA Y GINECOLOGIA
38(5):228-239, 1973.

"Prognostic value of the serum HCG radioimmunoassay in
threatened abortion," by E. Guerresi, et al. RIVISTA
ITALIANA DI GINECOLOGIA 56(3):201-214, May, 1975.

"Pro-lifers will challenge Democratic abortion plank," by
J. Castelli. OUR SUNDAY VISITOR MAGAZINE 65:1,
July 11, 1976.

"Pronatalist programmes in Eastern Europe," by R.
McIntyre. SOVIET STUDIES 27:366-380, July, 1975.

"Properties of the Brucella isolated from the aborted fetuses
of cows inoculated with strain 82 vaccine," by V. S.
Duranov. VETERINARIIA (11):32-33, November,
1975.

"Proposal for the management of the current regulations
under Paragraph 218," by P. Stoll, et al. FORT-
SCHRITTE DU MEDIZIN 94(27):1468-1471, September 23, 1976.

"Proposed decree on abortion and nurses' role," by S. A.
Jegede. NIGERIAN NURSE 7(1):33-34, January-March,
1975.

"A prospective study of drugs and pregnancy," by S.
Kullander, et al. ACTA OBSTETRICIA ET GYNE-
COLOGICA SCANDINAVICA 55(1):25-33, 1976.
(Bio. Abstrs. 1976, 1144)

"Prostaglandin F2 alpha as abortifacient agent. Practical
aspects," by M. Bygdeman. LAKARTIDNINGEN 76(32):
2621-2623, August 4, 1976.

"Prostaglandin gel for the induction of abortion and labor
in fetal death," (proceedings), by T. Modly, et al.
ARCHIV FUR GYNAEKOLOGIE 219(1-4):498-499,
November 18, 1975.

"Prostaglandins and post-abortion luteolysis in early
pregnancy," by A. Leader, et al. PROSTAGLANDINS
10(5):889-897, November, 1975.

"Prostaglandins as early abortifacients. pp. 484-489," by
N. Wiqvist, et al. In: Segal SJ, et al., ed. The

regulation of mammalian reproduction. Springfield, Ill. , Thomas, 1973. W3 F049 no. 8 1973.

"Prostaglandins: basic reproductive consideration and new clinical applications. pp. 157-181," by F. Naftolin. In: Kahn RH, Lands WE, ed. Prostaglandins and cyclic AMP. New York, Academic Press, 1973. QU 90 S991p 1972.

"Protestant anti-abortion leader scores prejudice." OUR SUNDAY VISITOR 65:2, October 24, 1976.

"Protestant leaders back Catholic pro-life stand." OUR SUNDAY VISITOR 64:2, December 14, 1975.

"Protestant pro-life women launch national task force." OUR SUNDAY VISITOR 64:2, May 2, 1976.

"Protestants back Catholic efforts against abortion." OUR SUNDAY VISITOR 64:1, March 7, 1976.

"Psychiatric and mental health nursing. Pre-abortion emotional counseling," by S. Gedan. ANA CLINICAL SESSIONS :217-125, 1973.

"Psychiatric aspects of abortion in Hong Kong," by K. Singer. INTERNATIONAL JOURNAL OF SOCIAL PSYCHIATRY 21(4):303-306, Winter, 1975.

"Psychological bases of the two-child norm," by R. D. Kahoe. CATALOG OF SELECTED DOCUMENTS IN PSYCHOLOGY 5, 282, Summer, 1975.

"Psychological causes and impact of abortion," by P. Jadoul. REVUE MEDICALE DE LIEGE 30(8):258-261, April 15, 1975.

"Psychological correlates of delayed decisions to abort," by M. B. Bracken, et al. HEALTH EDUCATION MONOGRAPHS 4:6-44, Spring, 1976.

97

"Psychological factors in contraceptive failure and abortion request," by D. Everingham. MEDICAL JOURNAL OF AUSTRALIA 2(15):617-618, October 11, 1975.

"Psychological sequelae of therapeutic abortion." (editorial). BRITISH MEDICAL JOURNAL 1(6020):1239, May 22, 1976.

"Psychological sequelae of therapeutic abortion," (letter, by J. Kellett. BRITISH MEDICAL JOURNAL 2(6026): 45, July 3, 1976.

"Psychological-sociological views on S 218 (study on 379 pregnant women and women in puerperium)," by J. M. Wenderlein. ZENTRALBLATT FUR GYNAEKOLOGIE 98(9):527-532, 1976.

"Psychosocial aspects of abortion in the United States," by J. D. Osofsky, et al. MOUNT SINAI JOURNAL OF MEDICINE, NEW YORK 42(5):456-467, September-October, 1975.

"Psychosocial aspects of abortion. A review of issues and needed research," by R. Illsley, et al. BULLETIN OF THE WORLD HEALTH ORGANIZATION 53(1):83-106, 1976.

"Psychosocial aspects of pregnancy control: women and perceptions," by M. Murphy. ANA CLINICAL SESSIONS :66-70, 1974.

"Psychosocial consequences of therapeutic abortion King's termination study III," (letter), by H. S. Greer, et al. BRITISH JOURNAL OF PSYCHIATRY 128:74-79, January, 1976.

"Psychotherapy in abortion," by C. M. Donovan. CURRENT PSYCHIATRIC THERAPIES 15:77-83, 1975.

"Public health facilities issue new abortion policy." HOSPITALS 50:17, January 1, 1976.

"Public opinion and legal abortion in New Zealand," by B. J.
Kirkwood, et al. NEW ZEALAND MEDICAL JOURNAL
83(556):43-47, January 28, 1976.

"Putting the clock back on abortion," by P. Ferris.
OBSERVER 10, February 16, 1975.

"Putting a stop to the abortion industry," by L. Abse.
TIMES 14, July 29, 1976.

"Quantitative determination of antitriphoblastic IgG, IgA and
IgM in habitual abortion (research with radial immuno-
diffusion). pp. 157-165," by N. S. Cavallaro, et al.
In: Marchesi F, Cittadini E, ed. Fertilità e sterilità.
Taormina, Minerva medica, 1974. WP 570 S679f 1973.

"Quebec Halts Trial of Abortion Doctor," by H. Giniger."
THE NEW YORK TIMES December 12, 21:1, 1976.

"A question of clinical freedom," by B. Watkin. NURSING
MIRROR AND MIDWIVES' JOURNAL 142(18):42,
April 29, 1976.

"A question of conscience." (letter). BRITISH MEDICAL
JOURNAL 2(6026):43, July 3, 1976.

"A question of conscience," (letter), by R. Salm. BRITISH
MEDICAL JOURNAL 1(6025):1593, June 26, 1976.

"A question of conscience," by R. Walley. BRITISH
MEDICAL JOURNAL 1(6023):1456-1458, June 12, 1976.

"Questions of life...," by P. Clarke, et al. GUARDIAN
11, February 4, 1976.

"Radiation effects in early pregnancy as a medical indication
for its artificial interruption," by L. Dakov, et al.
AKUSHERSTVO I GINEKOLOGIIA (Sofia) 15(2):120-126,
1976.

"Radioimmunologic determination of placental lactogenic hormone in threatened spontaneous abortion. Prognostic value compared with determination of chorionic gonadotrophic hormone (HCG)," by R. Hechtermans, et al. JOURNAL DE GYNECOLOGIE, OBSTETRIQUE ET BIOLOGIE DE LA REPRODUCTION 2(1):53-62, January-February, 1973.

"Radioimmunological study of human chorionic gonadotropin in cases of abortion," by G. Castellari, et al. MINERVA GINECOLOGIA 27(9):717-721, September, 1975.

"Radiological studies on habitual abortion and prognosis of pregnancy," by G. Ohmura. JAPANESE JOURNAL OF FERTILITY AND STERILITY 20(3):92-107, 1975. (Bio. Abstrs. 1976, 28720)

"Rally Demands Ban on Abortion," by M. Talchin. THE NEW YORK TIMES (M), January 23, 20:3, 1976.

"Random thoughts on abortion attitudes," by K. Solomon. AMERICAN JOURNAL OF PUBLIC HEALTH 66(9): 905-906, September, 1976.

"Rape and abortion: is the argument valid?" by M. Sonsmith. LIGUORIAN 64:45-47, June, 1976.

"Reagan Affirms Antiabortion Stand." THE NEW YORK TIMES (M), February 8, 44:3, 1976.

"The real issues about abortions," by A. Bowden. DAILY TELEGRAPH 16, July 29, 1976.

"Recent developments in the abortion area," by A. Scanlan. CATHOLIC LAWYER 21:315-321, Fall, 1975.

"Recent French law on interruption of pregnancy," by R. Bourg. BRUXELLES-MEDICAL 55(4):201-206, April, 1975.

"Recovery after prolonged anuria following septic abortion,"
by D. S. Emmanoulel, et al. OBSTETRICS AND GYNE-
COLOGY 47(1):36S-39S, January, 1976.

"Recurrent abortions and paternal balanced translocation
t(lq-;13q≠)," by D. Rozynkowa, et al. HUMANGENETIK
28(4):349-351, August 25, 1975.

"Redefining the issues in fetal experimentation," by E. F.
Diamond. JOURNAL OF THE AMERICAN MEDICAL
ASSOCIATION 236:281-283, July 19, 1976.

"Reflections on abortion, a current and ageless problem," by
L. Dérobert. MEDECINE LEGALE ET DOMMAGE
CORPOREL 7(4):289-291, October-December, 1974.

"Reforms accepted." ECONOMIST 257:36, October 25, 1975.

"The relationship between abortion attitudes and Catholic
religiosity," by A. J. Blasi, et al. SOCIAL SCIENCE
50, 1:34-39, Winter, 1975. (Socio. Abstrs. 1976,
76I2502)

"The relationship between legal abortion and marriage," by
K. E. Bauman, et al. SOCIAL BIOLOGY 22, 2:117-124,
Summer, 1975. (Socio. Abstrs. 1976, 76I0401)

"The relative risks of sterilization alone and in combination
with abortion," by K. G. B. Edstrom. BULLETIN OF
THE WORLD HEALTH ORGANIZATION 52(2):141-148,
1975. (Bio. Abstrs. 1976, 16962)

"Religion and voting on abortion reform: a follow-up study,"
by J. T. Richardson, et al. JOURNAL FOR THE
SCIENTIFIC STUDY OF RELIGION 14, 2:159-164, June,
1975. (Socio. Abstrs. 1976, 76I0933)

"Religious freedom and abortion," by E. Lio. L'OSSERVA-
TORE ROMANO 9(413):8 passim, February 26, 1976.

"Religious groups plan abortion rights drive," by J. Fogarty.

NATIONAL CATHOLIC REPORTER 12:6, February 6, 1976.

"Remarks on abortion, abandonment, and adoption opportunities," by R. M. Herbenick. PHILOSOPHY & PUBLIC AFFAIRS 5, 1:98-104, Fall, 1975. (Socio. Abstrs. 1976, 76I2512)

"Remarks on the proposal for new qualifications in interruption of pregnancy," by S. Cammelli. PROFESSIONI INFERMIERISTICHE 28(2):45-49, April-June, 1975.

"Repeat aborters," by S. M. Schneider, et al. AMERICAN JOURNAL OF OBSTETRICS AND GYNECOLOGY 126(3): 316-320, October 1, 1976.

"Repeat abortion [examines the repeat abortion experience of New York city residents during July 1, 1970, to June 30, 1972, on the basis of a probability model that generates repeat abortion ratios as a function of assumptions about fecundity, contraceptive efficiency, and exposure lenghts]," by R. G. Potter, et al. DEMOGRAPHY 13:65-82, February, 1976.

"Repeated abortion. pp. 213-218," by C. Serrao. In: Marchesi F, Cittadini E, ed. Fertilità e sterilità. Taormina, Minerva medica, 1974. WP 570 S679f 1973.

"Repeated legal abortions," by L. Jacobsson, et al. LAKARTIDNINGEN 73(22):2100-2103, May 26, 1976.

"Repercussions of legal abortion on subsequent pregnancies," by R. Renaud, et al. JOURNAL DE GYNECOLOGIE, OBSTETRIQUE BIOLOGIE DE LA REPORCUDTION 3(4): 577-594, June, 1974.

"Report of study group on prostaglandin. pp. 5-8." In: Bergström S, ed. Report from meetings of the Prostaglandin Task Force Steering Committee. Stockholm, 1973. QV 175 W927r 1972-1973.

"Reported live births following induced abortion: two and one-half years' experience in Upstate New York," by G. Stroh, et al. AMERICAN JOURNAL OF OBSTETRICS AND GYNECOLOGY 126(1):83-90, September 1, 1976.

"Reproductive failure secondary to chromosome abnormalities," by A. Boué, et al. ACTA EUROPAEA FERTILITATIS 6(1):39-55, March, 1975.

"Reproductive performance after treatment of intrauterine adhesions," by E. Caspi, et al. INTERNATIONAL JOURNAL OF FERTILITY 20(4):249-252, 1975. (Bio. Abstrs. 1976, 46114)

"Republican Feminists Prepare to Fight for Convention Delegates, Rights Amendment and Abortion." THE NEW YORK TIMES (M), February 19, 25:1, 1976.

"Requests for termination of pregnancy: psychogeneis and assistance," by G. Resta. MINERVA GINECOLOGIA 27(8):600-606, August, 1975.

"Restrictions in Missouri abortion statute upheld." JOURNAL OF THE MISSISSIPPI STATE MEDICAL ASSOCIATION 16(12):382, December, 1975.

"Results of therapeutic abortion induction using extra-amniotically administered prostaglandin F2 alpha," by H. Lahmann, et al. ARCHIV FUR GYNAEKOLOGIE 219(1-4):499-500, November 18, 1975.

"Results with intra-amniotic administration. pp. 33-36," by W. Brenner, et al. In: Bergström S, ed. Report from meetings of the Prostaglandin Task Force Steering Committee. Stockholm, 1973. QV 175 W927r 1972-1973.

"A Retrial in Abortion Case is Ordered in Canada," by R. Trumbull. THE NEW YORK TIMES (M), January 23, 2:4, 1976.

"A retrospective study of patients seeking pregnancy advice,"

by R. Coles. JOURNAL OF BIOSOCIAL SCIENCE 7, 4:
357-366, October, 1975. (Socio. Abstrs. 1976, 7612701)

"Reversible hypernatremic coma following therapeutic abortion with hypertonic saline," by A. Reches, et al.
HAREFUAH 89(5):209-211, September 1, 1975.

"Right to life." CHRISTIANITY TODAY 20:55, February 13,
1976.

"The right to life," by F. Donaldson. CHRISTIAN STANDARD
8, January 11, 1976.

"Rights of the retarded." (letter). INQUIRY 6(4):4, 30-3,
August, 1976.

"Roe v. Wade (93 Sup Ct 705): its impact on rights of choice
in human reproduction." COLUMBIA HUMAN RIGHTS
LAW REVIEW 5:497-521, Fall, 1973.

"Role of the fibrin stabilizing factor (factor XIII) in early
placental abruption," by M. Brandt, et al. ZENTRAL-
BLATT FUR GYNAEKOLOGIE 97(19):1184-1186, 1975.

"Running scared on abortion." NEW STATESMAN 90:489,
October 24, 1975.

"Saline abortion and lupus erythematosus," by J. F.
Jewett. NEW ENGLAND JOURNAL OF MEDICINE
294(14):782-783, April 1, 1976.

"Salty tears, salty death; the saline mode of abortion: a
comparison," by F. Frech. LIGUORIAN 64:29-31,
October, 1976.

"Search for antifertility agents from indigenous medicinal
plants," by A. Pakrashi, et al. INDIAN JOURNAL OF
MEDICAL RESEARCH 63(3):378-381, March, 1975.

"Scientists Develop Device for Inducing Abortions." THE

NEW YORK TIMES (S), November 21, 26:6, 1976.

"The Senates Vote on Abortion." THE NEW YORK TIMES
(S), August 29, IV, 4:1, 1976.

" 'Second generation' prostaglandins: midtrimester pregnancy termination by intramuscular injection of a 15-
methyl analog of prostaglandin F2alpha," by J. Robins,
et al. FERTILITY AND STERILITY 27(1):104-109,
January, 1976.

"Second thoughts on abortion from the doctor who led the
crusade for it," by C. Remsberg, et al. GOOD
HOUSEKEEPING 182:69 passim, March, 1976.

"Second trimester abortion. A symposium by correspond-
ence," by F. P. Zuspan, et al. JOURNAL OF REPRO-
DUCTIVE MEDICINE 16(2):47-64, February, 1976.

"Second trimester spontaneous abortion, the IUD, and
infection," by S. H. Eisinger. AMERICAN JOURNAL
OF OBSTETRICS AND GYNECOLOGY 124(4):393-397,
1976. (Bio. Abstrs. 1976, 5211)

"Section 401(b) of the health programs extension act: an
abortive attempt by Congress to resolve a constitutional
dilemma." WILLIAM AND MARY LAW REVIEW 17:
303-331, Winter, 1975.

"Secular press snubs abortion death report," by J.
Scheidler. OUR SUNDAY VISITOR MAGAZINE 64:1
passim, March 14, 1976.

"Select committee on abortion." (letter). LANCET
2(7980):306, August 7, 1976.

"Select committee under the abortion law," (letter), by
H. C. McLaren. LANCET 2(7942):986, November 15,
1975.

"Senate Rejects Abortion Curb," by D. E. Rosenbaum.

THE NEW YORK TIMES (M), August 26, 15:1, 1976.

"Senate votes against even considering pro-life bill." OUR
SUNDAY VISITOR 65:2, May 16, 1976.

"Senator Church Joins Presidential Race," by L. Carlton.
THE NEW YORK TIMES (L), March 19, 18:7, 1976.

"Sensitization of women to fetal tissue and leukocytic antigens and its role in miscarriage," by L. F. Kiseleva,
et al. VOPROSY OKHRANY MATERINSTVA I DETSTVA
21(7):65-67, June, 1976.

"Septic abortion and its socio-economical aspects," by J.
Duva Palacios, et al. REVISTA CHILENA DE
OBSTETRICIA Y GINECOLOGIA 39(1):15-19, 1974.

"Septic abortion associated with a Lippes loop," by A. K.
Thomas. BRITISH MEDICAL JOURNAL 3(5986):747-748,
September 27, 1975.

"Septic abortion, excluding those caused by Bacillus perfringens," by M. Herrera, et al. REVISTA CHILENA
DE OBSTETRICIA Y GINECOLOGIA 38(4):176-186,
1973.

"Septic abortion in women using intrauterine devices," by
P. Williams, et al. BRITISH MEDICAL JOURNAL
4(5991):263-264, November 1, 1975.

"Septic abortion. Personal experience and management,"
by R. H. Schwarz. ANTIBIOTICS AND CHEMOTHERAPY
21:46-49, 1976.

"Septic shock in obstetrical clinic," by B. L. Gurtovoi,
et al. AKUSHERSTVO I GINEKOLOGIIA (Moscow)
(3):68-72, March, 1976.

"Septic spontaneous abortion associated with the Dalkon
Shield. pp. 417-428," by E. J. Preston, et al. In:
Hefnawi F, Segal SJ, ed. Analysis of intrauterine

contraception. Amsterdam, North-Holland, 1975. W3 IN182AI 1974a.

"Serial intramuscular injections of 15(S)-15-methyl-prostaglandin F2alpha in the induction of abortion," by N. H. Lauersen, et al. PROSTAGLANDINS 10(6): 1029-1036, December, 1975.

"Serious complications of septic abortions. Pelviperitoneal complications (II)," by S. Musso, et al. MINERVA GINECOLOGIA 27(12):1054-1059, December, 1975.

"Serum fibrinogen-fibrin related antigen and protamine sulfate test in patients with septic abortion and acute renal failure," by I. Crisnic, et al. REVUE ROUMAINE DE MEDECINE [Now MEDECINE INTERNE] 14(1):47-51, 1976. (Bio. Abstrs. 1976, 41222)

"Serum hormone levels in women undergoing abortion with intra-amniotic, extra-amniotic or intra-muscular administration of 15(S) 15-methyl-prosaglandin F2a," by C. P. Puri, et al. PROSTAGLANDINS 11(5):905-923, 1976. (Bio. Abstrs. 1976, 62680)

"Serum level of enzymes during abortion (with simultaneous administration of beta mimetics and beta blocking agents," by E. Szabo, et al. ORVOSI HETILAP 117(11):652-655, March 14, 1976.

"Serum levels of estradiol and progesterone during administration of PGF2 alpha for induction of abortion and labour," by A. Kivikoski, et al. ACTA OBSTETRICIA ET GYNECOLOGICA SCANDINAVICA 55(2):188-190, 1976.

"Serum levels of progesterone, estradiol, and hydrocortisone in ewes after abortion due to Listeria monocytogenes type 5," by J. L. Carter, et al. AMERICAN JOURNAL OF VETERINARY RESEARCH 37(9):1071-1073, September, 1976.

"Severe complications of septic abortion. I. Nephrovascular complications," by G. Musso, et al. MINERVA GINECOLOGICA 27(9):690-697, September, 1975.

"Shifts in public opinion toward abortion," by W. R. Arney, et al. INTELLECT 104:280, January, 1976.

"Significance of HLA and blood-group incompatibility in spontaneous abortion," by J. G. Lauritsen, et al. CLINICAL GENETICS 9(6):575-582, 1976. (Bio. Abstrs. 1976, 66537)

"The significance of oral contraceptives in causing chromosome anomalies in spontaneous abortions," by J. G. Lauritsen. ACTA OBSTETRICIA ET GYNECOLOGICA SCANDINAVICA 54(3):261-264, 1975. (Bio. Abstrs. 1976, 54717)

"Significance of placenta lactogen and placenta isoenzyme of alkaline phosphatase in the diagnosis of threatened gravidity," by J. Sedlák, et al. CASOPIS LEKARU CESKYCH 115(2-3):79-81, January 23, 1976.

"Simone Veil: driving force behind France's abortion law," by A. F. Gonzalez, Jr. AMERICAN MEDICAL NEWS 19; IMPACT/9, June 28, 1976.

"Simone Veil: 20 million Frenchwomen won't be wronged," by C. Servan-Schreiber. MS MAGAZINE 4:104-105 passim, February, 1976.

"Single extra-amniotic injection of prostaglandins in viscous gel to induce abortion," by I. Z. Mackenzie, et al. BRITISH JOURNAL OF OBSTETRICS AND GYNAECOLOGY 83(6):505-507, June, 1976.

"Six More Italians Undergo Abortion." THE NEW YORK TIMES (S), August 20, IV, 17:8, 1976.

"A sliding scale for abortions?" by R. Gillon. OBSERVER 19, July 6, 1975.

"Smoking during pregnancy, stillbirth and abruptio placentae," by J. Goujard, et al. BIOMEDICINE EXPRESS (Paris) 23(1):20-22, February 10, 1975.

"Social-hygienic characteristics of abortion in the Checheno-Ingush ASSR, by M. T. Inderbiev. ZDRAVOOKHRANENIE ROSSIISKAI FEDERATSII (5):24-26, May, 1975.

"Social medicine aspects in pregnancy interruption," by U. Fritsche, et al. ZEITSCHRIFT FUR AERZTLICHE FORTBILDUNG 69(21):1131-1136, November 1, 1975.

"Somatic complications after induced abortion," (letter), by E. Arnesen, et al. TIDSSKRIFT FOR DEN NORSKE LAEGEFORENING 96(15):899-900, May 30, 1976.

"Somatic complications following induced abortions," by K. Molne, et al. TIDSSKRIFT FOR DEN NORSKE LAEGE-FORENING 96(8):483-488, March 20, 1976.

"Somatic complications of induced abortion," (editorial), by P. Bergsjö. TIDSSKRIFT FOR DEN NORSKE LAEGEFORENING 96(8):524-525, March 20, 1976.

"Some forensic problems of commissions for the interruption of pregnancy," by J. Lysican. CESKOSLOVENSKA GYNEKOLOGIE 40(10):737-738, December, 1975.

"Some Leptospira agglutinins deleted in domestic animals in British Columbia," by C. E. Andress, et al. CANADIAN JOURNAL OF COMPARATIVE MEDICINE 40(2):215-217, 1976. (Bio. Abstrs. 1976, 28688)

"Some reflections on the abortion issue," by D. Gustafson. WESTERN HUMANITIES REVIEW 30:181-198, Summer, 1976.

"Sonar in the diagnosis of threatened abortion," by P. L. Ceccarello, et al. MINERVA GINECOLOGIA 27(12):983-987, December, 1975.

"Sonar in early abnormal pregnancy. pp. 273-279," by P.
L. Ceccarello, et al. In: Kazner E, et al., ed. Ultrasonics in medicine. Amsterdam, Excerpta Medica,
1975. W3 EX89 no.363 1975.

"Spina bifida and anencephaly: miscarriage as possible
cause," by C. Clarke, et al. BRITISH MEDICAL
JOURNAL 4(5999):743-746, December 27, 1975.

"Spontaneous abortion as a screening device. The effect
of fetal survival on the incidence of birth defects," by
Z. Stein, et al. AMERICAN JOURNAL OF EPIDEMI-
OLOGY 102(4):275-290, October, 1975.

"Spontaneous abortions in working women," by G. Geshev.
AKUSHERSTVO I GINEKOLOGIIA (Sofia) 15(2):115-120,
1976.

"Spontaneous fetal loss: a note on rates and some impli-
cations," by P. Cutright. JOURNAL OF BIOSOCIAL
SCIENCE 7, 4:421-433, October, 1975. (Socio.
Abstrs. 1976, 7612508)

"St. Louis action tops in fight against abortion," by R.
Casey. NATIONAL CATHOLIC REPORTER 12:1-2
passim, March 26, 1976.

"State legislation on abortion after Roe v. Wade: selected
constitutional issues," by M. D. Bryant, Jr. AMERICAN
JOURNAL OF LAW AND MEDICINE 2(1):101-132,
Summer, 1976.

"A state-registered abortionist?" (editorial). LANCET
2(7941):912-913, November 8, 1975.

"A state-registered abortionists," (letter), by D. P. Cocks,
et al. LANCET 2(7948):1308-1309, December 27, 1975.

"Statistical study of the etiology of habitual abortion. pp. 149-
152," by N. S. Cavallaro, et al. In: Marchesi F,
Cittadini E, ed. Fertilità e sterilità. Taormina, Minerva

medica, 1974. WP 570 S679f 1973.

"Stoking hell's fire." ECONOMIST 257:40, December 20, 1975.

"Strategy questioned," by D. Thorman. NATIONAL CATHOLIC REPORTER 12:8, December 12, 1975.

"Studies in pregnant women on fetomaternal immunization to HL-A alloantigens and ABO and Rh antigens: II. Clinical observations on the course of pregnancy," by Z. Zdebski. FOLIA MEDICA CRACOVIENSIA 16(3): 341-354, 1974. (Bio. Abstrs. 1976, 14408)

"Studies on immediate post-abortion copper 'T' device," by I. Gupta, et al. INDIAN JOURNAL OF MEDICAL RESEARCH 63(5):736-739, May, 1975.

"Study Finds Democratic Nations Stay with Liberalized Abortion." THE NEW YORK TIMES (S), February 20, 2:1, 1976.

"Study Finds Rise in Abortion Here," by E. E. Asbury. THE NEW YORK TIMES (M), January 25, 52:1, 1976.

"Study of the amniotic fluid of sheep in the normal course of pregnancy and in abortion," by S. Georgiev. VETERINARNO-MEDITSINSKI NAUKI 12(5):37-44, 1975.

"Study of the complications occurring in the interruption of pregnancy on demand based on data from the obstetrical and gynecological ward in Ruse over a 10-year period," by Kh. Durveniashki. AKUSHERSTVO I GINEKOLOGIIA (Sofia) 15(2):126-130, 1976.

"Study of the outcome of pregnancy in sheep with positive serologic reactions to toxoplasmosis according to the complement fixation test," by A. Donev. VETERINARNO-MEDITSINSKI NAUKI 12(1):64-68, 1975.

"Study of the transplacental passage of fetal erythrocytes in

100 abortions," by C. Quereux, et al. JOURNAL DE
GYNECOLOGIE, OBSTETRIQUE BIOLOGIE DE LA
REPRODUCTION 1(5 Suppl 2):215-218, 1972.

"Study of Y-chromatin in the human buccal epithelium," by
A. M. Zakharov, et al. ARKHIV ANATOMII GISTOLOGII
I EMBRIOLOGII 68(5):18-23, 1975. (Bio. Abstrs. 1976,
60555)

"Study shows more nurses than before favor abortion," by
J. McCann. NATIONAL CATHOLIC REPORTER 12:5,
March 26, 1976.

"Suboptimal pregnancy outcome among women with prior
abortions and premature births," by S. J. Funderburk,
et al. AMERICAN JOURNAL OF OBSTETRICS AND
GYNECOLOGY 126(1):55-60, September 1, 1976.

"Successive spontaneous abortions with diverse chromosomal
aberrations in human translocation heterozygote," by
G. Kohn, et al. TERATOLOGY; JOURNAL OF ABNOR-
MAL DEVELOPMENT 12(3):283-289, December, 1975.

"Sudden infant death syndrome and subsequent pregnancy,"
by F. Mandell, et al. PEDIATRICS 56:774-776,
November, 1975.

"Summary of Actions Taken by U.S. Supreme Court." THE
NEW YORK TIMES April 27, 15:2, 1976.

"Summary of Actions Taken by U.S. Supreme Court." THE
NEW YORK TIMES (S), July 7, 39:2, 1976.

"Supreme court and abortion." SOCIETY 13:6-9, March,
1976.

"Supreme Court rejects spousal and parental rights in abortion decision," by G. E. Reed. HOSPITAL PROGRESS
57:18 passim, August, 1976.

"Supreme Court to hear abortion cases in '77." OUR

SUNDAY VISITOR 65:2, July 25, 1976.

"Supreme Court unwilling to settle state action conflict," by
P. F. Geary. HOSPITAL PROGRESS 57(5):6, 12, May,
1976.

"Surgical treatment of the abortion at the Gynecologic-
Obstetrical Department of the General Hospital in
Zrenjanin in the period 1967-1974," by B. Nedejković,
et al. MEDICINSKI PREGLED 29(5-6)231-235, 1976.

"A survey of the relationship of infection with toxoplasmosis
in Asian women and its possible effects on their pregnancy outcome," by R. C. Francis. SINGAPORE
MEDICAL JOURNAL 16(4):290-296, 1975. (Bio.
Abstrs. 1976, 45953)

"Survey shows New York is abortion capital of nation."
OUT SUNDAY VISITOR 64:2, February 8, 1976.

"The Switcher Issues," by W. Safire. THE NEW YORK
TIMES (M), February 23, 25:5, 1976.

"Symposium on intrauterine genetics. Reproductive failures
in relation to chromosome abnormalities," by A. Boué,
et al. UNION MEDICALE DU CANADA 104(12):1775-
1781, December, 1975.

"The synergistic effect of calcium and prostaglandin F2alpha
in second trimester abortion. A pilot study," by L.
Weinstein, et al. OBSTETRICS AND GYNECOLOGY
48(4):469-471, October, 1976.

"Synergetic effect of hypertonic NaCl solution and PGF 2
alpha in induced abortion of the second trimester," by
N. Vujaković, et al. JUGOSLOVENSKA GINEKOLIGIJA
I OPSTETRICIJA 16(1):59-64, January-February, 1976.

"Systemic and local administration of prostaglandins for
postconceptional fertility control. pp. 108-115," by M.
Toppozada, et al. In: Bergström S, ed. Report from

meetings of the Prostaglandin Task Force Steering
Committee. Stockholm, 1973. QV 175 W927r 1972-1973.

"Talked out." ECONOMIST 256:18, August 9, 1975.

"Teen-age Abortions Without Family Consent Hang in
the Balance," by G. Dullea. THE NEW YORK TIMES
(M), June 22, 40:1, 1976.

"Teenagers: fertility control behavior and attitudes before
and after abortion, childbearing or negative pregnancy
test," by J. R. Evans, et al. FAMILY PLANNING
PERSPECTIVES 8(4):192-200, July-August, 1976.

"Temporal changes in circulating steroids during prostaglandin F2 alpha induced abortion in the rat and rabbit,"
by I. F. Lau, et al. PROSTAGLANDINS 11(5):859-869,
May, 1976.

"10,000 Antiabortionists Attend a Protest Rally," by P.
Kihss. THE NEW YORK TIMES July 12, III, 21:7, 1976.

"Terbutaline inhibition of midtrimester uterine activity
induced by prostaglandin F2alpha and hypertonic saline,"
by K. E. Andersson, et al. BRITISH JOURNAL OF
OBSTETRICS AND GYNAECOLOGY 82(9):745-749,
September, 1975.

"Term delivery through a cervicovaginal fistula," by
M. A. Pelosi, et al. AMERICAN JOURNAL OF
OBSTETRICS AND GYNECOLOGY 122(6):789-790, 1975.
(Bio. Abstrs. 1976, 53718)

"The termination of human pregnancy with prostaglandin
analogs," by G. D. Gutknecht, et al. JOURNAL OF
REPRODUCTIVE MEDICINE 15(3):93-96, September, 1975.

"Termination of hypertensive pregnancies with intra-amniotic
urevert," by S. Roopnarinesingh. WEST INDIAN MEDICAL
JOURNAL 24(3):164-168, September, 1975.

"Termination of late first-tirmester and early second-trimester gestations with intramuscular 15 (S)-15-methyl-prostaglandin F2alpha," by R. J. Bolognese, et al. JOURNAL OF REPRODUCTIVE MEDICINE 16(2): 81-84, February, 1976.

"Termination of late-term pregnancy in intra-amniotic administration of prostaglandin and hypertonic saline solution," by E. A. Chernukha, et al. AKUSHERSTVO I GINEKOLOGIIA (Moscow) (6):19-24, June, 1975.

"Termination of midtrimester pregnancy by serial intra-muscular injections of 15(S)-15-methyl-prostaglandin F2alpha," by N. H. Lauersen, et al. AMERICAN JOURNAL OF OBSTETRICS AND GYNECOLOGY 124(2):169-176, January 15, 1976.

"Termination of pregnancy," by A. McQueen. NURSING MIRROR AND MIDWIVES' JOURNAL 142:45-47, June 17, 1976.

"Termination of pregnancy by sheep anti-LHRH gamma golublin in rats," by N. Nishi, et al. ENDOCRINOLOGY 98(4):1024-1030, April, 1976.

"Termination of pregnancy in cases of fetal death in utero by intravenous prostaglandin F2alpha," by A. P. Lange, et al. PROSTAGLANDINS 11(1):101-108, January, 1976.

"Termination of pregnancy with double prostaglandin impact," by A. I. Csapo, et al. AMERICAN JOURNAL OF OBSTE-TRICS AND GYNECOLOGY 124(1):1-13, January 1, 1976.

"Termination of pseudopregnancy by administration of prostaglandin F2alpha and termination of early pregnancy by administration of prostaglandin F2alpha or colchicine or by removal of embryo in mares," by L. K. Kooistra, et al. AMERICAN JOURNAL OF VETERINARY RESEARCH 37(1):35-39, January, 1976.

"Territorial differences in abortion rate in Czechoslovakia

in 1969 and 1970," by H. Wynnyczuková. DEMOGRAFIE
15, 2:110-120, 1973. (Socio. Abstrs. 1976, 76I0154)

"Therapeutic abortion," (letter), by R. N. Ough.
CANADIAN MEDICAL ASSOCIATION JOURNAL 113(9):
818-821, November 8, 1975.

"Therapeutic abortion and its aftermath," by M. Stone.
MIDWIFE, HEALTH VISITOR AND COMMUNITY NURSE
11:335-338, October, 1975.

"Therapeutic abortion and its psychological implications: the
Canadian experience," by E. R. Greenglass. CANADIAN
MEDICAL ASSOCIATION JOURNAL 113:794-797,
October 18, 1976.

"Therapeutic abortion in a midwestern city," by L. Melamed.
PSYCHOLOGICAL REPORTS 37(3 Pt 2):1143-1146,
December, 1975.

"Therapeutic abortion--some psychiatric aspects," by F.
Shane. PSYCHIATRIC NURSING 17(2):11-13, March-
April, 1976.

"Therapeutic midtrimester abortion by the intra-uterine
administration of prostaglandins. Experience of Groote
Schuur Hospital, 1974-1975," by G. Sher. SOUTH
AFRICAN MEDICAL JOURNAL 50(30):1173-1177, July 14,
1976.

"There Just Wasn't Room in Our Lives Now For Another
Baby." THE NEW YORK TIMES May 14, I, 27:3, 1976.

"They exploded the abortion myth," by M. Burson. OUR
SUNDAY VISITOR MAGAZINE 64:1 passim, January 18,
1976.

"Thoughts on Abortion," by J. Schrank. THE NEW YORK
TIMES February 16, 18:3, 1976.

"Thousands march in national capital in protest against

legalized abortion," by C. Foster. OUR SUNDAY VISITOR 64:1, February 8, 1976.

"Threatened or protected risky gravidity," by V. Kliment, et al. CESKOSLOVENSKA GYNEKOLOGIE 41(1):30-31, March, 1976.

"3Beta-hydroxy-20-oxo-pregn-5-ene-16 alpha-carbonitrile, a potent catatoxic steroid devoid of an abortifacient effect," by Y. Taché, et al. ENDOCRINOLOGY 97(3): 731-734, September, 1975.

"Three against abortion: none of them Catholic," by R. Cormier. ST. ANTHONY MESSENGER 84:18-22, 1976.

"350 requests of abortion. What happens just two years before?" by A. M. Lanoy, et al. PRAXIS 64(10):295-298, March 11, 1975.

"3 Italian Women in Toxic-Gas Area Undergo Abortion." THE NEW YORK TIMES (S), August 14, 4:5, 1976.

"Three levels of discussion about abortion," by J. Carlson. DIMENSION 8:37-45, September, 1976.

"Three years is too long." CHRISTIANITY TODAY 20:38 passim, February 13, 1976.

"Time to stop fiddling about with the Abortion Act," by D. Steel. TIMES 16, February 2, 1976.

"Today's moral symmetry principle," by R. L. Trammell. PHILOSOPHY AND PUBLIC AFFAIRS 5, 305-313, Spring, 1976.

"Toward an abortion counseling strategy for pro-life counselors," by P. J. Armstrong. SCHOOL COUNSELOR 24:36-38, September, 1976.

"Trans-isthmicocervical intra-amniotic instillation of

hypertonic sodium solutions for termination of pregnancy after the 1st trimester," by I. Kosowski. ZENTRAL-BLATT FUR GYNAEKOLOGIE 97(18):1130-1135, 1975.

"Transplacental hemorrhage in abortion (incidence, entity and immunizing value). pp. 145-147," by S. di Leo, et al. In: Marchesi F, Cittadini E, ed. Fertilità e sterilità. Taormina, Minerva medica, 1974. WP 570 S679f 1973.

"Treatment of the focus in septic gnyecologic infection," by F. Rocha. REVISTA CHILENA DE OBSTETRICIA Y GINECOLOGIA 39(6):268-278, 1974.

"Treatment of perforation of the large intestine due to illegal abortion," by H. G. Mayer. ZENTRALBLATT FUR GYNAEKOLOGIE 97(12):734-737, 1975.

"Treatment of threatened and habitual abortions with Turinal preparations," by H. Szucka-May, et al. GINEKOLOGIA POLASKA 46(12):1265-1269, December, 1975.

"Treatment of threatened abortion in a serotonin antagonist. Clinico-statistical data," by M. Goisis, et al. MINERVA GINECOLOGIA 27(9):773-778, September, 1975.

"Treatment of threatened early abortion (6th-16th week of pregnancy) of Th 1165a (Partusisten)," by H. Bärmig, et al. ZENTRALBLATT FUR GYNAEKOLOGIE 98(13): 792-794, 1976.

"Treatment of women suffering from habitual miscarriage," by N. T. Gudakova. AKUSHERSTVO I GINEKOLOGIIA (Moscow) (3):64-65, March, 1976.

"Trends in attitudes toward abortion, 1972-1975," by W. R. Arney, et al. FAMILY PLANNING PERSPECTIVES 8:117-124, May-June, 1976.

"Trichomonas fetus-induced abortion," by J. W. Kendrick.

THERIOGENOLOGY 5(3):150-152, 1976. (Bio. Abstrs. 1976, 27484)

"Trisomy 21 in mother and daughter," by D. Francesconi, et al. CLINICAL GENETICS 9(3):346, 1976. (Bio. Abstrs. 1976, 25789)

"A 22/22 translocation carrier with recurrent abortions demonstrated by a Giemsa banding technique," by T. Maeda, et al. HUMAN GENETICS 31(2):243-245, February 29, 1976.

"The two faces of Women's Liberation." OUR SUNDAY VISITOR MAGAZINE 65:1 passim, June 27, 1976.

"Two forms of simian-virus-40-specific T-antigen in abortive and lytic infection," by C. Ahmad-Zadeh, et al. PROCEEDINGS OF THE NATIONAL ACADEMY OF SCIENCES OF THE UNITED STATES OF AMERICA 73(4):1097-1101, 1976. (Bio. Abstrs. 1976, 26824)

"Ultrasound in the management of elective abortion," by R. C. Sanders, et al. AMERICAN JOURNAL OF ROENT-GENOLOGY 125(2):469-473, October, 1975.

"UN study group reports, Msgr. McHugh dissents; study paper on abortion." OUR SUNDAY VISITOR 64:2, March 7, 1976.

"Understanding adolescent pregnancy and abortion," by S. L. Hatcher. PRIMARY CARE; CLINICS IN OFFICE PRACTICE 3(3):407-425, September, 1976.

"Unexpectedly cautious." ECONOMIST 260:29-30, July 31, 1976.

"The unmet need for legal abortion services in the U.S.," by C. Tietze, et al. FAMILY PLANNING PERSPECTIVES 7(5):224-230, September-October, 1975.

"The unwanted child: caring for the fetus born alive after
an abortion." HASTINGS CENTER REPORT 6(5):10-15,
October, 1976.

"Unwanted pregnancies and abortion," (letter), by L. A.
Woolf. MEDICAL JOURNAL OF AUSTRALIA 2(9):368-
369, August 30, 1975.

"Unwanted pregnancy and abortion," by M. J. Castro.
REVISTA DE NEURO-PSIQUIATRIA 38(3-4):177-186,
September-December, 1975.

"Ureter-uterus fistula after abortion," by W. Hardt, et al.
ZEITSCHRIFT FUR UROLOGIE UND NEPHROLOGIE
68(10):761-764, October, 1975.

"USA and abortion," by J. Noonan. TABLET 230:494-496,
May 22, 1976.

"U.S. Catholic Conference files brief asking Supreme Court
give unborn legal protection," by J. Castelli. OUR
SUNDAY VISITOR 64:3, January 25, 1976.

"U.S. Court Overturns Curb on Medicaid Abortions," by
M. H. Siegel. THE NEW YORK TIMES (M), October 23,
1:3, 1976.

"U.S. Courts Bar Curb on Funding Some Abortion," by
M. H. Siegel. THE NEW YORK TIMES (M), October 2,
1:2, 1976.

"U.S. money backs international abortion cartel," by M.
Bunson. OUR SUNDAY VISITOR MAGAZINE 65:1
passim, June 13, 1976.

"U.S. Supreme Court lets lower court decision stand on
right of hospital to refuse abortion." OUR SUNDAY
VISITOR 64:1, December 14, 1975.

"Use of combination prostaglandin F2alpha and hypertonic
saline for midtrimester abortion. Department of

Obstetrics and Gynecology Harvard Medical School, Beth
Israel Hospital, Boston, Massachusetts." PROSTA-
GLANDINS 12(4):625-630, October, 1976.

"Use of E-aminocaproic acid for blocking uterine contractions
in threatened, premature labor and late abortion," by A.
Donchev. AKUSHERSTVO I GINEKOLOGIIA (Sofia)
14(5):368-371, 1975.

"The use of human abortuses in the search for teratogens.
pp. 189-196," by G. P. Oakley, Jr. In: Shepard TH
et al., ed. Methods for detection of environmental
agents that produce congenital defects. Amsterdam,
North-Holland, 1975. QS 675 M592 1974. 1974.

"Use of prostaglandins for induction of abortion," by E. A.
Chernukha. AKUSHERSTVO I GINEKOLOGIIA (Moscow)
(7):7-10, July, 1975.

"Use of prostaglandins in gynecology and obstetrics," by
B. I. Nesheim. TIDSSKRIFT FOR DEN NORSKE
LAEGEFORENING 96(6):375-376, February 28, 1976.

"The use of silastic vaginal device containing (15S)-15
methyl prostaglandin F2 alpha methyl ester for early
first trimester pregnancy termination," by J. Robins.
PROSTAGLANDINS 12 Suppl:123-134, 1976.

"The use of surgery to avoid childbearing among Navajo
and Hopi Indians. pp. 9-21," by S. J. Kunitz, et al.
In: Kaplan BA, ed. Anthropological studies of human
fertility. Detroit, Wayne State Univ Press, 1976.
GN 241 S989a 1975.

"Uterine rupture complicating mid-trimester abortion in a
young woman of low parity," by R. H. Hayashi, et al.
INTERNATIONAL JOURNAL OF GYNAECOLOGY AND
OBSTETRICS 13(5):229-232, 1975. (Bio. Abstrs. 1976,
22789)

"Vacuum aspiration at therapeutic abortion: effect of Cu-IUD insertion at operation on post-operative blood loss," by F. Solheim, et al. CONTRACEPTION 13(6):707-713, 1976. (Bio. Abstrs. 1976, 40215)

"Vaginal cytology in induced abortion," by S. Dossland, et al. TIDSSKRIFT FOR DEN NORSKE LAEGEFORENING 96(16):937-938, June 10, 1976.

"Vaginally administered 16, 16-dimethyl-PGE2 for the induction of midtrimester abortion," by J. N. Martin, Jr., et al. PROSTAGLANDINS 11(1):123-132, 1976. (Bio. Abstrs. 1976, 4269)

"Value conflicts and the uses of research: the example of abortion." MAN AND MEDICINE 1:29-41, Autumn, 1975.

"Value of intradermal hormone tests in the diagnosis of causes of threatened abortion," by L. P. Peshev. VOPROSY OKHRANY MATERINSTVA I DETSTVA 20(9):67-70, September, 1975.

"The value of prostaglandins in the treatment of missed abortion," by N. Exalto, et al. NEDERLANDS TIJDSCHRIFT VOOR GENEESKUNDE 120(30):1289-1292, July 24, 1976.

"Vascular lesions of the endometrium in spontaneous abortion," by L. Orcel, et al. ANNALES D'ANATOMIE PATHOLOGIQUE 20(2):109-120, March-April, 1975.

"Viability and abortion," by C. Macaluso. KENTUCKY LAW JOURNAL 64, 1:146-164, 1976. (Socio. Abstrs. 1976, 76I2441)

"Viewpoint: abortion revisited," by H. Moody. CHRISTI-ANITY AND CRISIS 35:166-168, July 21, 1975.

"Violent perforations of the uterus in the 10-year material of the Gynecologic-Obstetrical Department in Bitola," by T. Pasanku. MEDICINSKI ARHIV 28(3):337-339,

May–June, 1974.

"Virus-induced abortion. Studies of equine herpesvirus 1 (abortion virus) in hamsters," by J. D. Burek, et al. LABORATORY INVESTIGATION 33(4):400–406, October, 1975.

"Voluntary abortion and resistance to contraception," by M. Bourgeois, et al. ANNALES MEDICO-PSYCHOLOGI-QUES 2(2):366–377, July, 1975.

"Voluntary abortion, the global picture and danger for our society," by J. Botella Llusiá. CUADERNOS DE REALIDADES SOCIALES 4:77–84, May, 1974. (Socio. Abstrs. 1976, 76I0109)

"Votes in Congress." THE NEW YORK TIMES May 2, 58:4, 1976.

"Votes in Congress." THE NEW YORK TIMES July 4, 39:7, 1976.

"Votes in Congress." THE NEW YORK TIMES August 29, 47:3, 1976.

"Wallace Pressing the Abortion Issue," by R. Reed. THE NEW YORK TIMES (M), March 3, 17:6, 1976.

"Water intoxication associated with oxytocin infusion," by A. J. Ahmad, et al. POSTGRADUATE MEDICAL JOURNAL 51(594):249–252, April, 1975.

"We are lovers of life, Archbishop Sheen says." OUR SUNDAY VISITOR 65:2, July 11, 1976.

"We ask protection for the unborn: pastoral letter," by Card. T. Manning. L'OSSERVATORE ROMANO 6(410): 10, February 5, 1976.

"West German abortion decision: a contrast to Roe v. Wade

(93 Sup Ct 705) Preface," by J. D. Gorby, et al. JOHN
MARSHALL JOURNAL 9:551-684, Spring, 1976.

"What are the bonds between the fetus and the uterus," by
V. Adamkiewicz. INFIRMIÉRE CANADIENNE 18(2):
26-28, February, 1976.

"What are the bonds between the fetus and the uterus?" by
V. W. Adamkiewicz. CANADIAN NURSE 72(2):26-28,
February, 1976.

"What are the father's rights in abortion?" by R. Blackwood.
JOURNAL OF LEGAL MEDICINE 3(9):28-36, October,
1975.

"What for?" ECONOMIST 258:34, February 14, 1976.

"What I saw at the abortion," by R. Selzer. CHRISTIANITY
TODAY 20:11-12, January 16, 1976.

"What I saw at the abortion; continued from ESQUIRE,
January, 1976," by R. Selzer. CATHOLIC DIGEST 40:
47-50, July, 1976.

"What is distress?" ECONOMIST 257:42, 45, October 18,
1975.

"What therapeutic abortion?" by A. Bompiani. L'OSSERVA-
TORE ROMANO 15(419):9, April 8, 1976.

"When being unwanted is a capital crime," by M. White.
TIMES 10, July 21, 1975.

"When is killing the unborn a homicidal action?" by P.
Coffey. LINACRE 43:85-93, May, 1976.

"When is life," by N. Pyle. FAITH FOR THE FAMILY
3, November-December, 1975.

"Where have all the conceptions gone?" by C. J. Roberts,
et al. LANCET 1(7905):498-499, 1975. (Bio. Abstrs.

1976, 1153)

"Where the Women Stand on Controversial Issues." THE
NEW YORK TIMES (M), April 12, 24:6, 1976.

"Whistle-stops abortion out as top national issue," by
R. Casey. NATIONAL CATHOLIC REPORTER 12:3, O
October 1, 1976.

"The WHO Prostaglandin Task Force. (Protocol manual).
Phase IIb clinical trials comparing intra-amniotic
prostaglandin F2alpha and 15-methyl PGE2alpha.
(Trial No. 103). pp. 65-78." In: Bergström, S, ed.
Report from meetings of the Prostaglandin Task Force
Steering Committee. Stockholm, 1973. QV 175
W927r 1972-1973.

--Phase III clinical trials of intra-amniotic prostaglandin
F2alpha versus hypertonic saline (trial no. 101) and
extra-amniotic prostaglandin F2alpha (trial no. 102).
pp. 12-27." In: Bergström S, ed. Report from meetings
of the Prostaglandin Task Force Steering Committee.
Stockholm, 1973. QV 175 W927r 1972-1973.

"The WHO Prostaglandin Task Force. Report from the Prostaglandin Task Force Meeting, Geneva, February 26--28,
1973. pp. 31-32." In: Bergström S, ed. Report from meetings of the Prostaglandin Task Force Steering Committee.
Stockholm, 1973. QV 175 W927r 1972-1973.

--Report from the Prostaglandin Task Force Meeting,
Stockholm, October 2-3, 1972. pp. 9-11." In:
Bergström S, ed. Report from meetings of the
Prostaglandin Task Force Steering Committee. Stock-
holm, 1973. QV 175 W927r 1972-1973.

"Whose interests?" by J. Turner. NURSING TIMES
71(45):1763, November 6, 1975.

"Why new uproar over abortion: pushing to the foreground
of '76 politics is an issue candidates would like to avoid;

the reason: it's trouble - no matter what they say."
U.S. NEWS AND WORLD REPORT 80:14-15, March 1,
1976.

"Woman's choice." ECONOMIST 260:35-36, July 10, 1976.

"Woman's Rights." THE NEW YORK TIMES (M), February 9, 21:7, 1976.

"Women, anger and abortion," by R. C. Wahlberg.
CHRISTIAN CENTURY 92:622-623, July 7, 1976.

"Women's experience of local anethesia in early legal
abortions," by U. Idahl, et al. LAKARTIDNINGEN 73
(34):2745-2746, August 18, 1976.

"Women's experience of the abortion procedure," by L.
Jacobsson, et al. SOCIAL PSYCHIATRY 10(4):155-160,
October, 1975.

"World as reality, as resource, and as pretense," by R.
Stith. AMERICAN JOURNAL OF JURISPRUDENCE
20:141-153, 1975.

"Zinc and copper in pregnancy, correlations to fetal and
maternal complications," by S. Jameson. ACTA
MEDICA SCANDINAVICA SUPPLEMENT (593):5-20,
1976.

"Zinc deficiency in malabsorption states: a cause of infertility?" by S. Jameson. ACTA MEDICA SCANDI-
NAVICA SUPPLEMENT (593):38-49, 1976.

PERIODICAL LITERATURE

SUBJECT INDEX

ABNORMALITIES
see: Complications

ABORTION (GENERAL)
"G. B. Drayson, M. P." NEW HUMANIST 92:287-288,
March, 1976.

"A note on the unborn person," by R. Masiello. LINACRE
43:112-114, May, 1976.

"Pregnant stewardess - should she fly?" by P. Scholten.
AVIATION SPACE AND ENVIRONMENTAL MEDICINE
47(1):77-81, 1976.

ABORTION ACT
see: Laws and Legislation

ABORTION: AUSTRIA

ABORTION: BELGIUM

ABORTION: CANADA
"Acquittal of Canadian Physician In Illegal-Abortion Case
Upheld," by R. Trumbull. THE NEW YORK TIMES (M)
January 21, 21:4, 1976.

"All Charges Withdrawn in Quebec Abortion Case." THE
NEW YORK TIMES (S) December 11, 9:6, 1976.

"Canada's Top Court Bars Move to Reverse Abortion Acquittal." THE NEW YORK TIMES (M) March 16, 4:5, 1976.

"Canadian Abortion Doctor Wins Third Acquittal." THE NEW YORK TIMES (S) September 19, 7:1, 1976.

"The Canadian abortion law," (letter), by P. G. Coffey. CANADIAN MEDICAL ASSOCIATION JOURNAL 115(3): 211-216, August 7, 1976.

"The Canadian abortion law," (letter), by M. Cohen, et al. CANADIAN MEDICAL ASSOCIATION JOURNAL 114(7): 593, April 3, 1976.

"Canadian Physician, Jailed in Abortion Case, Is Freed." THE NEW YORK TIMES (S) January 27, 2:5, 1976.

"Dilemma." (pictorial). CANADIAN NURSE 72:51-55, August, 1976.

"Eugenic recognition in Canadian law," by B. M. Dickens. OSGOODE HALL LAW JOURNAL 13: 547-577, October, 1975.

"The Morgentaler case," (letter), by G. Carruthers. CANADIAN MEDICAL ASSOCIATION JOURNAL 113 (9):818, November 8, 1975.

"Morgentaler freed, new trial ordered," by B. Richardson. HUMANIST 36:50, March, 1976.

"Quebec Halts Trial of Abortion Doctor," by H. Giniger. THE NEW YORK TIMES December 12, 21:1, 1976.

"A Retrial in Abortion Case is Ordered in Canada," by R. Trumbull. THE NEW YORK TIMES (M) January 23, 2:4, 1976.

ABORTION: CANADA

"Therapeutic abortion and its psychological implications:
the Canadian experience," by E. B. Greenglass.
CANADIAN MEDICAL ASSOCIATION JOURNAL 113:
794-797, October 18, 1976.

ABORTION: CAROLINE ISLANDS

ABORTION: CHILE

ABORTION: CHINA
"Potential anti-fertility plants from Chinese medicine,"
by Y. C. Kong, et al. AMERICAN JOURNAL OF
CHINESE MEDICINE 4(2):105-128, Summer, 1976.

"Psychiatric aspects of abortion in Hong Kong," by K.
Singer. INTERNATIONAL JOURNAL OF SOCIAL
PSYCHIATRY 21(4):303-306, Winter, 1975.

"A survey of the relationship of infection with toxoplasmosis in Asian women and its possible effects on
their pregnancy outcome," by R. C. Francis.
SINGAPORE MEDICAL JOURNAL 16(4):290-296, 1975.

ABORTION: CUBA

ABORTION: CZECHOSLOVAKIA
"Influence of Abortion-Rate in Czechoslovakia on the
Selected Phenomena of Reproduction-Processes," by
H. Wynnyczuková, et al. DEMOGRAFIE 17, 3, 193-
204, 1975.

"Territorial Differences in Abortion Rate in Czechoslovakia in 1969 and 1970," by H Wynnyczuková, et
al. DEMOGRAFIE 15, 2, 110-120, 1973.

ABORTION: DENMARK
"The impact of liberalized abortion legislation on contraceptive practice in Denmark," by R. L. Somers,
et al. STUDIES IN FAMILY PLANNING 7(8):218-223,
August, 1976.

ABORTION: DENMARK

"Legal abortion in the county of Funen in relation to the
liberalized Danish legislation," by F. H. Nielsen, et
al. UGESKRIFT FOR LAEGER 138(6):369-375,
February 2, 1976.

ABORTION: EUROPE
"European Communist states turn away from abortion,"
by H. Szablya. OUR SUNDAY VISITOR 64:3, January 25, 1976.

"Problem of abortions in the European socialist countries,"
by V. V. Bodrova. ZDRAVOOKHRANENIE ROSSIISKOI
FEDERATSII (5):34-40, May, 1975.

"Pronatalist programmes in Eastern Europe," by R.
McIntyre. SOVIET STUDIES 27:366, July, 1975.

ABORTION: FINLAND

ABORTION: FRANCE
"Acute renal failure in the postpartum and post-abortion
periods observed in the maternity department of the
Hôpital Charles Nicolle," by B. Farza, et al.
JOURNAL DE GYNECOLOGIE, OBSTETRIQUE ET
BIOLOGIE DE LA REPRODUCTION 1(5 Suppl 2):443-
447, 1972.

"French Critize Medical Society," by J. F. Clarity. THE
NEW YORK TIMES (M) April 11, 19:1, 1976.

"Paris Counts 45,085 Abortions in First Year After Change
in Law." THE NEW YORK TIMES (S) November 17, I,
19:1, 1976.

"Recent French law on interruption of pregnancy," by R.
Bourg. BRUXELLES-MEDICAL 55(4):201-206, April,
1975.

"Simone Veil: driving force behind France's abortion law,"

ABORTION: FRANCE

by A. F. Gonzalez, Jr. AMERICAN MEDICAL NEWS
19: IMPACT/9, June 28, 1976.

"Simone Veil: 20 million Frenchwomen won't be wronged,"
by C. Servan-Schreiber. MS MAGAZINE 4:104-105
passim, February, 1976.

ABORTION: GERMANY
"Ethics in embryo: abortion and the problem of mor-
ality in post-war German literature," by A. F.
Keele." GERMANIC REVIEW 51:299-241, May, 1976.

"Legal abortions at the University-Gynecological Clinic
Mannheim during 1971-1974," by W. von Mühlenfels,
et al. FORTSCHRITTE DU MEDIZIN 93(31):1530-
1532, November 6, 1975.

"Procedures in the termination of pregnancy, 'Mannheim'
proposal - document symbol Paragraph 218/new 76,"
by S. Sievers, et al. FORTSCHRITTE DU MEDIZIN
94(27):1471-1472, September 23, 1976.

"West German abortion decision: a contrast to Roe v.
Wade (93 Sup Ct 705)," by J. D. Gorby, et al.
JOHN MARSHALL JOURNAL 9:551-684, Spring, 1976.

"What is distress." ECONOMIST 257:42 passim, October 18, 1975.

ABORTION: GHANA
"Incomplete abortions in Accra and Bangkok University
Hospitals 1972-1973," by I. C. Chi, et al. INTER-
NATIONAL JOURNAL OF GYNAECOLOGY AND
OBSTETRICS 13(4):148-161, 1975.

ABORTION: HUNGARY
"The effect of the legalization of abortion on public health
and some of its social concomitants in Hungary," by
M. Miklos. DEMOGRAFIA 16, 1, 70-113, 1973.

ABORTION: HUNGARY

"The impact of induced abortions on fertility," by M.
Károly, et al. DEMOGRAFIA 13, 4, 413-420, 1970.

"Legal aspects of some methods of birth-control," by
N. Endre. DEMOGRAFIA 13, 4, 355-385, 1970.

"Mortality and morbidity associated with legal abortions
in Hungary, 1960-1973," by Z. Bognar, et al.
AMERICAN JOURNAL OF PUBLIC HEALTH 66:568-
575, June, 1976.

ABORTION: INDIA
"Abortion in India," by R. P. Mohan. SOCIAL SCIENCE
50, 3, 141-143, Summer, 1975.

"Medical interruption of pregnancy in India," by T.
Chandy. MUENCHENER MEDIZINISCHE WOCHEN-
SCHRIFT 117(34):1349-1352, August 22, 1975.

"419,000 Abortions in India." THE NEW YORK TIMES (S)
August 21, 18:2, 1976.

"A survey of the relationship of infection with toxoplasmosis in Asian women and its possible effects on
their pregnancy outcome," by R. C. Francis.
SINGAPORE MEDICAL JOURNAL 16(4):290-296, 1975.

ABORTION: ITALY
"Abortion Backers on March in Rome." THE NEW YORK
TIMES (S) April 4, 20:1, 1976.

"Abortion Debate Heats up in Italy," by C. Lord. THE
NEW YORK TIMES (M) August 9, 7:1, 1976.

"Dangerous developments on the subject of therapeutic
abortion: Italy's decisions after the Seveso contamination," by G. Guzzetti. L'OSSERVATORE ROMANO
39(443)11, September 23, 1976.

"Declaration of Permanent Council of Italian Bishops' Conference; abortion issue." L'OSSERVATORE ROMANO 1(405):9, January 1, 1976.

"Exemption on Abortion Reported in Italy." THE NEW YORK TIMES (S) August 3, 2:4, 1976.

"Fitting the Bill," by J. Cook. GUARDIAN 11, October 21, 1975.

"Gun or slow poison." TIME 207:61-62, April 29, 1976.

"How to abort a government." ECONOMIST 259:62, April 10, 1976.

"In defence of life and love; homily," by Card. G. Colombo. L'OSSERVATORE ROMANO 20(424):4-5, May 13, 1976.

"Italian bishops get flack because of anti-Communism." OUR SUNDAY VISITOR 64:2, January 4, 1975.

"Italian Catholic jurists on question of abortion." L'OSSERVATORE ROMANO 14(418):4, April 1, 1976.

"Italian Party Chief, in One-Man Drive, Seeks a National Consensus on Policy," by A. Shuster. THE NEW YORK TIMES (M) April 7, 2:4, 1976.

"Italy Allocates Funds for Gassed Region." THE NEW YORK TIMES (S) August 11, 2:6, 1976.

"Italy in a Political Crisis Over Abortion," by A. Shuster. THE NEW YORK TIMES (M) April 3, 9:4, 1976.

"Our decision, say women." ECONOMIST 257:49, December 13, 1975.

ABORTION: ITALY

"Poisonous Clouds' Effects Still Baffle Italy's Officials,"
by S. V. Roberts. THE NEW YORK TIMES (L)
August 13, I, 3:1, 1976.

"Political Crisis Plagues Italy," by A. Shuster. THE
NEW YORK TIMES (M) April 13, 10:4, 1976.

"Pope Denies View is Outdated " THE NEW YORK
TIMES (S) January 22, 32:1, 1976.

"Six More Italians Undergo Abortion." THE NEW YORK
TIMES (S) August 20, IV, 17:8, 1976.

"Stoking hell's fire." ECONOMIST 257:40, December 20,
1975.

"3 Italian Women in Toxic-Gas Area Undergo Abortion."
THE NEW YORK TIMES (S) August 14, 4:5, 1976.

ABORTION: JAMAICA

ABORTION: JAPAN
"Fertility control transition from abortion to contraception in Japan since 1948," by T. Aso. INTER-
NATIONAL REVIEW OF MODERN SOCIOLOGY 4, 1,
43-53, Spring, 1974.

ABORTION: MALAYSIA
"Abortions-government hospitals Peninsular Malaysia
1960-1972," by J. A. Thambu. MEDICAL JOURNAL
OF MALAYSIA 29(4):258-262, June, 1975.

"Maternal mortality from septic abortions in University
Hospital, Kuala Lumpur from March 1968 to February
1974," by K. H. Ng, et al. MEDICAL JOURNAL OF
MALAYSIA 30(1):52-54, September, 1975.

"A survey of the relationship of infection with toxoplasmosis in Asian women and its possible effects

ABORTION: MALAYSIA

on their pregnancy outcome," by R. C. Francis.
SINGAPORE MEDICAL JOURNAL 16(4):290-296,
1975.

ABORTION: MEXICO

ABORTION: NETHERLANDS
"Interruption of pregnancy in the Netherlands." (letter).
ZEITSCHRIFT FUR ALLGEMEINMEDIZIN; DU
LANDARZT 51(10):493-499, April 10, 1975.

ABORTION: NEW ZEALAND
"Abortion in New Zealand," by A. D. Trlin. AUS-
TRALIAN JOURNAL OF SOCIAL ISSUES 20, 3, 179-
296, August, 1975.

"Abortion practice in NZ public hospitals." NURSING
FORUM (Auckl) 3(4):5-7, November-December, 1975.

"Contraception, sterilisation and abortion in NZ."
NURSING FORUM (Auckl) 4:6-9, June/July, 1976.

"Morbidity of therapeutic abortion in Auckland," by M.
A. Baird. NEW ZEALAND MEDICAL JOURNAL
83(565):395-399, June, 1976.

"Public opinion and legal abortion in New Zealand," by
B. J. Kirkwood, et al. NEW ZEALAND MEDICAL
JOURNAL 83(556):43-47, January 28, 1976.

ABORTION: NIGERIA
"Proposed decree on abortion and nurses' role," by S.
A. Jegede. NIGERIAN NURSE 7(1):33-34, January-
March, 1975.

ABORTION: NORWAY

ABORTION: PAKISTAN
"Pakistan may allow abortion as part of a new deal for

ABORTION: PAKISTAN

women," by H. Akhtar. TIMES 6, August 20, 1976.

ABORTION: POLAND

ABORTION: PORTUGAL
"Abortions in Portugal a Complex Controversy," by M.
Howe. THE NEW YORK TIMES (M) March 13, 13:6, 1976

ABORTION: PUERTO RICO

ABORTION: RHODESIA

ABORTION: SCANDINAVIA
"Abortion development in the Scandinavian countries
1965-1974," by P. C. Matthiessen. UGESKRIFT
FOR LAEGER 138(60):351-353, February 2, 1976.

"Abortion incidence and medical legislation in
Scandinavia," by K. Sundström. LAKARTIDNINGEN
73(36):2896, September 1, 1976.

"Abortion increase in Scandinavia in 1975." NORDISK
VETERINAER MEDICA 91(4):115, April, 1976.

ABORTION: SINGAPORE

ABORTION: SWEDEN

ABORTION: TAIWAN
"A comparison of four methods for determing prevalence
of induced abortion, Taiwan, 1970-1971," by R. V.
Rider, et al. AMERICAN JOURNAL OF EPIDEMI-
OLOGY 103(1):37-50, January, 1976.

"Competition between spontaneous and induced abortion,"
by R. G. Potter, et al. DEMOGRAPHY 12:129-141,
February, 1975.

"Induced abortion and contraceptive practice: an experience

ABORTION: TAIWAN

in Taiwan," by I. H. Su, et al. STUDIES IN FAMILY
PLANNING 7:224-230, August, 1976.

"The influence of induced abortion on Taiwanese fertility,"
by J. M. Sullivan, et al. STUDIES IN FAMILY
PLANNING 7(8):231-238, August, 1976.

ABORTION: THAILAND
"Comparison of culdoscopic and lararoscopic tubal
sterilization," by S. Koetsawang, et al. AMERICAN
JOURNAL OF OBSTETRICS AND GYNECOLOGY
124(6):601-606, 1976. (Bio. Abstrs. 1976, 11031)

"Incomplete abortions in Accra and Bangkok University
Hospitals 1972-1973," by I. C. Chi, et al. INTER-
NATIONAL JOURNAL OF GYNAECOLOGY AND
OBSTETRICS 13(4):148-161, 1975.

ABORTION: UGANDA

ABORTION: UNITED KINGDOM
"Abortion: how we won the battle and nearly lost the war,"
by P. Ashdown-Sharp. NOVA 62-64, October, 1975.

"The abortion issue; England," by D. Sullivan. TABLET
230:710-711, July 24, 1976.

"The abortion law and legal paradox," by J. Crawford.
MONTH 9:97-100, March, 1976.

"Abortion law: what for?" ECONOMIST 258:34, February 14, 1976.

"Abortion: let the whole truth be heard," by R. Butt.
TIMES 16, April 24, 1975.

"Abortion needs another look," by J. White. TIMES
12, February 9, 1976.

"Abortion since 1967," by M. Simms. NEW HUMANIST
91:269-271, February, 1976.

"Abortion: stop shielding the facts with a white coat,"
by R. Butt. TIMES 14, May 8, 1975.

"Abortion: what the trends are," by P. Harrison. NEW
SOCIETY 33, 669, 242-244, July 31, 1975.

"The battle of abortion," by J. Turner. NEW SOCIETY
541-542, March 11, 1976.

"Behind the day-care abortion decision," by D. Loshak.
DAILY TELEGRAPH 13, January 30, 1976.

"The case for day care abortion," by J. Turner. NEW
HUMANIST 91:231-232, January, 1976.

"Counsel for abortion, " J. Turner. GUARDIAN 11
August 15, 1975.

"Days of hope, " by J. Turner. GUARDIAN 9 November 12, 1975.

"Illegal abortions and the Abortion Act 1967," by P.
Cavadino. BRITISH JOURNAL OF CRIMINOLOGY
16:63-67, January, 1976.

"The Irish emigrant and the abortion crisis. " WORLD
OF IRISH NURSING 4(10):1-2, October, 1975.

"James White's bid for reform," by J. White.
GUARDIAN 11, July 30, 1976.

"Moral ethics seminar; opening address of medical
ethics seminar in Dublin," by D. Ryan. L'OSSER-
VATORE ROMANO 49(401):9, December 4, 1975.

"No going back," by D. Gould. NEW STATESMAN

132, January 31, 1975.

"None but the brave?" by D. Gould. NEW STATESMAN
89:774, June 13, 1975.

"A plain woman's guide to abortion," by A. McHardy.
GUARDIAN 9, August 5, 1976.

"Politics of abortion." NEW STATESMAN 91:275,
March 5, 1976.

"Pregnancies of Irish residents terminated in England
and Wales in 1973," by D. Walsh. IRISH MEDICAL
JOURNAL 69(1):16-18, January 17, 1976.

"Putting the clock back on abortion," by P. Ferris.
OBSERVER 10, February 16, 1975.

"Putting a stop to the abortion industry," by L. Abse.
TIMES 14, July 29, 1976.

"Questions of life ... , " by P. Clarke, et al. GUARDIAN
11, February 4, 1976.

"The real issues about abortions," by A. Bowden.
DAILY TELEGRAPH 16, July 29, 1976.

"Reforms accepted." ECONOMIST 257:36, October 25,
1975.

"Running scared on abortion." NEW STATESMAN 90:
489, October 24, 1975.

"Talked out." ECONOMIST 256:18, August 9, 1975.

"Therapeutic abortion and its aftermath," by M. Stone.
MIDWIFE, HEALTH VISITOR AND COMMUNITY
NURSE 11:335-338, October, 1975.

ABORTION: UNITED KINGDOM

"Time to stop fiddling about with the Abortion Act," by D. Steel. TIMES 16, February 2, 1976.

"Unexpectedly cautious." ECONOMIST 260:29-30, July 31, 1976.

"What for?" ECONOMIST 258:34, February 14, 1976.

"Where have all the conceptions gone?" by C. J. Roberts, et al. LANCET 1(7905):498-499, 1975.

ABORTION: UNITED STATES
ARIZONA
"The use of surgery to avoid childbearing among Navajo and Hopi Indians. pp. 9-21," by S. J. Kunitz, et al. In: Kaplan BA, ed. Anthropological studies of human fertility. Detroit, Wayne State Univ Press, 1976. GN 241 S989a 1975.

ARKANSAS

CALIFORNIA

CHICAGO

CINCINNATI

COLORADO

CONNECTICUT
"Connecticut Loses Suit Over Minor's Abortions." THE NEW YORK TIMES (S) October 3, 41:1, 1976.

"Connecticut physicians' attitudes toward abortion," by G. L. Pratt, et al. AMERICAN JOURNAL OF PUBLIC HEALTH 66:288-290, March, 1976; Reply with rejoinder, K. Solomon 66:905-906, September, 1976.

ABORTION: UNITED STATES

CONNECTICUT
    "Votes in Congress." THE NEW YORK TIMES
      May 2, 58:4, 1976.

    "Votes in Congress." THE NEW YORK TIMES
      July 4, 39:7, 1976.

    "Votes in Congress." THE NEW YORK TIMES
      August 29, 47:3, 1976.

FLORIDA

GEORGIA
    "A comparison of saline and prostaglandin abortions
    at the Medical Center of Central Georgia," by
    J. R. Harrison, et al. JOURNAL OF THE
    MEDICAL ASSOCIATION OF GEORGIA 65(2):53-
    54, February, 1976.

HAWAII
    "Method of payment--relation to abortion complica-
    tions," by R. G. Smith, et al. HEALTH AND
    SOCIAL WORK 1:5-28, May, 1976.

ILLINOIS

INDIANA
    "Indiana Abortion Rule Voided." THE NEW YORK
    TIMES (S) June 17, 36:8, 1976.

IOWA

LOUISIANA

MARYLAND

MASSACHUSETTS
    "Analysis of the 1974 Massachusetts abortion statute
    and a minor's right to abortion." NEW ENGLAND

ABORTION: UNITED STATES

MASSACHUSETTS
    LAW REVIEW 10:417-454, Spring, 1975.

    "Doctor asks Court to Overturn His Conviction in
    Fetus Death." THE NEW YORK TIMES (S)
    April 6, 25:2, 1976.

    "Doe v. Doe [(Mass) 314 N E 2d 128]: the wife's
    right to an abortion over her husband's objec-
    tions." NEW ENGLAND LAW REVIEW 11:205-
    224, Fall, 1975.

    "Edelin case rekindles right-to-life hopes," by R.
    Adams. FAITH FOR THE FAMILY 9, November-
    December, 1975.

    "Massachusetts Poll Hints Deep Democrat Rifts," by
    R. Reinhold. THE NEW YORK TIMES (M) March 4,
    18:3, 1976.

    "Use of combination prostaglandin F2alpha and
    hypertonic saline for midtrimester abortion. De-
    partment of Obstetrics and Gynecology Harvard
    Medical School, Beth Israel Hospital, Boston,
    Massachusetts." PROSTAGLANDINS 12(4):625-
    630, October, 1976.

MICHIGAN

MINNESOTA

MISSISSIPPI

MISSOURI
    "Abortion Ruling is Expected to Affect Restrictive
    Laws in at Least 26 States," by S. S. King.
    THE NEW YORK TIMES (M) July 2, I, 8:3, 1976.

    "Husband's consent for abortion struck down by U.S.

ABORTION: UNITED STATES

MISSOURI
   Supreme Court: Missouri." HOSPITALS 50:22,
   August 1, 1976.

   "Restriction in Missouri abortion statute upheld."
   JOURNAL OF THE MISSISSIPPI STATE MEDICAL
   ASSOCIATION 16(12):382, December, 1975.

   "St. Louis action tops in fight against abortion," by
   R. Casey. NATIONAL CATHOLIC REPORTER
   12:1-2 passim, March 26, 1976.

MONTANA

NEBRASKA

NEW HAMPSHIRE
   "New Hampshire Held Liable On All Welfare Abortions." THE NEW YORK TIMES (S) January 20, 16:
   4, 1976.

NEW JERSEY
   "Culture Lacking Jerseyans Feel." THE NEW YORK
   TIMES (M) March 25, 76:6, 1976.

   "E.R.A. and Abortion Face Senate Test," by M.
   Waldron. THE NEW YORK TIMES (M) December 5,
   XI, 6:5, 1976.

   "Medicaid Stayed on Abortion Curb," by W. E.
   Waggoner. THE NEW YORK TIMES (M) January 17,
   56:8, 1976.

   "Main Street Now: Burgers' 'n Sex," by F. Ferretti. THE
   NEW YORK TIMES (M) February 1, XI, 1:1, 1976.

   "New Jersey Briefs: 4 hospitals Said to Violate Rights."
   THE NEW YORK TIMES (S) June 4, II, 21:1, 1976.

NEW JERSEY

"New Jersey Briefs. Medicaid Restrictions Enjoined."
THE NEW YORK TIMES (S) February 3, 67:7, 1976.

"New Jersey Court Rules for Abortion." THE NEW
YORK TIMES (S) November 21, VI, 7:4, 1976.

"New Security Measures Will Protect Assembly," by
M. Waldron. THE NEW YORK TIMES (S) April 27,
75:8, 1976.

"New York Times/New Jersey Poll," by J. F.
Sullivan. THE NEW YORK TIMES (L) March 21, XI,
17:2, 1976.

"Nonsectarian Hospitals in Jersey Are Ordered to
Permit Abortions," by A. A. Narvaez. THE NEW
YORK TIMES (M) November 18, 1:1, 1976.

"Votes in Congress." THE NEW YORK TIMES
May 2, 58:4, 1976.

"Votes in Congress." THE NEW YORK TIMES
July 4, 39:7, 1976.

"Votes in Congress." THE NEW YORK TIMES
August 29, 47:3, 1976.

NEW YORK

"Albany Changes Bill in Abortion," by R. Smothers.
THE NEW YORK TIMES (M) May 26, 34:3, 1976.

"The Antiabortion Bill Is Vetoed by Carey," by I.
Peterson. THE NEW YORK TIMES (M) June 23,
42:2, 1976.

"Assembly Revives An Abortion Bill," by L. Brown.
THE NEW YORK TIMES (M) June 3, 74:5, 1976.

NEW YORK

"Assembly's Abortion Bill Advances, Then Falters,"
by R. Smothers. THE NEW YORK TIMES (M)
May 14, II, 4:7, 1976.

"The bad old days: clandestine abortions among the
poor in New York City before liberalization of the
abortion law," by S. Polgar, et al. FAMILY
PLANNING PERSPECTIVES 8(3):125-127, May-
June, 1976.

"Court Lifts Medicaid Ban for Voluntary Abortions."
THE NEW YORK TIMES (S) March 11, 42:6, 1976.

"Death Bill." (editorial). THE NEW YORK TIMES
May 11, 32:2, 1976.

"Health Aides and Abortion Groups Assail Proposed
Medicaid Control," by J. Maynard. THE NEW
YORK TIMES (M) September 18, 9:1, 1976.

"Legal abortion: a half-decade of experience," by J.
Pakter, et al. FAMILY PLANNING PERSPEC-
TIVES 7(6):248-255, November-December, 1975.

"Long Island Poll," by F. Lynn. THE NEW YORK
TIMES (M) May 2, XXI, 31:1, 1976.

"Measure Passed by Albany Legislature," by R.
Smothers. THE NEW YORK TIMES (M) June 11, II,
4:1, 1976.

"Medicaid coverage of abortions in New York City:
costs and benefits," by M. Robinson, et al.
FAMILY PLANNING PERSPECTIVES 6, 4, 202-
208, Fall, 1974. (Socio. Abstrs. 1976, 7610425)

"Medical License Seized from an Abortion Doctor
Charged With Ineptitude." THE NEW YORK

NEW YORK
TIMES (S) October 26, 36:2, 1976.

"No Chance is Seen of Overriding Carey's Veto of
Abortion Bill," by L. Greenhouse. THE NEW
YORK TIMES (M) June 24, 66:5, 1976.

"On Long Island's Mind: Some Surprises in a Poll,"
by F. Lynn. THE NEW YORK TIMES (L) April 18,
XXI, 1:1, 1976.

"Repeat abotion [examines the repeat abortion
experience of New York city residents during
July 1, 1970 to June 30, 1972, on the basis of a
probability model that generates repeat abortion
ratios as a function of assumptions about fecundity,
contraception efficiency, and exposure lengths],"
by R. G. Potter, et al. DEMOGRAPHY 13:65-82,
February, 1976.

"Reported live births following induced abortion: two
and one-half years' experience in Upstate New
York," by G. Stroh, et al. AMERICAN JOURNAL
OF OBSTETRICS AND GYNECOLOGY 126(1):83-
90, September 1, 1976.

"Study Finds Rise in Abortion Here," by E. E.
Asbury. THE NEW YORK TIMES (M) January 25,
52:1, 1976.

"Summary of Actions Taken by U.S. Supreme Court."
THE NEW YORK TIMES (S) April 27, 15:2, 1976.

"Survey shows New York is abortion capital of nation,"
OUR SUNDAY VISITOR 64:2, February 8, 1976.

"10,000 Antiabortionists Attend a Protest Rally," by
R. Kihss. THE NEW YORK TIMES June 12, III,
21:7, 1976.

ABORTION: UNITED STATES

NEW YORK
    "Votes in Congress." THE NEW YORK TIMES
        May 2, 58:4, 1976.

    "Votes in Congress." THE NEW YORK TIMES
        July 4, 39:7, 1976.

    "Votes in Congress." THE NEW YORK TIMES
        August 29, 47:3, 1976.

NORTH CAROLINA

OKLAHOMA

OREGON

PENNSYLVANIA
    "A new look at the etiology of cervical incompetence:
    with review of seven-year experience at Pennsyl-
    vania Hospital," by U. C. Nwosu. INTERNATIONAL
    JOURNAL OF GYNAECOLOGY AND OBSTETRICS
    13(5):201-205, 1975. (Bio. Abstrs. 1976, 28723)

RHODE ISLAND

SOUTH DAKOTA

TENNESSEE

TEXAS
    "Induced abortion in Texas," by L. H. Roht, et al.
        TEXAS MEDICINE 72(4):84-91, April, 1976.

VERMONT
    "Incidence of infections associated with the intra-
    uterine contraceptive device in an isolated com-
    munity," by P. B. Mead, et al. AMERICAN
    JOUNRAL OF OBSTETRICS AND GYNECOLOGY
    125(1):79-82, 1976. (Bio. Abstrs. 1976, 34365)

ABORTION: UNITED STATES

    WISCONSIN

ABORTION: USSR
    "Social-hygienic characteristics of abortion in the
    Checheno-Ingush USSR," by M. T. Inderbiev.
    ZDRAVOOKHRANENIE ROSSIISKOI FEDERATSSI
    (5):24-26, May, 1975.

ABORTION: YUGOSLAVIA
    "Low birth weight subsequent to induced abortion: A
    historical prospective study of 948 women in Skopje,
    Yugoslavia," by C. J. Hogue. AMERICAN JOURNAL
    OF OBSTETRICS AND GYNECOLOGY 123(7):675-681,
    1975.

ADOPTION
    see: Family Planning

ALUPENT

AMERICAN COLLEGE OF OBSTETRICIANS AND GYNE-
    COLOGISTS

AMERICAN HOSPITAL ASSOCIATION

AMERICAN PUBLIC HEALTH ASSOCIATION

AMOGLANDIN

AMOXICILLIN

ANESTHESIA
    see also: Induced Abortion
             Therapeutic Abortion

    "Ambulatory anesthesia for induced abortion," by P. P.
    Olsen. UGESKRIFT FOR LAEGER 138(30):1814-
    1817, July 19, 1976.

ANESTHESIA

"Anaesthetics and abortions," (letter), by D. I. Rushton.
LANCET 2(7977):141, July 17, 1976.

"Inhalation anesthetics--more vinyl chloride?" by T. H.
Corbett. ENVIRONMENTAL RESEARCH 9:211-214,
June, 1975.

"Outpatient legal abortion. 500 operations with paracervical anesthesia," by J. Prest, et al. UGESKRIFT
FOR LAEGER 138(6):333-335, February 2, 1976.

"Outpatient legal abortion using a modified Vabra
aspirator and paracervical anesthesia," by J.
Praest, et al. UGESKRIFT FOR LARGER 138(6):
336-338, February 2, 1976.

"Women's experience of local anesthesia in early legal
abortions," by U. Idahl, et al. LAKARTIDNINGEN
73(34):2745-2746, August 18, 1976.

ANTIBODIES
"Detection of anti-HL-A serum antibodies in habitual
abortion (possibilities of the use of the leukoagglutination method). pp. 167-172, " by S. Nigro,
et al. In: Marchesi F, Cittadini E, ed. Fertilità
e sterilità. Taormina, Minerva medica, 1974.
WP 570 S679f 1973.

"Detection of anti-Toxoplasma gondii antibodies in subjects with repeated abortions, perinatal mortality
and malformed infants," by A. Castro, et al.
ANNALI SCLAVO 18(1):75-81, January-February,
1976.

ARACHIDONIC ACID

ARTIFICIAL ABORTION
see: Induced Abortion

ASPIRIN

ASPIRIN
"Effect of aspirin on bleeding time during elective abortion," by R. Waltman, et al. OBSTETRICS AND GYNECOLOGY 48(1):108-110, 1976. (Bio. Abstrs. 1976, 58163)

"The influence of aspirin on the course of induced midtrimester abortion," by J. R. Niebyl, et al. AMERICAN JOURNAL OF OBSTETRICS AND GYNECOLOGY 124(6):607-610, 1976. (Bio. Abstrs. 1976, 16218)

BEHAVIOR
see: Sociology and Behavior

BIBLIOGRAPHY

BIRTH CONTROL
see also: Family Planning.

"Abortion: the last resort," by M. C. Segers. AMERICA 133:456-458, December 27, 1975; Discussion 134: 22, January 17, 1976.

"Abortion: a lucrative business," by J. Hewitt. FAITH FOR THE FAMILY 10 , November-December, 1975.

"Abortion revisited," by H. Moody. CHRISTIANITY AND CRISIS 166, July 21, 1975.

"Abortion: weighing the decision," by M. Osterhaven. CHRISTIAN HERALD 6, May 30, 1975.

"Catholic alternatives center open to counsel on birth control," by J. Buckley. NATIONAL CATHOLIC REPORTER 13:6, November 5, 1976.

"Is abortion ever a 'last resort'." AMERICA 140, February 21, 1976.

BIRTH CONTROL

"Lament for one million fetuses," by M. Mulder.
BANNER 4, August 15, 1975.

"Legal aspects of some methods of birth-control," by
N. Endre. DEMOGRAFIA 13, 4, 355-385, 1970.

"The right to life," by F. Donaldson   CHRISTIAN
STANDARD 8, January 11, 1976.

"When is life," by N. Pyle. FAITH FOR THE FAMILY
3, November-December, 1975.

BLOOD
"Application of radioimmunologic determination of
placental lactogen hormone to the prognosis of
spontaneous threatened abortion," by R. Hechtermans,
et al. JOURNAL DE GYNECOLOGIE, OBSTETRIQUE
ET BIOLOGIE DE LA REPRODUCTION 1(5 Suppl 2):
331-334, 1972.

"Behavior of serum magnesium level during abortion,"
by M. Cilensek, et al. ZENTRALBLATT FUR
GYNAEKOLOGIE 97(19):1176-1178, 1975.

"Endocrine assessment of threatened abortion," (proceedings), by R. E. Rewell. JOURNAL OF
CLINICAL PATHOLOGY 28(9):757, September, 1975.

"Evidence of serum HPL level for prognosis of
threatening abortion," by P. Tykal, et al. ARCHIV
FUR GYNAEKOLOGIE 219(1-4):418-419, November 18, 1975

"HCG, HPL, oestradiol, progesterone and AFP in
serum in patients with threatened abortion," by J.
Kunz, et al. BRITISH JOURNAL OF OBSTETRICS
AND GYNAECOLOGY 83(8):640-644, August, 1976.

"Human placental lactogen levels in the serum during

151

early pregnancy," by R. Dudenhausen, et al.
JOURNAL OF PERINATAL MEDICINE 2(2):93-100, 1974.

"Massive invasion of fetal lymphocytes into the
mother's blood at induced abortion," by R. Zilliaus,
et al. SCANDINAVIAN JOURNAL OF IMMUNOLOGY
4(5-6):601-605, September, 1975.

"Molecular aspects of defibrination in a Reptilase-treated case of 'dead fetus syndrome'," by R.
Hafter, et al. THROMBOSIS RESEARCH 7(3):391-399, September, 1975.

"Prognostic value of the serum HCG radioimmunoassay
in threatened abortion," by E. Guerresi, et al.
RIVISTA ITALIANA DI GINECOLOGIA 56(3):201-214,
May, 1975.

"Radioimmunologic determination of placental lactogenic
hormone in threatened spontaneous abortion. Prognostic value compared with determination of chorionic
gonadotrophic hormone (HCG)," by R. Hechtermans,
et al. JOURNAL DE GYNECOLOGIE, OBSTETRIQUE
ET BIOLOGIE DE LA REPRODUCTION 2(1):53-62,
January-February, 1973.

"Role of the fibrin stablizing factor (factor XIII) in early
placental abruption," by M. Brandt, et al. ZENTRAL-BLATT FUR GYNAEKOLOGIE 97(19):1184-1186,
1975.

"Serum level of enzymes during abortion (with simultaneous administration of beta mimetics and beta
blocking agents," by E. Szabo, et al. ORVOSI
HETILAP 117(11): 652-655, March 14, 1976.

CAMPAIGN ISSUES
see: Politics

CANDIDIASIS

CANDIDIASIS
see: Complications

CARDIOVASCULAR SYSTEM
see: Complications

CEPHALOTHIN

CERVICAL INCOMPETENCE AND INSUFFICIENCY
"Diagnostic and therapeutic studies of abortion caused by
cervix insufficiency based on our case records from
1964 to the present. pp. 173-193," by S. Mangiameli.
In: Marchesi F, Cittadini E, ed. Fertilità e sterilità.
Taormina, Minerva medica, 1974. WP 570 S679f
1973.

"A new look at the etiology of cervical incompetence:
with review of seven-year experience at Pennsylvania
Hospital," by U. C. Nwosu. INTERNATIONAL
JOURNAL OF GYNAECOLOGY AND OBSTETRICS
13(5):201-205, 1975. (Bio. Abstrs. 1976, 28723)

CHLORMADINONE

CLINICAL ASPECTS
"Abortion Abuses." THE NEW YORK TIMES May 2,
57:1, 1976.

"Biological and clinical aspects of legal abortion," by
G. Pescetto. ANNALI DI OSTETRICIA, GINECOL-
OGIA MEDICINA PERINATALE 96(4):215-227,
July-August, 1975.

"Clinical aspects and treatment of puerperal and post-
abortion staphylococcal sepsis," by V. I. Kuznetsova,
et al. PEDIATRIIA AKUSHERSTVO I GINDKOLOGIIA
:55-58, May-June, 1976.

"Clinical experience using intraamniotic prostaglandin

F2alpha for midtrimester abortion in 600 patients," by
G. G. Anderson, et al. OBSTETRICS AND GYNE-
COLOGY 46(5):591-595, November, 1975.

"Clinical observation of the prevention of RH isoim-
munization with immunoglobulin anti-D. ," by S.
Hisanaga, et al. ACTA OBSTETRICA ET GYNAE-
COLOGICA JAPONICA 21(2):97-102, 1974.

"Clinical observations with a prostaglandin-containing
silastic vaginal device for pregnancy termination,"
by C. H. Hendricks, et al. PROSTAGLANDINS 12
Suppl:99-122, 1976.

"I'm here to scrub your tummy; abortion clinic," by M.
Amundson. MS MAGAZINE 4:20, June, 1976.

"Menstrual induction: its place in clinical practice,"
by K. R. Irani, et al. OBSTETRICS AND GYNE-
COLOGY 46(5):596-598, November, 1975.

"Methodology for determining the optimal design of a
free standing abortion clinic," by H. S. Gitlow.
MANAGEMENT SCIENCE: JOURNAL OF THE
INSTITUTE OF MANAGEMENT SCIENCE 22:1289-
1298, August, 1976.

"Prostaglandins: basic reproductive consideration and
new clinical applications. pp. 157-182," by F.
Naftolin. In: Kahn Rh, Lands WE, ed. Prostaglandins
and cyclic AMP. New York, Academic Press, 1973.
QU 90 S991p 1972.

"A question of clinical freedom," by B. Watkin.
NURSING MIRROR AND MIDWIVES JOURNAL 142
(18):42, April 29, 1976.

CLOMIPHENE

COLLEGE WOMEN

COLLEGE WOMEN
  see: Youth

COMPLICATIONS
  see also: Hemorrhage

"Abortions in 1973 in Linköping--contraceptive technics
  postoperative complications," by U. Larsson-Cohn.
  LAKARTIDNINGEN 72(44):4282-4284, October 29,
  1975.

"Abruptio placentae complicated by retinal artery
  thrombosis," by A. T. Coopland. AMERICAN
  JOURNAL OF OBSTETRICS AND GYNECOLOGY
  123(8):917-918, December 15, 1975.

"Abruptio placentae following a negative oxytocin
  challenge test," by J. C. Seski, et al. AMERICAN
  JOURNAL OF OBSTETRICS AND GYNECOLOGY
  125(2):276, May 15, 1976.

"Acute coagulation disorders in missed abortion," by
  R. Almuna. REVISTA CHILENA DE OBSTETRICIA
  Y GINECOLOGIA 38(6):272-285, 1973.

"Acute complications of abortion," by E. Obel. UGE-
  SKRIFT FOR LAEGER 138(6):319-323, February 2,
  1976.

"Acute renal failure in the postpartum and post-abortion
  periods observed in the maternity department of the
  Hôpital Charles Nicolle," by B. Farza, et al.
  JOURNAL DE GYNECOLOGIE, OBSTETRIQUE ET
  BIOLOGIE DE LA REPRODUCTION 1(5 Suppl 2):
  443-447, 1972.

"Aetiology of anencephaly and spina bifida." (letter).
  BRITISH MEDICAL JOURNAL 1(6007):455-456,
  February 21, 1976.

"Artificial interruption and female morbidity," by A.
Kotásek, et al. CESKOSLOVENSKA GYNEKOLOGIE
41(1):31-33, March, 1976.

"Association between maternal bleeding during gestation
and congenital anomalies in the offspring," by A.
Ornoy, et al. AMERICAN JOURNAL OF OBSTE-
TRICS AND GYNECOLOGY 124(5):474-478, 1976.

"Attempt to elucidate the causes of certain complications following artificial abortion using radioisotopes,"
by A. Atanasov, et al. AKUSHERSTVO I GINEKOL-
OGIIA (Sofia) 14(5):372-375, 1975.

"Bronchoconstriction and pulmonary hypertension during
abortion induced by 15-ethyl-prostaglandin F2a," by
E. K. Weir, et al. AMERICAN JOURNAL OF MEDI-
CINE 60(4):556-562, 1976.

"Chorionic haemangiomata and abruptio placentae. Case
report and review," by H. G. Kohler, et al. BRITISH
JOURNAL OF OBSTETRICS AND GYNAECOLOGY
83(8):667-670, August, 1976.

"Clinical aspects and treatment of puerperal and post-
abortion staphylococcal sepsis," by V. I. Kuznetsova,
et al. PEDIATRIIA AKUSHERSTVO I GINEKOLOGIIA
:55-58, May-June, 1976.

"A clotting defect following pregnancy termination by
dilatation and curettage," by R. J. Solyn. INTER-
NATIONAL SURGERY 61(2):86-87, February, 1976.

"Coagulation disorders after hypertonic-saline abortion," (letter), by J. W. Ten Cate, et al. LANCET
1(7952):205, January 24, 1976.

"Coagulation disorders after hypertonic-saline abortion," by J. R. O'Brien. LANCET 1(7955):367,
February 14, 1976.

COMPLICATIONS

"Coagulation disorders and abortion using hypertonic
solutions," (letter), by I. Craft, et al. LANCET
1(7956):428, February 21, 1976.

"Comparative studies on the cytohormonal and cytochemical
exponents of estrogens-progesterone activity in the
vaginal lining epithelium in women with pregnancy complications. I. Threatened abortion," by J. Dudkiewicz.
GINEKOLOGIA POLASKA 46(11):1133-1146, November,
1975.

"A comparative study of intra-amniotic saline and two prostaglandin F2a dose schedules for midtrimester abortion,"
by D. A. Edlrman et al. AMERICAN JOURNAL OF
OBSTETRICS AND GYNECOLOGY 125(2):188-195, 1976.

"Complications after abortion. Hospitalization for early
post-abortion morbidity after voluntary abortion," by
G. E. Feichter. FORTSCHRITTE DU MEDIZIN 94(16):
965-967, June 3, 1976.

"Complications following ambulatory abortion," by G.
Wolters. FORTSCHRITTE DU MEDIZIN 94(27):1473-
1475, September 23, 1976.

"Concurrent use of prostaglandin F2a and laminaria tents
for induction of midtrimester abortion," by J. H.
Duenhoelter, et al. OBSTETRICS AND GYNECOLOGY
47(4):469-472, 1976. (Bio. Abstrs. 1976, 33635)

"Congenital abnormalities and selective abortion," by M. J.
Seller. JOURNAL OF MEDICAL ETHICS 2(3):138-141,
September, 1976.

"Delayed morbidity following prostaglandin-induced abortion," by I. Z. Mackenzie, et al. INTERNATIONAL
JOURNAL OF GYNAECOLOGY AND OBSTETRICS
13(5):209-214, 1975. (Bio. Abstrs. 1976, 23175)

COMPLICATIONS

"Disseminated intravascular coagulation in abruptio
placentae--report of a case," by N. Saito, et al.
ACTA OBSTETRICA ET GYNAECOLOGICA
JAPONICA 22(2):113-118, April, 1975.

"Early complications and late sequelae of induced abortion: A review of the literature," by K. G. B. Edström.
BULLETIN OF THE WORLD HEALTH ORGANIZATION
52(2):123-139, 1975. (Bio. Abstrs. 1976, 16899)

"Ectopic pregnancy after postcoital diethylstillestrol," by
A. R. Smythe, et al. AMERICAN JOURNAL OF
OBSTETRICS AND GYNECOLOGY 121(2):284-285, 1975.
(Bio. Abstrs. 1976, 11530)

"Endometrial ossification," by C. Hus. BRITISH JOURNAL
OF OBSTETRICS AND GYNAECOLOGY 82(10):836-839,
October, 1975.

"Evaluation of a preevacuated endometrial suction apparatus
in general obstetric-gynecologic practice," by M. J.
Padawer, et al. NEW YORK STATE JOURNAL OF
MEDICINE 76(6):885-888, June, 1976.

"Fatal complication of pregnancy interruption (Karman
method)," (letter), by H. Larrieu, et al. NOUVELLE
PRESSE MEDICALE 4(38):2733, November 8, 1975.

"The fate of the child after threatened abortion," by H. J.
Wallner. JOURNAL OF PERINATAL MEDICINE
2(1):54-60, 1974.

"Focal glomerulonephritis, pregnancy and miscarriage,"
(letter), by E. Lusvarghi. NEPHRON 16(4):322-323,
1976.

"Genital cytologic abnormalities in patients having
therapeutic abortion," by C. T. Creasman, et al.
SOUTHERN MEDICAL JOURNAL 69(2):199-200, February, 1976.

COMPLICATIONS

"Gonorrhea in obstetric patients," by D. E. Jones, et al.
JOURNAL OF THE AMERICAN VENERAL DISEASE
ASSOCIATION 2(3):30-32, 1976. (Bio. Abstrs. 1976,
28653)

"Incidence of infections associated with the intrauterine
contraceptive device in an isolated community," by
P. B. Mead, et al. AMERICAN JOURNAL OF
OBSTETRICS AND GYNECOLOGY 125(1):79-82,
1976. (Bio. Abstrs. 1976, 34365)

"Induced abortion and secondary infertility," by D.
Trichopoulos, et al. BRITISH JOURNAL OF OBSTE-
TRICS AND GYNAECOLOGY 83(8):645-650, August,
1976.

"Influence of abortions and interruptions of pregnancies on
subsequent deliveries. I. Course of pregnancy," by
P. Knorre. ZENTRALBLATT FUR GYNAEKOLOGIE
98(10):587-590, 1976.

--II. Course of labor," by P. Knorre. ZENTRALBLATT
FUR GYNAEKOLOGIE 98(10):591-594, 1976.

--III. After-labor-period and puerperium," by P. Knorre.
ZENTRALBLATT FUR GYNAEKOLOGIE 98(10):595-599,
1976.

"Intrauterine adhesions secondary to elective abortion.
Hysteroscopic diagnosis and management," by C. M.
March, et al. OBSTETRICS AND GYNECOLOGY 48
(4):422-444, October, 1976.

"Late complications following abortus provocatus," by E.
Obel. UGESKRIFT FOR LAEGER 138(6):323-328,
February 2, 1976.

"Legal abortion: An appraisal of its health impact," by G.
S. Berger. INTERNATIONAL JOURNAL OF GYNAE-

COLOGY AND OBSTETRICS 13(4):165-170, 1975. (Bio. Abstrs. 1976, 22866)

"Legal aspects of menstrual regulation: some preliminary observations," by L. T. Lee, et al. JOURNAL OF FAMILY LAW 14:181-221, 1975.

"Low birth weight subsequent to induced abortion: A historical prospective study of 948 women in Skopje, Yugoslavia," by C. J. Hogue. AMERICAN JOURNAL OF OBSTETRICS AND GYNECOLOGY 123(7):675-681, 1975. (Bio Abstrs. 1976, 5154)

"Massive form of Couvelaire's syndrome with preservation of the uterus," by T. Pasanku. MEDICINSKI PREGLED 28(3-4):145-147, 1975.

"Maternal mortality from septic abortions in University Hospital, Kuala Lumpur from March 1968 to February 1974," by K. H. Ng, et al. MEDICAL JOURNAL OF MALAYSIA 30(1):52-54, September, 1975.

"Morbidity of therapeutic abortion in Auckland," by M. A. Baird. NEW ZEALAND MEDICAL JOURNAL 83(565): 395-399, June, 1976.

"Mortality and morbidity associated with legal abortions in Hungary, 1960-1973," by Z. Bognar, et al. AMER-ICAN JOURNAL OF PUBLIC HEALTH 66:568-575, June, 1976.

"Neonatal death after induced abortion," by R. Prywes, et al. HAREFUAH 90(10):453-456, May 16, 1976.

"Obstetric complications after treatment of intrauterine synechiae (Asherman's syndrome)," by R. Jewelewicz, et al. OBSTETRICS AND GYNECOLOGY 47(6):701-705, 1976. (Bio. Abstrs. 1976, 46115)

COMPLICATIONS

"Occult manifestations of septic abortion," by J. E.
Dewhurst, et al. NURSING MIRROR AND MIDWIVES'
JOURNAL 142:62-63, April 29, 1976.

"Pathological features of the placenta in fetal death," by
A. Ornoy, et al. ARCHIVES OF PATHOLOGY AND
LABORATORY MEDICINE 100(7):367-371, 1976.
(Bio. Abstrs. 1976, 59485)

"The possible deleterious effects of the intramyometrial
injection of hypertonic urea," by T. H. Parmley, et
al. OBSTETRICS AND GYNECOLOGY 47(2):210-212,
February, 1976.

"Postabortal and postpartum tetanus. A review of 19
cases," by M. J. Bennett. SOUTH AFRICAN MED-
ICAL JOURNAL 50(13):513-516, March 24, 1976.

"Post-abortal tetanus," by C. Newman, et al. CON-
NECTICUT MEDICINE 39(12):773-774, December, 1975.

"Problem of causative relation between pregnancy interruption and following premature termination of pregnancy," by R Voigt, et al. ZENTRALBLATT FUR
GYNAEKOLOGIE 97(22):1375-1377, 1975.

"Recovery after prolonged anuria following septic abortion," by D. S. Emmanouelel, et al. OBSTETRICS AND
GYNECOLOGY 47(1):36S-39S, January, 1976.

"The relative risks of sterilization alone and in combination with abortion," by K. G. B. Edström. BULLETIN
OF THE WORLD HEALTH ORGANIZATION 52(2):141-
148, 1975. (Bio. Abstrs. 1976, 16962)

"Requests for termination of pregnancy: psychogenesis
and assistance," by G. Resta. MINERVA GINECOL-
OGIA 27(8):600-606, August, 1975.

"Reversible hypernatremic coma following therapeutic abortion with hypertonic saline," by A. Reches, et al. HAREFUAH 89(5):209-211, September 1, 1975.

"Role of the fibrin stabilizing factor (factor XIII) in early placental abruption," by M. Brandt, et al. ZENTRAL-BLATT FUR GYNAEKOLOGIE 97(19):1184-1186, 1975.

"Saline abortion and lupus erythematosus," by J. F. Jewett. NEW ENGLAND JOURNAL OF MEDICINE 294(14):782-783, April 1, 1976.

"Second-trimester spontaneous abortion, the IUD, and infection," by S. H. Eisinger. AMERICAN JOURNAL OF OBSTETRICS AND GYNECOLOGY 124(4):393-397, 1976. (Bio. Abstrs. 1976, 5211)

"Septic shock in obstetrical clinic," by B. L. Gurtovoi, et al. AKUSHERSTVO I GINEKOLOGIIA (Moscow) (3):68-72, March, 1976.

"Serious complications of septic abortions. Pelviperi-toneal complications (II)," by S. Musso, et al. MINERVA GINECOLOGIA 27(12):1054-1059, December, 1975.

"Serum fibrinogen-fibrin related antigen and protamine sulfate test in patients with septic abortion and acute renal failure," by I. Crisnic, et al. REVUE ROUMAINE DE MEDECINE [now: MEDECINE INTERNE] 14(1):47-51, 1976. (Bio. Abstrs. 1976, 41222)

"Severe complications of septic abortion. I. Nephro-vascular complications," by G. Musso, et al. MINERVA GINECOLOGICA 27(9):690-697, September, 1975.

"Smoking during pregnancy, stillbirth and abruptio placentae," by J. Goujard, et al. BIOMEDICINE

COMPLICATIONS

EXPRESS (Paris) 23(1):20-22, February 10, 1975.

"Somatic complications after induced abortion," (letter),
by E. Arnesen, et al. TIDSSKRIFT FOR DEN
NORSKE LAEGEFORENING 96(15):899-900, May 30,
1976.

"Somatic complications following induced abortions," by
K. Molne, et al. TIDSSKRIFT FOR DEN NORSKE
LAEGEFORENING 96(8):483-488, March 20, 1976.

"Somatic complications of induced abortion," (editorial),
by P. Bergsjö. TIDSSKRIFT FOR DEN NORSKE
LAEGEFORENING 96(8):524-525, March 20, 1976.

"Spina bifida and anencephaly: miscarriage as possible
cause," by C. Clarke, et al. BRITISH MEDICAL
JOURNAL 4(5999):743-746, December 27, 1975.

"Study of the complications occurring in the interruption
of pregnancy on demand based on data from the
obstetrical and gynecological ward in Ruse over a
10-year period," by Kh. Durveniashki. AKUSHERSTVO
I GINEKOLOGIIA (Sofia) 15(2):126-130, 1976.

"Study of the transplacental passage of fetal erythrocytes
in 100 abortions," by C. Quereux, et al. JOURNAL
DE GYNECOLOGIE, OBSTETRIQUE ET BIOLOGIE DE
LA REPRODUCTION 1(5 Suppl 2):215-218, 1972.

"Term delivery through a cervicovaginal fistula," by
M. A. Pelosi, et al. AMERICAN JOURNAL OF
OBSTETRICS AND GYNECOLOGY 122(6):789-790,
1975. (Bio. Abstrs. 1976, 53718)

"Therapeutic abortion and its aftermath," by M. Stone.
MIDWIFE, HEALTH VISITOR AND COMMUNITY
NURSE 11:335-338, October, 1975.

COMPLICATIONS

"3Beta-hydroxy-20-oxo-pregn-5-ene-16 alpha-carbonitrile, a potent catatoxic steroid devoid of an abortifacient effect," by Y. Taché, et al. ENDOCRINOLOGY 97(3): 731-734, September, 1975.

"Ureter-uterus fistula after abortion," by W. Hardt, et al. ZEITSCHRIFT FUR UROLOGIE UND NEPHROL-OGIE 68(10):761-764, October, 1975.

"Uterine rupture complicating mid-trimester abortion in a young woman of low parity," by R. H. Hayashi, et al. INTERNATIONAL JOURNAL OF GYNAECOLOGY AND OBSTETRICS 13(5):229-232, 1975. (Bio. Abstrs. 1976, 22789)

"Zinc and copper in pregnancy, correlations to fetal and maternal complications," by S. Jameson. ACTA MEDICA SCANDINAVICA SUPPLEMENT (593):5-20, 1976.

CONTRACEPTION

"Abortion and contraception information during first period under new legislation," by K. Sundström. LAKARTIDNINGEN 72(38):3531-3533, September 17, 1975.

"Abortion in 1975: the psychiatric perspective and contra-ception in adolescence," by P. D. Barglow. JOGN; JOURNAL OF OBSTETRIC, GYNECOLOGIC AND NEONATAL NURSING 5:41-47, January/February, 1976.

"Abortion in 1975: The psychiatric perspective, with a discussion of abortion and contraception in adoles-cence," by P. D. Barglow. JOGN; JOURNAL OF OBSTETRIC, GYNECOLOGIE AND NEONATAL NURSING 5(1):41-48, January-February, 1976.

"Contraception alone will not allow us to control population," by T. Smith. TIMES 12, July 7, 1975.

"Contraception, sterilisation & abortion in NZ." NURS-
ING FORUM (Auckl) 4:6-9, June/July, 1976.

"Contraceptive practice and prevention as alternative to
legitimization of indiscriminate abortion," by I.
Vandelli, et al. ANNALI DI OSTETRICIA, GINECOL-
OGIA, MEDICINA PERINATALE 96(4):254-273, July-
August, 1975.

"Fertility control transition from abortion to contraception
in Japan since 1948," by T. Aso. INTERNATIONAL
REVIEW OF MODERN SOCIOLOGY 4,1:43-53, Spring,
1974.

"Incidence of abortion and contraception patterns during
1968-1974," by R. L. Somers, et al. UGESKRIFT
FOR LAEGER 138(6):353-355, February 2, 1976.

"Induced abortion and contraceptive practice: an experience in Taiwan," by I. H. Su, et al. STUDIES IN
FAMILY PLANNING 7:224-230, August, 1976.

"IUD and induced abortion," by S. O. Skouby. UGESKRIFT
FOR LAEGER 138(6):339-341, February 2, 1976.

"Legal abortion. Abortion as a form of contraception? A
prospective study of 608 women applying for abortion,"
by P. Diederich, et al. UGESKRIFT FOR LAEGER
138(6):355-359, February 2, 1976.

"The outcome of pregnancy in former oral contraceptive
users." BRITISH JOURNAL OF OBSTETRICS AND
GYNAECOLOGY 83(8):608-616, August, 1976.

"Patterns of contraceptive failures: the role of motivation
re-examined," by W. G. Cobliner, et al. JOURNAL
OF BIOSOCIAL SCIENCE, 7, 3:307-318, July, 1975.

CONTRACEPTION

(Socio. Abstrs. 1976, 76H9180)

"Population control in Australia today: contraception, sterilization and abortion," by J. Leeton. MEDICAL JOURNAL OF AUSTRALIA 2(17):682-685, October 25, 1975.

"Post-partum and post-abortum contraception," by B. Fonty, et al. JOURNAL DE GYNECOLOGIE, OBSTE-TRIQUE ET BIOLOGIE DE LA REPRODUCTION 4(3): 395-404, 1975. (Bio. Abstrs. 1976, 22786)

"Postpartum contraception: subsequent pregnancy, delivery and abortion rates," J. J. Shulman, et al. FERTILITY AND STERILITY 27(1):97-103, January, 1976.

"Psychological factors in contraceptive failure and abortion request," (letter), by D. Everingham. MEDICAL JOURNAL OF AUSTRALIA 2(15):617-618, October 11, 1975.

"The significance of oral contraceptives in causing chromosome anomalies in spontaneous abortions," by J. G. Lauritsen. ACTA OBSTETRICIA ET GYNECOLOGICA SCANDINAVICA 54(3):261-264, 1975. (Bio. Abstrs. 1976, 54717)

"Voluntary abortion and resistance to contraception," by M. Bourgeois, et al. ANNALES MEDICO-PSYCHOLOGI-QUES 2(2):366-377, July, 1975.

CRIMINAL ABORTION
see: Laws and Legislation

DEMOGRAPHY
see also: Population

"The American birth rate: evidences of a coming rise," by J. Sklar, et al. SCIENCE 189(4204):693-700, 1975.

DEMOGRAPHY

(Bio. Abstrs. 1976, 51944)

"Characteristics of pregnant women who report previous abortions," by S. Harlap, et al. BULLETIN OF THE WORLD HEALTH ORGANIZATION 52(2):149-154, 1975. (Bio. Abstrs. 1976, 16900)

"Conceptual problems in our public health demograpy," by A. A. Curbelo. REVISTA DE SANIDAD E HIGIENE PUBLICA 48(11):1015-1019, November, 1974.

"The demographic effect of induced abortion," by C. Tietze, et al. OBSTETRICAL AND GYNECOLOGICAL SURVEY 31(10):699-709, October, 1976.

"Incomplete abortions in Accra and Bangkok University Hospitals 1972-1973," by I. C. Chi, et al. INTER-NATIONAL JOURNAL OF GYNAECOLOGY AND OBSTETRICS 13(4):148-161, 1975. (Bio. Abstrs. 1976, 22865)

"A pilot study of demographic and psychosocial factors in medical termination of pregnancy," by R. Goraya, et al. JOURNAL OF THE INDIAN MEDICAL ASSO-CIATION 64(11):309-315, June 1, 1975.

"Territorial differences in abortion rate in Czechoslovakia in 1969 and 1970," by H. Wynncyczuková. DEMO-GRAFIE 15, 2:110-120, 1973. (Socio. Abstrs. 1976, 76I0154)

DIAGNOSIS
"Anencephaly: early ultrasonic diagnosis and interruption of pregnancy. Apropos of a case," by R. Chef, et al. JOURNAL DE GYNECOLOGIE, OBSTETRIQUE ET BIOLOGIE DE LA REPRODUCTION 3(1):93-104, January-February, 1974.

"Application of a radioeceptorassay of human chorionic

gonadotropin in the diagnosis of early abortion," by
T. P. Rosal, et al. FERTILITY AND STERILITY
26(11):1105-1113, November, 1975.

"Asherman's syndrome (Fritsch-Asherman)," by E. G.
Waters. JOURNAL OF THE MEDICAL SOCIETY OF
NEW JERSEY 73(9):745-747, September, 1976.

"Comparison of the MMPI and Mini-Mult with women who
request abortion," by W. F. Gayton, et al. JOURNAL
OF CLINICAL PSYCHOLOGY 32(3):648-650, July,
1976.

"Correlation of the diagnostic value of vaginal cytology
and estimation of total urinary oestrogens in threatened
pregnancies," by I. Misinger, et al. CESKOSLOVENSKA
GYNEKOLOGIE 40(7):512-514, August, 1975.

"The diagnosis and treatment of threatened miscarriage,"
by B. Faris. AUSTRALASIAN NURSES JOURNAL
4:7, October, 1975.

"Diagnosis of Asherman's syndrome (intrauterine
synechiae)," by I. Berta, et al. ZENTRALBLATT
FUR GYNAEKOLOGIE 98(8):495-503, 1976.

"The diagnosis of early pregnancy failure by sonar," by
H. P. Robinson. BRITISH JOURNAL OF OBSTE-
TRICS AND GYNAECOLOGY 82(11):849-857,
November, 1975.

"Diagnosis, treatment and prognosis of threatened abortion," by H. Wilken, et al. ZENTRALBLATT FUR
GYNAEKOLOGIE 98(10):577-586, 1976.

"Diagnosis and therapy of the asherman's syndrome," by
K. Poradovský, et al. CESKOSLOVENSKA GYNE-
KOLOGIE 40(7):502-503, August, 1975.

"Diagnostic examination methods in threatened pregnancy. Panel discussion." ARCHIV FUR GYNAEKOLOGIE 219(1-4):399 passim, November 18, 1975.

"Effectiveness of ultrasonic diagnosis in abortion," by W. W. Stein, et al. ARCHIV FUR GYNAEKOLOGIE 219(1-4):549-550, November 18, 1975.

"Establishment of prognosis in threatened abortion. Value of the combined use of diagnostic ultrasound and quantitative determination of chorionic gonadotropin hormone," by S. Levi, et al. JOURNAL DE GYNECOLOGIE, OBSTETRIQUE ET BIOLOGIE DE LA REPRODUCTION 2(2):155-160, March, 1973.

"Evaluation of the chorionic gonadotropin level, determined by the immunological method, in the prognosis of threatened abortion," by C. Croce, et al. MINERVA GINECOLOGIA 28(2):112-117, February, 1976.

"Functional colpocytology in threatened abortion and internal abortion. pp. 153-155," by N. Marotta, et al. In: Marchesi F, Cittadini E, ed. Fertilità e sterilità Taormina, Minerva medica, 1974. WP 570 S679f 1973.

"Measurements by ultrasonics of the gestation sac in threatened abortion," by S. Levi. JOURNAL DE GYNECOLOGIE, OBSTETRIQUE ET BIOLOGIE DE LA REPRODUCTION 5(3):359-365, April-May, 1976.

"The predictive value of thyroid 'test profile' in habitual abortion," by D. Winikoff, et al. BRITISH JOURNAL OF OBSTETRICS AND GYNAECOLOGY 82(9):760-766, September, 1975.

"Prenatal diagnosis of trisomy 9," by U. Francke, et al. HUMANGENETIK 29(3):243-250, 1975.

"The problem of prognostication in disturbed pregnancies," by E. Picha. WIEN KLIN WOCHENSCHRIFT
87(20):702-704, October 31, 1975.

"Prognosis in threatened abortion: a comparison between
predictions made by sonar urinary hormone assays
and clinical judgement," by G. B. Duff. BRITISH
JOURNAL OF OBSTETRICS AND GYNAECOLOGY
82(11):858-862, November, 1975.

"Prognostic and diagnostic value of bidimensional
ecthography in threatened abortion," by N. Rodriguez.
REVISTA CHILENA DE OBSTETRICIA Y GINECOLOGIA
38(5):228-239, 1973.

"Prognostic value of the serum HCG radioimmunoassay
in threatened abortion," by E. Guerresi, et al.
RIVISTA ITALIANA DI GINECOLOGIA 56(3):201-214,
May, 1975.

"Radioimmunologic determination of placental lactogenic
hormone in threatened spontaneous abortion. Prognostic value compared with determination of chorionic
gonadotrophic hormone (HCG)," by R. Hechtermans,
et al. JOURNAL DE GYNECOLOGIE, OBSTETRIQUE
ET BIOLOGIE DE LA REPRODUCTION 2(1):53-62,
January-February, 1973.

"Significance of placenta lactogen and placenta isoenzyme
of alkaline phosphatase in the diagnosis of threatened
gravidity," by J. Sedlák, et al. CASOPIS LEKARU
CESKYCH 115(2-3):79-81, January 23, 1976.

"Sonar in the diagnosis of threatened abortion," by P. L.
Ceccarello, et al. MINERVA GINECOLOGIA 27(12):
983-987, December, 1975.

"Sonar in early abnormal pregnancy. pp. 273-279," by
P. L. Ceccarello, et al. In: Kazner E, et al., ed.

DIAGNOSIS

Ultrasonics in medicine. Amsterdam, Excerpta
Medica, 1975. W3 EX89 no. 363 1975.

"Value of intradermal hormone tests in the diagnosis
of causes of threatened abortion," by L. P. Peshev.
VOPROSY OKHRANY MATERINSTVA I DETSTVA
2C(9):67-70, September, 1975.

DIAZEPAM

DIETHYLSTILBESTROL
"Ectopic pregnancy after postcoital diethylstilbestrol," by
A. R. Smythe, et al. AMERICAN JOURNAL OF OB-
STETRICS AND GYNECOLOGY 121(2):284-285, 1975.
(Bio. Abstrs. 1976, 11530)

DINOPROST THOMETHAMINE

DOXICILLIN

DRUG THERAPY
see: Induced Abortion
Surgical Treatment and Management
Techniques of Abortion
Under Specific Drugs

E-AMINOCAPROIC ACID
"Use of E-aminocaproic acid for blocking uterine contractions in threatened, premature labor and late
abortion," by A. Donchev. AKUSHERSTVO I
GINEKOLOGIIA (Sofia) 14(5):368-371, 1975.

EDUCATION
"Abortion as a problem of medical education," by J.
Jiménez-Vargas, et al. REVISTA DE MEDICINA DE
LA UNIVERSIDAD DE NAVARRA 17(3):273-279,
September, 1973.

ENDOTOXIN

ESTRADIOL

ESTRADIOL
"Serum levels of estradiol and progesterone during
administration of PGF2 alpha for induction of abor-
ion and labour," by A. Kivikoski, et al. ACTA
OBSTETRICIA ET GYNECOLOGICA SCANDINAVICA
55(2):188-190, 1976.

ETHYL ALCOHOL

ETIDOCAINE
"Paracervical block with etidocaine for out-patient
abortion," by G. Willdeck-Lund, et al. ACTA
ANAESTHESIOLOGICA SCANDINAVICA. SUPPLE-
MENT (60):106-109, 1975.

EUTHANASIA
"A new ethical approach to abortion and its implications
for the euthanasia dispute," by R. F. Gardner.
JOURNAL OF MEDICAL ETHICS 1(3):127-131,
September, 1975.

"On the bounds of freedom: from the treatment of fetuses
to euthanasia," by H. T. Englehardt, Jr. CONNETI-
CUT MEDICINE 40(1):51-54, January, 1976.

"Orthodox Church condemns abortion and euthanasia."
OUR SUNDAY VISITOR 64:3, December 7, 1975.

FAMILY PLANNING
see also: Sociology and Behavior

"Advances in Planned Parenthood," by R. M. Wynn.
EXCERPTA MEDICA 10, 4:52, 1975.

"Advances in Planned Parenthood," by R. M. Wynn.
EXCERPTA MEDICA 11, 1:51, 1976.

"Attitude of some elites towards introduction of abortion
as a method of family planning in Bangladesh," by

FAMILY PLANNING

R. H. Chaudhury. BANGLADESH DEVELOPMENT
STUDIES 3:479-494, October, 1975.

"Comparative study of the causes of induced abortion
and the knowledge of family planning," by M. D.
Ramos Netto. REVISTA ENFERMAGEM EM NOVAS
DIMENSOES 1(4):172, September-October, 1975.

"Pregnancy counseling and abortion referral for patients
in Federally funded family planning programs," by
J. I. Rosoff. FAMILY PLANNING PERSPECTIVES
8(1):43-46, January-February, 1976.

"Pregnancy planning/abortion," by C. Tietze. FAMILY
PLANNING PERSPECTIVES 7(6):247, November-
December, 1975.

"Trends in attitudes toward abortion, 1972-1975," by
W. R. Arney, et al. FAMILY PLANNING PER-
SPECTIVES 8:117-124, May/June, 1976.

FAUSTAN

FEES AND PUBLIC ASSISTANCE
see also: Laws and Legislation
Sociology and Behavior

"Abortion." THE NEW YORK TIMES (S) January 27, 12:3,
1976.

"Abortion Curb Defeated." THE NEW YORK TIMES (S)
June 29, 14:3, 1976.

"Abortion Ruling." THE NEW YORK TIMES (S) October 24, IV, 6:6, 1976.

"Battle underway on funding of abortions by government."
OUR SUNDAY VISITOR 65:2, August 8, 1976.

"Compromise reached on use of federal funds for abortions," by T. P. Southwick. CONGRESSIONAL QUARTERLY WEEKLY REPORT 34:2541, September 18, 1976.

"Conference Vote Ban on Medical Funds for Most Abortions," by D. E. Rosenbaum. THE NEW YORK TIMES (M) September 16, 1:3, 1976.

"Congress Acts on Abortions." (editorial). THE NEW YORK TIMES (S) September 19, IV, 2:2, 1976.

"Congress Approves Curb on Abortions, But Veto is Likely," by D. E. Rosenbaum. THE NEW YORK TIMES (M) September 18, 1:6, 1976.

"Congress Overrides Ford's Veto of Bill of Social Services," by R. D. Lyons. THE NEW YORK TIMES (M) October 1, I, 1:1, 1976.

"Court Lifts Medicaid Ban for Voluntary Abortions." THE NEW YORK TIMES (S) March 11, 42:6, 1976.

"End of Medicaid for Abortions Feared," by G. Goodman, Jr. THE NEW YORK TIMES (M) February 14, 12:4, 1976.

"Group Plans to Sue to Bar Any Change in Rules on Abortion," by J. Cummings. THE NEW YORK TIMES (S) September 29, 19:5, 1976.

"H.E.W. Funds Bill Stalled in House by Abortion Issue." THE NEW YORK TIMES (S) August 11, 71:4, 1976.

"Legal abortion in gynecological departments following free access to abortion," by F. Lundvall. UGESKRIFT FOR LAEGER 138(6):360-363, February 2, 1976.

"Medicaid Stayed on Abortion Curb," by W. E. Waggoner.

FEES AND PUBLIC ASSISTANCE

THE NEW YORK TIMES (M) January 17, 56:8, 1976.

"New Hampshire Held Liable on All Welfare Abortions."
THE NEW YORK TIMES (S) January 20, 16:4, 1976.

"Summary of Actions Taken by U.S. Supreme Court."
THE NEW YORK TIMES April 27, 15:2, 1976.

"U.S. Court Overturns Curb on Medicad Abortions," by
M. H. Siegel. THE NEW YORK TIMES (M) October 23,
1:3, 1976.

"U.S. Courts Bar Curb on Funding Some Abortions," by
M. H. Siegel. THE NEW YORK TIMES (M) October 2,
1:2, 1976.

FERTILITY
see: Sterility

FETUS
"Abortion for the fetus's own sake?" by P. F. Camenisch.
HASTINGS CENTER REPORT 6(2):38-41, April,
1976.

"The action of the vaccinia virus upon placenta and fetus
in revaccinated pregnants," by V. Topciu, et al.
ZENTRABLATT FUR BAKTERIOLOGIE [Originale,
Reihe B] 161(5-6):551-556, March, 1976.

"Alpha-fetoprotein levles in maternal plasma and amniotic
fluid during prostaglandin-induced mid-trimester abortions: the relation to fetal distress and death," by
R. H. Ward, et al. BRITISH JOURNAL OF OBSTE-
TRICS AND GYNAECOLOGY 83(4):299-302, April, 1976.

"Determination of Rh blood group of fetuses in abortions
by suction curettage," by R. M. Greendyke, et al.
TRANSFUSION 16(3):267-269, May-June, 1976.

175

"Fetal membranes. Microscopic aspects in abortions and intrauterine deaths with retention," by A. Turcas, et al. JOURNAL DE GYNECOLOGIE, OBSTETRIQUE ET BIOLOGIE DE LA REPRODUCTION 2(1):23-32, January-February, 1973.

"Fetus papyraceus," (letter), by R. P. Balfour. OBSTETRICS AND GYNECOLOGY 47(4):507, April, 1976.

"Fetus papyraceus," by A. Targaszewska, et al. POLSKI TYGODNIK LEKARSKI 30(41):1713-1714, October 13, 1975.

"Give us our daily bread (a feature on aborting abnormal fetus," by H. Yeager. CATHOLIC MIND 28, September 1975.

"The intravenous infusion of prostaglandin F2alpha in the management of intrauterine death of the fetus," by N. Moe. ACTA OBSTETRICIA ET GYNECOLOGICA SCANDINAVICA 55(2):113-114, 1976.

"Management of patients at risk for fetal malformation," by M. Watt. NURSING MIRROR AND MIDWIVES' JOURNAL 142:61-63, May 6, 1976.

"On the bounds of freedom: from the treatment of fetuses to euthanasia," by H. T. Engelhardt, Jr. CONNETI-CUT MEDICINE 40(1):51-54, 57, January, 1976.

"Redefining the issues in fetal experimentation," by E. F. Diamond. JOURNAL OF THE AMERICAN MEDICAL ASSOCIATION 236:281-283, July 19, 1976.

"Termination of pregnancy in cases of fetal death in utero by intravenous prostaglandin F2 alpha," by A. P. Lange, et al. PROSTAGLANDINS 11(1):101-108, January, 1976.

FETUS

"The unwanted child: caring for the fetus born alive after an abortion." HASTINGS CENTER REPORT 6(5):10-15, October, 1976.

"What are the bonds between the fetus and the uterus?" by V. W. Adamkiewicz. CANADIAN NURSE 72(2):26-28, February, 1976.

"What are the bonds between the fetus and the uterus," by V. W. Adamkiewicz. INFIRMIÈRE CANADIENNE 18(2):26-28, February, 1976.

FLAVOXATE

FLUMETHASONE

GENETICS

"Aetiology of spontaneous abortion. A cytogenetic and epidemiological study of 288 abortuses and their parents," by J. G. Lauritsen. ACTA OBSTETRICIA ET GYNECOLOGICA SCANDINAVICA SUPPLEMENT (52):1-29, 1976.

"Association of pericentric inversion of chromosome 9 and reproductive failure in ten unrelated families," by J. Boué, et al. HUMANGENETIK 30(3):217-224, September 20, 1975.

"Balanced homologous translocation t(22q22q) in a phenotypically normal woman with repeated spontaneous abortion," by L. M. Farah, et al. HUMAN-GENETIK 28(4):357-360, August 25, 1975.

"A case of ring 18 chromosome in a sibship with multiple spontaneous abortions," by R. Coco, et al. ANNALES DE GENETIQUE 18(2):135-237, June, 1975.

"Chromosomal aberrations and disorders of evolution in repeated spontaneous abortions," by A. Zwinger, et al.

CESKOSLOVENSKA GYNEKOLOGIE 41(2):121-126,
April, 1976.

"Chromosomal and anatomic studies of pregnancies after
discontinuation of steroid contraceptives," by A. Boué,
et al. JOURNAL DE GYNECOLOGIE, OBSTETRIQUE
ET BIOLOGIE DE LA REPRODUCTION 2(2):141-154,
March, 1973.

"Chromosomal study of 65 couples with spontaneous abor-
tions," by J. L. Taillemite, et al. JOURNAL DE
GYNECOLOGIE, OBSTETRIQUE ET BIOLOGIE DE
LA REPRODUCTION 5(3):343-349, April-May, 1976.

"Chromosome aberrations as a cause of spontaneous
abortion," by J. Kleinebrecht, et al. ZEITSCHRIFT
FUR ALLGEMEINMEDIZIN; DU LANDARZT 51(22):
974-977, August 10, 1975.

"Chromosome studies in couples with repeated spontaneous
abortions," by C. Tsenghi, et al. OBSTETRICS AND
GYNECOLOGY 47(4):463-468, 1976. (Bio. Abstrs.
1976, 42979)

"Congenital malformations of the central nervous system
in spontaneous abortions, by M. R. Creasy, et al.
JOURNAL OF MEDICAL GENETICS 13(1):9-16, 1976.
(Bio. Abstrs. 1976, 14103)

"Chromosome studies in 500 induced abortions," by M.
Yamamoto, et al. HUMANGENETIK 29(1):9-14,
August 29, 1975.

"Cytogenetic studies in reproductive loss," by R. Schmidt
et al. JAMA; JOURNAL OF THE AMERICAN MEDICA
ASSOCIATION 236(4):369-373, 1976. (Bio. Abstrs. 19'
54722)

"Cytogenetic study of families with habitual abortions," by

G. Vulkova, et al. AKUSHERSTVO I GINEKOLOGIIA (Moscow) 15(2):111-115, 1976.

"A cytogenetic study of human spontaneous abortions using banding techniques," by M. R. Creasy, et al. HUMAN GENETICS 31(2):177-196, February 29, 1976. (Bio. Abstrs. 1976, 31538)

"Cytogenetics of fetal wastage," by H. J. Kim, et al. NEW ENGLAND JOURNAL OF MEDICINE 293(17):844-847, October 23, 1975.

"Evaluation of the causes of habitual abortion and malformation in children based on cytogenetic examination of parents," by E. Samochowiec, et al. ZENTRAL-BLATT FUR GYNAEKOLOGIE 97(7):419-425, 1975.

"Familial C/D translocation t(9;13)(9p23.13q21) in a male associated with recurrent abortion," by D. Singh-Kahlon, et al. HUMAN GENETICS 33(3):223-230, August 30, 1976.

"Fetal loss and familial chromosome 1 translocations," by J. H. Garrett, et al. CLINICAL GENETICS 8(5):341-348, November, 1975.

"45,XO Turner's syndrome without evidence of mosaicism in a patient with two pregnancies," by J. Philip, et al. ACTA OBSTETRICIA ET GYNECOLOGICA SCANDIN-AVICA 55(3):283-286, 1976. (Bio. Abstrs. 1976, 54731)

"Four familial translocations ascertained through spontaneous abortions," by D. H. Carr, et al. HUMAN GENETICS 31(1):93-96, 1976. (Bio. Abstrs. 1976, 25779)

"A further chromosome analysis in induced abortions," by M. Yamamoto, et al. HUMAN GENETICS 34(1):69-71,

September 10, 1976.

"Genetic analysis of families with reciprocal translocations," by I. V. Lur'e, et al. GENETIKA 9(11):
159-164, November, 1973.

"Genetic aspects of habitual abortion. pp. 31-41," by
F. Mollica. In: Marchesi F, Cittadini E, ed.
Fertilità e sterilità. Taormina, Minerva medica,
1974. WP 570 S679f 1973.

"Genetic examination of patients in consultation for
sterility or miscarriages," by M. M. Freund, et al.
JOURNAL DE GENETIQUE HUMAINE 23 Suppl:112-
113, October, 1975.

"Histological analysis of spontaneous abortions with
trisomy 2: first description of an embryo," by J.
Kleinebrecht, et al. HUMANAGENETIK 29(1):15-
22, August 29, 1975.

"Identification of C trisomies in human abortuses," by
J. Boué, et al. JOURNAL OF MEDICAL GENETICS
12(3):265-268, 1975. (Bio. Abstrs. 1976, 60541)

"Immunologic rejection of chromosomally abnormal
fetuses," by T. Kushnick. PERSPECTIVES IN
BIOLOGY AND MEDICINE 18(2):292-293, Winter,
1975.

"Karyotype of the parents after spontaneous abortion?
Translocation 46 XY t (2p-;21q+) detected in the
husband of a woman who presented with 2 early
spontaneous abortion," by D. Rabineau, et al.
JOURNAL DE GYNECOLOGIE, OBSTETRIQUE ET
BIOLOGIE DE LA REPRODUCTION 3(2):265-270,
March, 1974.

"Karyotypes of spontaneous human abortuses and several

aspects of their phenotypic presentation," by N. M.
Slozina, et al. TSITOLOGIIA 17(8):989-993, August,
1975.

"Karyotyping of in cases of spontaneous abortions," by
L. Wisniewski, et al. GINEKOLOGIA POLASKA
47(1):57-66, January, 1976.

"A large pericentric inversion of human chromosome 8,"
by R. Herva, et al. AMERICAN JOURNAL OF HUMAN
GENETICS 28(3):208-212, May, 1976.

"Maternal factors associated with fetal chromosomal
anomalies in spontaneous abortions," by E. Alberman,
et al. BRITISH JOURNAL OF OBSTETRICS AND
GYNAECOLOGY 83(8):621-627, August, 1976.

"Origin of the extra chromosome in trisomy 16," by J.
G. Lauritsen, et al. CLINICAL GENETICS 10(3):
156-160, September, 1976.

"Phenotypic expression of lethal chromosomal anomalies
in human abortuses," by J. Boué, et al. TERATOL-
OGY; JOURNAL OF ABNORMAL DEVELOPMENT
14(1):3-19, August, 1976.

"Phosphoglucomutase phenotypes and prenatal selection.
Studies of spontaneous and induced abortions," by G.
Beckman, et al. HUMAN HEREDITY 25(3):172-176,
1975.

"Prenatal diagnosis of trisomy 9," by U. Franke, et al.
HUMANGENETIK 29(3):243-250, 1975.

"Prenatal genetic diagnosis in 350 amniocenteses," by
B. F. Crandall. OBSTETRICS AND GYNECOLOGY
48(2):158-162, 1976. (Bio. Abstrs. 1976, 66501)

"Recurrent abortions and paternal balanced translocation

t(1q-;13q⊅)," by D. Rozynkowa, et al. HUMAN-
GENETIK 28(4):349-351, August 25, 1975.

"Reproductive failure secondary to chromosome abnormalities," by A. Boué, et al. ACTA EUROPAEA
FERTILITATIS 6(1):39-55, March, 1975.

"The significance of oral contraceptives in causing
chromosome anomalies in spontaneous abortions," by
J. G. Lauritsen. ACTA OBSTETRICIA ET GYNE-
COLOGICA SCANDINAVICA 54(3):261-264, 1975.
(Bio. Abstrs. 1976, 54717)

"Study of Y-chromatin in the human buccal epithelium,"
by A. M. Zakharov, et al. ARKHIV ANATOMII
GISTOLOGII I EMBRIOLOGII 68(5):18-23, 1975.
(Bio. Abstrs. 1976, 60555)

"Successive spontaneous abortions with diverse chromosomal aberrations in human translocation hetero-
zygote," by G. Kohn, et al. TERATOLOGY;
JOURNAL OF ABNORMAL DEVELOPMENT 12(3):
283-289, December, 1975.

"Symposium on intrauterine genetics. Reproductive
failures in relation to chromosome abnormalities," by
A. Boué, et al. UNION MEDICALE DU CANADA
104(120:1775-1781, December, 1975.

"Trisomy 21 in mother and daughter," by D. Francesconi,
et al. CLINICAL GENETICS 9(3):346, 1976. (Bio.
Abstrs. 1976, 25789)

"A 22/22 translocation carrier with recurrent abortions
demonstrated by a Giemsa banding technique," by T.
Maeda, et al. HUMAN GENETICS 31(2):243-245,
February 29, 1976.

"Where have all the conceptions gone?" by C. J. Roberts,

GENETICS

et al. LANCET 1(7905):498-499, 1975. (Bio. Abstrs. 1976, 1153)

GENTAMICIN GARAMYCIN

GESTANON

GONORRHEA
see: Complications

GYNECOLOGY
"The impact of voluntary abortion on American obstetrics and gynecology," by D. P. Swartz. MOUNT SINAI JOURNAL OF MEDICINE, NEW YORK 42(5): 468-478, September-October, 1975.

"Possibilities for work organization in the abortion sections of district gynecology department," by D. Andreev, et al. AKUSHERSTVO I GINEKOLOGIIA (Sofia) 13(6):466-471, 1974.

"The problem of abortion. Viewpoint of a gynecologist," by A. Wery. REVUE MEDICALE DE LIEGE 30(8): 253-258, April 25, 1975.

"Use of prostaglandins in gynecology and obstetrics," by B. I. Nesheim. TIDSSKRIFT FOR DEN NORSKE LAEGEFORENING 96(6):375-376, February 28, 1976.

"Violent perforations of the uterus in the 10-year material of the Gynecologic-Obstetrical Department in Bitola," by T. Pasanku. MEDICINSKI ARHIV 28(3):337-339, May-June, 1974.

GYNESTHESIN

HABITUAL ABORTION
"Anti-PP1Pk (anti-Tja) and habitual abortion," by D. B. Weiss, et al. FERTILITY AND STERILITY 26(9):

901-903, September, 1975.

"Asherman's syndrome (Fritsch-Asherman)," by E. G.
Waters. JOURNAL OF THE MEDICAL SOCIETY
OF NEW JERSEY 73(9):745-747, September, 1976.

"Asherman's syndrome, the Massouras Duck's Foot-IUD
(MDF-IUD) and Peacock Hook. Treatment and prevention
pp. 265-272," by H. G. Massouras. In: da Paz AC,
et al., ed. Recent advances in human reproduction.
Amsterdam, Excerpta Medica, 1976. W3 EX89 no.
370 1974.

"Chromosomal aberrations and disorders of evolution in
repeated spontaneous abortions," by A. Zwinger, et
al. CESKOSLOVENSKA GYNEKOLOGIE 41(2):121-
126, April, 1976.

"Cytogenetic study of families with habitual abortions,"
by G. Vulkova, et al. AKUSHERSTVO I GINEKOLOGIIA
(Moscow) 15(2):111-115, 1976.

"Detection of anti-HL-A serum antibodies in habitual
abortion (possibilities of the use of the leukoagglutination method) pp. 167-172," by N. S. Cavallaro,
et al. In: Marchesi F, Cittadini E, ed. Fertilità e
sterilità. Taormina, Minerva medica, 1974. WP 570
S679f 1973.

"Detection of anti-Toxoplasma gondii antibodies in subjects with repeated abortions, perinatal mortality and
malformed infants," by A. Castro, et al. ANNALI
SCLAVO 18(1):75-81, January-February, 1976.

"Diagnosis of Asherman's syndrome (intrauterine
synechiae)," by I. Berta, et al. ZENTRALBLATT
FUR GYNAEKOLOGIE 98(8):495-503, 1976.

"Diagnostic and therapeutic studies of abortion caused

by cervix insufficiency based on our case records
from 1964 to the present. pp. 173-193," by S.
Mangiameli. In: Marchesi F, Cittandidi E, ed.
Fertilità e sterilità. Taormina, Minerva medica,
1974. WP 570 S679f 1973.

"Diagnosis and therapy of asherman's syndrome,"
by K. Poradovsky, et al. CESKOSLOVENSKA
GYNEKOLOGIE 40(7):502-503, August, 1975.

"Endocrine habitual abortion. pp. 63-76," by C.
Montoneri. In: Marchesi F, Cittadini E, ed.
Fertilità e sterilità. Taormina, Minerva medica,
1974. WP 570 S679f 1973.

"Etiopathogenesis of habitual abortion. pp. 3-9," by I.
Panella, et al. In: Marchesi F, Cittadidi E, ed.
Fertilità e sterilità. Taormina, Minerva medica,
1974. Wp 570 S679f 1973.

"Evaluation of the causes of habitual abortion and malformation in children based on cytogenetic examination
of parents," by E. Samochowiec, et al. ZENTRAL-
BLATT FUR GYNAEKOLOGIE 97(7):419-425, 1975.

"Familial C/D translocation t(9;13)(9p23.13q21) in a
male associated with recurrent abortion," by D.
Singh-Kahlon, et al. HUMAN GENETICS 33(3):223-
230, August 30, 1976.

"Fetal loss and familial chromosome 1 translocations,"
by J. H. Garrett, et al. CLINICAL GENETICS
8(5):341-348, November, 1975.

"Genetic aspects of habitual abortion. pp. 31-41," by
F. Mollica. In: Marchesi F, Cittadidi E, ed.
Fertilità e sterilità. Taormina, Minerva medica,
1974. WP 570 S679f 1973.

"Genital listeriosis (a case report," by P. Jagtap, et
al. JOURNAL OF POSTGRADUATE MEDICINE
21(3):157-160, July, 1975.

"Habitual abortion and pathology of the seminal fluid.
pp. 195-202," by R. Agostini, et al. In: Marchesi F,
Cittadini E, Ed. Fertilità e sterilità. Taormina,
Minerva medics, 1974. WP 570 S679f 1973.

"Habitual abortion: biochemical aspects. pp. 77-90,"
by L. Iachello. In: Marchesi F, Cittadidi E, ed.
Fertilità e sterilità. Taormina, Minerva medica,
1974. WP 570 S679f 1973.

"Habitual abortion: causes and pathogenetic aspects.
pp. 11-29," by S. di Leo. In: Marchesi F, Cittadini
E, ed. Fertilita e sterilita. Taormin, Minerva
medica, 1974. WP 570 S679f 1973.

"Habitual abortion studied in the light of our seminological knowledge. pp. 203-212," by G. Nicora, et
al. In: Marchesi F, Cittadini E, ed. Fertilità e
sterilità. Taormina, Minerva medica, 1974.
WP 570 S679f 1973.

"Hormonal treatment in habitual abortions," by S.
Grigorov, et al. AKUSHERSTVO I GINEKOLOGIIA
(Sofia) 14(3):171-175, 1975.

"Immunological aspects of habitual abortion. pp. 43-
61," by N. S. Cavallaro. In: Marchesi F, Cittadini
E, ed. Fertilità e sterilità. Taormina, Minerva
medica, 1974. WP 570 S679f 1973.

"A nursing care study of tracheloplasty on a 25 year
old woman," by C. C. Nwaekpe. NIGERIAN NURSE
8(1):26-28, January-March, 1976.

"Obstetric complications after treatment of intrauterine

synechiae (Asherman's syndrome)," by R. Jewelewicz, et al. OBSTETRICS AND GYNECOLOGY 47(6):701-705, 1976. (Bio. Abstrs. 1976, 46115)

"Outcome and quality of pregnancies obtained by ovulation inducers in infertile women: apropos of 229 pregnancies in 91 women, of whom 42 were treated for spontaneous abortion and 49 treated for ovarian sterility," by J. Henry-Suchet, et al. JOURNAL DE GYNECOLOGIE, OBSTETRIQUE ET BIOLOGIE DE LA REPRODUCTION 2(6):653-672, September, 1973.

"Possible andrological factor as cause of spontaneous abortion," by R. Schoysman. VERHANDELINGEN; KONINKLIJKE ACADEMIE VOOR GENEESKUNDE VON BELGIE 37(2):33-41, 1975.

"Postpartum and postabortal ovarian vein thrombophlebitis," by T. R. Allan, et al. OBSTETRICS AND GYNECOLOGY 47(5):525-528, 1976. (Bio. Abstrs. 1976, 24056)

"Preclinical abortion. pp. 125-144," by S. Cianci, et al. In: Marchesi F, Cittadini E, ed. Fertilità e sterilità. Taormina, Minerva medica, 1974. WP 570 S679f 1973.

"The predictive value of thyroid 'test profile' in habitual abortion," by D. Winikoff, et al. BRITISH JOURNAL OF OBSTETRICS AND GYNAECOLOGY 82(9):760-766, September, 1975.

"Prevention and therapy of habitual abortion. pp. 101-124," by P. Spanio, et al. In: Marchesi F, Cittadini E, ed. Fertilità e sterilità. Taormina, Minerva medica, 1974. WP 570 S679f 1973.

"Quantitative determination of antitriphoblastic IgG, IgA and IgM in habitual abortion (research with radial immunodiffusion. pp. 157-165," by N. S. Cavallaro, et al. In: Marchesi F, Cittadini E, ed. Fertilità e sterilità. Taormina, Minerva medica, 1974. WP 570 S679f 1973.

"Radiological studies on habitual abortion and prognosis of pregnancy," by G. Ohmura. JAPANESE JOURNAL OF FERTILITY AND STERILITY 20(3):92-107, 1975. (Bio. Abstrs. 1976, 28720)

"Recurrent abortions and paternal balanced translocation t(1q-;13q/)," by D. Rozynkowa, et al. HUMAN-GENETIK 28(4):349-351, August 25, 1975.

"Repeat abortion [examines the repeat abortion experience of New York city residents]," by R. G. Potter, et al. DEMOGRAPHY 13:65-82, February, 1976.

"Repeated abortion. pp. 213-218," by C. Serrao. In: Marchesi F, Cittandini E, ed. Fertilità e sterilità. Taormina, Minerva medica, 1974. WP 570 S679f 1973.

"Statistical study of the etiology of habitual abortion. pp. 149-152," by N. S. Cavallaro, et al. In: Marchesi F, Cittandini E, ed. Fertilità e sterilità. Taormina, Minerva medica, 1974. WP 570 S679f 1973.

"Successive spontaneous abortions with diverse chromosomal aberrations in human translocation heterozygote," by G. Kohn, et al. TERATOLOGY; JOURNAL OF ABNORMAL DEVELOPMENT 12(3):283-289, December, 1975.

"Treatment of threatened and habitual abortions with Turinal preparations," by H. Szucka-May, et al. GINEKOLOGIA POLASKA 46(12):1265-1269, December, 1975.

HABITUAL ABORTION

"Treatment of women suffering from habitual miscarriage," by N. T. Gudakova. AKUSHERSTVO I GINEKOLOGIIA (3):64-65, March, 1976.

"A 22/22 translocation carrier with recurrent abortions demonstrated by a Giemsa banding technique," by T. Maeda, et al. HUMAN GENETICS 31(2):243-245, February 29, 1976.

HALOTHANE
"The abortive effect of halothane," by A. Doenicke, et al. ANESTHESIE, ANALGESIE, REANIMATION 32(1):41-46, January-February, 1975.

HEMORRHAGE
see also: Complications

"Transplacental hemorrhage in abortion (incidence, entity and immunizing value). pp. 145-147," by S. di Leo, et al. In: Marchesi F, Cittadini E, ed. Fertilità e sterilità. Taormina, Minerva medica, 1974. WP 570 S679f 1973.

HEPARIN
"Intra-abdominal bleeding following subcutaneous heparin application in septic abortion," by D. Susemihl, et al. GEBURTSHILFE UND FRAUENHEILKUNDE 36(2): 126-127, February, 1976.

HEXENAL
"Case of the lack of effect of anesthetization in the intravenous administration of sombrevin and hexenal," by P. M. Veropotvelian, et al. PEDIATRIIA AKUSHERSTVO I GINEKOLOGIIA (5):62, 1975.

HISTORY
"Abortion in India," by R. P. Mohan. SOCIAL SCIENCE 50, 3:141-143, Summer, 1975.

HISTORY

"Historical record explains Bartlett Amendment defeat,"
(letter), by P. G. Driscoll. HOSPITAL PROGRESS
56(11):6, November, 1975.

"History of the relation between pregnancy and pulmonary
tuberculosis and therapeutic abortion," by T. M.
Caffaratto. MINERVA GINECOLOGIA 28(2):192-201,
February, 1976.

"Induced abortion: epidemiological aspects," by D. Baird.
JOURNAL OF MEDICAL ETHICS 1(3):122-126, September, 1975.

"Legal abortion: a half-decade of experience," by J.
Pakter, et al. FAMILY PLANNING PERSPECTIVES
7(6):248-255, November-December, 1975.

"Marie Stopes Memorial Lecture 1975. The compulsory
pregnancy lobby--then and now," by M. Simms.
JOURNAL OF THE ROYAL COLLEGE OF GENERAL
PRACTITIONERS 25(159):709-719, October, 1975.

HORMONES
"Hormonal consequences of the therapeutic interruption
of pregnancy by an intraamniotic injection of concentrated sodium chloride solution. pp. 21-33," by
H. de Watteville, et al. In: Vokaer R, De Bock G, ed.
Reproductive endocrinology. Oxford, Pergamon Press,
1975. WQ 200 F673r 1973.

"Hormonal surveillance in the 1st trimester of pregnancy," by E. van Bogaert, et al. BRUXELLES-
MEDICAL 55(2):71-78, February, 1975.

"Hormonal treatment in habitual abortions," by S.
Grigorov, et al. AKUSHERSTVO I GINEKOLOGIIA
(Sofia) 14(3):171-175, 1975.

"Hormone release and abortifacient effectiveness of a

190

newly developed silastic device containing 15-ME-
PGF2alpha methyl ester in concentrations of 0.5%
and 1.0%," by N. H. Lauersen, et al. PROSTA-
GLANDINS 12 Suppl:63-79, 1976.

HOSPITALS

"Abortions-government hospitals Peninsular Malaysia
1960-1972," by J. A. Thambu. MEDICAL JOURNAL
OF MALAYSIA 29(4):258-262, June, 1975.

"Day-care abortion: facts and fantasies," by C. Tomalin.
HEALTH AND SOCIAL SERVICE JOURNAL 86:353,
February 21, 1976.

"Federal hospitals to follow Supreme Court abortion
rules." MODERN HEALTHCARE, SHORT-TERM
CARE EDITION 5:16b, February, 1976.

"Hospital Sued Over Abortion." THE NEW YORK TIMES
(S) March 18, 45:1, 1976.

"Hospitals--a current analysis of the right to abortions
and sterilizations in the Fourth circuit: state action
and the church amendment." NORTH CAROLINA
LAW REVIEW 54:1307-1316, September, 1976.

"Intrauterine injection of 15(S)-15-methyl-prostaglandin
F2alpha for termination of early pregnancy in outpatient," by O. Ylikorkala, et al. PROSTAGLANDINS
10(2):333-341, August, 1975.

"Legal abortion. A prospective study of outpatient legal
abortion in the Municipal hospital in Arhus during
a 1 year period," by B. R. Moller, et al. UGESKRIFT
FOR LAEGER 138(6):329-333, February 2, 1976.

"Legal abortion. Review after introduction of outpatient
abortions," by P. C. Davidsen, et al. UGESKRIFT
FOR LAEGER 138(6):375-378, February 2, 1976.

"May hospitals prohibit abortions and sterilizations?"
by J. A. Turpin. MEDICO-LEGAL BULLETIN
24(9):1-9, September, 1975.

"New Jersey Briefs: 4 hospitals said to violate rights."
THE NEW YORK TIMES (S) June 4, II, 21:1, 1976.

"New Security Measures Will Protect Assembly," by M.
Waldron. THE NEW YORK TIMES (S) April 27,
75:8, 1976.

"Outpatient legal abortion. 500 operations with paracervical anesthesia," by J. Prest, et al. UGESKRIFT
FOR LAEGER 138(6):333-335, February 2, 1976.

"Outpatient legal abortion using a modified Vabra aspirator and paracervical anesthesia," by J. Praest, et al.
UGESKRIFT FOR LAEGER 138(6):336-338, February 2, 1976.

"Patterns of contraceptive failures: the role of motivation
re-examined," by W. G. Cobliner, et al. JOURNAL
OF BIOSOCIAL SCIENCE 7, 3:307-318, July, 1975.
(Socio. Abstrs. 1976, 76H9180)

"Private Hospitals to Decide Soon Whether to Challenge
Abortion Ruling," by A. A. Narvaez. THE NEW
YORK TIMES (M) November 19, II, 19:3, 1976.

IMMUNITY

"Abortion: a hypothesis on the role of ABO blood groups
and placental alkaline phosphatase," by E. Bottini.
SOCIAL BIOLOGY 22(3):221-228, 1975. (Bio.
Abstrs. 1976, 24579)

"Anti-PP1Pk (anti-Tja) and habitual abortion," by D. B.
Weiss, et al. FERTILITY AND STERILITY 26(9):
901-903, September, 1975.

"Certain immunologic indicators in miscarriage," by M. A. Omarov, et al. AKUSHERSTVO I GINEKOLOGIIA (Moscow) (9):61-62, September, 1975.

"Clinical observation of the prevention of RH isoimmunization with immunoglobulin anti-D," by S. Hisanaga, et al. ACTA OBSTETRICA ET GYNAECOLOGICA JAPONICA 21(2):97-102, 1974. (Bio. Abstrs. 1976, 14294)

"Detection of anti-HL-A serum antibodies in habitual abortion (possibilities of the use of the leukoagglutination method). pp. 167-172," by N. S. Cavallaro, et al. In: Marchesi F, Cittadini E, ed. Fertilità e sterilità. Taormina, Minerva medica, 1974. WP 570 S679f 1973.

"Immunologic rejection of chromosomally abnormal fetuses," by T. Kushnick. PERSPECTIVES IN BIOLOGY AND MEDICINE 18(2):292-293, Winter, 1975.

"Immunological aspects of habitual abortion. pp. 43-61," by N. S. Cavallaro. In: Marchesi F, Cittadini E, ed. Fertilità e sterilità. Taormina, Minerva medica, 1974. WP 570 S679f 1973.

"Prevention of Rh hemolytic disease: ten years' clinical experience with Rh immune globulin," by V. J. Freda, et al. NEW ENGLAND JOURNAL OF MEDICINE 292(19):1014-1016, 1975. (Bio. Abstrs. 1976, 14306)

"Prevention of RH immunization in therapeutic abortion," by M. Bulić. LIJECNICKI VJESNIK 98(2):103-104, Feburary, 1976.

"Quantitative determination of antitriphoblastic IgG, IgA and IgM in habitual abortion (research with radial immunodiffusion). pp. 157-165," by N. S. Cavallaro, et al. In: Marchesi F, Cittadini E, ed. Fertilità e sterilità. Taormina, Minerva medica, 1974. WP 570 S679f 1973.

"Sensitization of women to fetal tissue and leukocytic antigens and its role in miscarriage," by L. F. Kieseleva, et al. VOPROSY OKHRANY MATERINSTVA I DETSTVA 21(7):65-67, June, 1976.

"Significance of HLA and blood-group incompatibility in spontaneous abortion," by J. G. Lauritsen, et al. CLINICAL GENETICS 9(6):575-582, 1976. (Bio. Abstrs. 1976, 66537)

"Studies in pregnant women on fetomaternal immunization to HL-A alloantigens and ABO and Rh antigens: II. Clinical observations on the course of pregnancy," by Z. Zdebski. FOLIA MEDICA CRACOVIENSIA 16(3):341-354, 1974. (Bio. Abstrs. 1976, 14408)

"Transplacental hemorrhage in abortion (incidence, entity and immunizing value). pp. 145-147," by S. di Leo, et al. In: Marchesi F, Cittadini E, ed. Fertilità e sterilità. Taormina, Minerva medica, 1974. WP 570 S679f 1973.

INDOMETHACIN

INDUCED ABORTION
see also: Techniques of Abortion

"Abortifacient efficiency of 15(S) 15-methyl-prostaglandin F2alpha-methyl ester administered vaginally during early pregnancy," by O. Yikorkala, et al. PROSTA-GLANDINS 12(4):609-624, October, 1976.

"Abortion and maternal deaths," (letter), by C. Brook. BRITISH MEDICAL JOURNAL 2(6034):524-525, August 28, 1976.

"Abortion and maternal deaths," (letter), by C. B.
Goodhart. BRITISH MEDICAL JOURNAL 2(6033):
477, August 21, 1976.

"Abortion and maternal deaths," (letter), by A. M.
Smith. BRITISH MEDICAL JOURNAL 2(6031):368,
August 7, 1976.

"Abortion attitudes among Catholic college students," by
P. D. Bardis. ADOLESCENCE 10(39):433-441, Fall,
1975.

"Abortion development in the Scandinavian countries
1965-1974," by P. C. Matthiessen. UGESKRIFT FOR
LAEGER 138(6):351-353, February 2, 1976.

"Abortion: for the fetus's own sake?" by P. F. Camenisch.
HASTINGS CENTER REPORT 6(2):38-41, April, 1976.

"Abortion induction using prostaglandin E2," by K.
Felshart. ARCHIV FUR GYNAEKOLOGIE 219(1-4):
500-501, November 18, 1975.

"The abortion issue." (editorial). JOURNAL OF MEDI-
CAL ETHICS 1(3):109-110, September, 1975.

"Abortion--the medical facts," by L. Machol, et al.
FAMILY HEALTH 8:42-45 passim, February, 1976.

"Abortion: perception and contemporary genocide myth:
a comparative study among low-income pregnant
Black and Puerto Rican women," by B. R. Hughes.
DISSERTATION ABSTRACTS INTERNATIONAL 34(6-A):
3542-3543, December, 1973.

"Abortion practice: could drugs replace doctors?" by S.
Whitehead. NURSING TIMES 72(15):564-565, April 15,
1976.

"Abortion-seeking women's views on the importance of social benefits as an alternative to induced abortion," by T. Ganes, et al. TIDSSKRIFT FOR DEN NORSKE LAEGEFORENING 96(13):768-770, May 10, 1976.

"Abortion today," by A. Ruppersberg, Jr. OHIO STATE MEDICAL JOURNAL 72(3):161-163, March, 1976.

"Abortions in 1973 in Linköping--contraceptive technics and postoperative complications," by U. Larsson-Cohn. LAKARTIDNINGEN 72(44):4282-4284, October 29, 1975.

"The abortive effect of halothane," by A. Doenicke, et al. ANESTHESIE, ANALGESIE, REANIMATION 32(1):41-46, January-February, 1975.

"Abortogenic activity of antiserum to alpha-foetoprotein," by G. L. Mizejewski, et al. NATURE 259(5540):222-224, January 22, 1976.

"Acute complications of abortion," by E. Obel. UGE-SKRIFT FOR LAEGER 138(6):319-323, February 2, 1976.

"Acute renal failure in the postpartum and post-abortion periods observed in the maternity department of the Hôpital Charles Nicolle," by B. Farza, et al. JOURNAL DE GYNECOLOGIE, OBSTETRIQUE ET BIOLOGIE DE LA REPRODUCTION 1(5 Suppl 2):443-447, 1972.

"Adolescent pregnancy and abortion," by D. D. Youngs, et al. MEDICAL CLINICS OF NORTH AMERICA 59(6):1419-1427, November, 1975.

"Adrenaline and noradrenaline excretion during an induced abortion," by M. Bokiniec, et al. ANNALES UNIVER-SITATIS MARIAE CURIE-SKLODOWSKA; SECTIO D:

MEDICINA 29:151-156, 1974.

"Alpha-fetoprotein levels in maternal plasma and
amniotic fluid during prostaglandin-induced midtrimester abortions: the relation to fetal distress and
death," by R. H. Ward, et al. BRITISH JOURNAL
OF OBSTETRICS AND GYNAECOLOGY 83(4):299-302,
April, 1976.

"Alpha-fetoprotein during mid-trimester induced abortion,"
(letter), by Y. Beyth, et al. LANCET 2(7937):709,
October 11, 1975.

"Ambulatory anesthesia for induced abortion," by P. P.
Olsen. UGESKRIFT FOR LAEGER 138(30):1814-1817,
July 19, 1976.

"Anmiotic fluid removal prior to saline abortion," by
A. C. Mehta, et al. ANNALES CHIRURGIAE ET
GYNAECOLOGIAE FENNIAE 65(1):68-71, 1976.

"Anaesthetics and abortions," (letter), by D. I. Tushton.
LANCET 2(7977):141, July 17, 1976.

"Anencephaly: early ultrasonic diagnosis and interruption
of pregnancy. Apropos of a case," by R. Chef, et al.
JOURNAL DE GYNECOLOGIE, OBSTETRIQUE ET
BIOLOGIE DE LA REPRODUCTION 3(1):93-104),
January-February, 1974.

"Artificial abortion: reasons and management," by A. C.
Drogendijk, Jr. NEDERLANDS TIJDSHRIFT VOOR
GENEESKUNDE 120(19):809-814, May, 1976.

"Artificial abortion: reasons and management," by T. A.
Eskes. NEDERLANDS TIJDSHRIFT VOOR GENEES-
KUNDE 120(19):815-816, May, 1976.

"Artificial interruption and female morbidity," by A.

Kotásek, et al. CESKSLOVENSKA GYNEKOLOGIE
41(1):31-33, March, 1976.

"Attempt to elucidate the causes of certain complications
following artificial abortion using radioisotopes," by
A. Atanasov, et al. AKUSHERSTVO I GINEKOLOGIIA
(Sofia) 14(5):372-375, 1975.

"The attitude of women to anticonception after artificial
interruption of gravidity," by D. Fukalová, et al.
CESKOSLOVENSKA GYNEKOLOGIE 40(9):680-681,
November, 1975.

"Biological and clinical aspects of legal abortion," by G.
Pescetto. ANNALI DI OSTETRICIA, GINECOLOGIA
MEDICINA PERINATALE 96(4):215-227, July-August,
1975.

"Blood coagulation studies in prostaglandin abortion,"
(proceedings), by R. Lang, et al. ARCHIV FUR
GYNAEKOLOGIE 219(1-4):501-502, November 18,
1975.

"Bronchoconstriction and pulmonary hypertension during
abortion induced by 15-ethyl-prostaglandin F2a," by
E. K. Weir, et al. AMERICAN JOURNAL OF
MEDICINE 60(4):556-562, 1976. (Bio. Abstrs. 1976,
23180)

"Case of the lack of effect of anesthetization in the intra-
venous administration of sombrevin and hexenal," by
P. M. Veropotvelian, et al. PEDIATRIIA AKUSHER-
STVO I GINEKOLOGIIA (5):62, 1975.

"Causes of unwanted pregnancies and reasons for their
interruption," by A. Meyer. ZENTRALBLATT FUR
GYNAEKOLOGIE 97(23):1444-1449, 1975.

"Cervical diameter after suction termination of preg-

nancy," (letter), by M. M. Black, et al. BRITISH
MEDICAL JOURNAL 1(6014):902, April 10, 1976.

"Cervical diameter after suction termination of pregnancy," by F. D. Johnstone, et al. BRITISH
MEDICAL JOURNAL 1(6001):68-69, January 10, 1976.

"Cervical dilatation and pregnancy interruption using
Rivanol for intrauterine filling," by I. Máthé, et al.
ORVOSI HETILAP 116(47):2782-2785, November 23,
1975.

"Characteristics of pregnant women who report previous
abortions," by S. Harlap, et al. BULLETIN OF THE
WORLD HEALTH ORGANIZATION 52(2):149-154,
1975. (Bio. Abstrs. 1976, 16900)

"Chromosome studies in 500 induced abortions," by M.
Yamamoto, et al. HUMANGENETIK 29(2):9-14,
August 29, 1975.

"Clinical conference: abortion and sterilization."
JOURNAL OF MEDICAL ETHICS 1(1):45-48, April,
1975.

"Clinical experience using intraamniotic prostaglandin
F2alpha for midtrimester abortion in 600 patients,"
by G. G. Anderson, et al. OBSTETRICS AND
GYNECOLOGY 46(5):591-595, November, 1975.

"Coagulation changes during second-trimester abortion
induced by intra-amniotic prostaglandin E2 and
hypertonic solutions," by I. Z. Mackenzie, et al.
LANCET 2(7944):1066-1069, 1975. (Bio. Abstrs.
1976, 5680)

"Coagulation disorders after hypertonic-saline abortion,"
(letter), by J. W. ten Cate, et al. LANCET 1(7952):
205, January 24, 1976.

"Coagulation disorders after hypertonic-saline abortion,"
(letter), by J. R. O'Brien, Jr. LANCET 1(7955):
367, February 14, 1976.

"Coagulation disorders and abortion using hypertonic
solutions," (letter), by I. Craft, et al. LANCET
1(7956):428, February 21, 1976.

"Comparative evaluation of quantitative variation of 5 per
cent intra-amniotic saline for mid-trimester abortion,"
by A. K. Ghosh. JOURNAL OF THE INDIAN MEDICAL
ASSOCIATION 64(11):305-306, June 1, 1975.

"Comparative study of the causes of induced abortion and
the knowledge of family planning," by M. D. Ramos
Netto. REVISTA ENFERMAGEM EM NOVAS
DIMENSOES 1(4):172, September-October, 1975.

"A comparative study of intra-amniotic saline and two
prostaglandin F2a dose schedules for midtrimester
abortion," by D. A. Edleman, et al. AMERICAN
JOURNAL OF OBSTETRICS AND GYNECOLOGY
125(2):188195, 1976. (Bio. Abstrs. 1976, 39271)

"A comparison of four methods for determining preval-
ence of induced abortion, Taiwan, 1970-1971," by R.
V. Rider, et al. AMERICAN JOURNAL OF EPIDEMI-
OLOGY 103(1):37-50, January, 1976.

"Comparison of intra-amniotic prostaglandin F2 alpha
and hypertonic saline for induction of second-trimester
abortion." BRITISH MEDICAL JOURNAL 1(6022):
1373-1376, June 5, 1976.

"A comparison of metal and plastic cannulae for performing vacuum," by S. S. Moghadam, et al. JOURNAL OF
REPRODUCTIVE MEDICINE 17(3):181-187, September,
1976.

"Competition between spontaneous and induced abortion,"
by R. G. Potter, et al. DEMOGRAPHY 12:129-141,
February, 1975.

"The complexity of compiling abortion statistics," by
J. C. Smith. PUBLIC HEALTH REPORTS 90(6):
502-503, November-December, 1975.

"Complications after abortion. Hospitalization for
early post-abortion morbidity after voluntary abortion," by G. E. Feichter. FORTSCHRITTE DE
MEDIZIN 94(16):965-967, June 3, 1976.

"Complications following ambulatory abortion," by G.
Wolters. FORTSCHRITTE DU MEDIZIN 94(27):
1473-1375, September 23, 1976.

"Concurrent use of prostaglandin F2a and laminaria
tents for induction of midtrimester abortion," by
J. H. Duenhoelter, et al. OBSTETRICS AND
GYNECOLOGY 47(4):469-472, 1976. (Bio. Abstrs.
1976, 33635)

"Congenital abnormalities and selective abortion," by
M. J. Seller. JOURNAL OF MEDICAL ETHICS
2(3):138-141, September, 1976.

"Connecticut physicians' attitudes toward abortion," by
G. L. Pratt, et al. AMERICAN JOURNAL OF PUBLIC
HEALTH 66:288-290, March, 1976; Reply with rejoinder
by K. Solomon 66:905-906, September, 1976.

"Counselling for abortion," by M. Blair. MIDWIFE
HEALTH VISITOR AND COMMUNITY NURSE 11(11):
355-356, November, 1975.

"The culturability of fibroblasts from the skin of abortuses
after intra-amniotic instillation of urea or prostaglandin," by K. S. Ju, et al. AMERICAN JOURNAL OF

OBSTETRICS AND GYNECOLOGY 125(8):1155,
August 15, 1976.

"Declaration on procured abortion," by J. Hamer.
C.I.C.I.A.M.S. NOUVELLES (2):7-18, 1975.

"The demographic effect of induced abortion," by C.
Tietze, et al. OBSTETRICAL AND GYNECOLOGICAL
SURVEY 31(10):699-709, October, 1976.

"The development of instruments to measure attitudes
toward abortion and knowledge of abortion," by S.
Snegroff. JOURNAL OF SCHOOL HEALTH 46(5):273-
277, May, 1976.

"Delayed morbidity following prostaglandin-induced abortion," by I. Z. Mackenzie, et al. INTERNATIONAL
JOURNAL OF GYNAECOLOGY AND OBSTETRICS
13(5):209-214, 1975. (Bio. Abstrs. 1976, 23175)

"Determination of Rh blood group of fetuses in abortions
by suction curettage," by R. M. Greendyke, et al.
TRANSFUSION 16(3):267-269, May-June, 1976.

"The distribution within the placenta, myometrium, and
decidua of 24Na-labelled hypertonic saline solution
following intra-amniotic or extra-amniotic injection,"
by B. Gustavil. BRITISH JOURNAL OF OBSTETRICS
AND GYNAECOLOGY 82(9):734-739, September, 1975.

"Early complications and late sequelae of induced abor-
tion: a review of the literature," by K. G. B.
Edström. BULLETIN OF THE WORLD HEALTH
ORGANIZATION (Bio. Abstrs. 1976, 16899)

"Early pregnancy interruption by 15(S) 15 methyl
prostaglandin F2a methyl ester," by M. Bygdeman,
et al. OBSTETRICS AND GYNECOLOGY 48(2):221-
224, 1976. (Bio. Abstrs. 1976, 56848)

INDUCED ABORTION

"Early termination of pregnancy: a comparative study
of intrauterine prostaglandin F2alpha and vacuum
aspiration," by M. I. Ragab, et al. PROSTAGLAN-
DINS 11(2):261-273, February, 1976.

"Early vacuum aspiration: minimizing procedures to non-
pregnant women," by E. R. Miller, et al. FAMILY
PLANNING PERSPECTIVES 8(1):33-38, January-
February, 1976.

"Effect of aspirin on bleeding time during elective
abortion," by R. Waltman, et al. OBSTETRICS
AND GYNECOLOGY 48(1):108-110, 1976. (Bio.
Abstrs. 1976, 58163)

"The effect of meperidine analgesia on midtrimester
abortions induced with intra-amniotic prostaglandin
F2a," by L. G. Staurovsky, et al. AMERICAN
JOURNAL OF OBSTETRICS AND GYNECOLOGY
125(2):185-187, 1976. (Bio. Abstrs. 1976, 50604)

"The effects of attitude and direction of true-false
interspersed questions on the learning of a prose
passage on a controversial topic," by S. S. El-Azzabi.
DISSERTATION ABSTRACTS INTERNATIONAL 34
(11-A), 7039, May, 1974.

"Effects of legal termination on subsequent pregnancy,"
by J. A. Richardson, et al. BRITISH MEDICAL
JOURNAL 1(6021):1303-1304, May 29, 1976.

"Effects of prostaglandin E2 and F2alpha therapy," by
I. S. Fraser. COMPREHENSIVE THERAPY 2(9):
55-59, September, 1976.

"The efficacy and safety of intramuscularly administered
15(S) 15 methyl prostaglandin E2 methyl ester for
induction of artificial abortion," by W. E. Brenner,
et al. AMERICAN JOURNAL OF OBSTETRICS AND

GYNECOLOGY 123(1):19-29, September 1, 1975.

"The efficacy of intravaginal 15 methly prostaglandin F2alpha methyl ester in first and second trimester abortion," by T. F. Dillon, et al. PROSTAGLANDINS 12 Suppl:81-98, 1976.

"Endometrial aspiration in fertility control. A report of 500 cases," by R. P. Bendel, et al. AMERICAN JOURNAL OF OBSTETRICS AND GYNECOLOGY 125(3):328-332, June 1, 1976.

"Error during abortion--2 physicians got warning." LAKARTIDNINGEN 73(4):231-232, January 21, 1976.

"Estrogen content of the amniotic fluid, plasma and placental tissue during abortion induced by prostaglandin F2 alpha and 15-methyl-prostaglandin F2 alpha," by V. G. Orlova, et al. AKUSHERSTVO I GINEKOLOGIE (Moscow) (6):24-28, June, 1975.

"Evaluation of abortion techniques: recent and future trends. pp. 164-173," by R. J. Pion, et al. In: Moghissi KS, Evans TN, ed. Regulation of human fertility. Detroit, Wayne State Univ Press, 1976. W3 HA292 1973r.

"Evaluation of intramuscular 15(s)-15 methyl prostaglandin F2 alpha tromethamine salt for induction of abortion medications to attenuate side effects, and intracervical laminaria tents," by W. Gruber, et al. FERTILITY AND STERILITY 27(9):1009-1023, September, 1976.

"Evaluation of vaginal delivery systems containing 15(s)15-methyl PGF2alpha methyl ester," by C. H. Spilman, et al. PROSTAGLANDINS 12 Suppl:1-16, 1976.

"Experience with 276 intra-amniotic prostaglandin F2a induced midtrimester abortions," by M. S. Golbus, et al. PROSTAGLANDINS 11(5):841-851, 1976. (Bio. Abstrs. 1976, 62686)

"Extra-amniotic 15 (S)-15 methyl PGF2alpha to induce abortion: a study of three administration schedules," by I. Z. Mackenzie, et al. PROSTAGLANDINS 12(3):443-453, September, 1976.

"Extra-amniotic mannitol for pregnancy termination," by M. A. Deshmukh, et al. JOURNAL OF POST-GRADUATE MEDICINE 22(1):23-25, January, 1976.

"Facing a grand jury." AMERICAN JOURNAL OF NURSING 76:398-400, March, 1976.

"Factor analysis of attitudes toward abortion," by B. Corenblum, et al. PERCEPTUAL AND MOTOR SKILLS 40(2):587-591, April, 1975.

"Fatal case of nivaquine poisoning. Medica-legal and toxicological study," by H. J. Lazarini, et al. MEDECINE LEGALE ET DOMMAGE CORPOREL 7(4):332, October-December, 1974.

"Fatal complication of pregnancy interruption (Karman method)," (letter), by H. Larrieu, et al. NOUVELLE PRESSE MEDICALE 4(38):2733, November 8, 1975.

"Fetomaternal transfusion in abortion and pregnancy interruptions and Rh-prevention," by H. Radzuweit, et al. ZENTRALBLATT FUR GYNAEKOLOGIE 97(22):1367-1374, 1975.

"First and repeat abortions: a study of decision-making and delay," by M. B. Bracken, et al. JOURNAL OF BIOSOCIAL SCIENCE 7, 4:473-491, October, 1975. (Socio. Abstrs. 1976, 76I2866)

"First experiences with a (15S)-15-methyl prostaglandin
F2alpha vaginal device for termination of early first
trimester pregnancy with serial sonographic observations," by J. H. Duenhoelter, et al. PROSTA-
GLANDINS 12 Suppl:135-145, 1976.

"Foreign workers and pregnancy interruption," by
E. Burckhardt-Tamm, et al. THERAPEUTISCHE
UMSCHAW 32(9):577-579, September, 1975.

"A further chromosome analysis in induced abortions,"
by M. Yamamoto, et al. HUMAN GENETICS 34(1):
69-71, September 10, 1976.

"Guidance prior to abortion," by V. Sele. UGESKRIFT
FOR LAEGER 138(6):379, February 2, 1976.

"Health personnel organization for professional self-
determination," by B. Brekke. SYKEPLEIEN 61
(22):1145-1147, November 20, 1974.

"A histologic study of the placentas of patients with
saline- and prostaglandin-induced abortion," by
S. Purl, et al. OBSTETRICS AND GYNCEOLGOY
48(2):216-220, 1976. (Bio. Abstrs. 1976, 56851)

"Histological studies on hemostasis in abortions in the
second and third month of pregnancy: comparison with
post partum hemostasis," by R. Slunsky. ARCHIV
FUR GYNAEKOLOGIE 220(4):325-338, 1976.
(Bio. Abstrs. 1976, 51867)

"Historical record explains Bartlett Amendment defeat,"
(letter), by P. G. Driscoll. HOSPITAL PROGRESS
56(11):6, November, 1975.

"Hormone release and abortifacient effectiveness of a
newly developed silastic device containing 15-ME-
PGF2alpha methyl ester in concentrations of 0.5%

and 1.0%," by N. H. Lauersen, et al. PROSTA-
GLANDINS 12 Suppl:63-79, 1976.

"Illegal abortions in the United States: 1972-1974," by
W. Cates, Jr., et al. FAMILY PLANNING PER-
SPECTIVES 8(2):86-92, March-April, 1976.

"The impact of induced abortions on fertility," by
M. Károly. DEMOGRAFIA 13, 4:413-420, 1970.
(Socio. Abstrs. 1976, 76I0122)

"Incidence of abortion during treatment with ovulation
inducers. pp. 219-224," by G. Guastella, et al.
In: Marchesi F, Cittadini E, ed. Fertilità e
sterilità. Taormina, Minerva medica, 1974.
WP 570 S679f 1973.

"Incomplete abortions in Accra and Bangkok University
Hospitals 1972-1973," by I. C. Chi, et al. INTER-
NATIONAL JOURNAL OF GYNAECOLOGY AND
OBSTETRICS 13(4):148-161, 1975. (Bio. Abstrs.
1976, 22865)

"An inconvenient fetus." NURSING MIRROR AND MID-
WIVES' JOURNAL 141:76, July 17, 1975.

"Indications and contraindications for the interruption
in dermatologic diseases," by N. Sönnichsen.
THERAPEUTISCHE UMSCHAW 31(5):301-306,
May, 1974.

"Induced abortion," by K. W. Andersen, et al.
UGESKRIFT FOR LAEGER 137(46):2716, November 10, 1975.

"Induced abortion and contraceptive practice: an experience in Taiwan," by I. H. Su, et al. STUDIES
IN FAMILY PLANNING 7:224-230, August, 1976.

"Induced abortion and the course of the next pregnancy,
labor and puerperium," by H. Zrubek, et al.
GINEKOLOGIA POLASKA 47(1):32-37, January, 1976.

"Induced abortion and secondary infertility," by D.
Trichopoulos, et al. BRITISH JOURNAL OF OBSTE-
TRICS AND GYNAECOLOGY 83(8):645-650, August,
1976.

"Induced abortion: epidemiological aspects," by D.
Baird. JOURNAL OF MEDICAL ETHICS 1(3):122-
126, September, 1975.

"Induced abortion in the 8-9th week of pregnancy with
vaginally administered 15-methyl PGF2alpha methyl
ester," by A. Leader, et al. PROSTAGLANDINS
12(4):631-637, October, 1976.

"Induced abortion in Texas," by L. H. Roht, et al.
TEXAS MEDICINE 72(4):84-91, April, 1976.

"Induced abortion, Jewish law and Jewish morality," by
F. Rosner. MAN AND MEDICINE 1:213-224,
Spring, 1976.

"Induced abortion--a new major study." JOURNAL OF
THE ROYAL COLLEGE OF GENERAL PRACTITIONERS
26(169):558-559, August, 1976.

"Induced abortion: 1975 factbook," by C. Tietze, et al.
REPORTS ON POPULATION-FAMILY PLANNING
(14):1-75, December, 1975.

"Induced abortions and spontaneous abortions. Psychopathological aspects apropos of a preliminary sample
of 411 requests for pregnancy interruption," by M.
Bourgeois, et al. ANNALES MEDICO-PSYCHO-
LOGIQUES 2(2):339-366, July, 1975.

"Induced legal abortions of juveniles," by M. Farkas,
    et al. DEMOGRAFIA 17, 2:236-243, 1974. (Socio.
    Abstrs. 1976, 76I1399)

"Induction of abortion by vaginal administration of
    15(s)15-methyl prostaglandin F2alpha methyl ester. A
    comparison of two delivery systems," by M. Bygdeman,
    et al. PROSTAGLANDINS 12 Suppl:27-51, 1976.

"Induction of abortion with anti-feto-placental antibody,"
    by Y. Amano. CLINICAL ENDOCRINOLOGY 24(7):
    625-629, July, 1976.

"Induction of abortion with intra-amniotic or intra-
    muscular 15(S)-15-methyl-prostaglandin F2alpha,"
    by O. Ylikorkaia, et al. PROSTAGLANDINS 10(3):
    423-434, September, 1975.

"Induction of midtrimester abortion by serial intra-
    vaginal administration of 15(S)-15-methyl-prostaglandin
    F2alpha (THAM) suppositories," by N. H. Lauersen,
    et al. PROSTAGLANDINS 19(6):1037-1045, December,
    1975.

"Induction of midtrimester abortion with intraamniotic
    urea, intravenous oxytocin and laminaria," by I. M.
    Golditch, et al. JOURNAL OF REPRODUCTIVE
    MEDICINE 15(6):225-228, December, 1975.

"Induction of second trimester abortion by infusion of
    intraamniotic hypertonic and extraamniotic physio-
    logical slaine solution," by M. Blum, et al.
    GEBURTSHILFE UND FRAUENHEILKUNDE 36(5):
    444-447, May, 1976.

"Influence of abortions and interruptions of pregnancies
    on subsequent deliveries. I. Course of pregnancy,"
    by P. Knorre. ZENTRALBLATT FUR GYNAEKOLOGIE
    98(10):587-590, 1976.

"Influence of abortions and interruptions of pregnancies on subsequent deliveries. II. Course of labor," by P. Knorre. ZENTRALBLATT FUR GYNAEKOLOGIE 98(10):591-594, 1976.

--III. After-labor-period and puerperium," by P. Knorre. ZENTRALBLATT FUR GYNAEKOLOGIE 98(10):595-599, 1976.

"The influence of aspirin on the course of induced mid-trimester abortion," by J. R. Niebyl, et al. AMERICAN JOURNAL OF OBSTETRICS AND GYNECOLOGY 124(6):607-610, 1976. (Bio. Abstrs. 1976, 16218)

"The influence of induced abortion on Taiwanese fertility," by J. M. Sullivan, et al. STUDIES IN FAMILY PLANNING 7(8):231-238, August, 1976.

"Inhibitory effect of progesterone on the lactogenic and abortive action of prostaglandin F2alpha," by N. T. Vermouth, et al. JOURNAL OF ENDOCRINOLOGY 66(1):21-29, July, 1975.

"Intra-amniotic administration of 15(S)-15-methyl-prostaglandin F2alpha for the induction of midtrimester abortion," by J. R. Dingfelder, et al. AMERICAN JOURNAL OF OBSTETRICS AND GYNECOLOGY 125(6):821-826, July, 1976.

"Intra-amniotic administration of prostaglandin F2 alpha 12-methyl-prostaglandin F2 alpha and hypertonic sodium chloride solution for induction of abortion in second-trimester pregnancy," by L. S. Persianinov, et al. ZENTRALBLATT FUR GYNAEKOLOGIE 97(19):1153-1159, 1975.

"Intra-amniotic urea and prostaglandin F2 alpha for midtrimester abortion: a modified regimen," by

R. T. Burkman, et al. AMERICAN JOURNAL OF
OBSTETRICS AND GYNECOLOGY 126(3):328-333,
October 1, 1976.

"Intrauterine adhesions secondary to elective abortion.
Hysteroscopic diagnosis and management," by C. M.
March, et al. OBSTETRICS AND GYNECOLOGY
48(4):422-424, October, 1976.

"Intra-uterine administration of prostaglandin F2alpha
for induction of abortion. pp. 27-30." In: Bergström S, ed. Report from meetings of the Prostaglandin Task Force Steering Committee. Stockholm, 1973.
QV 175 W927r 1972-1973.

"Intra-uterine administration of prostaglandin F2alpha
or 15-methyl PGF2alpha for induction of abortion.
Intra-amniotic method. pp. 79." In: Bergström S,
ed. Report from meetings of the Prostaglandin
Task Force Steering Committee. Stockholm, 1973.
QV 175 W927r 1972-1973.

"Intrauterine aspiration in humans in the early fetal
period," by M. Yu. Makkaveeva. ARKHIV PATHOL-
OGIE 37(12):41-46, 1975. (Bio. Abstrs. 1976, 36105)

"Intrauterine extra-amniotic 15(s)-15-methyl prostaglandin F2alpha for induction of early midtrimester
abortion," by A. G. Shapiro. FERTILITY AND
STERILITY 27(9):1024-1028, September, 1976.

"Intrauterine injection of 15(S)-15-methyl-prostaglandin
F2alpha for termination of early pregnancy in outpatient," by O. Ylikorkala, et al. PROSTAGLANDINS
10(2):333-341, August, 1975.

"An interdisciplinary cause in human sexuality for medical
and nursing students," by F. H. Mims. DISSERTATION
ABSTRACTS INTERNATIONAL 35(3-A), 1506,

September, 1974. (Psycho. Abstrs. 1976, 12899)

"The intravenous infusion of prostaglandin F2alpha in the management of intrauterine death of the fetus," by N. Moe. ACTA OBSTETRICIA ET GYNECOLOGICA SCANDINAVICA 55(2):113-114, 1976.

"Invited discussion: the use of induced abortuses for monitoring. pp. 197-203," by T. Tanimura. In: Shepard TH et al. , ed. Methods for detection of environmental agents that produce congenital defects. Amsterdam, North-Holland, 1975. QS 675 M592 1974. 1974.

"The Irish emigrant and the abortion crisis." WORLD OF IRISH NURSING 4(10):1-2, October, 1975.

"IUD and induced abortion," by S. O. Skouby. UGESKRIFT FOR LAEGER 138(6):339-341, February 2, 1976.

"Kinetic and metabolic studies of 15-methyl-prostaglandin F2a administered intra-amniotically for induction of abortion," by K. Green. PROSTAGLANDINS 11(4): 699-711, 1976. (Bio. Abstrs. 1976, 50694)

"Kyematopathological studies in cases of late abortion," by D. Lüthje, et al. ARCHIV FUR GYNAEKOLOGIE 219:(1-4):285, November 18, 1975.

"Labor induction by intra-amniotic administration of prostaglandin F 2 alpha," by H. Halle, et al. ZENTRALBLATT FUR GYNAEKOLOGIE 97(19): 1160-1165, 1975.

"Laminaria augmentation of intra-amniotic PGF2 for midtrimester pregnancy termination," by P. G. Stubblefield, et al. PROSTAGLANDINS 10(3):413-422, September, 1975.

"Laminaria augmentation of midtrimester pregnancy termination by intramuscular prostaglandin 15 (S) 15-methyl F2 alpha," by J. Robins, et al. JOURNAL OF REPRODUCTIVE MEDICINE 16(6):334-336, June, 1976.

"Laminaria in abortion. Use in 1368 patients in first trimester," by W. M. Hern. ROCKY MOUNTAIN MEDICAL JOURNAL 72(9):390-395, September, 1975.

"Late complications following abortus provocatus," by E. Obel. UGESKRIFT FOR LAEGER 138(6):323-328, February 2, 1976.

"Low birth weight subsequent to induced abortion: a historical prospective study of 948 women in Skopje, Yugoslavia," by C. J. Hogue. AMERICAN JOURNAL OF OBSTETRICS AND GYNECOLGOY 123(7):675-681, 1975. (Bio. Abstrs. 1976, 5154)

"Law for the nurse supervisor," by H. Creighton. SUPERVISOR NURSE 6:10-11 passim, April, 1975.

"Legal abortion--1000 women. Data concerning contraception, age and obstetric history," by F. Lundvall. UGESKRIFT FOR LAEGER 138(6):363-369, February 2, 1976.

"Legal abortion. A prospective study of outpatient legal abortion in the Municipal hosptial in Arhus during a 1 year period," by B. R. Moller, et al. UGESKRIFT FOR LAEGER 138(6):329-333, February 2, 1976.

"Legal abortions at the University-Gynecological Clinic Mannheim during 1971-1974," by W. von Mühlenfels, et al. FORTSCHRITTE DU MEDIZIN 93(31):1530-1536, November 6, 1975.

"Legal aspects of some methods of birth-control," by
N. Endre. DEMOGRAFIA 13, 4:355-385, 1970.
(Socio. Abstrs. 1976, 76I0044)

"Legal consequences of the 'right' to abortion," by L.
E. Rozovsky. DIMENSIONS IN HEALTH SERVICE
53(4):14-15, April, 1976.

"Management of failed prostaglandin abortion," by N. H.
Lauersen, et al. OBSTETRICS AND GYNECOLOGY
47(4):473-378, 1976. (Bio. Abstrs. 1976, 16203)

"Massive invasion of fetal lymphocytes into the mother's
blood at induced abortion," by R. Zilliacus, et al.
SCANDINAVIAN JOURNAL OF IMMUNOLOGY 4(5-6):
601-605, September, 1975.

"May hospitals prohibit abortions and sterilizations?"
by J. A. Turpin. MEDICO-LEGAL BULLETIN
24(9):1-9, September, 1975.

"Mechanism of action of prostaglandin F2 alpha and its
clinical use in obstetrics," by L. S. Persianinov.
AKUSHERSTVO I GINEKOLOGIIA (Moscow) (6):7-15,
June, 1975.

"Menstrual induction by the vaginal application of ICI
81008 gel," by A. I. Csapo, et al. PROSTAGLANDINS
12(3):455-461, September, 1976.

"Menstrual induction: its place in clinical practice," by
K. R. Irani, et al. OBSTETRICS AND GYNECOLOGY
46(5):596-598, November, 1975.

"Menstrual induction with the PGF2alpha analogue ICI
81008," by A. I. Csapo, et al. PROSTAGLANDINS
11(1):155-162, January, 1976.

"Menstrual regulation." (editorial). LANCET 1(7966):

947, May 1, 1976.

"Menstrual regulation (a new procedure for fertility control," by C. S. Dawn, et al. JOURNAL OF THE INDIAN MEDICAL ASSOCIATION 64(11):293-296, June 1, 1975.

"Methodological observations on research concerning the effects of induced abortions," by R. Andorka, et al. DEMOGRAFIA 17, 1:63-73, 1974. (Socio. Abstrs. 1976, 76I1392)

"Midtrimester abortion induced by serial intramuscular injections of 15(S)-15-methyl-prostaglandin E2 methyl ester," by N. H. Lauersen, et al. AMERICAN JOURNAL OF OBSTETRICS AND GYNECOLOGY 123(7):665-670, December 1, 1975.

"Midtrimester pregnancy termination by intramuscular injection of a 15-methyl analogue of prostaglandin F2 alpha," by J. Robins, et al. AMERICAN JOURNAL OF OBSTETRICS AND GYNECOLGOY 123(6):625-631, November 15, 1975.

"Midtrimester pregnancy termination with prostaglandin E2 vaginal suppositories," by M. Hochman, et al. JOURNAL OF REPRODUCTIVE MEDICINE 16(5):263-268, May, 1976.

"Midtrimester prostaglandin-induced abortion: gross and light microscopic findings in the placenta," by L. H. Honore. PROSTAGLANDINS 11(6):1019-1032, 1976. (Bio. Abstrs. 1976, 62674)

"Mid-trimester termination." (editorial). BRITISH MEDICAL JOURNAL 1(6022):1357-1358, June 5, 1976.

"Mid-trimester termination," (letter), by R. V. Clements, et al. BRITISH MEDICAL JOURNAL 2(6035):587,

September 4, 1976.

"Modern use of the laminaria tent," by K. R. Niswander.
MOUNT SINAI JOURNAL OF MEDICINE, NEW YORK
42(5):424-430, September-October, 1975.

"Miscarriage and abortion: I. Induced and spontaneous
abortion. Psychopathological aspects in connection
with a first sample of 411 requests for interruption
of pregnancy," by M. Bourgeois, et al. ANNALES
MEDICO-PSYCHOLOGIQUES 2(2):339-366, July,
1975. (Psycho. Abstrs. 1976, 12347)

--II. Voluntary abortion and resistance to contraception,"
by M. Bourgeois, et al. ANNALES MEDICO-PSYCHO-
LOGIQUES 2(2):366-377, July, 1975. (Psycho. Abstrs.
1976, 12348)

"Morphological studies on cases of early abortion with
special reference to HCG excretion," by M. Hölzl, et
al. ARCHIV FUR GYNAEKOLOGIE 219(1-4):550-551,
November 18, 1975.

"The need for more facts about abortion?" (editorial).
JOURNAL OF THE ROYAL COLLEGE OF GENERAL
PRACTITIONERS 25(153):235-236, April, 1975.

"Neonatal death after induced abortion," by R. Prywes,
et al. HAREFUAH 90(10):453-456, May 16, 1976.

"A new ethical approach to abortion and its implications
for the euthanasia dispute," by R. F. Gardner.
JOURNAL OF MEDICAL ETHICS 1(3):127-131,
September, 1975.

"Observation of the behavior of aborted women in the days
immediately following abortion," by M. Houmont.
REVUE MEDICALE DE LIEGE 30(8):261-265,
April 15, 1975.

INDUCED ABORTION

"The outcome of pregnancy in former oral contraceptive
users." BRITISH JOURNAL OF OBSTETRICS AND
GYNAECOLOGY 83(8):608-616, August, 1976.

"Outpatient legal abortion. 500 operations with paracervical anesthesia," by J. Prest, et al. UGE-
SKRIFT FOR LAEGER 138(6):333-335, February 2,
1976.

"Outpatient legal abortion using a modified Vabra aspir-
ator and paracervical anesthesia," by J. Prest, et al.
UGESKRIFT FOR LAEGER 138(6):336-338,
February 2, 1976.

"Outpatient postconceptional fertility control with vaginally
administered 15(S) 15-methyl-PGF2alpha-methyl ester,"
by M. Bygdeman, et al. AMERICAN JOURNAL OF
OBSTETRICS AND GYNECOLOGY 124(5):495-498,
March 1, 1976.

"Paracervical block with etidocaine for out-patient
abortion," by G. Willdeck-Lund, et al. ACTA
ANAESTHESIOLOGICA SCANDINAVICA. SUPPLE-
MENT (60):106-109, 1975.

"Pathophysiology of disseminated intravascular coagulation
in saline-induced abortion," by R. K. Laros, Jr., et
al. OBSTETRICS AND GYNECOLOGY 48(3):353-356,
September, 1976.

"Performing second-trimester abortions. Rationale for
inpatient basis," by G. Stroh, et al. NEW YORK
STATE JOURNAL OF MEDICINE 75(12):2168-2171,
October, 1975.

"PGE2 as a vaginal abortifacient - diaphragm effect,"
(letter), by S. L. Corson, et al. PROSTAGLANDINS
10(3):543-544, September, 1975.

217

"Phosphoglucomutase phenotypes and prenatal selection. Studies of spontaneous and induced abortions," by G. Beckman, et al. HUMAN HEREDITY 25(3):172-176, 1975.

"The placental and fetal response to the intra-amniotic injection of prostaglandin F2alpha in midtrimester abortions," by P. Jouppila, et al. BRITISH JOURNAL OF OBSTETRICS AND GYNAECOLOGY 83(4):303-306, April, 1976.

"Placental cultures for cytogenetic assessment in saline-aborted fetuses," by H. A. Gardner, et al. AMERICAN JOURNAL OF OBSTETRICS AND GYNE-COLOGY 126(3):350-352, October 1, 1976.

"Plasma levels of the methyl ester of 15-methyl PGF2a in connection with intravenous and vaginal administration to the human," by K. Green, et al. PROSTA-GLANDINS 11(5):879-892, 1976. (Bio. Abstrs. 1976, 62691)

"Plasma renin activity in abortion," by P. Soveri, et al. ACTA OBSTETRICIA ET GYNECOLOGICA SCANDI-NAVICA 55(2):175-177, 1976. (Bio. Abstrs. 1976, 30739)

"Possibilities for work organization in the abortion sections of district gynecology departments," by D. Andreev, et al. AKUSHERSTVO I GINEKOLOGIIA (Sofia) 13(6):466-471, 1974.

"Postabortion insertion of the intrauterine copper T (TCu 200). pp. 115-118," by K. G. Nygren, et al. In: Hefnawi F, Segal SJ, ed. Analysis of intrauterine contraception. Amsterdam, North-Holland, 1975. W3 IN182AI 1974a.

"Pregnancy and abortion in adolescence. Report of a

WHO meeting." WORLD HEALTH ORGANIZATION
TECHNICAL REPORT SERIES (583):1-27, 1975.

"Pregnancy interruption by vacuum aspiration," (letter),
by G. Gergely. ORVOSI HETILAP 116(46):2748-2749,
November 16, 1975.

"Pregnancy planning/abortion," (letter), by C. Tietze.
FAMILY PLANNING PERSPECTIVES 7(6):247,
November-December, 1975.

"The problem of abortion. Viewpoint of the general
practitioner," by J. Henrion. REVUE MEDICALE
DE LIEGE 30(8):249-253, April 15, 1975.

"The problem of abortion. Viewpoint of a gynecologist,"
by A. Wery. REVUE MEDICALE DE LIEGE
April 15, 1975.

"Problem of abortions in the European socialist countries,"
by V. V. Bodrova. ZDRAVOOKHRANENIE ROSSIISKOI
FEDERATSII (5):34-40, May, 1975.

"Problem of causative relation between pregnancy interruption and following premature termination of pregnancy," by R. Voigt, et al. ZENTRALBLATT FUR
GYNAEKOLOGIE 97(22):1375-1377, 1975.

"Preliminary trials of vaginal silastic devices containing
(15s)-15 methyl prostaglandin F2 alpha methyl ester
for the induction of menses and for pregnancy termination summary of brook lodge workshop (January 29,
1976)," by E. M. Southern. PROSTAGLANDINS
12 Suppl:147-152, 1976.

"Problems of decision making of interruption commissions,"
by D. Fukalova. CESKOSLOVENSKA GYNEKOLOGIE
40(9):669-671, November, 1975.

"Progesterone levels in amniotic fluid and maternal plasma in prostaglandin F2alpha-induced midtrimester abortion,' by Z. Koren, et al. OBSTETRICS AND GYNECOLOGY 48(4):427 passim, October, 1976.

"Prostaglandin F2 alpha as abortifacient agent. Practical aspects," by M. Bydgeman. LAKARTIDNINGEN 76(32): 2621-2623, August 4, 1976.

"Prostaglandin gel for the induction of abortion and labor in fetal death," (proceedings), by T. Modly, et al. ARCHIV FUR GYNAEKOLOGIE 219(1-4):498-499, November 18, 1975.

"Prostaglandins and post-abortion luteolysis in early pregnancy," by A. Leader, et al. PROSTAGLANDINS 10(5):889-897, November, 1975.

"Prostaglandins: basic reproductive consideration and new clinical applications. pp. 157-181," by F. Naftolin. In: Kahn RH, Lands WE, ed. Prostaglandins and cyclic AMP. New York, Academic Press, 1973. QU 90 S991p 1972.

"Psychosocial aspects of abortion. A review of issues and needed research," by R. Illsley, et al. BULLETIN OF THE WORLD HEALTH ORGANIZATION 53(1):83-106, 1976.

"Psychological bases of the two-child norm," by R. D. Kahoe. CATALOG OF SELECTED DOCUMENTS IN PSYCHOLOGY 5, 282, Summer, 1975. (Psycho. Abstrs. 1976, 9619)

"Psychological causes and impact of abortion," by P. Jadoul. REVUE MEDICALE DE LIEGE 30(8):258-261, April 15, 1975.

"A question of clinical freedom," by B. Watkin. NURSING

MIRROR AND MIDWIVES JOURNAL 142(18):42,
April 29, 1976.

"A question of conscience," (letter), by R. Salm.
BRITISH MEDICAL JOURNAL 1(6025):1593, June 26,
1976.

"A question of conscience," by R. Walley. BRITISH
MEDICAL JOURNAL 1(6023):1456-1458, June 12, 1976.

"Reflections on abortion, a current and ageless problem,"
by L. Derobert. MEDECINE LEGALE ET DOMMAGE
CORPOREL 7(4):289-291, October-December, 1974.

"The relative risks of sterilization alone and in combination with abortion," by K. G. B. Edström. BULLETIN
OF THE WORLD HEALTH ORGANIZATION 52(2):141-
148, 1975. (Bio. Abstrs. 1976, 16962)

"Report of study group on prostaglandin. pp. 5-8." In:
Bergström S, ed. Report from meetings of the
Prostaglandin Task Force Steering Committee.
Stockholm, 1973. QV 175 W927r 1972-1973.

"Reported live births following induced abortion: two and
one-half years' experience in Upstate New York," by
G. Stroh, et al. AMERICAN JOURNAL OF OBSTE-
TRICS AND GYNECOLOGY 126(1):83-90, September 1,
1976.

"Requests for termination of pregnancy: psychogenesis
and assistance," by G. Resta. MINERVA GINECOL-
OGIA 27(8):600-606, August, 1975.

"Results with intra-amniotic administration. pp 33-36,"
by W. Brenner, et al. In: Bergström S, ed. Report
from meetings of the Prostaglandin Task Force
Steering Committee. Stockholm, 1973. QV 175
W927r 1972-1973.

"Somatic complications after induced abortion," (letter), by E. Arnesen, et al. TIDSSKRIFT FOR DEN NORSKE LAEGEFORENING 96(15):899-900, May 30, 1976.

"Somatic complications following abortions," by K. Molne, et al. TIDSSKRIFT FOR DEN NORSKE LAEGEFOREN-ING 96(8):483-488, March 20, 1976.

"Somatic complications of induced abortion," (editorial), by P. Bergsjö. TIDSSKRIFT FOR DEN NORSKE LAEGEFORENING 96(8):524-525, March 20, 1976.

"Some forensic problems of commissions for the inter-ruption of pregnancy," by J. Lysican. CESKOSLO-VENSKA GYNEKOLOGIE 40(10):737-738, December, 1975.

"A state-registered abortionist?" (editorial). LANCET 2(7941):912-913, November 8, 1975.

"Suboptimal pregnancy outcome among women with prior abortions and premature births," by S. J. Funderburk, et al. AMERICAN JOURNAL OF OBSTETRICS AND GYNECOLOGY 126(1):55-60, September 1, 1976.

"Supreme Court unwilling to settle state action conflict," by P. F. Geary. HOSPITAL PROGRESS 57(5):6, 12, May, 1976.

"The synergistic effect of calcium and prostaglandin F2alpha in second trimester abortion. A pilot study," by L. Weinstein, et al. OBSTETRICS AND GYNECOL-OGY 48(4):469-471, October, 1976.

"Synergetic effect of hypertonic NaCl solution and PGF 2 alpha in induced abortion of the second trimester," by N. Vujakovic, et al. JUGOSLOVENSKA GINEKOL-OGIJA I OPSTETRICIJA 16(1):59-64, January-February, 1976.

"Systemic and local administration of prostaglandins for postconceptional fertility control. pp. 108-115," by M. Toppozada, et al. In: Bergström S, ed. Report from meetings of the Prostaglandin Task Force Steering Committee. Stockholm, 1973. QV 175 W927r 1972-1973.

"Teenagers: fertility control behavior and attitudes before and after abortion, childbearing or negative pregnancy test," by J. R. Evans, et al. FAMILY PLANNING PERSPECTIVES 8(4):192-200, July-August, 1976.

"Terbutaline inhibition of midtrimester uterine activity induced by prostaglandin F2alpha and hypertonic saline," by K. E. Andersson, et al. BRITISH JOURNAL OF OBSTETRICS AND GYNAECOLOGY 82(9):745-749, September, 1975.

"The termination of human pregnancy with prostaglandin analogs," by G. D. Gutknecht, et al. JOURNAL OF REPRODUCTIVE MEDICINE

"Termination of late first-trimester and early second-trimester gestations with intramuscular 15 (S)-15-methyl prostaglandin F2alpha," by R. J. Bolognese, et al. JOURNAL OF REPRODUCTIVE MEDICINE 16(2):81-84, February, 1976.

"Termination of late-term pregnancy in intra-amniotic administration of prostaglandin and hypertonic saline solution," by E. A. Chernukha, et al. AKUSHERSTVO I GINEKOLOGIIA (Moscow) (6):19-24, June, 1975.

"Termination of midtirmester pregnancy by serial intra-muscular injections of 15(S)-15-methyl-prostaglandin F2alpha," by N. H. Lauersen, et al. AMERICAN JOURNAL OF OBSTETRICS AND GYNECOLOGY 124 (2):169-176, January 15, 1976.

"Termination of pregnancy," by A. McQueen. NURSING MIRROR AND MIDWIVES' JOURNAL 142:45-47, June 17, 1976.

"Termination of pregnancy in cases of fetal death in utero by intravenous prostaglandin F2alpha," by A. P. Lange, et al. PROSTAGLANDINS 11(1):101-108, January, 1976.

"Termination of pregnancy with double prostaglandin impact," by A. I. Csapo, et al. AMERICAN JOURNAL OF OBSTETRICS AND GYNECOLOGY 124(1):1-13, January 1, 1976.

"350 requests of abortion. What happens just two years before?" by A. M. Lanoy, et al. PRAXIS 64(10): 295-298, March 11, 1975.

"Trans-isthmicocervical intra-amniotic instillation of hypertonic sodium solutions for termination of pregnancy after the 1st trimester," by I. Kosowski. ZENTRALBLATT FUR GYNAEKOLOGIE 97(18):1130-1135, 1975.

"Trends in attitudes toward abortion, 1972-1975," by W. R. Arney, et al. FAMILY PLANNING PERSPECTIVES 8:117-124, May-June, 1976.

"Ultrasound in the management of elective abortion," by R. C. Sanders, et al. AMERICAN JOURNAL OF ROENTGENOLOGY 125(2):469-473, October, 1975.

"The unwanted child: caring for the fetus born alive after an abortion." HASTINGS CENTER REPORT 6(5):10-15, October, 1976.

"Ureter-uterus fistula after abortion," by W. Hardt, et al. ZEITSCHRIFT FUR UROLOGIE UND NEPHROLOGIE 68(10):761-764, October, 1975.

"Use of combination prostaglandin F2alpha and hypertonic saline for midtirmester abortion. Department of Obstetrics and Gynecology Harvard Medical School, Beth Israel Hospital, Boston, Massachusetts." PROSTAGLANDINS 12(4):625-630, October, 1976.

"Use of prostaglandins in gynecology and obstetrics," by B. I. Nesheim. TIDSSKRIFT FOR DEN NORSKE LAEGEFORENING 96(6):375-376, February 28, 1976.

"Use of prostaglandins for induction of abortion," by E. A. Chernukha. AKUSHERSTVO I GINEKOLOGIIA (Moscow) (7):7-10, July, 1975.

"The use of silastic vaginal device containing (15S)-15 methyl prostaglandin F2 alpha methyl ester for early first trimester pregnancy termination," by J. Robins. PROSTAGLANDINS 12 Suppl:123-134, 1976.

"The use of surgery to avoid childbearing among Navajo and Hopi Indians. pp. 9-21," by S. J. Kunitz, et al. In: Kaplan BA, ed. Anthropological studies of human fertility. Detroit, Wayne State Univ Press, 1976. GN 241 S989a 1975.

"Vaginal cytology in induced abortion," by S. Dossland, et al. TIDSSKRIFT FOR DEN NORSKE LAEGEFORENING 96(16):937-938, June 10, 1976.

"Vaginally administered 16, 16-dimethyl-PGE2 for the induction of midtrimester abortion," by J. N. Martin, Jr., et al. PROSTAGLANDINS 11(1):123-132, 1976. (Bio. Abstrs. 1976, 4269)

"Violent perforations of the uterus in the 10-year material of the Gynecologic-Obstetrical Department in Bitola," by T. Pasanku. MEDICINSKI ARKIV 28(3):337-339, May-June, 1974.

"What are the bonds between the fetus and the uterus?"
by V. W. Adamkiewicz. CANADIAN NURSE 72(2):
26-28, February, 1976.

"What are the bonds between the fetus and the uterus,"
by V. Adamkiewicz. INFIRMIÈRE CANADIENNE
18(2):26-28, February, 1976.

"The WHO Prostaglandin Task Force. (Protocol manual).
Phase IIb clinical trials comparing intra-amniotic
prostaglandin F2alpha and 15-methyl PGE2alpha.
(Trial No. 103). pp. 65-78." In: Bergström S, ed.
Report from meetings of the Prostaglandin Task
Force Steering Committee. Stockholm, 1973. QV 175
W927r 1972-1973.

--Phase III clinical trials of intra-amniotic prostaglandin
F2alpha versus hypertonic saline (trial no. 101) and
extra-amniotic prostaglandin F2alpha (trial no. 102).
pp. 12-27." In: Bergström S, ed. Report from meetings
of the Prostaglandin Task Force Steering Committee.
Stockholm, 1973. QV 175 W927r 1972-1973.

"The WHO Prostaglandin Task Force. Report from the
Prostaglandin Task Force Meeting, Geneva, February 26-
28, 1973. pp. 31-32." In: Bergström S, ed. Report
from meetings of the Prostaglandin Task Force Steering
Committee. Stockholm, 1973. QV 175 W927r 1972-1973.

--Report from the Prostaglandin Task Force Meeting,
Stockholm, October 2-3, 1972. pp. 9-11." In:
Bergström S, ed. Report from meetings of the Prostaglandin Task Force Steering Committee. Stockholm,
1973. QV 175 W927r 1972-1973.

"Women's experience of the abortion procedure," by L.
Jacobsson, et al. SOCIAL PSYCHIATRY 10(4), 155-160,
October, 1975.

INDUCED ABORTION

"Women's experience of local anesthesia in early legal
abortions," by U. Idahl, et al. LAKARTIDNINGEN
73(34):2745-2746, August 18, 1976.

INFANTICIDE

INFECTION
see: Complications

ISOPTIN

ISOXSUPRINE
"Interpretative analysis of 50 cases of tocolysis treated
with isoxsuprine," by A. Tomassini, et al.
MINERVA GINECOLOGIA 27(11):861-873, November,
1975.

LAW ENFORCEMENT
see: Laws and Legislation

LAWS AND LEGISLATION
"Abortion." (editorial). LANCET 2(7980):296, August 7,
1976.

"Abortion." THE NEW YORK TIMES (S) January 27,
12:3, 1976.

"Abortion," (editorial), by W. R. Barclay. JAMA;
JOURNAL OF THE AMERICAN MEDICAL ASSOCIATION
236(4):388, July 26, 1976.

"Abortion (amendment) bill," (letter), by J. B. Metcalfe.
BRITISH MEDICAL JOURNAL 3(5982):544, August 30,
1975.

"Abortion and the constitution: the need for a life-
protective amendment," by R. A. Destro. CALIFOR-
NIA LAW REVIEW 63:1250-1351, September, 1975.

"Abortion and contraception information during first
period under new legislation," by K. Sundström.
LAKARTIDNINGEN 72(38):35313533, September 17,
1975.

"Abortion and fertility control (a brief world review),"
by R. Dutta. JOURNAL OF THE INDIAN MEDICAL
ASSOCIATION 64(11):315-320, June 1, 1975.

"Abortion and inalienable rights in classical liberalism,"
by G. D. Glenn. AMERICAN JOURNAL OF JURIS-
PRUDENCE 20:62-80, 1975.

"Abortion and maternal deaths." (editorial). BRITISH
MEDICAL JOURNAL 2(6027):70, July 10, 1976.

"Abortion because of other the desired fetal sex?" by E.
Schwinger. BEITRAEGE ZUR GERICHTLICHEN
MEDIZIN 33:46-48, 1975.

"Abortion, conscience and the constitution: an examination
of federal institutional conscience clauses," by H. F.
Pilpel. COLUMBIA HUMAN RIGHTS LAW REVIEW
6:279-305, Fall-Winter, 1974-1975.

"Abortion conscience clauses." COLUMBIA JOURNAL
OF LAW AND SOCIAL PROBLEMS 11:571-627,
Summer, 1975.

"Abortion Curb Defeated." THE NEW YORK TIMES (S)
June 29, 14:3, 1976.

"The Abortion Decision." (editorial). THE NEW YORK
TIMES July 3, 20:1, 1976.

"Abortion decision and evolving limits on state intervention," by D. MacDougal, et al. HAWAII BAR
JOURNAL 11:51-72, Fall, 1974.

"Abortion: how we won the battle and nearly lost the war," by P. Ashdown-Sharp. NOVA 62-64, October, 1975.

"Abortion: the husband's constitutional rights," by W. D. H. Teo. ETHICS 85:337-342, July, 1975; Reply by L. M. Purdy 86:247-251, April, 1976.

"Abortion in India," by R. P. Mohan. SOCIAL SCIENCE 50, 3:141-143, Summer, 1975.

"Abortion in 1975: the psychiatric perspective, with a discussion of abortion and contraception in adolescence," by P. D. Barglow. JOGN; JOURNAL OF OBSTETRIC, GYNECOLOGIC AND NEONATAL NURSING 5(1):41-48, January-February, 1976.

"Abortion incidence and medical legislation in Scandinavia," by K. Sundström. LAKARTIDNINGEN 73(36):2896, September 1, 1976.

"Abortion increase in Scandinavia in 1975." NORDISK VETERINAER MEDICA 91(4):115, April, 1976.

"The abortion law and legal paradox," by J. Crawford. MONTH 9:97-100, March, 1976.

"An abortion law update," by A. H. Bernstein. HOSPITALS 50(11):90-92, June 1, 1976.

"Abortion law: what for?" ECONOMIST 258:34, February 11, 1976.

"Abortion liberalization: a worldwide trend," by L. R. Brown, et al. FUTURIST 10:140-143, June, 1976.

"Abortion: a logical oddity," by J. M. Crawford. NEW LAW JOURNAL 126:252-254, 298-299, March 11-18, 1976.

"Abortive Medicaid." (editorial). THE NEW YORK
TIMES (M) September 17, I, 22:1, 1976.

"Abortion: Medicaid's unwanted child?" WOMEN'S
RIGHTS LAW REPORTER 3:22-27, September, 1975.

"Abortion need and services in the United States, 1974-
1975," by E. Weinstock, et al. FAMILY PLANNING
PERSPECTIVES 8(2):58-69, March-April, 1976.

"Abortion: Perception and contemporary genocide myth:
a comparative study among low-income pregnant
Black and Puerto Rican women," by B. R. Hughes.
DISSERTATION ABSTRACTS INTERNATIONAL 34
(6-A):3542-3543, December, 1973. (Psycho. Abstrs.
1976, 4369)

"Abortion, the public morals, and the police power: the
ethical function of substantive due process," by M. J.
Perry. U.C.L.A. LAW REVIEW 23:689-736,
April, 1976.

"Abortion recommendations accepted." BRITISH MEDI-
CAL JOURNAL 4(5991):293-294, November 1, 1975.

"Abortion: rights and risks," by D. Rice. HARPERS
BAZAAR 109:71 passim, June, 1976.

"Abortion Ruling." THE NEW YORK TIMES (S) October 24, IV, 6:6, 1976.

"Abortion Ruling is Expected to Affect Restrictive Laws in
at Least 26 States," by S. S. King. THE NEW YORK
TIMES (M) July 2, I, 8:3, 1976.

"Abortion Ruling 'Monumental' to Some, 'Appalling' to
Others," by T. Goldstein. THE NEW YORK TIMES
(M) July 2, I, 9:1, 1976.

"Abortion-seeking women's views on the importance of
social benefits as an alternative to induced abortion,"
T. Ganes, et al. TIDSSKRIFT FOR DEN NORSKE
LAEGEFORENING 96(13):768-770, May 10, 1976.

"Abortion: an unresolved issue--are parental consent
statutes unconstitutional?" NEBRASKA LAW REVIEW
55:256-282, 1976.

"Abortion vs. manslaughter," (letter), by W. V. Dolan.
ARCHIVES OF SURGERY 111(1):93, January, 1976.

"Abortions denied," by L. Lader. NATION 223:38-39,
July 17, 1976.

"Acquittal of Canadian Physician in Illegal-Abortion Case
Upheld," by R. Trumbull. THE NEW YORK TIMES
(M) January 21, 12:4, 1976.

"Administrative law--social security--availability of
medicaid funds for elective abortions." WAYNE
LAW REVIEW 22:857-870, March, 1976.

"Albany Changes Bill on Abortion," by R. Smothers.
THE NEW YORK TIMES (M) May 26, 34:3, 1976.

"All Charges Withdrawn in Quebec Abortion Case."
THE NEW YORK TIMES (S) December 11, 9:6, 1976.

"Allied health board on abortion: Patients have to be
favored more than the personnel." LAKARTIDNINGEN
72(51):5042, December 17, 1975.

"Analysis of the 1974 Massachusetts abortion statute and
a minor's right to abortion." NEW ENGLAND LAW
REVIEW 10:417-454, Spring, 1975.

"Annual abortion action," by C. Ingham. MS MAGAZINE
4:79, February, 1976.

"Another opinion on abortion." SYGEPLEJERSKEN
75(33):13-14, August 20, 1975.

"The Antiabortion Bill is Vetoed by Carey," by I.
Peterson. THE NEW YORK TIMES (M) June 23,
42:2, 1976.

"Anti-abortion Unit Calls for Inquiry." THE NEW YORK
TIMES (S) July 4, 18:8, 1976.

"Assembly Revives an Abortion Bill," by L. Brown. THE
NEW YORK TIMES (M) June 3, 74:5, 1976.

"Assembly's Abortion Bill Advances, Then Falters," by
R. Smothers. THE NEW YORK TIMES (M) May 14,
II, 4:7, 1976.

"Availability of abortion, sterilization, and other medical
treatment for minor patients," by L. J. Dunn, Jr.
UNIVERSITY OF MISSOURI AT KANSAS CITY LAW
REVIEW 44:1-22, Fall, 1975.

"The bad old days: clandestine abortions among the poor
in New York City before liberalization of the abortion
law," by S. Polgar, et al. FAMILY PLANNING
PERSPECTIVES 8(3):125-127, May-June, 1976.

"Ban all abortions? Yes--1 million lives are destroyed
each year; interview with Archbishop J. L. Bernardin;
No--we believe in a woman's right to make her own
choice; interview with Rabbi R. S. Sternberger."
U.S. NEWS AND WORLD REPORT 81:27-28, September 27, 1976.

"Battle underway on funding of abortions by government."
OUR SUNDAY VISITOR 65:2, August 8, 1976.

"Bill Restricting Abortions Passed by Senate in Albany,"
by R. Smothers. THE NEW YORK TIMES (M)

March 31, 18:3, 1976.

"Bishop asks Catholics join Washington March for Life."
OUR SUNDAY VISITOR 64:3, January 18, 1976.

"Canada's Top Court Bars Move to Reverse Abortion
Acquittal." THE NEW YORK TIMES (M) March 16,
4:5, 1976.

"The Canadian abortion law," (letter), by P. G. Coffey.
CANADIAN MEDICAL ASSOCIATION JOURNAL
115(3):211-216, August 7, 1976.

"The Canadian abortion law," (letter), by M. Cohen, et
al. CANADIAN MEDICAL ASSOCIATION JOURNAL
114(7):593, April 3, 1976.

"Canadian Physician, Jailed in Abortion Case, is Freed."
THE NEW YORK TIMES (S) January 27, 2:5, 1976.

"Compromise reached on use of federal funds for abortions," by T. P. Southwick. CONGRESSIONAL
QUARTERLY WEEKLY REPORT 34:2541, September 18, 1976.

"Compulsory abortion: next challenge to liberated women?"
by G. S. Swan. OHIO NORTHERN UNIVERSITY
LAW REVIEW 3:152-175, 1975.

"Conference Vote Ban on Medicaid Funds for Most Abortions," by D. E. Rosenbaum. THE NEW YORK
TIMES (M) September 16, 1:3, 1976.

"Confronting objections to an anti-abortion amendment,"
by R. Byrn. AMERICA 134:529-534, June 19, 1976.

"Congress Acts on Abortion." (editorial). THE NEW
YORK TIMES (S) September 19, IV, 2:2, 1976.

"Congress Approves Curb on Abortions, but Veto is Likely," by D. E. Rosenbaum. THE NEW YORK TIMES (M) September 18, 1:6, 1976.

"Congress Overrides Ford's Veto of Bill of Social Services," by R. D. Lyons. THE NEW YORK TIMES (M) October 1, I, 1:1, 1976.

"Connecticut Loses Suit Over Minor's Abortions." THE NEW YORK TIMES (S) October 3, 41:1, 1976

"Conscience clause may be next target of proabortion forces," by E. J. Schulte. HOSPITAL PROGRESS 57:19 passim, August, 1976.

"Conscience of the law," by J. E. Hogan. CAHTOLIC LAWYER 21:190-196, Summer, 1975.

"Consent question--parental and spousal consent for abortions," by C. D. Davis. TEX HOSPITALS 32:27-30, September, 1976.

"Constitutional law--abortion--parental and spousal consent requirements violate right to privacy in abortion decision." KANSAS LAW REVIEW 24: 446-462, Winter, 1976.

"Constitutional law--abortion--Utah statute requiring notification of husband by physician upheld." WESTERN STATE UNIVERSITY LAW REVIEW 3:313-323, Spring, 1976.

"Constitutional law--commercial speech doctrine--a clarification of the protection afforded advertising under the first amendment." BRIGHAM YOUNG UNIVERSITY LAW REVIEW 1975:797-811, 1975.

"Constitutional law--denial of equal protection to patient as also constituting denial of equal protection to

234

physician." UNIVERSITY OF TOLEDO LAW REVIEW
7:213-229, Fall, 1975.

"Constitutional law--first amendment--freedom of speech--
advertising cannot be denied first amendment protection, absent a showing by the state of a legitimate
public interest justifying its regulation." UNIVERSITY
OF CINCINNATI LAW REVIEW 44:852-859, 1975.

"Constitutional law--first amendment--newspaper
advertisement of abortion referral service entitled
to first amendment protection." UNIVERSITY OF
RICHMOND LAW REVIEW 10:427-433, Winter, 1976.

"Constitutional law--first amendment--United States
Supreme Court held that the first amendment protected
an abortion advertisement which conveyed information
of potential interest to an audience, despite its
appearance in the form of a paid commercial advertisement." INDIANA LAW REVIEW 8:890-897, 1975.

"Constitutional law--freedom of the press--prohibition of
abortion referral service advertising held unconstitutional." CORNELL LAW REVIEW 61:640-660, April,
1976.

"Constitutional right of privacy--minor's right to an
abortion--statutory requirement of spousal consent,
or parental consent in the case of an unmarried, minor
female, is an unconstitutional deprivation of a woman's
right to determine whether to undergo an abortion."
HOFSTRA LAW REVIEW 4:531-547, Winter, 1976.

"Constitutional validity of abortion legislation: a comparative note," by H. P. Glenn. MCGILL LAW
JOURNAL 21:673-684, Winter, 1975.

"Contraceptive practice and prevention as alternative to
legitimization of indiscriminate abortion," by I.

235

Vandelli, et al. ANNALI DI OSTETRICIA, GINE-
COLOGIA, MEDICINA PERINATALE 96(4):254-273,
July-August, 1975.

"Consultation for abortion. Experiences and results,"
by V. S. Sievers, et al. FORTSCHRITTE DU
MEDIZIN 94(2):70-72, January 15, 1976.

"Cooke, On Anniversary of Ruling, Scores Court's Abortion Position," by G. Dugan. THE NEW YORK TIMES
(M) January 23, 20:4, 1976.

"Courageous Veto." (editorial). THE NEW YORK
TIMES June 25, I, 26:2, 1976.

"Court abortion decisions draw strong criticisms."
OUR SUNDAY VISITOR 65:2, July 18, 1976.

"Court Lifts Medicaid Ban for Voluntary Abortions."
THE NEW YORK TIMES (S) March 11, 42:6, 1976.

"Criminal abortion using ruta roots (Ruta graveolens
L.)," by K. Wehr. BEITRAEGE ZUR GERICHTLICHEN
MEDIZIN 32:126-131, 1974.

"Criminal law: defence: charge of performing illegal
abortion." OTTAWA LAW REVIEW 8:59-69, Winter,
1976.

"Dangerous developments on the subject of therapeutic
abortion: Italy's decisions after the Seveso contamination," by G. Guzzetti. L'OSSERVATORE ROMANO
39[443]11, September 23, 1976.

"Death Bill." (editorial). THE NEW YORK TIMES
May 11, 32:2, 1976.

"Debating abortion: a non-Catholic and a scientist; amend
the constitution," by H. Arkes. WALL STREET

JOURNAL 188:26, October 26, 1976.

"Democrats for Life formed to work for an amendment."
OUR SUNDAY VISITOR 65:2, August 1, 1976.

"Disclosure on abortion," (letter), by P. J. Huntingford.
LANCET 1(7956):434-435, February 21, 1976.

"Dissent '76; amendment not answer to abortion," by
M. Bunson. NATIONAL CATHOLIC REPORTER
12:5, March 26, 1976.

"Doctor asks Court to Overturn His Conviction in Fetus
Death." THE NEW YORK TIMES (S) April 6, 25:2,
1976.

"Doe v. Doe [(Mass) 314 N E 2d 128]: the wife's right
to an abortion over her husband's objections." NEW
ENGLAND LAW REVIEW 11:205-224, Fall, 1975.

"Doe v. Beal (523 F 2d 611): abortion. Medicaid and
equal portection." VIRGINIA LAW REVIEW 62:
811-837, May, 1976.

"Domestic relations: minors and abortion--the requirements of parental consent." OKLAHOMA LAW RE-
VIEW 29:145-155, Winter, 1976.

"Draft letter on abortion sent bishops." NATIONAL
CATHOLIC REPORTER 12:14, January 9, 1976.

"Due process and equal protection: constitutional implications of abortion notice and reporting requirements."
BOSTON UNIVERSITY LAW REVIEW 56:522-541, May,
1976.

"Dutch Senate, by 7 Votes, Rejects Legal Abortions;
Coalition Crisis Allayed." THE NEW YORK TIMES
(S) December 15, I, 14:3, 1976.

LAWS AND LEGISLATION

"Economic value of statute reform: the case of liberalized abortion," by T. A. Deyak, et al. JOURNAL OF POLITICAL ECONOMY 84:83-99, February, 1976.

"Edelin case rekindles right-to-life hopes," by R. Adams. FAITH FOR THE FAMILY 9, November-December, 1975.

"Effects of legal termination and subsequent pregnancy," (letter), by R. E. Coles, et al. BRITISH MEDICAL JOURNAL 2(6026):45, July 3, 1976.

"Effects of legal termination on subsequent pregnancy," (letter), by G. Dixon, et al. BRITISH MEDICAL JOURNAL 2(6030):299, July 31, 1976.

"Effects of legal termination on subsequent pregnancy," by J. A. Richardson, et al. BRITISH MEDICAL JOURNAL 1(6021):1303-1304, May 29, 1976.

"The effects of a liberalized abortion law on pregnancy outcome. pp. 135-137," by J. T. Lanman, et al. In: Kelly S, et al. , ed. Birth defects: risks and consequences. New York, Academic Press, 1976. OS 675 B622 1974.

"An Emotional Issue's Status in the Courts," by L. Oelsner. THE NEW YORK TIMES (M) March 1, 28:1, 1976.

"End of Medicaid for Abortions Feared," by G. Goodman, Jr. THE NEW YORK TIMES (M) February 14, 12:4, 1976.

"E.R.A. and Abortion Face Senate Test," by M. Waldron. THE NEW YORK TIMES (M) December 5, XI, 6:5, 1976.

"Eugenic recognition in Canadian law," by B. M. Dickens.

OSGOODE HALL LAW JOURNAL 13:547-577,
October, 1975.

"Evidence of the Royal College of General Practitioners
to the Select Committee of Parilament on the Abortion
(Amendment) Bill." JOURNAL OF THE ROYAL
COLLEGE OF GENERAL PRACTITIONERS 25(159):
774-776, October, 1975.

"Facing a grand jury." AMERICAN JOURNAL OF NURS-
ING 76:398-400, March, 1976.

"Federal hospitals to follow Supreme Court abortion
rules." MODERN HEALTHCARE, SHORT-TERM
CARE EDITION 5:165, February, 1976.

"Group Plans to Sue to Bar Any Change in Rules on
Abortion," by J. Cummings. THE NEW YORK TIMES
(S) September 29, 19:5, 1976.

"Health Aides and Abortion Groups Assail Proposed
Medicaid Control," by J. Maynard. THE NEW
YORK TIMES (M) September 18, 9:1, 1976.

"H.E.W. Funds Bill Stalled in House by Abortion Issue."
THE NEW YORK TIMES (S) August 11, 71:4, 1976.

"High Court Affirms Lower Federal Court Ruling." THE
NEW YORK TIMES (S) November 30, 31:1, 1976.

"High court again gives approval for abortion in three
new decisions." OUR SUNDAY VISITOR 65:1, July 11,
1976.

"High Court Bars Challenge to Hosptial Abortion Curb,"
by L. Olesner. THE NEW YORK TIMES (M) March 2,
1:5, 1976.

"High Court Bars Giving a Husband Veto on Abortion," by

L. Oelsner. THE NEW YORK TIMES (M) July 2, I, 1:8, 1976.

"High court forbids parental, spouse veto over abortions [state laws that require a married woman to get her husband's consent or a minor to have her parent's or guardian's permission to obtain a first-trimester abortion were declared unconstitutional by the U.S. supreme court on July 1, 1976]." FAMILY PLANNING PERSPECTIVES 8:177-178, July-August, 1976.

"The High Courts' Last Full Week is its Fullest." THE NEW YORK TIMES (S) July 4, IV, 3:1, 1976.

"History of the relation between pregnancy and pulmonary tuberculosis and therapeutic abortion," by T. M. Caffaratto. MINERVA GINECOLOGIA 28(2):192-201, February, 1976.

"Hospitals--a current analysis of the right to abortions and sterilizations in the Fourth circuit: state action and the church amendment." NORTH CAROLINA LAW REVIEW 54:1307-1316, September, 1976.

"House Panel Hears Abortion Argument." THE NEW YORK TIMES (S) February 6, 36:5, 1976.

"House subcommittee hears wide range of testimony on pro-life amendment," by J. Maher. OUR SUNDAY VISITOR 64:2, February 22, 1976.

"House unit hears prelates, legal experts argue for, against abortion amendment." NATIONAL CATHOLIC REPORTER 12:32, April 2, 1976.

"Humane abortion services: a revolution in human rights and the delivery of a medical service," by M. S. Burnhill. MOUNT SINAI JOURNAL OF MEDICINE, NEW YORK 42(5):431-438, September-October, 1975.

LAWS AND LEGISLATION

"Husband's consent for abortion struck down by U.S. Supreme Court: Missouri." HOSPITALS 50:22, August 1, 1976.

"Illegal abortions and the Abortion Act 1967," by P. Cavadino. BRITISH JOURNAL OF CRIMINOLOGY 16:63-67, January, 1976.

"Illegal abortions in the United States: 1972-1974," by W. Cates, Jr., et al. FAMILY PLANNING PER- SPECTIVES 8(2):86-92, March-April, 1976.

"Impact of the abortion decisions upon the father's role," by J. P. Witherspoon. JURIST 35:32-65, 1975.

"The impact of liberalized abortion legislation on con- traceptive practice in Denmark," by R. I. Somers, et al. STUDIES IN FAMILY PLANNING 7(8):218- 223, August, 1976.

"The impact of voluntary abortion on American obstetrics and gynecology," by D. P. Swartz. MOUNT SINAI JOURNAL OF MEDICINE, NEW YORK 42(5):468-478, September-October, 1975.

"Incidence of abortion and contraception patterns during 1968-1974," by R. I. Somers, et al. UGESKRIFT FOR LAEGER 138(6):353-355, February 2, 1976.

"Indiana Abortion Rule Voided." THE NEW YORK TIMES (S) June 17, 36:8, 1976.

"Interruption of pregnancy in the Netherlands." (letter). ZEITSCHRIFT FUR ALLGEMEINMEDIZIN; DU LANDARZT 51(10):493-499, April 10, 1975.

"Justice Byron White gives disent on abortion cases," by J. Castelli. OUR SUNDAY VISITOR 65:3, July 18, 1976.

241

"Justices, Back Tomorrow, to Face Abortion and Death Penalty Issues," by L. Oelsner. THE NEW YORK TIMES (M) October 3, 1:4, 1976.

"Key weapon in fight for life; bishops outline a workable plan against abortion," by J. Fink. OUR SUNDAY VISITOR MAGAZINE 64:1 passim, January 25, 1976.

"Law and life sciences. Abortion and the Supreme Court: round two," by G. J. Annas. HASTINGS CENTER REPORT 6(5):15-17, October, 1976.

"Legal abortion. Abortion as a form of contraception? A prospective study of 608 women applying for abortion," by P. Diederich, et al. UGESKRIFT FOR LAEGER 138(6):355-359, February 2, 1976.

"Legal abortion: a half-decade of experience," by J. Pakter, et al. FAMILY PLANNING PERSPECTIVES 7(6):248-255, November-December, 1975.

"Legal abortion and hemostasis. Histological examinations and comparison to post partum hemostasis," by R. Slunsky. ARCHIV FUR GYNAEKOLOGIE 220(4):325-338, April 29, 1976.

"Legal abortion in the county of Funen in relation to the liberalized Danish legislation," by F. H. Nielsen, et al. UGESKRIFT FOR LAEGER 138(6):369-375, February 2, 1976.

"Legal abortion in gynecological departments following free access to abortion," by F. Lundvall. UGESKRIFT FOR LAEGER 138(6):360-363, February 2, 1976.

"Legal abortion. Organizational and medical problems," (editorial), by V. Sele. UGESKRIFT FOR LAEGER 138(6):350, February 2, 1976.

LAWS AND LEGISLATION

"Legal abortion. Review after introduction of outpatient
abortions," by P. C. Davidsen, et al. UGESKRIFT
FOR LAEGER 138(6):375-378, February 2, 1976.

"Legal aspects of menstrual regulation: some preliminary observations," by L. T. Leo, et al. JOURNAL
OF FAMILY LAW 14:181-221, 1975.

"Legal consequences of the 'right' to abortion," by L. E.
Rozovsky. DIMENSIONS IN HEALTH SERVICE 53(4):
14-15, April, 1976.

"Legal enforcement, moral pluralism and abortion," by
R. De George. AMERICAN CATHOLIC PHILOSOPHI-
CAL ASSOCIATION PROCEEDINGS 49:171-180, 1975.

"Legal problems related to abortion and menstrual regu-
lation," by A. M. Dourlen-Rollier. COLUMBIA
HUMAN RIGHTS LAW REVIEW 7:120-135, Spring-
Summer, 1975.

"Legal rights of minors to sex-related medical care," by
E. W. Paul. COLUMBIA HUMAN RIGHTS LAW
REVIEW 6:357-377, Fall-Winter, 1974-1975.

"Live birth: a condition precedent to recognition of rights."
HOFSTRA LAW REVIEW 4:805-836, Spring, 1976.

"March Against Abortion." THE NEW YORK TIMES (S)
January 25, IV, 3:2, 1976.

"Marchers for Life amass in D.C." NATIONAL CATHOLIC
REPORTER 12:6, February 6, 1976.

"Marie Stopes Memorial Lecture 1975. The compulsory
pregnancy lobby--then and now," by M. Simms.
JOURNAL OF THE ROYAL COLLEGE OF GENERAL
PRACTITIONERS 25(159):709-719, October, 1975.

243

"Measure Passed by Albany Legislature," by R. Smothers. THE NEW YORK TIMES (M) June 11, II, 4:1, 1976.

"Medicaid and the abortion right." GEORGE WASHINGTON LAW REVIEW 44:404-417, March, 1976.

"Medicaid coverage of abortions in New York City: Costs and benefits," by M. Robinson, et al. FAMILY PLANNING PERSPECTIVES 6, 4:202-208, Fall, 1974. (Socio. Abstrs. 1976, 76I0425)

"Medicaid Stayed on Abortion Curb," by W. E. Waggoner. THE NEW YORK TIMES (M) January 17, 56:8, 1976.

"Medical interruption of pregnancy in India," by T. Chandy. MUENCHENER MEDIZINISCHE WOCHENSCHRIFT 117(34):1349-1352, August 22, 1975.

"Medical License Seized from an Abortion Doctor Charged with Ineptitude." THE NEW YORK TIMES (S) October 26. 36:2, 1976.

"Medical Termination of Pregnancy Act, 1971 and the registered medical practitioners." (letter). JOURNAL OF THE INDIAN MEDICAL ASSOCIATION 65(11):320-321, December 1, 1975.

"The Medical Termination of Pregnancy Act, 1971 and the registered medical practitioners," by J. B. Mukherjee. JOURNAL OF THE INDIAN MEDICAL ASSOCIATION 65(1):13-17, July 1, 1975.

"Medico-social problems following the reform of para 218 - potential and limits of the future practice of abortion," by A. Trojan, et al. OEFFENTLICHE GESUNDHEITS-WESEN 37(11):693-699, November, 1975.

"Moral sentiment in judicial opinions on abortion," by E. N. Moore. SANTA CLARA LAWYER 15:591-634,

Spring, 1975.

"More on abortion," by S. Fraker, et al. NEWSWEEK 88:15, July 12, 1976.

"The Morgentaler case," (letter), by G. Carruthers. CANADIAN MEDICAL ASSOCIATION JOURNAL 113(9):818, November 8, 1975.

"Morgentaler freed, new trial ordered," by B. Richardson. HUMANIST 36:50, March, 1976.

"Mortality and morbidity associated with legal abortions in Hungary, 1960-1973," by Z. Bognar, et al. AMERICAN JOURNAL OF PUBLIC HEALTH 66:568-575, June, 1976.

"Most abortions by suction in 10th week or less; typical patient is young, unmarried, white, never-before pregnant." FAMILY PLANNING PERSPECTIVES 8(2):70-72, March-April, 1976.

"The motivation of the physician's behavior in correlation to the legislation of abortion," by G. Thomaschec. BEITRAEGE ZUR GERICHTLICHEN MEDIZIN 33:15-17, 1975.

"New Icelandic abortion law. Abortion on social indications before the 16th week." NORDISK MEDICIN 90(12):290, December, 1975.

"New Jersey Briefs: 4 hospitals said to violate rights." THE NEW YORK TIMES (S) June 4, II, 21:1, 1976.

"New Jersey Briefs: medicaid restrictions enjoined." THE NEW YORK TIMES (S) February 3, 67:7, 1976.

"New Jersey Court Rules for Abortion." THE NEW YORK TIMES (S) November 21, IV, 7:4, 1976.

"The new jurisprudence," by R. M. Bryn. JAMA;
    JOURNAL OF THE AMERICAN MEDICAL ASSOCIA-
    TION 236(4):359-360, July 26, 1976.

"New pro-life legislation: patterns and recommendations,"
    by J. P. Witherspoon. ST. MARY'S LAW JOURNAL
    7:637-697, 1976.

"New Security Measures Will Protect Assembly," by
    M. Waldron. THE NEW YORK TIMES (S) April 27,
    75:8, 1976.

"No Chance is Seen of Overriding Carey's Veto of Abortion
    Bill," by L. Greenhouse. THE NEW YORK TIMES (M)
    June 24, 66:5, 1976.

"No going back," by D. Gould. NEW STATESMAN 132,
    January 31, 1975.

"No Process of Law," by A. Lewis. THE NEW YORK
    TIMES April 8, 37:1, 1976.

"Nonsectarian Hospitals in Jersey Are Ordered to Permit
    Abortions," by A. A. Narvaez. THE NEW YORK
    TIMES (M) November 18, 1:1, 1976.

"Nor piety nor wit: the Supreme Court on abortion," by
    J. W. Dellapenna. COLUMBIA HUMAN RIGHTS LAW
    REVIEW 6:379-413, Fall-Winter, 1974-1975.

"Not much hope House will approve pro-life amendment,"
    by J. Maher. OUR SUNDAY VISITOR 64:2, February 22,
    1976.

"On abortion and right to life," (letter), by E. J. Kirsch.
    AMERICAN JOURNAL OF PUBLIC HEALTH 66(9):
    906, September, 1976.

"On the bounds of freedom: from the treatment of fetuses

to euthanasia," by H. T. Engelhardt, Jr. CONNETI-
CUT MEDICINE 40(1):51-54, 57, January, 1976.

"On the sociology and social ethics of abortion," by C.
Bagley. ETHICS IN SCIENCE AND MEDICINE 3(1):
21-32, May, 1976.

"Only amendment will save the unborn, professor says."
OUR SUNDAY VISITOR 65:3, October 31, 1976.

"Options in the abortion debate," by J. M. Wall.
CHRISTIAN CENTURY 93:139-140, February 18, 1976.

"Our resources for contraceptive advice and legal abortion," by J. Asplund. LAKARTIDNINGEN 72(47):4609-
4610, November 19, 1975.

"Override of fund bill veto leaves abortion ban intact."
NATIONAL CATHOLIC REPORTER 12:14, October 8,
1976.

"Pastoral letter for all bishops calls abortion laws unjust
and immoral; asks for action." OUR SUNDAY VISITOR
MAGAZINE 64:1, January 18, 1976.

"Perceptions of abortion. The circle of choice: a decision-
making process observed in women considering abortions," by G. K. Adams. ANA CLINICAL SESSIONS
:47-59, 1974.

"Performing abortions," by M. Denes. COMMENTARY
62:33-37, October, 1976.

"Pregnancies of Irish residents terminated in England
and Wales in 1973," by D. Walsh. IRISH MEDICAL
JOURNAL 69(1):16-18, January 17, 1976.

"Physician's decision-making role in abortion cases," by
J. J. R. Marcin, et al. JURIST 35:66-76, 1975.

"A pilot study of demographic and psychosocial factors in medical termination of pregnancy," by R. Goraya, et al. JOURNAL OF THE INDIAN MEDICAL ASSOCI-ATION 64(11):309-315, June 1, 1975.

"Planned Parenthood of Cent. Mo. v. Danforth, 96 Sup Ct 2831." OKLAHOMA LAW REVIEW 29:785-788, Summer, 1976.

"Post-abortal tetanus," by C. Newman, et al. CONNECTICUT MEDICINE 39(12):773-774, December, 1975.

"Pregnancy and abortion in adolescence: a comparative legal survey and proposals for reform," by L. T. Lee, et al. COLUMBIA HUMAN RIGHTS LAW REVIEW 6:307-355, Fall-Winter, 1974-1975.

"Pregnancy counseling and abortion referral for patients in Federally funded family planning programs," by J. I. Rosoff. FAMILY PLANNING PERSPECTIVES 8(1):43-46, January-February, 1976.

"President Vetoes $56 Billion Bill for Manpower, H.E.W. Programs," by P. Shabecoff. THE NEW YORK TIMES (M) September 30, 1:4, 1976.

"Private Hospitals to Decide Soon Whether to Challenge Abortion Ruling," by A. A. Narvaez. THE NEW YORK TIMES (M) November 19, II, 19:3, 1976.

"Problems of decision making of interruption commis-sions," by D. Fukalova. CESKOSLOVENSKA GYNE-KOLOGIE 40(9):669-671, November, 1975.

"Procedures in the termination of pregnancy, 'Mannheim' proposal - document symbol Paragraph 218/new 76," by S. Sievers, et al. FORTSCHRITTE DU MEDIZIN 94(27):1471-1472, September 23, 1976.

"Proposal for the management of the current regulations under Paragraph 218," by P. Stoll, et al. FORT-SCHRITTE DU MEDIZIN 94(27):1468-1471, September 23, 1976.

"Proposed decree on abortion and nurses' role," by S. A. Jegede. NIGERIAN NURSE 7(1):33-34, January-March, 1975.

"Protestant pro-life women launch national task force." OUR SUNDAY VISITOR 64:2, May 2, 1976.

"Psychological-sociological views on S 218 (study on 379 pregnant women and women in puerperium)," by J. M. Wenderlein. ZENTRALBLATT FUR GYNAEKOLOGIE 98(9):527-532, 1976.

"Psychotherapy in abortion," by C. M. Donovan. CURRENT PSYCHIATRIC THERAPIES 15:77-83, 1975.

"Public health facilities issue new abortion policy." HOSPITALS 50:17, January 1, 1976.

"Public opinion and legal abortion in New Zealand," by B. J. Kirkwood, et al. NEW ZEALAND MEDICAL JOURNAL 83(556):43-47, January 28, 1976.

"Putting the clock back on abortion," by P. Ferris. OBSERVER 10, February 16, 1975.

"Putting a stop to the abortion industry," by L. Abse. TIMES 14, July 29, 1976.

"Quebec Halts Trial of Abortion Doctor," by H. Giniger. THE NEW YORK TIMES December 12, 21:1, 1976.

"A question of conscience." (letter). BRITISH MEDICAL JOURNAL 2(6026):43, July 3, 1976.

"Rally Demands Ban on Abortion," by M. Talchin. THE NEW YORK TIMES (M) January 23, 20:3, 1976.

"Random thoughts on abortion attitudes," (letter), by K. Solomon. AMERICAN JOURNAL OF PUBLIC HEALTH 66(9):905-906, September, 1976.

"Rape and abortion: is the argument valid?" by M. Sonsmith. LIGUORIAN 64:45-47, June, 1976.

"The real issues about abortion," by A. Bowden. DAILY TELEGRAPH 16, July 29, 1976.

"Recent developments in the abortion area," by A. Scanlan. CATHOLIC LAWYER 21:315-321, Fall, 1975.

"Recent French law on interruption of pregnancy," by R. Bourg. BRUXELLES-MEDICAL 55(4):201-206, April, 1975.

"Redefining the issues in fotal experimentation," by E. F. Diamond. JOURNAL OF THE AMERICAN MEDICAL ASSOCIATION 236:281-283, July 19, 1976.

"The relationship between legal abortion and marriage," by K. E. Bauman, et al. SOCIAL BIOLOGY 22,2:117-124, Summer, 1975. (Socio. Abstrs. 1976, 76I0401)

"Remarks on abortion, abandonment, and adoption opportunities," by R. M. Herbenick. PHILOSOPHY AND PUBLIC AFFAIRS 5, 1:98-104, Fall, 1975. (Socio. Abstrs. 1976, 76I2512)

"Repeat aborters," by S. M. Schneider, et al. AMERICAN JOURNAL OF OBSTETRICS AND GYNECOLOGY 126(3): 316-320, October 1, 1976.

"Repeated legal abortions," by L. Jacobsson, et al.

LAKARTIDNINGEN 73(22):2100-2103, May 26, 1976.

"Repercussions of legal abortion on subsequent preg-
nancies," by R. Renaud, et al. JOURNAL DE GYNE-
COLOGIE, OBSTETRIQUE ET BIOLOGIE DE LA
REPRODUCTION 3(4):577-594, June, 1974.

"Restrictions in Missouri abortion statute upheld."
JOURNAL OF THE MISSISSIPPI STATE MEDICAL
ASSOCIATION 16(12):382, December, 1975.

"A Retrial in Abortion Case is Ordered in Canada," by
R. Trumbull. THE NEW YORK TIMES (M) January 23,
2:4, 1976.

"Rights of the retarded." (letter). INQUIRY 6(4):4, 30-33,
August, 1976.

"Roe v. Wade (93 Sup Ct 705): impact on rights of choice
in human reproduction." COLUMBIA HUMAN RIGHTS
LAW REVIEW 5:497-521, Fall, 1973.

"Section 401(b) of the health programs extension act: an
abortive attempt by Congress to resolve a constitutional dilemma." WILLIAM AND MARY LAW REVIEW
17:303-331, Winter, 1976.

"Select committee on abortion." (letter). LANCET
2(7980):306, August 7, 1976.

"Select committee under the abortion law," (letter), by
H. C. McLaren. LANCET 2(7942):986, November 15,
1975.

"Senate Rejects Abortion Curb," by D. E. Rosenbaum.
THE NEW YORK TIMES (M) August 26, 15:1, 1976.

"Senate votes against even considering pro-life bill."
OUR SUNDAY VISITOR 65:2, May 16, 1976.

"The Senates Vote on Abortion." THE NEW YORK TIMES (S) August 29, IV, 4:1, 1976.

"Simone Veil: driving force behind France's abortion law," by A. F. Gonzalez, Jr. AMERICAN MEDICAL NEWS 19; IMPACT 9, June 28, 1976.

"Social medicine aspects in pregnancy interruption," by U. Fritsche, et al. ZEITSCHRIFT FUR AERZTLICHE FORTBILDUNG 69(21):1131-1136, November 1, 1975.

"St. Louis action tops in fight against abortion," by R. Casey. NATIONAL CATHOLIC REPORTER 12:1-2 passim, March 26, 1976.

"State legislation on abortion after Roe v. Wade: selected constitutional issues," by M. D. Bryant, Jr. AMERICAN JOURNAL OF LAW AND MEDICINE 2(2):101-132, Summer, 1976.

"A state-registered abortionists?" (letter). by D. P. Cocks, et al. LANCET 2(7948):1308-1309, December 27, 1975.

"Strategy questioned," by D. Thorman. NATIONAL CATHOLIC REPORTER 12:8, December 12, 1975.

"Studies on immediate post-abortion copper 'T' device," by I. Gupta, et al. INDIAN JOURNAL OF MEDICAL RESEARCH 63(5):736-739, May, 1975.

"Summary of Actions Taken by U.S. Supreme Court." THE NEW YORK TIMES April 27, 15:2, 1976.

"Summary of Actions Taken by U.S. Supreme Court." THE NEW YORK TIMES (S) June 7, 39:2, 1976.

"Supreme court and abortion." SOCIETY 13:6-9, March, 1976.

"Supreme Court rejects spousal and parental rights in abortion decision," by C. E. Reed. HOSPITAL PROGRESS 57:18 passim, August, 1976.

"Supreme Court to hear abortion cases in '77." OUR SUNDAY VISITOR 65:2, July 25, 1976.

"Supreme Court unwilling to settle state action conflict," by P. F. Geary. HOSPITAL PROGRESS 57(5):6, 12, May, 1976.

"Therapeutic abortion and its aftermath," by M. Stone. MIDWIFE, HEALTH VISITOR AND COMMUNITY NURSE 11:335-338, October, 1975.

"Therapeutic abortion and its psychological implications: the Canadian experience," by E. B. Greenglass. CANADIAN MEDICAL ASSOCIATION JOURNAL 113: 754-757, October 18, 1976.

"Thousands march in national captial in protest against legalized abortion," by C. Foster. OUR SUNDAY VISITOR 64:1, February 8, 1976.

"Three years is too long." CHRISTIANITY TODAY 20: 38 passim, February 13, 1976.

"Time to stop fiddling about with the Abortion Act," by D. Steel. TIMES 16, February 2, 1976.

"Treatment of perforation of the large intestine due to illegal abortion," by H. G. Mayer. ZENTRALBLATT FUR GYNAEKOLOGY 97112):734-737, 1975.

"UN study group reports, Msgr. McHugh dissents; study paper on abortion." OUR SUNDAY VISITOR 64:2, March 7, 1976.

"Understanding adolescent pregnancy and abortion," by

S. L. Hatcher. PRIMARY CARE; CLINICS IN OFFICE
PRACTICE 3(3):407-425, September, 1976.

"Unexpectedly cautious." ECONOMIST 260:29-30, July 31,
1976.

"The unmet need for legal abortion services in the U.S.,"
by C. Tietze, et al. FAMILY PLANNING PERSPEC-
TIVES 7(5):224-230, September-October, 1975.

"Unwanted pregnancies and abortion," by L. A. Woolf.
MEDICAL JOURNAL OF AUSTRALIA 2(9):368-369,
August 30, 1975.

"U.S. Catholic Conference files brief asking Supreme
Court give unborn legal protection." OUR SUNDAY
VISITOR 64:3, January 25, 1976.

"U.S. Court Overturns Curb on Medicaid Abortions," by
M. H. Siegel. THE NEW YORK TIMES (M) October 23,
1:3, 1976.

"U.S. Courts Bar Curb on Funding Some Abortions," by
M. H. Siegel. THE NEW YORK TIMES (M) October 2,
1:2, 1976.

"U.S. money backs international abortion cartel," by
M. Bunson. OUR SUNDAY VISITOR MAGAZINE
65:1 passim, June 13, 1976.

"U.S. Supreme Court lets lower court decision stand on
right of hospital to refuse abortion." OUR SUNDAY
VISITOR 64:1, December 14, 1975.

"Viability and abortion," by C. Macaluso. KENTUCKY
LAW JOURNAL 64, 1:146-164, 1976.

"Votes in Congress." THE NEW YORK TIMES May 2,
58:4, 1976.

LAWS AND LEGISLATION

"Votes in Congress." THE NEW YORK TIMES (S)
July 4, 39:7, 1976.

"Votes in Congress." THE NEW YORK TIMES April 29,
47:3, 1976.

"West German abortion decision: a contrast to Roe v.
Wade (93 Sup Ct 705) Preface, J. D. Gorby, et al;
Introduction, J. D. Gorby; Dissenting remarks, R.
E. Jonas; Translation of the German federal
constitutional court decision." JOHN MARSHALL
JOURNAL 9:551-684, Spring, 1976.

"What are the father's rights in abortion?" by R.
Blackwood. JOURNAL OF LEGAL MEDICINE 3(9):
28-36, October, 1975.

"When being unwanted is a capital crime," by M. White.
TIMES 10, July 21, 1975.

"When is killing the unborn a homicidal action?" by P.
Coffey. LINACRE 43:85-93, May, 1976.

"Whose interests?" by J. Turner. NURSING TIMES
71(45):1763, November 6, 1976.

"Women, anger and abortion," by R. C. Wahlberg.
CHRISTIAN CENTURY 93:622-623, July 7, 1976.

"World as reality, as resource, and as pretense," by
P. Stith. AMERICAN JOURNAL OF JURISPRUDENCE
20:141-153, 1975.

"Women's experience of the abortion procedure," by L.
Jacobsson, et al. SOCIAL PSYCHIATRY 10(4):155-160,
October, 1975.

LISTERIOSIS

MALE ATTITUDES

MALE ATTITUDES
see: Sociology and Behavior

MARCH OF DIMES

MEFENAMIC ACID

MENSTRUATION
see: Complications
Induced Abortion

MENTALLY RETARDED
"Rights of the retarded." (letter). INQUIRY 6(4):4,
30-33, August, 1976.

MICROBIOLOGY
see: Research

MISCARRIAGES
"Certain immunologic indicators in miscarriage," by
M. A. Omarov, et al. AKUSHERSTVO I GINEKOL-
OLIIA (Moscow) (9):61-62, September, 1975.

"The diagnosis and treatment of threatened miscarriage,"
by B. Faris. AUSTRALASIAN NURSES JOURNAL
4:7, October, 1975.

"Effect of climatic-weather conditions on the incidence
of miscarriage," by I. I. Nikberg, et al. VOPROSY
OKHRANY MATERINSTVA I DETSTVA 21(1):28-31,
January, 1976.

"Focal glomerulonephritis, pregnancy and miscarriage,"
(letter), by E. Lusvarghi. NEPHRON 16(4):322-333,
1976.

"Miscarriage and abortion: I. Induced and spontaneous
abortion. Psychopathological aspects in connection
with a first sample of 411 requests for interruption

of pregnancy," by M. Bourgeois, et al. ANNALES
MEDICO-PSYCHOLOGIQUES 2(2):339-366, July,
1975. (Psycho. Abstrs. 1976, 12347)

--II. Voluntary abortion and resistance to contraception,"
by M. Bourgeois, et al. ANNALES MEDICO-
PSYCHOLOGIQUES 2(2):366-377, July, 1975.
(Psycho. Abstrs. 1976, 12348)

"Occupation and miscarriage," by W. Helbing. ZEIT-
SCHRIFT FUR DIE GESAMTE HYGIENE UND IHRE
GRENZGEBIETE 21(11):819-821, 1975.

"Sensitization of women to fetal tissue and leukocytic
antigens and its role in miscarriage," by L. F.
Kiseleva, et al. VOPROSY OKHRANY MATERINSTVA
I DETSTVA 21(7):65-67, June, 1976.

"Spina bifida and anencephaly: miscarriage as possible
cause," by C. Clarke, et al. BRITISH MEDICAL
JOURNAL 4(5999):743-746, December 27, 1975.

"Treatment of women suffering from habitual miscarriage,"
by N. T. Gudakova. AKUSHERSTVO I GINEKOLOGIIA
(Moscow) (3):64-65, March, 1976.

MORBIDITY
see: Complications

MORTALITY
see also: Complications
        Sepsis
        Septic Abortion and Septic Shock

"Abortion and maternal deaths." (editorial). BRITISH
MEDICAL JOURNAL 2(6027):70, July 10, 1976.

"Abortion and maternal deaths." (letter), by C. Brook.
BRITISH MEDICAL JOURNAL 2(6034):524-525,

August 28, 1976.

"Abortion and maternal deaths," (letter), by C. B. Goodhart. BRITISH MEDICAL JOURNAL 2(6033):477,
August 21, 1976.

"Abortion and maternal deaths," (letter), by A. M. Smith.
BRITISH MEDICAL JOURNAL 2(6031):368, August 7,
1976.

"Fatal case of nivaquine poisoning. Medico-legal and
toxicological study," by H. J. Lazarini, et al.
MEDICINE LEGALE ET DOMMAGE CORPOREL
7(4):332, October-December, 1974.

"Illegal abortions in the United States: 1972-1974," by
W. Cates, Jr., et al. FAMILY PLANNING PERSPEC-
TIVES 8(2):86-92, March-April, 1976.

"Legal abortion: an appraisal of its health impact," by
G. S. Berger. INTERNATIONAL JOURNAL OF
GYNAECOLOGY AND OBSTETRICS 13(4):165-170,
1975. (Bio. Abstrs. 1976, 22866)

"Maternal mortality from septic abortions in University
Hospital, Kuala Lumpur from March 1968 to February
1974," by K. H. Ng, et al. MEDICAL JOURNAL OF
MALAYSIA 30(1):52-54, September, 1975.

"Mortality and morbidity associated with legal abortions
in Hungary, 1960-1973," by Z. Bognar, et al.
AMERICAN JOURNAL OF PUBLIC HEALTH 66:568-
575, June, 1976.

"Postpartum and postabortal ovarian recin thrombo-
phlebitis," by T. R. Allan, et al. OBSTETRICS
AND GYNECOLOGY 47(5):525-528, 1976. (Bio.
Abstrs. 1976, 24056)

MYCOPLASMA
 "Mycoplasmas in humans: significance of Ureoplasma
   urealyticum," by R. B. Kundsin. HEALTH LABORA-
   TORY SCIENCE 12(2):144-151, 1976. (Bio. Abstrs.
   1976, 43909)

NAL
 see: Laws and Legislation

NCCB

NAPTHALENE

NEONATAL

NEURAMINIDASE

NURSES
 "Abortion--the nurse's feelings," by A. Danon. ANA
   CLINICAL SESSIONS :60-65, 1974.

 "Law for the nurse supervisor," by H. Creighton.
   SUPERVISOR NURSE 6:10-11 passim, April, 1975.

 "Nurse's attitudes to termination of pregnancy." NURSING
   FORUM (Auckl) 2(5):6-7, November-December, 1974.

 "Nurses who work to save live," by L. Curtin. OUR
   SUNDAY VISITOR MAGAZINE 64:16, January 25, 1976.

 "Postabortion psychiatric illness," by C. M. Donovan,
   et al. NURSING DIGEST 3:12-16, September-October,
   1975.

 --Nursing implications. Addendum," by C. A. Farrar.
   NURSING DIGEST 3:17, September-October, 1975.

 "Proposed decree on abortion and nurses' role," by S. A.
   Jegede. NIGERIAN NURSE 7(1):33-34, January-March,
   1975.

NURSES

"Study shows more nurses than before favor abortion,"
by J. McCann. NATIONAL CATHOLIC REPORTER
12:5, March 26, 1976.

NURSING HOMES

OBSTETRICS

"The impact of voluntary abortion on American obstetrics
and gynecology," by D. P. Swarts. MOUNT SINAI
JOURNAL OF MEDICINE, NEW YORK 42(5):468-
478, September-October, 1975.

"Mechanism of action of prostaglandin F2 alpha and its
clinical use in obstetrics," by L. S. Persianinov.
AKUSHERSTVO I GINEKOLOGIIA (Moscow) (6):7-15,
June, 1975.

"Use of prostaglandins in gynecology and obstetrics,"
by B. I. Nesheim. TIDSSKRIFT FOR DEN NORSKE
LAEGEFORENING 96(6):375-376, February 28, 1976.

"Violent perforations of the uterus in the 10-year material
of the Gynecologic-Obstetrical Department in Bitola,"
by T. Pasanku. MEDICINSKI ARHIV 28(3):337-339, M
May-June, 1974.

ORCIPRENALINE

OUTPATIENT ABORTION
see: Hospitals

OXYTOCIN

"Abruptio placentae following a negative oxytocin challenge
test," by J. C. Seski, et al. AMERICAN JOURNAL OF
OBSTETRICS AND GYNECOLOGY 125(2):276, May 15,
1976.

"Induction of midtrimester abortion with intraamniotic
urea, intravenous oxytocin and laminaria," by I. M.

OXYTOCIN

Golditch, et al. JOURNAL OF REPORDUCTIVE
MEDICINE 15(6):225-228, December, 1975.

"Uterine rupture complicating mid-trimester abortion
in a young woman of low parity," by R. H. Hayashi,
et al. INTERNATIONAL JOURNAL OF GYNAECOLOGY
AND OBSTETRICS 13(5):229-232, 1975. (Bio. Abstrs.
1976, 22789)

"Water intoxication associated with oxytocin infusion,"
by A. J. Ahmad, et al. POSTGRADUATE MEDICAL
JOURNAL 51(594):249-252, April, 1975.

PARAMEDICS

PARSLEY EXTRACT

PATIENT COUNSELING
see: Sociology and Behavior

PENTAZOCINE

PHARMACISTS

PHYSICIANS
see also: Psychology
Sociology and Behavior

"Application of Guttman scale analysis to physicians'
attitudes regarding abortion," by M. Koslowsky, et al.
JOURNAL OF APPLIED PSYCHOLOGY 61:301-304,
June, 1976.

"Connecticut physicians' attitudes toward abortion," by
G. L. Pratt, et al. AMERICAN JOURNAL OF PUBLIC
HEALTH 66:288-290, March, 1976; Reply with rejoin-
der by K. Solomon 66:905-906, September, 1976

"Doctor predicts abortion without death in future." OUR

SUNDAY VISITOR 64:1, March 7, 1976.

"Error during abortion--2 physicians got warning."
LAKARTIDNINGEN 73(4):231-232, January 21, 1976.

"The motivation of the physician's behavior in correlation
to the legalization of abortion," by G. Tomaschec.
BEITRAEGE ZUR GERICHTLICHEN MEDIZIN 33:15-
17, 1975.

"Physician's decision-making role in abortion cases," by
J. J. R. Marcin, et al. JURIST 35:66-76, 1976.

"The problem of abortion. Viewpoint of the general
practitioner," by J. Henrion. REVUE MEDICALE DE
LIEGE 30(8):249-253, April 15, 1975.

POLITICS
"Abortion and 1976 politics; with editorial comment,"
by R. N. Lynch. AMERICA 134:173, 177, 178,
March 6, 1976.

"Abortion and politics," by E. Doerr. HUMANIST 36:42,
March, 1976.

"Abortion Backers Seek out Carter." THE NEW YORK
TIMES (S) September 3, I, 9:4, 1976.

"The Abortion Debate," by J. A. O'Hare. THE NEW
TIMES (M) February 8, IV, 15:2, 1976.

"The Abortion Issue," by T. Wicker. THE NEW YORK
TIMES September 10, I, 25:2, 1976.

"Abortion: no middle ground," by M. Greenfield.
NEWSWEEK 87:92, February 16, 1976.

"Abortion politics," by S. Stencel. EDITORIAL RE-
SEARCH REPORTS 767-784, October 22, 1976.

POLITICS

"Abortion Stand by Carter Vexes Catholic Bishops," by
C. Mohr. THE NEW YORK TIMES (M) September 1,
1:5, 1976.

"Antiabortion Candidate Sparks Funding Debate," by
G. Vecsey. THE NEW YORK TIMES (M) February 9,
32:6, 1976.

"Archbishop Bernardin calls Ford stand disappointing,
asks support for the unborn." OUR SUNDAY
VISITOR 64:1, February 15, 1976.

"Archbishop Bernardin open to meeting with Carter."
L'OSSERVATORE ROMANO 32[436]6, August 5, 1976.

"As Carter Moves into Limelight He Becomes Highly
Visible and Vunerable," by J. T. Wooten. THE NEW
YORK TIMES (M) February 4, 15:1, 1976.

"Birth Curb Research Asked." THE NEW YORK TIMES
(S) February 29, 42:6, 1976.

"Bishops encouraged by Ford abortion stand," by R.
Casey. NATIONAL CATHOLIC REPORTER 12:1-2,
September 17, 1976.

"Bishops in politics: the big plunge: National conference
of Catholic bishops' Pastorial plan for pro-life
activities," by P. J. Weber. AMERICA 134:220-
223, March 20, 1976.

"Candidates on the issues: abortion," by E. Bowman,
et al. CONGRESSIONAL QUARTERLY WEEKLY
REPORT 34:463-466, February 28, 1976.

" 'Cannot be Neutral', on Abortion Issue, Cardinal
Proclaims," by G. Dugan. THE NEW YORK TIMES
(S) September 27, 37:6, 1976.

263

"Carey Welcomes Mondale," by L. Charlton. THE NEW YORK TIMES (M) August 26, 23:2, 1976.

"Carter and the Bishops." (editorial). THE NEW YORK TIMES September 2, 30:1, 1976.

"Carter and the Bishops," by K. A. Briggs. THE NEW YORK TIMES (M) September 3, I, 9:1, 1976.

"Carter Campaign Moving to Mollify Catholics After Dispute Over Democratic Party's Abortion Stand," by K. A. Briggs. THE NEW YORK TIMES (M) August 26, 20:1, 1976.

"Carter opposed to abortion but not for an amendment." OUR SUNDAY VISITOR 65:1, August 29, 1976.

"Carter says his abortion stand same as platform's." OUR SUNDAY VISITOR 65:1, August 1, 1976.

"Catholic League charges Carter endorsed abortion." OUR SUNDAY VISITOR 65:2, September 19, 1976.

"Catholic political leaders and abortion; a house divided; a look at the record of prominent Catholic national political leaders and their stance on pro-life legislation." OUR SUNDAY VISITOR MAGAZINE 65:1 passim, August 29, 1976.

"Democrats take stand against pro-lifers." OUR SUNDAY VISITOR 65:1, June 27, 1976.

"Dole campaign ad controversy revived [antiabortion ads]." EDITOR AND PUBLISHER-THE FOURTH ESTATE 109:34, September 4, 1976.

"Ellen McCormack: campaigning for the unborn," by B. Beckwith. ST. ANTHONY MESSENGER 83:30-36, May, 1976.

"Foe of Abortion Qualifies for U.S. Aid," by E. Shanahan.
THE NEW YORK TIMES (M) February 26, 21:3, 1976.

"Foley Pressing Antiabortion Issue," by M. Waldron.
THE NEW YORK TIMES (S) May 21, II, 21:1, 1976.

"Ford Abortion Stand Draws Criticism." THE NEW YORK
TIMES (M) February 5, 15:1, 1976.

"Ford Says Court 'Went to Far' on Abortion '73," by
M. J. Naughton. THE NEW YORK TIMES (M)
February 4, 1:3, 1976.

"Importance of Abortion." THE NEW YORK TIMES (S)
February 8, IV, 3:1, 1976.

"Jackson Abortion Stand is Disputed by His Wife." THE
NEW YORK TIMES (S) March 11, 34:1, 1976.

"Jimmy Carter and the Catholic Bishops," by W. V.
Shannon. THE NEW YORK TIMES September 5,
IV, 13:2, 1976.

"The MacNeil Report," by J. Hennesee. THE NEW
YORK TIMES (M) April 4, II, 25:1, 1976.

"Mail on Abortion." THE NEW YORK TIMES (S) July 25,
30:8, 1976.

"Massachusetts Poll Hints Deep Democrat Rifts," by R.
Reinhold. THE NEW YORK TIMES (M) March 4,
18:3, 1976.

"Mr. Ford on Abortion." (editoral). THE NEW YORK
TIMES February 5, 30:2, 1976.

"100,000 at 'World' Mass as Catholic Parley Closes."
THE NEW YORK TIMES (M) August 9, 1:3, 1976.

POLITICS

"1,703 Persons Queried in Times-CBS Survey." THE
NEW YORK TIMES (M) September 10, I, 19:1, 1976.

"Pinning down the politicians." ECONOMIST 258:40
passim, February 14, 1976.

"Political responsibility and abortion." AMERICA 134:
173, March 6, 1976.

"Politics and abortion." COMMONWEAL 103:131-132,
February 27, 1976.

"Politics and abortion," by C. Brandmeyer. COMMON-
WEAL 103:432-433, July 2, 1976.

"Politics of abortion," by J. Armstrong. CHRISTIAN
CENTURY 93:215, March 10, 1976.

"Pro-lifers will challenge Democratic abortion plank."
OUR SUNDAY VISITOR MAGAZINE 65:1, July 11,
1976.

"Reagan Affirms Antiabortion Stand." THE NEW YORK
TIMES (M) February 8, 44:3, 1976.

"Republican Feminists Prepare to Fight for Convention
Delagates, Rights Amendment and Abortion." THE
NEW YORK TIMES (M) February 19, 25:1, 1976.

"Senator Church Joins Presidential Race," by L. Carlton.
THE NEW YORK TIMES (L) March 19, 18:7, 1976.

"The Switcher Issues," by W. Safire. THE NEW YORK
TIMES (M) February 23, 25:5, 1976.

"10,000 Antiabortionists Attend a Protest Rally," by P.
Kihss. THE NEW YORK TIMES (M) July 12, III,
21:7, 1976.

POLITICS

"Thoughts on Abortion," by J. Schrank. THE NEW YORK
TIMES February 16, 18:3, 1976.

"Wallace Pressing the Abortion Issue," by R. Reed.
THE NEW YORK TIMES (M) March 3, 17:6, 1976.

"Where the Women Stand on Controversial Issues." THE
NEW YORK TIMES (M) April 12, 24:6, 1976.

"Whistle-stop: abortion out as top national issue," by R.
Casey. NATIONAL CATHOLIC REPORTER 12:3,
October 1, 1976.

"Why new uproar over abortions: pushing to the foreground of '76 politics is an issue candidates would
like to avoid; the reason: its trouble--no matter what
they say." U.S. NEWS AND WORLD REPORT 80:14-
15, March 1, 1976.

"Woman's Rights." THE NEW YORK TIMES (M)
February 9, 21:7, 1976.

POPULATION
see also: Demography

"Contraception alone will not allow us to control population," by T. Smith. TIMES 12, July 7, 1975.

"Population, abortion, birth rates," by J. Kettle.
EXECUTIVE 17:47-48, November, 1975.

"Population control in Australia today: contraception,
sterilization and abortion," by J. Leeton. MEDICAL
JOURNAL OF AUSTRALIA 2(17):682-685, October 25,
1975.

POTASSIUM AMPICILLIN

PREGNANCY INTERRUPTION
see: Induced Abortion

PROGESTERONE
"Comparative studies on the cytohormonal and cytochemical exponents of estrogens-progesterone activity
in the vaginal lining epithelium in women with pregnancy complications. I. Threatened abortion," by
J. Dudkiewica. GINEKOLOGIA POLASKA 46(11):
1135-1146, November, 1975.

"HCG, HPL, oestradiol, progesterone and AFP in serum
in patients with threatened abortion," by J. Kunz, et
al. BRITISH JOURNAL OF OBSTETRICS AND
GYNAECOLOGY 83(8):640-644, August, 1976.

"Inhibitory effect of progesterone on the lactogenic and
abortive action of prostaglandin F2alpha," by N. T.
Vermouth, et al. JOURNAL OF ENDOCRINOLOGY
66(1):21-29, July, 1975.

"Progesterone levels in amniotic fluid and maternal
plasma in prostaglandin F2alpha-induced midtrimester
abortion," by Z. Koren, et al. OBSTETRICS AND
GYNECOLOGY 48(4):427 passim, October, 1976.

PROSTAGLANDINS
"Abortifacient efficiency of 15 (S) 15-methyl-prostaglandin
F2alpha-methyl ester administered vaginally during
early pregnancy," by O. Ylikorkala, et al. PROSTA-
GLANDINS 12(4):609-624, October, 1976.

"Abortion induction using prostaglandin E2," by K.
Felshart. ARCHIV FUR GYNAEKOLOGIE 219(1-4):
500-501, November 18, 1975.

"Active pre-term management of severe osteogenesis
imperfecta," by J. Swinhoe, et al. ACTA OBSTE-
TRICIA ET GYNECOLOGICA SCANDINAVICA

55(1):81-83, 1976. (Bio. Abstrs. 1976, 1152)

"Alpha-fetoprotein levels in maternal plasma and
amniotic fluid during prostaglandin-induced midtrimester abortions: the relation to fetal distress
and death," by R. H. Ward, et al. BRITISH JOURNAL
OF OBSTETRICS AND GYNAECOLOGY 83(4):299-302,
April, 1976.

"Blood coagulation studies in prostaglandin abortion,"
(proceedings), by R. Lang, et al. ARCHIV FUR
GYNAEKOLOGIE 219(1-4):501-502, November 18,
1975.

"Bronchoconstriction and pulmonary hypertension during
abortion induced by 15-ethyl-prostaglandin F2a," by
E. K. Weir, et al. AMERICAN JOURNAL OF MEDI-
CINE 60(4):556-562, 1976. (Bio. Abstrs. 1976,
23180)

"Clinical experience using intramaniotic prostaglandin
F2alpha for midtrimester abortion in 600 patients,"
by G. G. Anderson, et al. OBSTETRICS AND
GYNECOLOGY 46(5):591-595, November, 1975.

"Clinical observations with a prostaglandin-containing
silastic vaginal device for pregnancy termination,"
by C. H. Hendricks, et al. PROSTAGLANDINS 12
Suppl:99-122, 1976.

"Coagulation changes during second-trimester abortion
induced by intra-amniotic prostaglandin E2 and
hypertonic solutions," by I. Z. Mackenzie, et al.
LANCET 2(7944):1066-1069, 1975. (Bio. Abstrs.
1976, 5680)

"Combination therapy for midtrimester abortion: laminaria and analogues of prostaglandins," by P. G.
Stubblefield, et al. CONTRACEPTION 13(6):723-729,

1976. (Bio. Abstrs. 1976, 39255)

"A comparative study of intra-amniotic saline and two
prostaglandin F2a dose schedules for midtrimester
abortion," by D. A. Edleman, et al. AMERICAN
JOURNAL OF OBSTETRICS AND GYNECOLOGY
125(2):188-195, 1976. (Bio. Abstrs. 1976, 39271)

"Comparison of intra-amniotic prostaglandin F2 alpha
and hypertonic saline for induction of second-trimester
abortion." BRITISH MEDICAL JOURNAL 1(6022):
1373-1376, June 6, 1976.

"A comparison of saline and prostaglandin abortions at
the Medical Center of Central Georgia," by J. R.
Harrison, Jr., et al. JOURNAL OF THE MEDICAL
ASSOCIATION OF GEORGIA 65(2):53-54, February,
1976.

"Concurrent use of prostaglandin F2a and laminaria tents
for induction of midtrimester abortion," by J. H.
Duenhoelter, et al. OBSTETRICS AND GYNECOLOGY
47(4):469-472, 1976. (Bio. Abstrs. 1976, 33635)

"The culturability of fibroblasts from the skin of abortuses
after intra-amniotic instillation of urea or prostaglandin," by K. S. Ju, et al. AMERICAN JOURNAL OF
OBSTETRICS AND GYNECOLOGY 125(8):1155,
August 15, 1976.

"The current status of prostaglandins as abortifacients,"
by W. E. Brenner. AMERICAN JOURNAL OF
OBSTETRICS AND GYNECOLOGY 123(3):306-328,
October 1, 1975.

"Delayed morbidity following prostaglandin-induced
abortion," by I. Z. Mackenzie, et al. INTERNATIONAL
JOURNAL OF GYNAECOLOGY AND OBSTETRICS 13(5):
209-214, 1975. (Bio. Abstrs. 1976, 23175)

"Early pregnancy interruption by 15(S) 15 methyl prostaglandin F2a methyl ester," by M. Bygdeman, et al. OBSTETRICS AND GYNECOLOGY 48(2):221-224, 1976. (Bio. Abstrs. 1976, 56848)

"Early termination of pregnancy: a comparative study of intrauterine prostaglandin F2alpha and vacuum aspiration," by M. I. Ragab, et al. PROSTA-GLANDINS 11(2):261-273, February, 1976.

"The effect of meperidine analgesia on midtrimester abortions induced with intra-amniotic prostaglandin F2a," by L. G. Staurovsky, et al. AMERICAN JOURNAL OF OBSTETRICS AND GYNECOLOGY 125(2):185-187, 1976. (Bio. Abstrs. 1976, 50604)

"Effects of prostaglandin E2 and F2alpha therapy," by I. S. Fraser. COMPREHENSIVE THERAPY 2(9): 55-59, September, 1976.

"The efficacy and safety of intramuscularly administered 15(S) 15 methyl prostaglandin E2 methyl ester for induction of artificial abortion," by W. E. Brenner, et al. AMERICAN JOURNAL OF OBSTETRICS AND GYNECOLOGY 123(1):19-29, September 1, 1975.

"The efficacy of intravaginal 15 methyl prostaglandin F2alpha methyl ester in first and second trimester abortion," by T. F. Dillon, et al. PROSTAGLANDINS 12 Suppl:81-98, 1976.

"Electorencephalographic changes following intra-amniotic prostaglandin F2a administration for therapeutic abortion," by A. Faden, et al. OBSTE-TRICS AND GYNECOLOGY 47(5):607-608, 1976. (Bio. Abstrs. 1976, 27851)

"Estrogen content of the amniotic fluid, plasma and placental tissue during abortion induced by prostaglan-

din F2alpha and 15-methyl-prostaglandin F2 alpha,"
by V. G. Orlova, et al. AKUSHERSTVO I GINE-
KOLOGIE (Moscow) (6):24-28, June, 1975.

"Evaulation of intramuscular 15(s)-15-methyl prostaglandin F2 alpha tromethamine salt for induction of
abortion, medications to attenuate side effects, and
intracervical laminaria tents," by W. Gruber, et
al. FERTILITY AND STERILITY 27(9):1009-1023,
September, 1976.

"Evaluation of vaginal delivery systems containing 15[s]
15-methyl PGF2alpha methyl ester," by C. H.
Spilman, et al. PROSTAGLANDINS 12 Suppl:1-16,
1976.

"Experience with 276 intra-amniotic prostaglandin F2a
induced midtrimester abortions," by M. S. Golbus,
et al. PROSTAGLANDINS 11(5):841-851, 1976.
(Bio. Abstrs. 1976, 62686)

"Extra-amniotic 15 (S)-15 methyl PGF2alpha to induce
abortion: a study of three administration schedules,"
by I. Z. Mackenzie, et al. PROSTAGLANDINS
12(3):443-453, September, 1976.

"First experiences with a (15S)-15-methyl prostaglandin
F2alpha vaginal device for termination pregnancy
with serial sonographic observations," by J. H.
Duenhoelter, et al. PROSTAGLANDINS 12 Suppl:
135-245, 1976.

"A histologic study of the placentas of patients with saline-
and prostaglandin-induced abortion," by S. Puri, et al.
OBSTETRICS AND GYNECOLOGY 48(2):216-220, 1976.
(Bio. Abstrs. 1976, 56851)

"Hormone release and abortifacient effectiveness of a
newly developed silastic device containing 15-ME-

PGF2alpha methyl ester in concentrations of 0.5% and 1.0%," by N. H. Lauersen, et al. PROSTA-GLANDINS 12 Suppl:63-79, 1976.

"Inhibitory effect of progesterone on the lactogenic and abortive action of prostaglandin F2alpha," by N. T. Vermouth, et al. JOURNAL OF ENDOCRINOLOGY 66(1):21-29, July, 1975.

"Induced abortion in the 8-9th week of pregnancy with vaginally administered 15-methyl PGF2alpha methyl ester," by A. Leader, et al. PROSTAGLANDINS 12(4):631-637, October, 1976.

"Induction of abortion by vaginal administration of 15(s) 15-methyl prostaglandin F2alpha methyl ester. A comparison of two delivery systems," by M. Bygdeman, et al. PROSTAGLANDINS 12 Suppl:27-51, 1976.

"Induction of abortion with intra-amniotic or intra-muscular 15(S)-15-methyl-prostaglandin F2alpha," by O. Ylikorkala, et al. PROSTAGLANDINS 10(3):423-434, September, 1975.

"Induction of midtrimester abortion by serial intra-vaginal administration of 15(S)-15-methyl-prosta-glandin F2alpha (THAM) suppositories," by N. H. Lauersen, et al. PROSTAGLANDINS 10(6):1037-1045, December, 1975.

"The influence of aspirin on the course of induced mid-trimester abortion," by J. R. Niebyl, et al. AMERICAN JOURNAL OF OBSTETRICS AND GYNE-COLOGY 124(6):607-610, 1976. (Bio. Abstrs. 1976, 16218)

"Intra-amniotic administration of 15(S)-15-methyl-prostaglandin F2alpha for the induction of midtrimester

abortion," by J. R. Dingfelder, et al. AMERICAN
JOURNAL OF OBSTETRICS AND GYNECOLOGY
125(6):821-826, July 15, 1976.

"Intra-amniotic administration of prostaglandin F 2
alpha, 12-methyl-prostaglandin F 2 alpha and hypertonic chloride solution for induction of abortion in
second-trimester pregnancy," by L. S. Persianinov,
et al. ZENTRALBLATT FUR GYNAEKOLOGIE
97(19):1153-1159, 1975.

"Intra-amniotic urea and prostaglandin F2 alpha for
midtrimester abortion: a modified regimen," by
R. T. Burkman, et al. AMERICAN JOURNAL OF
OBSTETRICS AND GYNECOLOGY 126(3):328-333,
October 1, 1976.

"Intramuscular (15S)-15-methyl prostaglandin F2alpha
for midtrimester and missed abortions," by S. D.
Sharma, et al. OBSTETRICS AND GYNECOLOGY
46(4):468-472, October, 1975.

"Intrauterine (extraamniotic) prostaglandins in the
management of unsuccessful pregnancy," by A. A.
Calder, et al. JOURNAL OF REPRODUCTIVE
MEDICINE 16(5):271-275, May, 1976.

"Intra-uterine administration of prostaglandin F2alpha
for induction of abortion. pp. 27-30." In:
Bergström S ed. Report from meetings of the Prostaglandin Task Force Steering Committee. Stockholm,
1973. QV 175 W927r 1972-1973.

"Intra-uterine administration of prostaglandin F2alpha
or 15-methyl PGF2 alpha for induction of abortion.
Intra-amniotic method. pp. 79." In: Bergström S, ed.
Report from meetings of the Prostgalndin Task Force
Steering Committee. Stockholm, 1973. QV 175 W927r
1972-1973.

"Intrauterine extra-amniotic 15(s)-15-methyl prosta-glandin f2alpha for induction of early midtrimester abortion," by A. G. Shapiro. FERTILITY AND STERILITY 27(9):1024-1028, September, 1976.

"Intrauterine injection of 15(S)-15-methyl-prostaglandin F2alpha for termination of early pregnancy in out-patient," by O. Ylikorkala, et al. PROSTAGLANDINS 10(2):333-341, August, 1975.

"The intravenous infusion of prostaglandin F2alpha in the management of intrauterine death of the fetus," by N. Moe. ACTA OBSTETRICIA ET GYNECOLOGICA SCANDINAVICA 55(2):113-114, 1976.

"Kinetic and metabolic studies of 15-methyl-prostaglandin F2a administered intra-amniotically for induction of abortion," by K. Green, et al. PROSTAGLANDINS 11(4):699-711, 1976. (Bio. Abstrs. 1976, 50694)

"Labor induction by intra-amniotic administration of prostaglandin F 2 alpha," by H. Halle, et al. ZENTRALBLATT FUR GYNAEKOLOGIE 97(19): 1160-1165, 1975.

"Laminaria augmentation of intra-amniotic PGF2 for midtrimester pregnancy termination," by P. G. Stubblefield, et al. PROSTAGLANDINS 10(3):413-422, Setpember, 1975.

"Laminaria augmentation of midtrimester pregnancy termination by intramuscular prostaglandin 15 (S) 15-methyl F2 alpha," by J. Robins, et al. JOURNAL OF REPRODUCTIVE MEDICINE 16(6):334-336, June, 1976.

"Luteolytic and abortifacient effects of serial intra-muscular injections of 15(S)-15-methyl-prostaglandin F2alpha in early pregnency," by N. H. Lauersen, et al.

AMERICAN JOURNAL OF OBSTETRICS AND GYNE-
COLOGY 124(4):425-429, February 15, 1976.

"Management of failed prostaglandin abortions," by N.
H. Lauersen, et al. OBSTETRICS AND GYNE-
COLOGY 47(4):473-478, 1976. (Bio. Abstrs. 1976,
16203)

"Management of intrauterine fetal demise and missed
abortion using prostaglandin E2 vaginal suppositories,"
by E. M. Southern, et al. OBSTETRICS AND GYNE-
COLOGY 47(5):602-606, 1976. (Bio. Abstrs. 1976,
24567)

"Management of spontaneous abortion and fetal death by
extra-amnial administration of a single dose of alpha
prostaglandin 2," by K. Lajos, et al. ORVOSI
HETILAP 117(30):1815-1817, July 25, 1976.

"Mechanism of action of prostaglandin F2 alpha and its
clinical use in obstetrics," by L. S. Persianinov.
AKUSHERSTVO I GINEKOLOGIIA (Moscow) (6):7-15,
June, 1975.

"Menstrual induction with PGF2alpha-analogue ICI
81008," by A. I. Csapo, et al. PROSTAGLANDINS
11(1):155-162, January, 1976.

"Midtrimester abortion induced by serial intramuscular
injections of 15(S)-15-methyl-prostaglandin E2 methyl
ester," by N. H. Lauersen, et al. AMERICAN
JOURNAL OF OBSTETRICS AND GYNECOLOGY 123
(7):665-670, December 1, 1975.

"Midtrimester pregnancy termination by intramuscular
injection of a 15-methyl analogue of prostaglandin
F2 alpha," by J. Robins, et al. AMERICAN
JOURNAL OF OBSTETRICS AND GYNECOLOGY 123
(6):625-631, November 15, 1975.

"Midtrimester pregnancy termination with prostaglandin
E2 vaginal suppositories," by M. Hochman, et al.
JOURNAL OF REPRODUCTIVE MEDICINE 16(5):
263-268, May, 1976.

"Midtrimester prostaglandin-induced abortion: gross
and light microscopic findings in the placenta," by
L. H. Honore. PROSTAGLANDINS 11(6):1019-1032,
1976. (Bio. Abstrs. 1976, 62674)

"Outpatient postconceptional fertility control with vaginally
administered 15(S) 15-methyl-PGF2alpha-methyl ester,"
by M. Bygdeman, et al. AMERICAN JOURNAL OF
OBSTETRICS AND GYNECOLOGY 124(5):495-498,
March 1, 1976.

"PGE2 as a vaginal abortifacient - diaphragm effect,"
(letter), by S. L. Corson, et al. PROSTAGLANDINS
10(3):543-544, September, 1975.

"The placental and fetal response to the intra-amniotic
injection of prostaglandin F2 alpha in midtrimester
abortions," by P. Jouppila, et al. BRITISH
JOURNAL OF OBSTETRICS AND GYNAECOLOGY
83(4):303-306, April, 1976.

"Plasma levels of the methyl ester of 15-methyl PGF2a
in connection with intravenous and vaginal administration to the human," by K. Green, et al. PROSTA-
GLANDINS 11(5):879-892, 1976. (Bio. Abstrs. 1976,
62691)

"Preliminary trials of vaginal silastic devices containing
(15s)-15 methyl prostaglandin f2 alpha methyl ester
for the induction of memses and for pregnancy termination summary of brook lodge workshop (January 29,
1976)," by E. M. Southern. PROSTAGLANDINS
12 Suppl:147-252, 1976.

"Preoperative cervical dilatation by small doses of
prostaglandin F2a," by R. Andriesse, et al.
CONTRACEPTION 14(1):93-99, 1976. (Bio. Abstrs.
1976, 50661)

"Progesterone levels in amniotic fluid and maternal plasma
in prostaglandin F2alpha-induced midtrimester abortion," by Z. Koren, et al. OBSTETRICS AND GYNE-
COLOGY 48(4):427 passim, October, 1976.

"Prostaglandin F2 alpha as abortifacient agent. Practical aspects," by M. Bygedman. LAKARTIDNINGEN
76(32):2621-2623, August 4, 1976.

"Prostaglandin gel for the induction of abortion and labor
in fetal death," (letter), by T. Modly, et al. ARCHIV
FUR GYNAEKOLOGIE 219(1-4):498-499, November 18,
1975.

"Prostaglandins as early abortifacients. pp. 484-489,"
by N. Wiqvist, et al. In: Segal SJ, et al., ed. The
regulation of mammalian reproduction. Springfield,
Ill., Thomas, 1973. W3 F049 no.8 1973.

"Prostaglandins and post-abortion luteolysis in early
pregnancy," by A. Leader, et al. PROSTAGLANDINS
10(5):889-897, November, 1975.

"Prostaglandins: basic reproductive consideration and
new clinical applications. pp. 157-181," by F.
Naftolin. In: Kahn RH, Lands WE, Ed. Prostaglandins and cyclic AMP. New York, Academic Press,
1973. QU 90 S991p 1972.

"Report of study group on prostaglandin. pp. 5-8." In:
Bergström S, ed. Report from meetings of the Prostaglandin Task Force Steering Committee. Stockholm,
1973. QV 175 W927r 1972-1973.

"Results of therapeutic abortion induction using extra-amniotically administered prostaglandin F2alpha," by H. Lahmann, et al. ARCHIV FUR GYNAEKOLOGIE 219(1-4):499-500, November 18, 1975.

"The synergistic effect of calcium and prostaglandin F2 alpha in second trimester abortion. A pilot study," by L. Weinstein, et al. OBSTETRICS AND GYNE-COLOGY 48(4):469-471, October, 1976.

"Systemic and local administration of prostaglandins for postconceptional fertility control. pp. 108-115," by M. Toppozada, et al. In: Bergström S, ed. Report from meetings of the Prostaglandin Task Force Steering Committee. Stockholm, 1973. QV 175 W927r 1972-1973.

"Terbutaline inhibition of midtrimester uterine activity induced by prostaglandin F2alpha and hypertonic saline," by K. E. Andersson, et al. BRITISH JOURNAL OF OBSTETRICS AND GYNAECOLOGY 82(9):745-749, September, 1975.

"The termination of human pregnancy with prostaglandin analogs," by G. D. Gutknecht, et al. JOURNAL OF REPRODUCTION MEDICINE 15(3):93-96, September, 1975.

"Termination of late first-trimester and early second-trimester gestations with intramuscular 15 (S)-15-methyl-prostaglandin F2alpha," by R. J. Bolognese, et al. JOURNAL OF REPRODUCTIVE MEDICINE 16(2):81-84, February, 1976.

"Termination of late-term pregnancy in intra-amniotic administration of prostaglandin and hypertonic saline solution," by E. A. Chernukha, et al. AKUSHERSTVO I GINEKOLOGIIA (Moscow) (6):19-24, June, 1975.

279

"Termination of midtrimester pregnancy by serial intramuscular injections of 15(S)-15methyl-prostaglandin
F2alpha," by N. H. Lauersen, et al. AMERICAN
JOURNAL OF OBSTETRICS AND GYNECOLOGY
124(2):169-176, January 15, 1976.

"Termination of pregnancy in cases of fetal death in
utero by intravenous prostaglandin F2alpha," by A. P.
Lange, et al. PROSTAGLANDINS 11(1):101-108,
January, 1976.

"Termination of pregnancy with double prostaglandin im-
pact," by A. I. Csapo, et al. AMERICAN JOURNAL
OF OBSTETRICS AND GYNECOLOGY 124(1):1-13,
January 1, 1976.

"Therapeutic midtrimester abortion by the intra-uterine
administration of prostaglandins. Experience of
Groote Schuur Hospital, 1974-1975," by G. Sher.
SOUTH AFRICAN MEDICAL JOURNAL 50(30):1173-
1177, July 14, 1976.

"Use of combination prostaglandin F2alpha and hypertonic
saline for midtrimester abortion. Department of
Obstetrics and Gynecology Harvard Medical School,
Beth Israel Hospital, Boston, Massachusetts."
PROSTAGLANDINS 12(4):625-630, October, 1976.

"Use of prostaglandins for induction of abortion," by E. A.
Chernukha. AKUSHERSTVO I GINEKOLOGIIA (Mos-
cow) (7):7-10, July, 1975.

"Use of prostaglandins in gynecology and obstetrics," by
B. I. Nesheim. TIDSSKRIFT FOR DEN NORSKE
LAEGEFORENING 96(6):375-376, February 28, 1976.

"The use of silastic vaginal device containing (15S)-15
methyl prostaglandin F2 alpha methyl ester for early
first trimester pregnancy termination," by J. Robins.

PROSTAGLANDINS 12 Suppl:123-134, 1976.

"Vaginally administered 16, 16-dimethyl-PGE2 for
the induction of midtrimester abortion," by J. N.
Martin, Jr. , et al. PROSTAGLANDINS 11(1):123-
132, 1976. (Bio. Abstrs. 1976, 4269)

"The value of prostaglandins in the treatment of missed
abortion," by N. Exalto, et al. NEDERLANDS
TIJDSCHRIFT VOOR GENEESKUNDE 120(30):1289-
1292, July 24, 1976.

"The WHO Prostaglandin Task Force. (Protocol manual).
Phase IIb clinical trials comparing intra-amniotic
prostaglandin F2alpha and 15-methyl PGE2alpha.
(Trial No. 103). pp. 65-78." In: Bergström S, ed.
Report from meetings of the Prostaglandin Task Force
Steering Committee. Stockholm, 1973. QV 175 W927r
1972-1973.

--Phase III clinical trials of intra-amniotic prostaglandin
F2alpha versus hypertonic saline (trial no. 101) and
extra-amniotic prostaglandin F2alpha (trial no. 102).
pp. 12-27." In: Bergström S, ed. Report from
meetings of the Prostaglandin Task Force Steering
Committee. Stockholm, 1973. QV 175 W927r
1972-1973.

PSYCHOLOGY
see also: Sociology and Behavior

"Abortion in 1975: the psychiatric perspective, with a
discussion of abortion and contraception in adolescence,"
by P. D. Barglow. JOGN; JOURNAL OF OBSTETRIC,
GYNECOLOGIC AND NEONATAL NURSING 5(1):41-48,
January-February, 1976.

"Abortion in 1975: the psychiatric perspective and contraception in adolescence," by P. D. Barglow. JOGN;

JOURNAL OF OBSTETRIC, GYNECOLOGIC AND
NEONATAL NURSING 5:41-47, January-February,
1976.

"Abortion: perception and contemporary genocide myth:
a comparative study among low-income pregnant
Black and Puerto Rican women," by B. R. Hughes.
DISSERTATION ABSTRACTS INTERNATIONAL 34
(6-A):3542-3543, December, 1973. (Psycho.
Abstrs. 1976, 4369)

"Amniocentesis-abortion woes: many who opt to end
pregnancy are unhappy about it later." MEDICAL
WORLD NEWS 12:72, July 12, 1976.

"Dilemma: therapeutic abortion following amniocentesis,"
by N. L. Rudd, et al. CANADIAN NURSE 72:51-56,
August, 1976.

"Grieving and unplanned pregnancy," by M. E. Swigar,
et al. PSYCHIATRY 39:72-80, Feburary, 1976.

"Induced abortions and spontaneous abortions. Psychopathological aspects apropos of a preliminary sample
of 411 requests for pregnancy interruption," by M.
Bourgeois, et al. AMMALES MEDICO-PSYCHO-
LOGIQUES 2(2):339-366, July, 1975.

"Observation of the behavior of aborted women in the days
immediately following abortion," by M. Houmont.
REVUE MEDICALE DE LIEGE 30(8):261-265,
April 15, 1975.

"Outcome following therapeutic abortion," by E. C. Payne,
et al. ARCHIVES OF GENERAL PSYCHIATRY 33(8):
725-733, June, 1976.

"Postabortion psychiatric illness," by C. M. Donovan,
et al. NURSING DIGEST 3:12-16, September-October,
1975.

--Nursing implications. Addendum," by C. A. Farrar. NURSING DIGEST 3:17, September-October, 1975.

"Psychiatric and mental health nursing. Pre-abortion emotional counseling," by S. Gedan. ANA CLINICAL SESSIONS :217-225, 1973.

"Psychiatric aspects of abortion in Hong Kong," by K. Singer. INTERNATIONAL JOURNAL OF SOCIAL PSYCHIATRY 21(4):303-306, Winter, 1975.

"Psychological bases of the two-child norm," by R. D. Kahoe. CATALOG OF SELECTED DOCUMENTS IN PSYCHOLOGY 5, 282, Summer, 1975. (Psycho. Abstrs. 1976, 9619)

"Psychological causes and impact of abortion," by P. Jadoul. REVUE MEDICALE DE LIEGE 30(8):258-261, April 15, 1975.

"Psychological factors in contraceptive failure and abortion request," by D. Everingham. MEDICAL JOURNAL OF AUSTRALIA 2(15):617-618, October 11, 1975.

"Psychological sequelae of therapeutic abortion." (editorial). BRITISH MEDICAL JOURNAL 1(6020): 1239, May 22, 1976.

"Psychological sequelae of therapeutic abortion," (letter), by J. Kellett. BRITISH MEDICAL JOURNAL 2(6026): 45, July 3, 1976.

"Psychological-sociological views on S 218 (study on 379 pregnant women and women in peurperium)," by J. M. Wenderlein. ZENTRALBLATT FUR GYNAEKOLOGIE 98(9):527-532, 1976.

"Psychosocial aspects of abortion in the United States," by J. D. Osofsky, et al. MOUNT SINAI JOURNAL OF

MEDICINE, NEW YORK 42(5):456-467, September-October, 1975.

"Psychosocial aspects of abortion. A review of issues and needed research," by R. Illsley, et al. BULLETIN OF THE WORLD HEALTH ORGANIZATION 53(1):83-106, 1976.

"Psychosocial aspects of pregnancy control: women and perceptions," by M. Murphy. ANA CLINICAL SESSIONS :66-70, 1974.

"Psychosocial consequences of therapeutic abortion King's termination study III," by H. S. Greer, et al. BRITISH JOURNAL OF PSYCHIATRY 128:74-79, January, 1976.

"Psychological correlates of delayed decisions to abort," by M. B. Bracken, et al. HEALTH EDUCATION MONOGRAPHS 4:6-44, Spring, 1976.

"Psychotherapy in abortion," by C. M. Donovan. CURRENT PSYCHIATRIC THERAPIES 15:77-83, 1975.

"Therapeutic abortion and its psychological implications: the Canadian experience," by E. P. Greenglass. CANADIAN MEDICAL ASSOCIATION JOURNAL 113: 794-797, 1976.

"Therapeutic abortion--some psychiatric aspects," by F. Shane. PSYCHIATRIC NURSING 17(2):11-13, March-April, 1976.

PUBLIC HEALTH
"The effect of the legalization of abortion on public health and some of its social concomitants in Hungary," by M. Miklos. DEMOGRAFIA 16, 1:70-113, 1973. (Socio. Abstrs. 1976, 7611408)

PUBLIC HEALTH

"Health care issues," by Sister M. A. A. Zasowska,
et al. HEALTH CARE DIMENSIONS :1-158, Fall,
1974.

"Public health facilities issue new abortion policy."
HOSPITALS 50:17, January 1, 1976.

RADIOLOGISTS

"Diagnostic X-ray Examination Called no Ground for
Abortion." THE NEW YORK TIMES (M) October 21,
16:1, 1976.

"Radiological studies on habitual abortion and prognosis
of pregnancy," by G. Ohmura. JAPANESE JOURNAL
OF FERTILITY AND STERILITY 20(3):92-107, 1975.
(Bio. Abstrs. 1976, 28720)

REFERRAL AGENCIES SERVICES
see: Sociology and Behavior

REGITINE

RELIGION AND ETHICS
see also: Sociology and Behavior

"Abortion," by J. Margolis. ETHICS 84, 1:51-61, 1973.
(Socio. Abstrs. 1976, 76I1759)

"Abortion and the concept of a person," by J. English.
CANADIAN JOURNAL OF PHILOSOPHY 5, 233-243,
October, 1975.

"Abortion and the right to life," by L. S. Carrier.
SOCIAL THEORY AND PRACTICE 3:381-401, Fall,
1975.

"Abortion and the sanctity of human life, by B. Brody. A
review," by P. J. Rossi. AMERICA 133:471, December 27, 1975.

"Abortion: the avoidable moral dilemma," by J. M.
Humber. THE JOURNAL OF VALUE INQUIRY
9, 282-302, Winter, 1975.

"Abortion: the class religion," by M. J. Sobran, Jr.
NATIONAL REVIEW 28:28-31, January 23, 1976.

"Abortion debate: finding a true pro-life stance," by
R. J. Westley. AMERICA 134:489-492, June 5, 1976.

"Abortion isn't a Catholic issue but an issue for all,
Protestant pro-life leaders say," by P. Dubec.
OUR SUNDAY VISITOR 64:1, December 21, 1975.

"The abortion issue; England," by D. Sullivan. TABLET
230:710-711, July 24, 1976.

"Abortion language and logic," by R. A. Hipkiss. ETC
33:207-210, June, 1976.

"Abortion: the last resort," by M. C. Segers. AMERICA
133:456-458, December 27, 1975; Discussion 134:22,
January 17, 1976.

"Abortion, the public morals, and the police power: the
ethical function of substantive due process," by M. J.
Perry. U.C.L.A. LAW REVIEW 23:689-736, April,
1976.

"Abortion: questions and answers from a Catholic perspective; the Catholic Church's view," by J.
Bernardin. L'OSSERVATORE ROMANO 45[449]9
passim, November 4, 1976.

"Abortion: privacy and fantasy," by R. M. Cooper.
ENCOUNTER (CHRISTIAN THEOLOGICAL SEMINARY)
37:181-188, Spring, 1976.

"Abortion will be an issue at Protestant conventions."

OUR SUNDAY VISITOR 65:2, June 13, 1976.

"Abortions in Portugal a Complex Controversy," by
M. Howe. THE NEW YORK TIMES (M) March 13,
13:6, 1976.

"Anti-abortion, the bishops and the crusaders," by J.
Castelli. AMERICA 134:442-444, May 22, 1976.

"Attitude of some elites towards introdution of abortion
as a method of family planning in Bangladesh," by
R. H. Chaudhury. BANGLADESH DEVELOPMENT
STUDIES 3:479-494, October, 1975.

"Ban all abortions? Yes--I million lives are destroyed
each year; interview with Arbp. J. L. Bernardin;
No--we believe in a woman's right to make her own
choice; interview with Rabbi R. S. Sternberger."
U.S. NEWS AND WORLD REPORT 81:27-28,
September 27, 1976.

"Baptists, in Shift, Ask Members to Seek Antiabortion
'Climate'," by K. A. Briggs. THE NEW YORK TIMES
(M) June 18, I, 11:1, 1976.

"Birth rights," by C. Dix, et al. GUARDIAN 11,
February 6, 1975.

"Bishop asks Catholics join Washington March for Life."
OUR SUNDAY VISITOR 64:3, January 18, 1976.

"Bishops in politics: the big plunge: National conference
of Catholic bishops' Pastoral plan for pro-life
activities," by P. J. Weber. AMERICA 134:220-223,
March 20, 1976.

"Bishops move." ECONOMIST 260:26, September 11, 1976.

"The bishops of Colombia for the defence of life."

L'OSSEVATORE ROMANO 15[419]8, April 8, 1976.

"Bishops Plan Drive to Ban Abortions." THE NEW
   YORK TIMES (S) January 3, 35:4, 1976.

"Bishops' plan for pro-life activities." AMERICA 133:
   454-455, December 27, 1975.

"Cardinal Terence Cooke on the rights of the unborn,"
   by Card. T. Cooke. L'OSSERVATORE ROMANO 41
   [445]11-12, October 7, 1976.

"Caring for all the people; respect life program on a
   parish level," by E. Mowery. LIGUORIAN 64:34-
   39, November, 1976.

"Catholic bishops: abortion the issue," W. F. Willoughby,
   CHRISTIANITY TODAY 20:35, December 19, 1975.

"Catholic vote: bishops' move." ECONOMIST 260:26,
   September 11, 1976.

"Catholics Promise to Oppose Abortion," by G. Dugan.
   THE NEW YORK TIMES (M) October 4, 10:3, 1976.

"Catholics' use of abortion," by J. J. Leon, et al.
   SOCIOLOGICAL ANALYSIS 36, 2:125-136, Summer,
   1975. (Socio. Abstrs. 1976, 76H9195)

"Church in the world: abortion and divorce: a change in
   attitude?" by J. Deedy. THEOLOGY TODAY 32:
   86-88, April, 1975.

"The Churches and abortion." NEW HUMANIST 92:32-35,
   May-June, 1976.

"Created in the image of God: man and abortion," by R.
   Slesinski. LINACRE 43:36-48, February, 1976.

"The defence of the true and complete values of life,"
by A. Vernaschi. L'OSSERVATORE ROMANO 17
[421]8-9, April 22, 1976.

"Discretionary killing," by G. F. Will. NEWSWEEK
88:96, September 20, 1976.

"Dutch Senate, by 7 Votes, Rejects Legal Abortion,
Coalition Crisis Allayed." THE NEW YORK TIMES
(S) December 15, I, 14:3, 1976.

"Evangelical looks at the abortion phenomenon," by
H. O. J. Brown. AMERICA 135:161-164, September 25, 1976.

"Facts and evils of free abortion; reprint from Civiltà
Cattolica, March 6, 1976," by G. Caprile.
L'OSSERVATORE ROMANO 21[425]5 passim,
May 20, 1976.

"The fight for life; it's up to you; some practical guidelines to make your voice heard," by M. Bunson.
OUR SUNDAY VISITOR MAGAZINE 64:1 passim,
May 2, 1976.

"Human being: the boundaries of the concept," by L. C.
Becker. PHILOSOPHY AND PUBLIC AFFAIRS
4:334-359, Summer, 1975.

"I was a spy at a Right-to-life convention," by L. Farr.
MS MAGAZINE 4:77-78 passim, February, 1976.

"Ideal family size as an intervening variable between
religion and attitudes towards abortion," by M. Rehzi.
JOURNAL FOR THE SCIENTIFIC STUDY OF RELIGION 14, 1:23-27, March, 1975.

"Induced abortion, Jewish law and Jewish morality," by
F. Rosner. MAN AND MEDICINE 1:213-224,

Spring, 1976.

"Is abortion a Catholic issue?" CHRISTIANITY TODAY 20:29, January 16, 1976.

"Is abortion only a Catholic issue?" by J. Higgins. LIGUORIAN 64:24-28, May, 1976.

"Is the pro-life movement dying at the grass-roots?" by F. Gannon. OUR SUNDAY VISITOR MAGAZINE 65:1 passim, August 8, 1976.

"Killing--mission of the physician?" by E. Trube-Becker. MEDIZINISCHE KLINIK 71(18):786-788, April 30, 1976.

"Let's lower our voices about abortion," by K. Axe. U.S. CATHOLIC 41:14-15, June, 1976.

"Let's not reject children of change," by A. Nowlan. THE ATLANTIC ADVOCATE 66:79, June, 1976.

"Long Island Poll," by F. Lynn. THE NEW YORK TIMES (M) May 2, XXI, 31:1, 1976.

"Magisterial teaching on life issues," by Card. H. Medeiros. L'OSSERVATORE ROMANO 36[440]4-5, September 2, 1976.

"Militancy and the Abortion Fight," by M. D. Dreger. THE NEW YORK TIMES (M) November 21, XXI, 26:1, 1976.

"Moral ethics seminar; opening address of medical ethics seminar in Dublin," by Abp. D. Ryan. L'OSSERVATORE ROMANO 49[401]9, December 4, 1975.

"Moral rights and abortion," by H. V. McLachlan.

CONTEMPORARY REVIEW 228:323-333, June, 1976.

"Moral sentiment in judicial opinions on abortion," by
E. N. Moore. SANTA CLARA LAWYER 15:591-
634, Spring, 1975.

"NFPC says bishops place too much emphasis on
abortion." OUR SUNDAY VISITOR 65:1, September 26,
1976.

"A new ethical approach to abortion and its implications
for the euthanasia dispute," by R. F. Gardner.
JOURNAL OF MEDICAL ETHICS 1(3):127-131,
September, 1975.

"The new jurisprudence," by R. M. Bryn. JAMA;
JOURNAL OF THE AMERICAN MEDICAL ASSOCI-
ATION 236(4):359-360, July 26, 1976.

"The new morality and abortion," by E. Lio. L'OSSER-
VATORE ROMANO 5[409]8-9, January 29, 1976.

"No bargaining about abortion; exhortation of bishops of
Lazio," by Card. U. Poletti. L'OSSERVATORE
ROMANO 45[449]11, November 4, 1976.

"No retreat on abortion," by J. D. Rockefeller, 3d.
NEWSWEEK 87:11, June, 21, 1976.

"Of many things: views of Catholic bishops," by J.
O'Hare. AMERICA 134:inside cover, January 31,
1976.

"On abortion and right to life," (letter), by E. J. Kirsch.
AMERICAN JOURNAL OF PUBLIC HEALTH 66(9):
906, September, 1976.

"Orthodox Church condemns abortion and euthanasia."
OUR SUNDAY VISITOR 64:3, December 7, 1975.

"Orthodox Rabbis Rebuke Jews Who Back Premissive Abortion," by I. Spiegel. THE NEW YORK TIMES (M) January 28, 36:2, 1976.

"Pastoral letter for all bishops calls abortion laws unjust and immoral; asks for action." OUR SUNDAY VISITOR MAGAZINE 64:1, January 18, 1976.

"A pastoral plan for pro-life activities." CATHOLIC MIND 74:55-64, March, 1976.

"Pastoral plan for pro-life activities; statement," by Card. T. Cooke, et al. L'OSSERVATORE ROMANO 1[405]3-4, January 1, 1976.

"Pax Romana, Catholic jurists against abortion." L'OSSERVATORE ROMANO 43[447]10, October 21, 1976.

"Pope Denies View is Outdated." THE NEW YORK TIMES (S) January 22, 32:1, 1976.

"Pope Praises Catholic Education in U.S." THE NEW YORK TIMES (S) June 25, I, 2:4, 1976.

"Potentiality in the abortion discussion," by F. C. Wade. REVIEW OF METAPHYSICS 29:239-255, December, 1975.

"Premarital sexual permissiveness and abortion: standards of college women," by A. M. Mirande, et al. PACIFIC SOCIOLOGICAL REVIEW 17, 4:485-503, October, 1974. (Socio. Abstrs. 1976, 76H8170)

"Protestant anti-abortion leader scores prejudice." OUR SUNDAY VISITOR 65:2, October 24, 1976.

"Protestant leaders back Catholic pro-life stand." OUR SUNDAY VISITOR 64:2, December 14, 1975.

"Protestants back Catholic efforts against abortion."
OUR SUNDAY VISITOR 64:1, March 7, 1976.

"A question of conscience," by R. Salm. BRITISH
MEDICAL JOURNAL 1(6025):1593, June 26, 1976.

"A question of conscience," by R. Walley. BRITISH
MEDICAL JOURNAL 1(6023):1456-1458, June 12,
1976.

"Reflections on abortion, a current and ageless prob-
lem," by L. Derobert. MEDECINE LEGALE ET
DOMMAGE CORPOREL 7(4):289-291, October-
December, 1974.

"The relationship between abortion attitudes and
Catholic religiosity," by A. J. Blasi, et al.
SOCIAL SCIENCE 50, 1:34-39, Winter, 1975.
(Socio. Abstrs. 1976, 76I2502)

"Religion and voting on abortion reform: a follow-up
study," by J. T. Richardson, et al. JOURNAL FOR
THE SCIENTIFIC STUDY OF RELIGION 14, 2:159-164,
June, 1975. (Socio. Abstrs. 1976, 76I0933)

"Religious freedom and abortion." L'OSSERVATORE
ROMANO 9[413]8 passim, February 26, 1976.

"Religious groups plan abortion rights drive," by J.
Fogarty. NATIONAL CATHOLIC REPORTER 12:6,
February 6, 1976.

"Remarks on abortion, abandonment, and adoption
opportunities," by R. M. Herbenick. PHILOSOPHY
& PUBLIC AFFAIRS 5, 1:98-104, Fall, 1975.
(Socio. Abstrs. 1976, 76I2512)

"Right to life." CHRISTIANITY TODAY 20:55, February 13, 1976.

"Second thoughts on abortion from the doctor who led the crusade for it," by C. Remsberg, et al. GOOD HOUSEKEEPING 182:69 passim, March, 1976.

"Secular press snubs abortion death report," by J. Scheidler. OUR SUNDAY VISITOR MAGAZINE 64:1 passim, March 14, 1976.

"Some reflections on the abortion issue," bu D. Gustafon. WESTERN HUMANITIES REVIEW 30:181-198, Summer, 1976.

"They exploded the abortion myth," by M. Bunson. OUR SUNDAY VISITOR MAGAZINE 64:1 passim, January 18, 1976.

"Three against abortion: none of them Catholic," by R. Cormier. ST. ANTHONY MESSENGER 84:18-22, June, 1976.

"Thousands march in national capital in protest against legalized abortion," by C. Foster. OUR SUNDAY VISITOR 64:1, February 8, 1976.

"Today's moral symmetry principle," by P. L. Trammell. PHILOSOPHY AND PUBLIC AFFAIRS 5, 305-313, Spring, 1976.

"Value conflicts and the uses of research: the example of abortion." MAN AND MEDICINE 1:29-41, Autumn, 1975.

"Viewpoint: abortion revisited," by H. Moody. CHRISTIANITY AND CRISIS 35:166-168, July 21, 1975.

"We are lovers of life, Archbishop Sheen says." OUR SUNDAY VISITOR 65:2, July 11, 1976.

RELIGION AND ETHICS

"We ask protection for the unborn; pastoral letter,"
by Card. T. Manning. L'OSSERVATORE ROMANO
6[410]10, February 5, 1976.

"What are the bonds between the fetus and the uterus?"
by V. W. Adamkiewicz. CANADIAN NURSE 72(2):
26-28, February, 1976.

"What I saw at the abortion," by R. Seizer. CHRISTI-
ANITY TODAY 20:11-12, January 16, 1976.

"What I saw at the abortion; continued from Esquire,
January, 1976." CATHOLIC DIGEST 40:47-50,
July, 1976.

"What therapeutic abortion?" by A. Bompiani. L'OSSER-
VATORE ROMANO 15[419]9, April 8, 1976.

RESEARCH
"Abortifacient effect of steroids from Ananas comosus
and their analogues on mice," by A. Pakrashi, et
al. JOURNAL OF REPRODUCTION AND FERTILITY
46(2):461-462, March, 1976.

"Abortifacient effects of Vibrio cholerae exo-enterotoxin
and endotoxin in mice," by G. J. Gasic, et al.
JOURNAL OF REPRODUCTION AND FERTILITY
45(2):315-322, November, 1975.

"Abortion and cannibalism in squirrel monkeys (Saimiri
sciureus) associated with experimental protein deficiency during gestation," by S. L. Manocha.
LABORATORY ANIMAL SCIENCE 26(4):649-650,
August, 1976.

"Abortion associated with Hemophilus somnus infection
in a bovine fetus," by A. A. van Dreumel, et al.
CANADIAN VETERINARY JOURNAL 16(12):367-
370, December, 1975.

295

RESEARCH

"Abortion associated with mixed Leptospira equid herpesvirus 1 infection," by W. A. Ellis, et al. VETERIN-
ARY RECORD 98(11):218-219, March 13, 1976.

"Abortion in cows as a probable consequence of mycosis,"
by B. Sielicka, et al. DERMATOLOGISCHE MONATS-
SCHRIFT 162(2):184-185, February, 1976.

"Abortions in cows caused by Aspergillus fumigatus
fresenius I, " by S. Venev. VETERINARNO-
MEDITSINSKI NAUKI 11(9):67-71, 1974.

"Abortion in sheep and goats in Cyprus caused by Coxiella
burnet," by R. W. Crowther, et al. VETERINARY
RECORD 99(2):29-30, July 10, 1976.

"Abortion research in Latin America," by S. G. Sainz.
STUDIES IN FAMILY PLANNING 7:211-217, August,
1976.

"Abortive action of 20 percent NaCL and alpha F2
prostaglandin solutions administered intra-amniotically
in rats," by N. S. Hung, et al. JOURNAL DE GYNE-
COLOGIE, OBSTETRIQUE ET BIOLOGIE DE LA
REPRODUCTION 3(8):1169-1188, December, 1974.

"The action of antitrophoblastic antibodies on pregnancy:
an experimental study," by P. Morin, et al.
JOURNAL DE GYNECOLOGIE, OBSTETRIQUE ET
BIOLOGIE DE LA REPRODUCTION 4(3):309-314, 1975.
(Bio. Abstrs. 1976, 17021)

"Antigenic analysis and immunological studies of the
uterotropic bacterial strains SH6 and 01 isolated from
aborted cows," by I. Gelev. VETERINARNO-MEDIT-
SINKI NAUKI 12(4):13-22, 1976.

"Bacterial infection in cows associated with abortion,
endometritis and infertility," by I. Gelev. ZENTRAL-

BLATT FUER VETERINAERMEDIZINE. JOURNAL
OF VETERINARY MEDICINE [B] 22(5):372-380, July,
1975.

"Bovine fetal cerebal absidiomycosis," by W. U. Knudtson,
et al. SABOURAUDIA; JOURNAL OF THE INTER-
NATIONAL SOCIETY FOR HUMAN AND ANIMAL
MYCOLOGY 13(3):299-302, 1975. (Bio. Abstrs. 1976,
24575)

"Bovine viral diarrhea virus-induced abortion," by J.
W. Kendrick. THERIOGENOLOGY 5(3):91-93, 1976.
(Bio. Abstrs. 1976, 32438)

"Brucella abortus infection in sheep: I. Field case," by
W. B. Shaw. BRITISH VETERINARY JOURNAL 132
(1):18-27, 1976. (Bio. Abstrs. 1976, 55552)

"Brucella abortus infection in sheep. II. Experimental
infection of ewes," by W. B. Shaw. BRITISH
VETERINARY JOURNAL 132(2):143-151, March-April,
1976.

"Case of rhinopneumonia in horses in Kirghizia," by A. V.
Mokrousova, et al. VETERINARIIA (2):57, February,
1976.

"Chlamydial abortion in sheep and goats," by Iu. D.
Karavaev. VETERINARIIA (6):96-97, June, 1976.

"Clinical and epizootiological aspects of bovine, caprine,
and ovine brucellosis in Greece," by P. A. Karvounaris.
DEVELOPMENTS IN BIOLOGICAL STANDARDIZATION
31:254-264, 1976.

"Comparative effects of hyperosmolar urea administered
by intraamniotic, intravenous, and intraperitoneal
routes in rhesus monkeys," by D. A. Blake, et al.
AMERICAN JOURNAL OF OBSTETRICS AND GYNE-

COLOGY 124(3):239-244, 1976. (Bio. Abstrs. 1976, 11034)

"Comparison of dexamethasone trimethylacetate and prostaglandin F-2alpha as abortifacients in the cow," (proceedings), by C. A. Sloan. JOURNAL OF RE-PRODUCTION AND FERTILITY 46(2):529, March, 1976.

"Corynebacterium pyogenes-induced abortion," by R. E. Smith. THERIOGENOLOGY 5(3):107-109, 1976. (Bio. Abstrs. 1976, 26769)

"Cystine aminopeptidase activity (oxytocinase) in pregnant guinea pigs: normal and infected with Campylobacter fetus," by R. Hrakak, et al. AMERICAN JOURNAL OF VETERINARY RESEARCH 37(3):343-344, 1976. (Bio. Abstrs. 1976, 36106)

"Dietary urea for dairy cattle: II. Effect of functional traits," by R. E. Erb, et al. JOURNAL OF DAIRY SCIENCE 59(4):656-667, 1976. (Bio. Abstrs. 1976, 23478)

"Dropsy of the fetal sacs in mares: induced and spontaneous abortion," by M. Vandeplassche, et al. VETERINARY RECORD 99(4):67-69, July 24, 1976.

"Early pregnancy testing and its relationship to abortion," by C. F. Irwin. JOURNAL OF REPRODUCTION AND FERTILITY [SUPPLEMENT] (23):485-488, October, 1975.

"The effect of dilysosomal macrophages on the development and the outcome of pneumonia induced by the agent of a enzootic abortion of ewes," by V. E. Pigarevskii, et al. BYULLETEN' EKSPERIMENTAL' NOI BIOLOGII I MEDITSENY 81(4):440-442, 1976. (Bio. Abstrs. 1976, 55559)

"Effect of the extracts from Aristolochia indica Linn on interception in female mice," by A. Pakrashi, et al. EXPERIENTIA 32(3):394-395, March 15, 1976.

"Effect of large daily doses of ascarlic acid on pregnancy in guinea pigs, rats and hamsters," by F. R. Alleva, et al. TOXICOLOGY AND APPLIED PHARMACOLOGY 35(2):393-395, 1976. (Bio. Absts. 1976, 7026)

"Effect of prostaglandin F2 alpha on the neurohypophysis: a histochemical study," by U. Singh, et al. ACTA MORPHOLOGICA ACADEMIA SCIENTIORUM HUNGARICAE 23(1):51-57, 1975. (Bio. Abstrs. 1976, (Bio. Abstrs. 1976, 13626)

"Effectiveness of vaccination against Chlamydia abortion in sheep," by W. A. Valder, et al. DEUTSCHE TIERAERZTLICHE WOCHENSCHRIFT 82(6):221-225, June 5, 1975.

"The effects of selective withdrawal of FSH or LH on spermatogenesis in the immature rat," by R. H. G. Madhwa. BIOLOGY OF REPRODUCTION 14(4):489-494, 1976. (Bio. Abstrs. 1976, 13477)

"Elimination of spontaneous and chemically induced chromosome aberrations in mice during early embryogenesis," by A. Basler, et al. HUMAN GENETICS 33(2):121-130, July 27, 1976.

"Epizontic bovine abortion," by J. W. Kendrick. THERIOGENOLOGY 5(3):99-101, 1976. (Bio. Abstrs. 1976, 26785)

"Equine rhinopneumonitis virus infection in horses," by R. G. Dijkstra. TIJDSCHRIFT VOOR DIERGENEESKUNDE 100(17):930-931, September 1, 1975.

"Equine virus abortion," (letter), by J. I. Phillip. VETERINARY RECORD 98(14):283, April 3, 1976.

"Experimental abortions in mice and guinea pigs caused by Aspergillus fumigatus spores," by S. Venev. VETERINARNO-MEDITSINSKI NAUKI 13(1):86-93, 1976.

"An experimental study of Salmonella dublin abortion in cattle," by G. A. Hall, et al. BRITISH VETERINARY JOURNAL 132(1):60-65, 1976. (Bio. Abstrs. 1976, 55553)

"Experimentally induced bovine abortion with Myco- plasma agalactiae subsp bovis," by O. H. Stalheim, et al. AMERICAN JOURNAL OF VETERINARY RESEARCH 37(8):879-883, August, 1976.

"Fertility and fertility problems in some beef herds in Sweden," by S. Einarsson, et al. NORDISK VETER- INAER MEDICIN 27(9):411-428, September, 1975.

"Fertility patterns in female mice following treatment with arginine vasotocin or melatonin," by M. K. Vaughan, et al. INTERNATIONAL JOURNAL OF FERTILITY 21(1):65-68, 1976. (Bio. Abstrs. 1976, 30927)

"Fertility problems caused by infectious agents pigs in the Netherlands," by J. P. Akkermans. TIJD- SCHRIFT VOOR DIERGENEESKUNDE 100(15):809- 820, August 1, 1975.

"Haemophilus parahemolyticus associated with abortion in swine," by R. W. Wilson, et al. CANADIAN VETERINARY JOURNAL 17(8):222, August, 1976.

"Induction of abortion in cattle with prostaglandin F2 alpha and oestradiol valerate," by A. Brand, et al.

TIJDESHRIFT VOOR DIERGENEESKUNDE 100(8): 432-435, April 15, 1975.

"Infectious bovine rhinotracheitis virus: experimental attempts at inducing bovine abortion with a New Zealand isolate," by P. J. Durham, et al. NEW ZEALAND VETERINARY JOURNAL 23(5):93-94, May, 1975.

"Infectious bovine rhinotracheitis virus-induced abortion," by C. A. Kirkbride. THERIOGENOLOGY 5(3):94-97, 1976. (Bio. Abstrs. 1976, 26841)

"Isolation and identification of a virus causing abortions and stillbirths in swine: a preliminary communication," by M. Dilovski, et al. VETERINARNO-MEDITSINSKI NAUKI 12(8):52-53, 1975. (Bio. Abstrs. 1976, 29133)

"Isolation of antigen in the diagnosis of enzootic abortion of sheep by use of the complement fixation test," by R. V. Borovik, et al. VETERINARIIA (6):51-53, June, 1975.

"Laboratory diagnosis of Vibrio fetus-induced abortion," by J. H. Bryner. THERIOGENOLOGY 5(3):129-138, 1976. (Bio. Abstrs. 1976, 26770)

"Laceration of umbilical artery and abruptio placentae secondary to amniocentesis," by J. D. James, et al. OBSTETRICS AND GYNECOLOGY 48(1 Suppl):44S-45S, July, 1976.

"Lead content of tissues of baby rats born of, and nourished by lead-poisoned mothers," by N. P. Singh, et al. JOURNAL OF LABORATORY AND CLINICAL MEDICINE 87(2):273-280, 1976. (Bio. Abstrs. 1976, 23141)

"Leptospirois-induced abortion," by C. S. Roberts.

THERIOGENOLOGY 5(3):110-122, 1976. (Bio. abstrs. 1976, 26768)

"Listeria monocytogenes-induced abortion," by R. E. Smith. THERIOGENOLOGY 5(3):123-127, 1976. (Bio. Abstrs. 1976, 32339)

"Morphologic and virologic studies of the fetus and placenta in neorickettsial abortion in cattle," by A. Angelov, et al. VETERINARNO-MEDITSINSKI NAUKI 12(7):20-27, 1975.

"Mycotic abortion," by C. Kirkbride. THERIOGENOLOGY 5(3):139-149, 1976. (Bio. Abstrs. 26804)

"Obtaining hyperimmune serum for the diagnosis of enzootic ovine abortion," by R. Kh. Khamadaev, et al. VETERINARIIA (10):36-38, October, 1975.

"Ovine chlamydial abortion in Alberta," by G. A. Chalmers, et al. CANADIAN VETERINARY JOURNAL 17(3):76-81, March, 1976.

"Pathogenicity of T. foetus after various periods of storage," by R. V. Kazeev, et al. VETERINARIIA (6):90-93, June, 1975.

"Pathologicoanatomic and histomorphological changes in the fetus in chlamydial abortion in swine," by A. I. Iatsyshin, et al. VETERINARIIA (4):80-84, April, 1976.

"Pathomorphological changes in sheep in experimental enzootic abortion," by Iu. T. Andrlishin. VETERINARIIA (8):72-76, August, 1975.

'Pharmacokinetics of intra-amniotically administered hyperosmolar urea in rhesus monkeys," by S. A. Blake, et al. AMERICAN JOURNAL OF OBSTETRICS

RESEARCH

AND GYNECOLOGY 124(3):245-250, February 1, 1976.

"Pneumonia associated with Torulopsis glabrata in an
aborted bovine fetus," by W. U. Knudtson, et al.
SABOURAUDIA; JOURNAL OF THE INTERNATIONAL
SOCIETY FOR HUMAN AND ANIMAL MYCOLOGY
14(1):43-45, March, 1976.

"Porcine abortion caused by Actinobacillus equuli," by
R. E. Werdin, et al. JOURNAL OF THE AMERICAN
VETERINARY MEDICAL ASSOCIATION 169(7):704-706,
October 1, 1976.

"Practical aspects of equine virus abortion in the United
Kingdom," by L. B. Jeffcott, et al. VETERINARY
RECORD 98(8):153-155, February 21, 1976.

"Pregnancy termination in dogs with novel nonhormonal
compounds," by G. Galliani, et al. AMERICAN
JOURNAL OF VETERINARY RESEARCH 37(3):263-
268, March, 1976.

"Progesterone withdrawal induced by ICI 81008 in
pregnant rats," by D. H. Warnock, et al. PROSTA-
GLANDINS 10(4):715-724, October, 1975.

"Properties of the Brucella isolated from the aborted
fetuses of cows inoculated with strain 82 vaccine,"
by V. S. Duranov. VETERINARIIA (11):32-33,
November, 1975.

"Search for antifertility agents from indigenous medicinal
plants," by A. Pakrashi, et al. INDIAN JOURNAL OF
MEDICAL RESEARCH 63(3):378-381, March, 1975.

"Serum levles of progesterone, estradiol, and hydrocortisone in ewes after abortions due to Listeria
monocytogenes type 5," by J. L. Carter, et al.
AMERICAN JOURNAL OF VETERINARY RESEARCH

303

37(9):1071-1073, September, 1976.

"Some Leptospira agglutinins detected in domestic animals in British Columbia," by C. E. Andress, et al. CANADIAN JOURNAL OF COMPARATIVE MEDICINE 40(2):215-217, 1976. (Bio. Abstrs. 1976, 28688)

"Study of the amniotic fluid of sheep in the normal course of pregnancy and in abortion," by S. Georgiev. VETERINARNO-MEDITSINSKI NAUKI 12(5):37-44, 1975.

"Study of the outcome of pregnancy in sheep with positive serologic reactions to toxoplasmosis according to the complement fixation test," by A. Donev. VETERINARO-MEDITSINSKI NAUKI 12(1):64-68, 1975.

"Temporal changes in circulating steroids during prosta-glandin F2 alpha induced abortion in the rat and rabbit," by I. F. Lau, et al. PROSTAGLANDINS 11(5):859-869, May, 1976.

"Termination of pregnancy by sheep anti-LHRH gamma globuin in rats," by N. Nishi, et al. ENDOCRINOLOGY 98(4):1024-1039, April, 1976.

"Termination of pseudopregnancy by administration of prostaglandin F2alpha and termination of early pregnancy by administration of prostaglandin F2alpha or colchicine or by removal of embryo in mares," by L. H. Kooistra, et al. AMERICAN JOURNAL OF VETERINARY RESEARCH 37(1):35-39, January, 1976.

"Trichomonas fetus-induced abortion," by J. W. Kendrick. THERIOGENOLOGY 5(3):150-152, 1976. (Bio. Abstrs. 1976, 27484)

"Two forms of simian-virus-40-specific T-antigen in abortive and lytic infection," by C. Ahmad-Zodeh, et al.

PROCEEDINGS OF THE NATIONAL ACADEMY OF
SCIENCES OF THE UNITED STATES OF AMERICA
73(4):1097-1101, 1976. (Bio. Abstrs. 1976, 26824)

"The use of human abortuses in the search for teratogens.
pp. 189-196," by G. P. Oakley, Jr. In: Shepard TH
et al., ed. Methods for detection of environmental
agents that produce congenital defects. Amsterdam,
North-Holland, 1975. QS 675 M592 1974. 1974.

"Virus-induced abortion. Studies of equine herpesvirus
1 (abortion virus) in hamsters," by J. D. Buerk, et
al. LABORATORY INVESTIGATION 33(4):400-406,
October, 1975.

RESPIRATORY SYSTEM
see: Complications

RIFAMPICIN

RIVANOL
"Cervical dilatation and pregnancy interruption using
Rivanol for intrauterine filling," by I. Mathe, et al.
ORVOSI HETILAP 116(47):2782-2785, November 23,
1975.

RUBELLA
see also: Complications

"Parity of women contracting rubella in pregnancy: impli-
cations with respect to rubella vaccination," by W.
C. Marshall. LANCET 1(7971):1231-1233, 1976.
(Bio. Abstrs. 1976, 45973)

"Personal experience with therapeutic abortion in cases
of rubella," by Y. Darbois, et al. JOURNAL DE
GYNECOLOGIE, OBSTETRIQUE ET BIOLOGIE DE LA
REPRODUCTION 3(6):943-954, September, 1974.

SEPSIS
"Post-partum and post-abortum contraception," by B.
Fonty, et al. JOURNAL DE GYNECOLOGIE, OBSTE-
TRIQUE ET BIOLOGIE DE LA REPRODUCTION
4(3):395-404, 1975. (Bio. Abstrs. 1976, 22786)

SEPTIC ABORTION AND SEPTIC SHOCK
see also: Complications
Sepsis

"Bacteriologic study of aerobes and anaerobes in the
vaginal flora of pregnant women and in incomplete
septic abortion," by G. Galan, et al. REVISTA
CHILENA DE OBSTETRICIA Y GINECOLOGIA 39(6):
238-243, 1974.

"A case report: septic midtrimester abortion with an
intrauterine device," by T. L. Connolly, et al.
NEBRASKA MEDICAL JOURNAL 60(11):435-438,
November, 1975.

"Clinical aspects and treatment of puerperal and post-
abortion syaphylococcal spesis," by V. I. Kuznetsova,
et al. PEDIATRIIA AKUSHERSTVO I GINEKOLOGIIA
:55-58, May-June, 1976.

"The end of the Dalkon shield." (editorial). MEDICAL
JOURNAL OF AUSTRALIA 2(14):542, October 4, 1975.

"Incidence of infections associated with the intrauterine
contraceptive device in an isolated community," by
P. B. Mead, et al. AMERICAN JOURNAL OF OBSTE-
TRICS AND GYNECOLOGY 125(1):79-82, 1976.

"Intra-abdominal bleeding following subcutaneous heparin
application in septic abortion," by D. Susemihl, et al.
GEBURTSHILFE UND FRAUENHEILKUNDE 36(2):
126-127, February, 1976.

"Maternal mortality from septic abortions in University
Hospital, Kuala Lumpur from March 1968 to February
1974," by K. H. Ng, et al. MEDICAL JOURNAL OF
MALAYSIA 30(1):52-54, September, 1975.

"Occult manifestations of septic abortion," by J. E.
Dewhurst, et al. NURSING MIRROR AND MIDWIVES'
JOURNAL 142:62-63, April 29, 1976.

"Recovery after prolonged anuria following septic abortion," by D. S. Emmanoulel, et al. OBSTETRICS
AND GYNECOLOGY 47(1):36S-39S, January, 1976.

"Second-trimester spontaneous abortion, the IUD, and
infection," by S. H. Eisinger. AMERICAN JOURNAL
OF OBSTETRICS AND GYNECOLOGY 124(4):393-397,
1976. (Bio. Abstrs. 1976, 5211)

"Septic abortion and its socio-economical aspects," by
J. Duva Palacios, et al. REVISTA CHILENA DE
OBSTETRICIA Y GINECOLOGIA 39(1):15-19, 1974.

"Septic abortion associated with a Lippes loop," by A. K.
Thomas. BRITISH MEDICAL JOURNAL 3(5986):747-
748, September 27, 1975.

"Septic abortion, excluding those caused by Bacillus
perfringens," by M. Herrera, et al. REVISTA
CHILENA DE OBSTETRICIA Y GINECOLOGIA 38(4):
176-186, 1973.

"Septic abortion in women using intrauterine devices," by
P. Williams, et al. BRITISH MEDICAL JOURNAL
4(5991):263-264, November 1, 1975.

"Septic abortion. Personal experience and management,"
by R. H. Schwarz. ANTIBIOTICS AND CHEMO-
THERAPY 21:46-49, 1976.

"Septic shock in obstetrical clinic," by B. L. Gurtovoi, et al. AKUSHERSTVO I GINEKOLOGIIA (Moscow) (3):68-72, March, 1976.

"Septic spontaneous abortion associated with the Dalkon Shield. pp. 417-428," by E. J. Preston, et al. In: Hefnawi F, Segal SJ, ed. Analysis of intrauterine contraception. Amsterdam, North-Holland, 1975. W3 IN182AI 1974a.

"Serious complications of septic abortions. Pelviperitoneal complications (II)," by S. Musso, et al. MINERVA GINECOLOGIA 27(12):1054-1059, December, 1975.

"Serum fibrinogen-fibrin related antigen and protamine sulfate test in patients with septic abortion and acute renal failure," by I. Crisnic, et al. REVUE ROUMAINE DE MEDECINE [Now MEDECINE INTERNE] 14(1):47-51, 1976. (Bio. Abstrs. 1976, 41222)

"Severe complications of septic abortion. I. Nephovascular complications," by G. Musso, et al. MINERVA GINECOLOGICA 27(9):690-697, September, 1975.

"Treatment of the focus in septic gynecologic infection," by F. Rocha. REVISTA CHILENA DE OBSTETRICIA Y GINECOLOGIA 39(6):268-278, 1974.

SOCIOLOGY AND BEHAVIOR
    see also: Family Planning
              Religion and Ethics

"Abortion attitudes among Catholic college students," by P. D. Bardis. ADOLESCENCE 10(39):433-441, Fall, 1975.

"Abortion: the danger of confusing responsibility with

punishment," by A. McLaren. TIMES 7, July 9, 1975.

"Abortion in New Zealand: a review," by A. D. Trlin.
AUSTRALIAN JOURNAL OF SOCIAL ISSUES 10, 3:
179-196, August, 1975. (Socio. Abstrs. 1976,
76H8920)

"Abortion need and services in the United States, 1974-
1975," by E. Weinstock, et al. FAMILY PLANNING
PERSPECTIVES 8(2):58-69, March-April, 1976.

"Abortion: a philosophical analysis," by F. Myrna.
FEM STUD 1, 49-63, Fall, 1972.

"Abortion: the problems that remain." MCCALLS 103:
33-34, March, 1976.

"Abortion: the woman's choice." ECONOMIST 260:35,
July 10, 1976.

"Abortionist's advertisement," by G. Monteiro.
WESTERN FOLKLORE 35:74, January, 1976.

"The antifeminism of abortion," by R. Kress. MARRIAGE
AND FAMILY LIVING 58:2-5, February, 1976.

"Are women becoming endangered species?" by J. Anderson. OUR SUNDAY VISITOR MAGAZINE 65:1, passim,
October 24, 1976.

"The Center for Disease Control." AORN JOURNAL;
ASSOCIATION OF OPERATING ROOM NURSES, INC.
24:333-334 passim, August, 1976.

"Childbirth or abortion? - problems of notification," by
J. Augustin. CESKOSLOVENSKA GYNEKOLOGIE
40(10):728-729, December, 1975.

"City setting and tolerance toward abortion: an exploratory

study of attitudes of coeds," by J. P. Reed. INTER-
NATIONAL JOURNAL OF SOCIOLOGY OF THE
FAMILY 5, 1:103-110, Spring, 1975. (Socio.
Abstrs. 1976, 76I2582)

"Counselling for abortion," by M. Blair. MIDWIFE
HEALTH VISITOR AND COMMUNITY NURSE 11(11):
355-356, November, 1975.

"Culture Lacking Jerseyans Feel." THE NEW YORK
TIMES (M) March 25, 76:6, 1976.

"The development of instruments to measure attitudes
toward abortion and knowledge of abortion," by S.
Snegroff. JOURNAL OF SCHOOL HEALTH 46(5):
273-277, May, 1976.

"Do the medical schools discriminate against anti-
abortion applicants?" LINACRE 43:29-35,
February, 1976.

"The effect of the legalization of abortion on public
health and some of its social concomitants in Hungary,"
by M. Miklos. DEMOGRAFIA 16, 1:70-113, 1973.
(Socio. Abstrs. 1976, 76I1408)

"The effects of attitude and direction of true-false interspersed questions on the learning of a prose passage
on a controversial topic," by S. S. El-Azzabi.
DISSERTATION ABSTRACTS INTERNATIONAL 34
(11-A), 7039, May 1974. (Psycho. Abstrs. 1976,
13140)

"Factor analysis of attitudes toward abortion," by B.
Corenblum, et al. PERCEPTUAL AND MOTOR
SKILLS 40(2):587-591, April, 1975.

"Guidance prior to abortion," by V. Sele. UGESKRIFT
FOR LAEGER 138(6):379, February 2, 1976.

"Hare on abortion," by R. Werner. ANALYSIS 36:177, June, 1976.

"Health and human rights," by N. Howard-Jones, et al. WORLD HEALTH ORGANIZATION :3-31, January, 1976.

"Health personnel organization for professional self-determination," by B. Brekke. SYKEPLEIEN 61(22): 1145-1147, November 20, 1974.

"How abortion spread to the Mideast and the Orient," by M. Bunson. OUR SUNDAY VISITOR MAGAZINE 65:1 passim, June 27, 1976.

"Human values and biotechnology," by M. A. Seibert, et al. MOMENTUM 7:4-12, February, 1976.

"Justifying 'wholesale slaughter," by D. Van De Veer. CANADIAN JOURNAL OF PHILOSOPHY 5, 245-258, October, 1975.

"Kill or cure," by J. Linklater. SPECTATOR 782, June 28, 1975.

"Life with Uncle," by R. Baker. THE NEW YORK TIMES (M) March 28, VI, 9, 1976.

"Media manipulation promotes world abortion craze," by M. Bunson. OUR SUNDAY VISITOR MAGAZINE 65:1 passim, June 20, 1976.

"Occult pregnancy. A pilot study," by S. K. Bloch. OBSTETRICS AND GYNECOLOGY 48(3):365-368, September, 1976.

"On the sociology and social ethics of abortion," by C. Bagley. ETHICS IN SCIENCE AND MEDICINE 3(1):21-32, May, 1976.

SOCIOLOGY AND BEHAVIOR

"A pilot study of demographic and psychosocial factors
in medical termination of pregnancy," by R. Goraya,
et al. JOURNAL OF THE INDIAN MEDICAL
ASSOCIATION 64(11):309-315, June 1, 1975.

"Pregnancy counseling and abortion referral for patients
in Federally funded family planning programs," by
J. I. Rosoff. FAMILY PLANNING PERSPECTIVES
8(1):43-46, January-February, 1976.

"Producing change in attitudes toward abortion," by R.
A. Lewis. THE JOURNAL OF SEX RESEARCH 9, 1:
52-68, February, 1973.

"The profilactic and therapeutic attitude in abortion," by
C. Tatic, et al. VIATA MEDICALA 23(9):57-60,
September, 1975.

"Pronatalist programmes in Eastern Europe," by R.
McIntyre. SOVIET STUDIES 27:366, July, 1975.

"Psychiatric and mental health nursing. Pre-abortion
emotional counseling," by S. Gedan. ANA CLINICAL
SESSIONS :217-225, 1973.

"Psychological factors in contraceptive failure and
abortion request," (letter), by D. Everingham.
MEDICAL JOURNAL OF AUSTRALIA 2(15):617-
618, October 11, 1975.

"Psychosocial aspects of abortion in the United States,"
by J. D. Osofsky, et al. MOUNT SINAI JOURNAL
OF MEDICINE, NEW YORK 42(5):456-467, September-
October, 1975.

"Psychosocial consequences of therapeutic abortion King's
termination study III," by H. S. Greer, et al. BRITISH
JOURNAL OF PSYCHIATRY 128:74-79, January, 1976.

"Ramdom thoughts on abortion attitudes," by K. Solomon.
AMERICAN JOURNAL OF PUBLIC HEALTH 66(9):
905-906, September, 1976.

"Septic abortion and its socio-economical aspects," by
J. Duva Palacios, et al. REVISTA CHILENA DE
OBSTETRICIA Y GINECOLOGIA 39(1):15-19, 1974.

"Shifts in public opinion toward abortion," by W. R.
Arney, et al. INTELLECT 104:280, January, 1976.

"A sliding scale for abortions?" by R. Gillon. OBSER-
VER 19, July 6, 1975.

"There Just Wasn't Room in Our Lives Now for Another
Baby," by J. Doe. THE NEW YORK TIMES May 14,
27:3, 1976.

"350 requests of abortion. What happens just two years
before?" by A. M. Lanoy, et al. PRAXIS 64(10):
295-298, March 11, 1975.

"Three levels of discussion about abortion," by J.
Carlson. DIMENSION 8:37-45, Spring, 1976.

"Toward an abortion counseling strategy for pro-life
counselors," by P. J. Armstrong. SCHOOL
COUNSELOR 24:36-38, September, 1976.

"The two faces of Women's Liberation." OUR SUNDAY
VISITOR MAGAZINE 65:1 passim, June 27, 1976.

"Unwanted pregnancy and abortion," by J. Castro
Morales. REVISTA DE NEURO-PSIQUIATRIA 38
(3-4):177-186, September-December, 1975.

"USA and abortion," by J. Noonan. TABLET 230:494-
496, May 22, 1976.

SOCIOLOGY AND BEHAVIOR

"Voluntary abortion and resistance to contraception,"
by M. Bourgeois, et al. ANNALES MEDICO-
PSYCHOLOGIQUES 2(2):366-377, July, 1975.

"Voluntary abortion, the global picture and danger for our
society," by J. Botella Llusia. CUADERNOS DE
REALIDADES SOCIALES 4:77-84, May, 1974. (Socio.
Abstrs. 1976, 76I0109)

"Woman's choice." ECONOMIST 260:35-36, July 10,
1976.

"Women, anger and abortion," by R. C. Wahlberg.
CHRISTIAN CENTURY 93:622-623, July 7, 1976.

SODIUM CHLORIDE
see: Prostaglandins
     Techniques of Abortion

SOMBREVIN
"Case of the lack of effect of anesthetization in the intra-
venous administration of sombrevin and hexenal," by
P. M. Veropotvelian, et al. PEDIATRIIA AKUSHER-
STVO I GINEKOLOGIIA (5):62, 1975.

S.P.U.C.
see: Religion and Ethics

SPONTANEOUS ABORTION
see also: Threatened Abortion

"Abortion: a hypothesis on the roll of ABO blood groups
and placental alkaline phosphatase," by E. Bottini.
SOCIAL BIOLOGY 22(3):221-228, 1975. (Bio. Abstrs.
1976, 24579)

"Aetiology of spontaneous abortion. A cytogenetic and
epidemiological study of 288 abortuses and their
parents," by J. G. Lauritsen. ACTA OBSTETRICIA

GYNECOLOGICA SCANDINAVICA SUPPLEMENT
(52):1-29, 1976.

"Area differences in the incidence of neural tube defect
and the rate of spontaneous abortion," by J. Fedrick,
et al. BRITISH JOURNAL OF PREVENTIVE AND
SOCIAL MEDICINE 30(1):32-35, March, 1976.

"Balanced homologous translocation t(22q22q) in a
phenotypically normal woman with repeated spontaneous abortions," by L. M. Farah, et al. HUMAN-
GENETIK 28(4):357-360, August 25, 1975.

"A case of ring 18 chromosome in a sibship with multiple
spontaneous abortions," by R. Coco, et al. ANNALES
DE GENETIQUE 18(2):135-137, June, 1975.

"Chromosomal aberrations and disorders of evolution in
repeated spontaneous abortions," by A. Zwinger, et al.
CESKOSLOVENSKA GYNEKOLOGIE 41(2):121-126,
April, 1976.

"Chromosomal study of 65 couples with spontaneous
abortions," by J. L. Taillemite, et al. JOURNAL DE
GYNECOLOGIE, OBSTETRIQUE ET BIOLOGIE DE LA
REPRODUCTION 5(3):343-349, April-May, 1976.

"Chromosome aberrations as a cause of spontaneous
abortion," by J. Kleinebrecht, et al. ZEITSCHRIFT
FUR ALLEGEMEINMEDIZIN; DE LANDARZT 51(22):
974-977, August 10, 1975.

"Chromosome studies in couples with repeated spontaneous
abortions," by C. Tsenghi, et al. OBSTETRICS AND
GYNECOLOGY 47(4):463-468, 1976. (Bio. Abstrs.
1976, 42979)

"Competition between spontaneous and induced abortion,"
by R. G. Potter, et al. DEMOGRAPHY 12:129-141,

February, 1975.

"Congenital malformations of the central nervous system in spontaneous abortions," by M. R. Creasy, et al. JOURNAL OF MEDICAL GENETICS 13(1):9-16, 1976. (Bio. Abstrs. 1976, 14103)

"A cytogenetic study of human spontaneous abortions using banding techniques," by M. R. Creasy, et al. HUMAN GENETICS 31(2):177-196, February 29, 1976. (Bio. Abstrs. 1976, 31538)

"Depressed mixed lymphocyte culture reactivity in mothers with recurrent spontaneous abortion," by J. G. Lauritsen, et al. AMERICAN JOURNAL OF OBSTE-TRICS AND GYNECOLOGY 125(1):35-39, 1976. (Bio. Abstrs. 1976, 34459)

"Effects of spontaneous abortions on the frequency of births of twins," by P. Lazar. COMPES RENDUS HEBDOMADAIRES DES SEANCES DE L'ACADEMIE DES SCIENCES; D: SCIENCES NATURELLES 282(2):243-246, January 12, 1976.

"Four familial translocations ascertained through spon-taneous abortions," by D. H. Carr, et al. HUMAN GENETICS 31(1):93-96, 1976. (Bio. Abstrs. 1976, 25779)

"The freqeuncy and causes of spontaneous abortion follow-ing artificial insemination," by A. Campana, et al. GEBURTSHILFE UND FRAUENHEILKUNDE 36(5): 421-429, May, 1976.

"Histological analysis of spontaneous abortions with trisomy 2: first description of an embryo," by J. Kleinebrecht, et al. HUMANGENETIK 29(1):15-22, August 29, 1975.

"Induced abortions and spontaneous abortions. Psychopathological aspects apropos of a preliminary sample of
411 requests for pregnancy interruption," by M. Bourgeois, et al. ANNALES MEDICO-PSYCHOLOGIQUES
2(2):339-366, July, 1975.

"Intrauterine aspiration in humans in the early fetal
period," by M. Makkaveeva. ARKHIV PATHOLOGIE
37(12):141-146, 1975. (Bio. Abstrs. 1976, 36105)

"Karyotype of the parents after spontaneous abortion?
Translocation 46 XY t(2p-;21q/) detected in the
husband of a woman who presented with 2 early
spontaneous abortions," by D. Rabineau, et al.
JOURNAL DE GYNECOLOGIE, OBSTETRIQUE ET BIO-
LOGIE DE LA REPRODUCTION 3(2):265-270, March,
1974.

"Karyotypes of spontaneous human abortuses and several
aspects of their phenotypic presentation," by N. M.
Slozina, et al. TSITOLOGIIA 17(8):989-993,
August, 1975.

"Karyotyping of in cases of spontaneous abortions," by
L. Wisniewski, et al. GINEKOLOGIA POLASKA 47
(1):57-66, January, 1976.

"Management of spontaneous abortion and fetal death by
extra-amnial administration of a single dose of alpha
prostaglandin 2," by K. Lajos, et al. ORVOSI
HETILAP 117(30):1815-1817, July 25, 1976.

"Maternal factors associated with fetal chromosomal
anomalies in spontaneous abortions," by E. Alberman,
et al. BRITISH JOURNAL OF OBSTETRICS AND
GYNAECOLOGY 83(8):621-627, August, 1976.

"Miscarriage and abortion: I. Induced and spontaneous
abortion. Psychopathological aspects in connection

with a first sample of 411 requests for interruption of pregnancy," by M. Bourgeois, et al. ANNALES MEDICO-PSYCHOLOGIQUES 2(2):339-366, July, 1975. (Psycho. Abstrs. 1976, 12347)

"Mycoplasmas in humans: significance of Ureaplasma urealyticum," by R. B. Kundsin. HEALTH LABORATORY SCIENCE 12(3):144-151, 1976. (Bio. Abstrs. 1976, 43909)

"Pathomorphological changes in an early spontaneous abortus with triploidy," by V. P. Kulazenko, et al. HUMAN GENETICS 32(2):211-215, 1976. (Bio. Abstrs. 1976, 60586)

"Plasma renin activity in abortion," by P. Soveri, et al. ACTA OBSTETRICIA GYNECOLOGICA SCANDINAVICA 55(2):175-177, 1976. (Bio. Abstrs. 1976, 30739)

"Possible andrological factor as cause of spontaneous abortion," by R. Schoysman. VERHANDELINGAN; KONINKLIJKE ACADEMIE VOOR GENESSKUNDE VON BELGIE 37(2):33-41, 1975.

"Second-trimester spontaneous abortion, the IUD, and infection," by S. H. Eisinger. AMERICAN JOURNAL OF OBSTETRICS AND GYNECOLOGY 124(4):393-397, 1976. (Bio. Abstrs. 1976, 5211)

"Septic spontaneous abortion associated with the Dalkon Shield. pp. 417-428," by E. J. Preston, et al. In: Hefnawi F, Segal SJ, ed. Analysis of intrauterine contraception. Amsterdam, North-Holland, 1975. W3 IN182AI 1974a.

"Significance of HLA and blood-group incompatibility in spontaneous abortion," by J. G. Lauritsen, et al. CLINICAL GENETICS 9(6):575-582, 1976. (Bio. Abstrs. 1976, 66537)

SPONTANEOUS ABORTION

"The significance of oral contraceptives in causing chromosome anomalies in spontaneous abortions," by J. G. Lauritsen. ACTA OBSTETRICIA ET GYNECOLOGICA SCANDINAVICA 54(3):261-264, 1975. (Bio. Abstrs. 1976, 54717)

"Spontaneous abortion as a screening device. The effect of fetal survival on the incidence of birth defects," by Z. Stein, et al. AMERICAN JOURNAL OF EPIDEMI-OLOGY 102(4):275-290, October, 1975.

"Spontaneous abortions in working women," by G. Beshev. AKUSHERSTVO I GINEKOLOGIIA (Sofia) 15(2):115-120, 1976.

"Spontaneous fetal loss: a note on rates and some impli-cations," by P. Cutright. JOURNAL OF BIOSOCIAL SCIENCE 7, 4:421-433, October, 1975. (Socio. Abstrs. 1976, 76I2508)

"Successive spontaneous abortions with diverse chromo-somal aberrations in human translocation hetero-zygote," by G. Kohn. TERATOLOGY; JOURNAL OF ABNORMAL DEVELOPMENT 12(3):283-289, Decem-ber, 1975.

"Vascular lesions of the endometrium in spontaneous abortion," by L. Orcel, et al. ANNALES D'ANATOMIE PATHOLOGIQUE 20(2):109-120, March-April, 1975.

"Where have all the conceptions gone?" by C. J. Roberts, et al. LANCET 1(7905):498-499, 1975. (Bio. Abstrs. 1976, 1153)

STATISTICS

"Abortion in New Zealand," by A. D. Trlin. AUSTRALIAN JOURNAL OF SOCIAL ISSUES 10, 3:179-196, August, 1975. (Socio. Abstrs. 1976, 76H8920)

STATISTICS

"The Availability of Abortion." THE NEW YORK TIMES
February 29, IV, 7:1, 1976.

"Chromosome studies in 500 induced abortions," by M.
Yamamoto, et al. HUMANGENETIK 29(1):9-14,
August 29, 1975.

"Clinical experience using intraamniotic prostaglandin
F2alpha for midtrimester abortion in 600 patients,"
by G. G. Anderson, et al. OBSTETRICS AND
GYNECOLOGY 46(5):591-595, November, 1975.

"The complexity of compiling abortion statistics," by J.
C. Smith. PUBLIC HEALTH REPORTS 90(6):502-503,
November-December, 1975.

"Delayed morbidity following prostaglandin-induced
abortion," by I. Z. Mackenzie, et al. INTERNATIONAL
JOURNAL OF GYNAECOLOGY AND OBSTETRICS
13(5):209-214, 1975. (Bio. Abstrs. 1976, 23175)

"The effect of the legalization of abortion on public health
and some of its social concomitants in Hungary," by
M. Miklos. DEMOGRAFIA 16, 1:70-113, 1973.
(Socio. Abstrs. 1976, 76I1408)

"First and repeat abortions: a study of decision-making
and delay," by M. B. Brucken, et al. JOURNAL OF
BIOSOCIAL SCIENCE 7, 4:473-491, October, 1975.
(Socio. Abstrs. 1976, 76I0866)

"Four familial translocations ascertained through spon--
taneous abortions," by D. H. Carr, et al. HUMAN
GENETICS 31(1):93-96, 1976. (Bio. Abstrs. 1976.
25779)

"Incomplete abortions in Accra and Bangkok University
Hospitals 1972-1973," by I. C. Chi, et al. INTER-
NATIONAL JOURNAL OF GYNAECOLOGY AND

320

OBSTETRICS 13(4):148-161, 1975. (Bio. Abstrs. 1976, 22865)

"Induced legal abortions of juveniles," by M. Farkas, et al. DEMOGRAFIA 17, 2:236-243, 1974. (Socio. Abstrs. 1976, 76I1399)

"Laminaria in abortion. Use in 1368 patients in first trimester," by W. M. Hern. ROCKY MOUNTAIN MEDICAL JOURNAL 72(9):390-395, September, 1975.

"Low birth weight subsequent to induced abortion: a historical prospective study of 948 women in Skopje, Yugoslavia," by C. J. Hogue. AMERICAN JOURNAL OF OBSTETRICS AND GYNECOLOGY 123(7):675-681, 1975. (Bio. Abstrs. 1976, 5154)

"Legal abortion. Abortion as a form of contraception? A prospective study of 608 women applying for abortion," by P. Diederich, et al. UGESKRIFT FOR LAEGER 138(6):355-359, February 2, 1976.

"Legal abortion: a half-decade of experience," by J. Pakter, et al. FAMILY PLANNING PERSPECTIVES 7(6):248-255, November-December, 1975.

"Legal abortion--1000 women. Data concerning contraception, age and obstetric history," by F. Lundvall. UGESKRIFT FOR LAEGER 138(6):363-369, February 2, 1976.

"Method of payment--relation to abortion complications," by R. G. Smith, et al. HEALTH AND SOCIAL WORK 1:5-28, May, 1976.

"On the method of mathematical statistical surveys connected with certain gestation processes," by M. Miklos. DEMOGRAFIA 17, 2:206-212, 1974. (Socio. Abstrs. 1976, 76I1279)

"Outcome and quality of pregnancies obtained by ovulation inducers in infertile women: apropos of 229 pregnancies in 91 women, of whom 42 were treated for spontaneous abortion and 49 treated for ovarian sterility," by J. Henry-Suchet, et al. JOURNAL DE GYNECOLOGIE, OBSTETRIQUES ET BIOLOGIE DE LA REPRODUCTION 2(6):653-672, September, 1973.

"Patterns of contraceptive failures: the role of motivation re-examined," by W. Cobliner, et al. JOURNAL OF BIOSOCIAL SCEINCE 7, 3:307-318, July, 1975. (Socio. Abstrs. 1976, 76H9180)

"A prospective study of drugs and pregnancy," by S. Kullander, et al. ACTA OBSTETRICIA ET GYNE-COLOGICA SCANDINAVICA 55(1):25-33, 1976. (Bio. Abstrs. 1144)

"Psychological-sociological views on S 218 (study on 379 pregnant women and women in puerperium," by J. M. Wenderlein. ZENTRALBLATT FUR GYNAEKOLOGIE 98(9):527-532, 1976.

"The relationship between legal abortion and marriage," by K. E. Brauman, et al. SOCIAL BIOLOGY 22, 2:117-124, Summer, 1975. (Socio. Abstrs. 1976, 76I0401)

"Reproductive performance after treatment of intra-uterine adhesions," by E. Caspi, et al. INTERNATION-AL JOURNAL OF FERTILITY 20(4):249-252, 1975. (Bio. Abstrs. 1976, 46114)

"Statistical study of the etiology of habitual abortion. pp. 149-152," by N. S. Cavallaro, et al. In: Marchesi F, Cittadini E, ed. Fertilità e sterilità. Taormina, Minerva medica, 1974. WP 570 S679f 1973.

"Study Finds Democratic Nations Stay with Liberalized

Abortion." THE NEW YORK TIMES (S) February 20,
2:1, 1976.

"Study Finds Rise in Abortion Here," by E. E. Asbury.
THE NEW YORK TIMES (M) January 25, 52:1, 1976.

"Study of the transplacental passage of fetal erythrocytes
in 100 abortions," by C. Quereux, et al. JOURNAL
DE GYNECOLOGIE, OBSTETRIQUE ET BIOLOGIE DE LA
REPRODUCTION 1(5 Suppl 2):215-218, 1972.

"Survey shows New York is abortion capital of nation."
OUR SUNDAY VISITOR 64:2, February 8, 1976.

"The unmet need for legal abortion services in the U.S.,"
by C. Tietze, et al. FAMILY PLANNING PERSPEC-
TIVES 7(5):224-230, September-October, 1975.

STERILITY
"Abortion and fertility control (a brief world review),"
by R. Dutta. JOURNAL OF THE INDIAN MEDICAL
ASSOCIATION 64(11):315-320, June 1, 1975.

"Endometrial aspiration in fertility control. A report of
500 cases," by R. P. Bendel, et al. AMERICAN
JOURNAL OF OBSTETRICS AND GYNECOLOGY
125(3):328-332, June 1, 1976.

"The epidemiology of infertility." WHO CHRONICLE
30(6):229-233, June, 1976.

"Genetic examination of patients in consultation for
sterility or miscarriage," by M. M. Freund, et al.
JOURNAL DE GENETIQUE HUMAINE 23 Suppl:112-
113, October, 1975.

"The impact of induced abortions on fertility," by M.
Karoly. DEMOGRAFIA 12, 4:413-420, 1970. (Socio.
Abstrs. 1976, 76I0122)

"The luteal phase defect," by G. S. Jones. FERTILITY
AND STERILITY 27(4):351-356, April, 1976.

"Menstrual regulation (a new procedure for fertility
control," by C. S. Dawn, et al. JOURNAL OF THE
INDIAN MEDICAL ASSOCIATION 64(11):293-296,
June 1, 1975.

"Outpatient postconceptional fertility control with
vaginally administered 15(S) 15-methyl-PGF2alpha-
methyl ester," by M. Bygdeman, et al. AMERICAN
JOURNAL OF OBSTETRICS AND GYNECOLOGY
124(5):495-498, March 1, 1976.

"Systemic and local administration of prostaglandins for
postconceptional fertility control. pp. 108-115," by
M. Toppozada, et al. In: Bergström S, ed. Report
from meetings of the Prostaglandin Task Force
Steering Committee. Stockholm, 1973. QV 175
W927r 1972-1973.

"Zinc deficiency in malabsorption states: a cause of
infertility?" by S. Jameson. ACTA MEDICA
SCANDINAVICA SUPPLEMENT (593):38-49, 1976.

STERILIZATION
"Availability of abortion, sterilization, and other
medical treatment for minor patients," by L. J. Dunn,
Jr. UNIVERSITY OF MISSOURI AT KANSAS CITY
LAW REVIEW 44:1-22, Fall, 1975.

"Clinical conference: abortion and sterilization."
JOURNAL OF MEDICAL ETHICS 1(1):45-48, April,
1975.

"Comparison of culdoscopic and lararoscopic tubal
sterilization," by S. Koetsawang, et al. AMERICAN
JOURNAL OF OBSTETRICS AND GYNECOLOGY 124
(6):601-606, 1976. (Bio. Abstrs. 1976, 11031)

STERILIZATION

"Contraception, sterilization and abortion in NZ."
NURSING FORUM (Akuckl) 4:6-9, June-July, 1976.

"High Court Bars Challenge to Hospital Abortion Curb,"
by L. Olesner. THE NEW YORK TIMES (M) March 2,
1:5, 1976.

"Hospitals - a current analysis of the right to abortions
and sterilizations in the Fourth circuit: state action
and the church amendment." NORTH CAROLINA
LAW REVIEW 54:1307-1316, September, 1976.

"May hospitals prohibit abortions and sterilizations?"
by J. A. Turpin. MEDICO-LEGAL BULLETIN
24(9):1-9, September, 1975.

"Population control in Australia today: contraception,
sterilization and abortion," by J. Leeton. MEDICAL
JOURNAL OF AUSTRALIA 2(17):682-685, October 25,
1975.

"The relative risks of sterilization alone and in combination with abortion," by K. G. B. Edström."
BULLETIN OF THE WORLD HEALTH ORGANIZATION
52(2):141-148, 1975. (Bio. Abstrs. 1976, 16962)

STILBESTROL

STUDENTS
see: Youth

SURGICAL TREATMENT AND MANAGEMENT
see also: Techniques of Abortion

"Asherman's syndrome, the Massouras Duck's Foot-IUD
(MDF-IUD) and Peacock Hook. Treatment and
prevention. pp. 265-272," by H. G. Massouras. In:
da Paz AC, et al. , ed. Recent advances in human
reproduction. Amsterdam, Excerpta Medica, 1976.

325

W3 EX89 no. 370 1974.

"Attempt to elucidate the causes of certain complications
following artificial abortion using radioisotopes," by
A. Atanasov, et al. AKUSHERSTVO I GINEKOLOGIIA
(Sofia) 14(5):372-375, 1975.

"Case of old uterine perforation after abortus mens II/III,"
by J. Laube, et al. ZENTRALBLATT FUR GYNAE-
KOLOGIE 97(22):1378-1379, 1975.

"The intravenous infusion of prostaglandin F2alpha in the
management of intrauterine death of the fetus," by
N. Moe. ACTA OBSTETRICIA ET GYNECOLOGICA
SCANDINAVICA 55(2):113-114, 1976.

"Management of failed prostaglandin abortions," by N.
H. Lauersen, et al. OBSTETRICS AND GYNECOLOGY
47(4):473-478, 1976. (Bio. Abstrs. 1976, 16203)

"Postabortion insertion of the intrauterine copper T
(TCu 200). pp. 115-118," by K. G. Nygren, et al.
In: Hefnawi F, Segal SJ, ed. Analysis of intrauterine
contraception. Amsterdam, North-Holland, 1975.
W3 IN182AI 1974a.

"Surgical treatment of the abortion at the Gynecologic-
Obstetrical Department of the General Hospital in
Zrenjanin in the period 1967-1974," by B. Nedejković,
et al. MEDICINSKI PREGLED 29(5-6):231-235, 1976.

"Treatment of perforation of the large intestine due to
illegal abortion," by H. G. Mayer. ZENTRALBLATT
FUR GYNAEKOLOGIE 97(12):734-737, 1975.

"The use of surgery to avoid childbearing among Navajo
and Hopi Indians. pp. 9-21," by S. J. Kunitz, et al.
In: Kaplan BA, ed. Anthropological studies of human
fertility. Detroit, Wayne State Univ Press, 1976.

SURGICAL TREATMENT AND MANAGEMENT

GN 241 S989a 1975.

SURVEYS
see: Sociology and Behavior

SYMPOSIA
"Symposium on intrauterine genetics. Reproductive
failures in relation to chromosome abnormalities,"
by A. Boué, et al. UNION MEDICALE DU CANADA
104(12):1775-1781, December, 1975.

SYNTOCINON

TECHNIQUES OF ABORTION
see also: Induced Abortion
Surgical Treatment and Management

"Abortion practice: could drugs replace doctors?" by
S. Whitehead. NURSING TIMES 72(15):564-565,
April 15, 1976.

"Abortions in 1973 in Linköping--contraceptive technics
and postoperative complications," by U. Larsson-Cohn.
LAKARTIDNINGEN 72(44):4282-4284, October 24, 1975.

"Active pre-term management of severe osteogenesis
imperfects," by J. Swinhoe, et al. ACTA OBSTE-
TRICIA ET GYNECOLOGICIA SCANDINAVICA 55
(1):81-83, 1976. (Bio. Abstrs. 1976, 1152)

"Amniotic fluid removal prior to saline abortion," by
A. C. Mehta, et al. ANNALES CHIRURGIAE ET
GYNAECOLOGIAE FENNIAE 65(1):68-71, 1976.

"A case report: septic midtrimester abortion with an
intrauterine device," by T. L. Connolly, et al.
NEBRASKA MEDICAL JOURNAL 60(11):435-438,
November, 1975.

"Cervical diameter after suction termination of pregnancy," (letter), by M. M. Black, et al. BRITISH MEDICAL JOURNAL 1(6014):902, April 10, 1976.

"Cervical diameter after suction termination of pregnancy," by F. D. Johnstone, et al. BRITISH MEDICAL JOURNAL 1(6001):68-69, January 10, 1976.

"Cervical dilatation and pregnancy interruption using Rivanol for intrauterine filling," by I. Máthé, et al. ORVOSI HETILAP 116(47):2782-2785, November 23, 1975.

"Clinical observations with a prostaglandin-containing silastic vaginal device for pregnancy termination," by C. H. Hendricks, et al. PROSTAGLANDINS 12 Suppl:99-122, 1976.

"A clotting defect following pregnancy termination by dilatation and curettage," by R. J. Solyn. INTERNATIONAL SURGERY 61(2):86-87, February, 1976.

"Coagulation disorders after hypertonic-saline abortion," (letter), by J. W. ten Cate, et al. LANCET 1(7952):205, January 24, 1976.

"Coagulation disorders after hypertonic-saline abortion," (letter), by J. R. O'Brien. LANCET 1(7955):367, February 14, 1976.

"Coagulation disorders and abortion using hypertonic solutions," (letter), by I. Craft, et al. LANCET 1(7956):428, February 21, 1976.

"Combination therapy for midtrimester abortion: laminaria and analogues of prostaglandins," by P. G. Stubblefield, et al. CONTRACEPTION 13(6):723-729, 1976. (Bio. Abstrs. 1976, 39255)

"Comparative evaluation of quantitative variation of 5 per cent intra-amniotic saline for mid-trimester abortion," by A. K. Ghosh. JOURNAL OF THE INDIAN MEDICAL ASSOCIATION 64(11):305-306, June 1, 1975.

"A comparison of metal and plastic cannulae for performing vacuum," by S. S. Moghadam, et al. JOURNAL OF REPRODUCTIVE MEDICINE 17(3):181-187, September, 1976.

"A comparison of saline and prostaglandin abortions at the Medical Center of Central Georgia," by J. R. Harrison, et al. JOURNAL OF THE MEDICAL ASSOCIATION OF GEORGIA 65(2):53-54, February, 1976.

"Concurrent use of prostaglandin F2a and laminaria tents for induction of midtrimester abortion," by J. H. Duenhoelter, et al. OBSTETRICS AND GYNECOLOGY 47(4):469-472, 1976. (Bio. Abstrs. 1976, 33635)

"The contribution of hysterosalpinography to the study of post partum and post abortum menstrual insufficiency," by M. Georgian, et al. RADIOLOGIA 14(1):27-34, 1975. (Bio. Abstrs. 1976, 16978)

"Criminal abortion using ruta roots (Ruta graveolens)," by K. Wehr. BEITRAEGE ZUR GERICHTLIEHEN MEDIZIN 32:126-131, 1974.

"Determination of Rh blood group of fetuses in abortions by suction curettage," by R. M. Greendyke, et al. TRANSFUSION 16(3):267-269, May-June, 1976.

"The distribution within the placenta, myometrium, and decidua of 24Na-labelled hypertonic saline solution following intra-amniotic or extra-amniotic injection," by B. Gustavil. BRITISH JOURNAL OF OBSTETRICS

AND GYNAECOLOGY 82(9):734-739, September, 1975.

"Early termination of pregnancy: a comparative study of intrauterine prostaglandin F2alpha and vacuum aspiration," by M. I. Ragab, et al. PROSTAGLANDINS 11(2):261-273, February, 1976.

"Early vacuum aspiration: minimizing procedures to nonpregnant women," by E. R. Miller, et al. FAMILY PLANNING PERSPECTIVES 8(1):33-38, January-February, 1976.

"Evaluation of abortion techniques: recent and future trends. pp. 164-173," by R. J. Pion, et al. In: Moghissi KS, Evans TN, ed. Regulation of human fertility. Detroit, Wayne State Univ Press, 1976. W3 HA292 1973r.

"Evaluation of intramuscular 15(s)-15-methyl prostaglandin F2 alpha tromethamine salt for induction of abortion, medications to attenuate side effects, and intracervical laminaria tents," by W. Gruber, et al. FERTILITY AND STERILITY 27(9):1009-1023, September, 1976.

"Evaluation of a preevacuated endometrial suction apparatus in general obstetric-gynecologic practice," by M. J. Padawer, et al. NEW YORK STATE JOURNAL OF MEDICINE 76(6):885-888, June, 1976.

"Experience with 276 intra-amniotic prostaglandin F2a induced midtrimester abortions," by M. S. Golbus, et al. PROSTAGLANDINS 11(5):841-851, 1976. (Bio. Abstrs. 1976, 62686)

"Fatal complication of pregnancy interruption," (letter), by H. Larrieu, et al. NOUVELLE PRESSE MEDICALE 4(38):2733, November 8, 1975.

"First trimester abortion by vacuum aspiration," by E.

Borko, et al. ANNALES CHIRURGIAE ET GYNAE-
COLOGIAE FENNIAE 64(5):320-325, 1975.

"Indications of choice for extra-amniotic perfusion of
physiologic serum," by M. Blum, et al. JOURNAL
DE GYNECOLOGIE, OBSTETRIQUE ET BIOLOGIE DE
LA REPRODUCTION 5(4):577-584, June, 1976.

"Induction of midtrimester abortion with intraamniotic
urea, intravenous oxytocin and laminaria," by I. M.
Golditch, et al. JOURNAL OF REPRODUCTIVE
MEDICINE 15(6):225-228, December, 1975.

"Induction of second trimester abortion by infusion of
intraamniotic hypertonic and extraamniotic
physiological saline solution," by M. Blum, et al.
GEBURTSHILFE UND FRAUENHEILKUNDE 36(5):
444-447, May, 1976.

"Induction of abortion with anti-feto-placental antibody,"
by Y. Amano. CLINICAL ENDOCRINOLOGY 24(7):
625-629, July, 1976.

"Intra-amniotic instillation of a hypertonic solution via
the cervical canal," by G. Geshev. AKUSHERSTVO I
GINEKOLOGIIA (Sofia) 14(4):275-278, 1975.

"Intrauterine aspiration in humans in the early fetal
period," by M. Makkaveeva. ARKHIV PATHOLOGIE
37(22):141-146, 1975. (Bio. Abstrs. 1976, 36105)

"Laminaria augmentation of intra-amniotic PGF2 for
midtrimester pregnancy termination," by P. G.
Stubblefield, et al. PROSTAGLANDINS 10(3):413-
422, September, 1975.

"Laminaria augmentation of midtrimester pregnancy
termination by intramuscular prostaglandin 15 (S)
15-methyl F2 alpha," by J. Robins, et al. JOURNAL

OF REPRODUCTIVE MEDICINE 16(6):334-336, June, 1976.

"Laminaria in abortion. Use in 1368 patients in first trimester," by W. M. Hern. ROCKY MOUNTAIN MEDICAL JOURNAL 72(9):390-395, September, 1975.

"Late therapeutic abortion induced by intra-amniotic injection of a hypertonic saline solution," by R. Wyss, et al. JOURNAL DE GYNECOLOGIE, OBSTETRIQUE ET BIOLOGIE DE LA REPRODUCTION 3(8):1189-1306, December, 1974.

"Medical interruption of pregnancy in India," by T. Chandy. MUENCHENER MEDIZINISCHE WOCHEN-SCHRIFT 117(34):1349-1352, August 22, 1975.

"Menstrual induction by the vaginal application of ICI 81008 gel," by A. I. Csapo, et al. PROSTAGLANDINS 12(3):455-461, September, 1976.

"Menstrual induction: its place in clinical practice," by K. R. Irani, et al. OBSTETRICS AND GYNECOLOGY 46(5):596-598, November, 1975.

"Menstrual induction with the PGF2alpha-analogue ICI 81008," by A. I. Csapo, et al. PROSTAGLANDINS 11(1):155-162, January, 1976.

"Modern use of the laminaria tent," by K. R. Niswander. MOUNT SINAI JOURNAL OF MEDICINE, NEW YORK 42(5):424-430, September-October, 1975.

"Most abortions by suction in 10th week or less; typical patient is young, unmarried, white, never-before pregnant." FAMILY PLANNING PERSPECTIVES 8(2):70-72, March-April, 1976.

"Outpatient legal abortion using a modified Vabra
aspirator and paracervical anesthesia," by J. Praest,
et al. UGESKRIFT FOR LAEGER 138(6):336-338,
February 2, 1976.

"Paracervical block with etidocaine for out-patient abortion," by G. Willdeck-Lund, et al. ACTA ANAESTHES-
IOLOGICA SCANDINAVICA. SUPPLEMENT (60):106-
109, 1975.

"Pathophysiology of disseminated intravascular coagulation
in saline-induced abortion," by R. K. Laros, Jr., et
al. OBSTETRICS AND GYNECOLOGY 48(3):353-356,
September, 1976.

"The placental and fetal response to the intra-amniotic
injection of prostaglandin F2alpha in midtrimester
abortions," by P. Jouppila, et al. BRITISH JOURNAL
OF OBSTETRICS AND GYNAECOLOGY 83(4):303-306,
April, 1976.

"Placental cultures for cytogenetic assessment in saline-
aborted fetuses," by H. A. Gardner, et al. AMERICAN
JOURNAL OF OBSTETRICS AND GYNECOLOGY 126
(3):350-352, October 1, 1976.

"Pregnancy interruption by vacuum aspiration," (letter),
by G. Gergely. ORVOSI HETILAP 116(46):2748-2749,
November 16, 1975.

"Preoperative cervical dilatation by small doses of
prostaglandin F2a," by R. Andriesse, et al. CONTRA-
CEPTION 14(1):93-99, 1976. (Bio. Abstrs. 1976,
50661)

"Saline abortion and lupus erythematosus," by J. F. Jewett.
NEW ENGLAND JOURNAL OF MEDICINE 294(14):782-
783, April 1, 1976.

TECHNIQUES OF ABORTION

"Salty tears, salty deaths: the saline mode of abortions:
a comparison," by F. Frech. LIGUORIAN 64:29-31,
October, 1976.

"Studies on immediate post-abortion copper 'T' device,"
by I. Gupta, et al. INDIAN JOURNAL OF MEDICAL
RESEARCH 63(5):736-739, May, 1975.

"Termination of pregnancy with double prostaglandin
impact," by A. I. Csapo, et al. AMERICAN JOURNAL
OF OBSTETRICS AND GYNECOLOGY 124(1):1-13,
January 1, 1976.

"Trans-isthmicocervical intra-amniotic instillation of
hypertonic sodium solutions for termination of pregnancy after the 1st trimester," by I. Kosowski.
ZENTRALBLATT FUR GYNAEKOLOGIE 97(18):1130-
1135, 1975.

"Ultrasound in the management of elective abortion," by
R. C. Sanders, et al. AMERICAN JOURNAL OF
ROENTGENOLOGY 125(2):469-473, October, 1975.

"The use of silastic vaginal device containing (15S)-15
methyl prostaglandin F2 alpha methyl ester for early
first trimester pregnancy termination," by J. Robins.
PROSTAGLANDINS 12 Suppl:123-134, 1976.

"Vacuum aspiration at therapeutic abortion: effect of
Cu-IUD insertion at operation on post-operative blood
loss," by F. Solheim, et al. CONTRACEPTION 13(6):
707-713, 1976. (Bio. Abstrs. 1976, 40215)

TETRACYCLINE

TH 1165a
"Treatment of threatened early abortion (6th-16th week of
pregnancy) of Th 1165a (Partusisten)," by H. Bärmig,
et al. ZENTRALBLATT FUR GYNAEKOLOGIE 98(13):

792-794, 1976.

THERAPEUTIC ABORTION
"Abortion as a problem of medical education," by J.
Jimenez-Vargas, et al. REVISTA DE MEDICINA
DE LA UNIVERSIDAD DE NAVARRA 17(3):273-279,
September, 1973.

"Abortion practice in NZ public hospitals." NURSING
FORUM (Auckl) 3(4):5-7, November-December, 1975.

"Consideration on the problem of pregnancy with inter-
occurrency of acute illness in the patient and the so
called therapeutic abortion," by J. E. dos Santos
Alves, et al. REVISTA DA ASSOCIACAO MEDICA
BRASILEIRA 22(1):21-28, January, 1976.

"Dilema: therapeutic abortion following amniocentesis,"
by N. L. Rudd, et al. CANADIAN NURSE 72:51-56,
August, 1976.

"Electroencephalographic changes following intraamniotic
prostaglandin F2a administration for therapeutic abortion," by A. Faden et al. OBSTETRICS AND GYNE-
COLOGY 47(5):607-608, 1976. (Bio. Abstrs. 27851)

"The evolution of ideas about therapeutic interruption of
pregnancy," by M. Monrozies. JOURNAL DE
GYNECOLOGIE, OBSTETRIQUE ET BIOLOGIE DE
LA REPRODUCTION 4(2):162-175, March, 1975.

"Genital cytologic abnormalities in patients having
therapeutic abortion," by W. T. Creasman, et al.
SOUTHERN MEDICAL JOURNAL 69(2):199-200,
February, 1976.

"History of the relation between pregnancy and pulmonary
tuberculosis and therapeutic abortion," by T. M.
Caffaratto. MINERVA GINECOLOGIA 28(2):192-201,

February, 1976.

"Hormonal consequences of the therapeutic interruption of pregnancy by an intraamniotic injection of concentrated sodium chloride solution. pp. 21-33," by H. de Watteville, et al. In: Vokaer R, De Bock G, ed. Reproductive endocrinology. Oxford, Pergamon Press, 1975. WQ 200 F673r 1973.

"Indications of choice for extra-amniotic perfusion of physiologic serum," by M. Blum, et al. JOURNAL DE GYNECOLOGIE, OBSTETRIQUE ET BIOLOGIE DE LA REPRODUCTION 5(4):577-584, June, 1976.

"Insertion of the Lippe's loop immediately after abrasio residuorum and interruptio graviditatis," by D. Mishev. AKUSHERSTVO I GINEKOLOGIIA (Sofia) 15(1):49-52, 1976.

"Intra-amniotic instillation of a hypertonic solution via the cervical canal," by G. Geshev. AKUSHERSTVO I GINEKOLOGIIA (Sofia) 14(4):275-278, 1975.

"Late therapeutic abortion induced by intra-amniotic injection of a hypertonic saline solution," by R. Wyss, et al. JOURNAL DE GYNECOLOGIE, OBSTETRIQUE ET BIOLOGIE DE LA REPRODUCTION 3(8):1189-1206, December, 1974.

"A life threatening pregnancy," by E. Moult. MATERNAL-CHILD NURSING JOURNAL 4(3):207-211, Fall, 1975.

"Medical counterindications for pregnancy," by J. C. Monnier. LILLE MEDICAL 20:242-246, 1975.

"The medical indications of therapeutic abortion yesterday and today," by D. Stucki, et al. PRAXIS 65(2):49-53, January 13, 1976.

"Morbidity of therapeutic abortion in Auckland," by M.
    A. Baird. NEW ZEALAND MEDICAL JOURNAL
    83(565):395-399, June, 1976.

"Nurse's attitudes to termination of pregnancy."
    NURSING FORUM (Auckl) 2(5):6-7, November-
    December, 1974.

"Outcome following therapeutic abortion," by E. C.
    Payne, et al. ARCHIVES OF GENERAL PSYCHIATRY
    33(6):725-733, June, 1976.

"Personal experience with therapeutic abortion in cases
    of rubella," by Y. Darbois, et al. JOURNAL DE
    GYNECOLOGIE, OBSTETRIQUE ET BIOLOGIE DE
    LA REPRODUCTION 3(6):943-954, September, 1974.

"Population control in Australia today: contraception,
    sterilization and abortion," by J. Leeton. MEDICAL
    JOURNAL OF AUSTRALIA 2(17):682-685, October 25,
    1975.

"Postpartum contraception: subsequent pregnancy,
    delivery, and abortion rates," by J. J. Shulman, et al.
    FERTILITY AND STERILITY 27(1):97-103, January,
    1976.

"Pregnancy with concurrent acute disease and the so-called
    therapeutic abortion," by J. E. Alves, et al. REVISTA
    DA ASSOCIACAO MEDICA BRASILEIRA 22(1):21-28,
    January, 1976.

"Prevention of RH immunization in therapeutic abortion,"
    by M. Bulić. LIJECNICKI VJESNIK 98(2):103-104,
    February, 1976.

"Psychiatric aspects of abortion in Hong Kong," by K.
    Singer. INTERNATIONAL JOURNAL OF SOCIAL
    PSYCHIATRY 21(4):303-306, Winter, 1975.

"Psychological sequelae of therapeutic abortion."
(editorial). BRITISH MEDICAL JOURNAL 1(6020):
1239, May 22, 1976.

"Psychological sequelae of therapeutic abortion," (letter),
by J. Kellett. BRITISH MEDICAL JOURNAL 2(6026):
45, July 3, 1976.

"Psychosocial consequences of therapeutic abortion King's
termination study III," by H. S. Greer, et al. BRITISH
JOURNAL OF PSYCHIATRY 128:74-79, January, 1976.

"Radiation effects in early pregnancy as a medical indication for its artificial interruption," by L. Dakov,
et al. AKUSHERSTVO I GINEKOLOGIIA (Sofia)
15(2):120-126, 1976.

"Remarks on the proposal for new qualifications in interruption of pregnancy," by S. Cammelli. PROFESSIONI
INFERMIERISTICHE 28(2):45-49, April-June, 1975.

"Results of therapeutic abortion induction using extra-
amniotically administered prostaglandin F2alpha,"
by H. Lahmann, et al. ARCHIV FUR GYNAEKOLOGIE
219(1-4):499-500, November 18, 1975.

"Reversible hypernatremic coma following therapeutic
abortion with hypertonic saline," by A. Reches, et
al. HAREFUAH 89(5):209-211, September 1, 1975.

"Saline abortion and lupus erythematosus," by J. F.
Jewett. NEW ENGLAND JOURNAL OF MEDICINE
294(14):782-783, April 1, 1976.

"Study of the complications occurring in the interruption
of pregnancy on demand based on data from the obstetrical and gynecological ward in Ruse over a 10-year
period," by Kh. Durveniashki. AKUSHERSTVO I
GINEKOLOGIIA (Sofia) 15(2):126-130, 1976.

"Termination of hypertensive pregnancies with intra-
amniotic urevert," by S. Roopnarinesingh. WEST
INDIAN MEDICAL JOURNAL 24(3):164-168,
September, 1975.

"Therapeutic abortion," (letter), by R. N. Ough.
CANADIAN MEDICAL ASSOCIATION JOURNAL
113(9):818-821, November 8, 1975.

"Therapeutic abortion and its aftermath," by M. Stone.
MIDWIFE, HEALTH VISITOR AND COMMUNITY
NURSE 11:335-338, October, 1975.

"Therapeutic abortion and its psychiatric implications:
the Canadian experience," by E. B. Greenglass.
CANADIAN MEDICAL ASSOCIATION JOURNAL
113:754-757, October 18, 1975.

"Therapeutic abortion in a midwestern city," by L.
Melamed. PSYCHOLOGICAL REPORTS 37(3 PT 2):
1143-1146, December, 1975.

"Therapeutic abortion--some psychiatric aspects," by F.
Shane. PSYCHIATRIC NURSING 17(2):11-13, March-
April, 1976.

"Therapeutic midtrimester abortion by the intra-uterine
administration of prostaglandins. Experience of
Groote Schuur Hospital, 1974-1975," by G. Sher.
SOUTH AFRICAN MEDICAL JOURNAL 50(30):1173-
1177, July 14, 1976.

"Vacuum aspiration at therapeutic abortion: effect of
Cu-IUD insertion at operation on post-operative blood
loss," by F. Solheim, et al. CONTRACEPTION 13(6):
707-713, 1976. (Bio. Abstrs. 1976, 40215)

"Water intoxication associated with oxytocin infusion,"
by A. J. Ahmad, et al. POSTGRADUATE MEDICAL

THERAPEUTIC ABORTION

JOURNAL 51(594):249-252, April, 1975.

"What therapeutic abortion?" by A. Bompiani.
L'OSSERVATORE ROMANO 15[419]9, April 8, 1976.

THREATENED ABORTION
"Application of a radioeceptorassay of human chorionic
gonadotropin in the diagnosis of early abortion," by
T. P. Rosal, et al. FERTILITY AND STERILITY
26(11):1105-1112, November, 1975.

"Application of radioimmunologic determination of placental
lactogen hormone to the prognosis of spontaneous
threatened abortion," by R. Hechtermans, et al.
JOURNAL DE GYNECOLOGIE, OBSTETRIQUE ET
BIOLOGIE DE LA REPORDUCTION 1(5 Suppl 2):331-
334, 1972.

"Are progestational agents indicated in threatened abortion?" NEDERLANDS TIJDSCHRIFT VOOR GENEES-
KUNDE 119(48):1904-1905, November 29, 1975.

"Are progestational agents indicated in threatened
abortion? (letter). by J. Wildschut. NEDERLANDS
TIJDSHRIFT VOOR GENEESKUNDE 120(7):296-297,
February 14, 1976.

"Association between maternal bleeding during gestation
and congenital anomalies in the offspring," by A. Ornay,
et al. AMERICAN JOURNAL OF OBSTETRICS AND
GYNECOLOGY 124(5):474-478, 1976. (Bio. Abstrs.
1976, 12921)

"Certain indicators of the functional state of fetoplacental
complex in pregnancy complicated by late toxemia and
threatened abortion," by M. I. Anisimova, et al.
VOPROSY OKHRANY MATERINSTVA DETSTVA 19(4):
62-66, April, 1974.

THREATENED ABORTION

"Certain problems of the pathogenesis, clinical course
and therapy of threatened abortion (to aid the
practicing physician)," by S. M. Bekker, et al.
VOPROSY OKHRANY MATERINSTVA I DETSTVA
20(7):73-79, July, 1975.

"Comparative studies on the cytohormonal and cytochemical exponents of estrogens-progesterone activity
in the vaginal lining epithelium in women with pregnancy
complications. I. Threatened abortion," by J.
Dudkiewicz. GINEKOLOGIA POLASKA 46(11):1133-
1146, November, 1975.

"Correlation of the diagnostic value of vaginal cytology
and estimation of total urinary oestrogens in threatened
pregnancies," by I. Misinger, et al. CESKOSLOVENSKA
GYNEKOLOGIE 40(7):512-514, August, 1975.

"The diagnosis and treatment of threatened miscarriage,"
by B. Faris. AUSTRALASIAN NURSES JOURNAL
4:7, October, 1975.

"Diagnosis, treatment and prognosis of threatened abortion," by H. Wilken, et al. ZENTRALBLATT FUR
GYNAEKOLOGIE 98(10):577-586, 1976.

"Diagnostic examination methods in threatened pregnancy.
Panel discussion." ARCHIV FUR GYNAEKOLOGIE
219(1-4):399 passim, November 18, 1975.

"Endocrine assessment of threatened abortion," (proceedings), by R. E. Rewell. JOURNAL OF CLINICAL
PATHOLOGY 28(9):757, September, 1975.

"Establishment of prognosis in threatened abortion. Value
of the combined use of diagnostic ultrasound and quantitative determination of chorionic gonadotropin hormone,"
by S. Levi, et al. JOURNAL DE GYNECOLOGIE,
OBSTETRICUQ ET BIOLOGIE DE LA REPRODUCTION

2(2):155-160, March, 1973.

"Evaluation of the chorionic gonadotropin level, determined by the immunological method, in the prognosis of threatened abortion," by C. Croce, et al. MINERVA GINECOLOGIA 28(2):112-117, February, 1976.

"Evidence of serum HPL level for prognosis of threatening abortion," by P. Tykal, et al. ARCHIV FUR GYNAE- KOLOGIE 219(1-4):418-419, November 18, 1975.

"Fatal fulminating diabetes mellitus," by J. F. Jewett. NEW ENGLAND JOURNAL OF MEDICINE 294(23): 1289-1290, June 3, 1976.

"The fate of the child after threatened abortion," by H. J. Wallner. JOURNAL OF PERINATAL MEDICINE 2(1): 54-60, 1974.

"Functional colpocytology in threatened abortion and internal abortion. pp. 153-155," by N. Marotta, et al. In: Marchesi F, Cittadini E, ed. Fertilità e sterilità. Taormina, Minerva medica, 1974. WP 570 S679f 1973.

"Gravibinan in the treatment of threatened abortion," by J. Krzysiek, et al. GINEKOLOGIA POLASKA 47(3):321- 325, March, 1976.

"HCG, HPL, oestradiol, progesterone and AFP in serum in patients with threatened abortion," by J. Kunz, et al. BRITISH JOURNAL OF OBSTETRICS AND GYNE- COLOGY 83(8):640-644, August, 1976.

"Hormonal surveillance in the 1st trimester of pregnancy," by E. van Bogaert, et al. BRUXELLES-MEDICAL 55(2):71-78, February, 1975.

"Implications of pregnanediol titre pattern on the fate of

threatened abortion," by R. N. Ghosh. JOURNAL OF THE INDIAN MEDICAL ASSOCIATION 66(1):4-6, January 1, 1976.

"Interpretative analysis of 50 cases of tocolysis treated with isoxsuprine," by A. Tomassini, et al. MINERVA GINECOLOGIA 27(11):861-873, November, 1975.

"Management of threatened abortion." (editorial). BRITISH MEDICAL JOURNAL 1(6017):1034, May 1, 1976.

"Management of threatened abortion," (letter), by D. H. Darwish. BRITISH MEDICAL JOURNAL 1(6022): 1402, June 5, 1976.

"Measurements by ultrasonics of the gestation sac in threatened abortion," by S. Levi. JOURNAL DE GYNECOLOGIE, OBSTETRIQUE ET BIOLOGIE DE LA REPRODUCTION 5(3):359-365, April-May, 1976.

"Premature labor in the Palmanova Hospital in the period 1963-1973," by S. Garofalo, et al. MINERVA GINE-COLOGIA 28(2):118-123, February, 1976.

"The problem of prognostication in disturbed pregnancies," by E. Picha. WIENER KLINISCHE WOCHENSCHRIFT 87(20):702-704, October 31, 1975.

"Prognosis in threatened abortion: a comparison between predictions made by sonar urinary hormone assays and clinical judgement," by G. B. Duff. BRITISH JOURNAL OF OBSTETRICS AND GYNAECOLOGY 82(11):858-862, November, 1975.

"Prognostic and diagnostic value of bidimensional echo-graphy in threatened abortion," by N. Rodriguez. REVISTA CHILENA DE OBSTETRICIA Y GINECOLOGIA 38(5):228-239, 1973.

"Prognostic value of the serum HCG radioimmunoassay
in threatened abortion," by E. Guerresi, et al.
RIVISTA ITALIANA DI GINECOLOGIA 56(3):201-214,
1975.

"Radioimmunologic determination of placental lactogenic
hormone in threatened spontaneous abortion. Prognostic value compared with determination of chorionic
gonadotrophic hormone (HCG)," by R. Hechtermans,
et al. JOURNAL DE GYNECOLOGIE, OBSTETRIQUE
ET BIOLOGIE DE LA REPRODUCTION 2(1):53-62,
January-February, 1973.

"Radioimmunological study of human chorionic gonadotropin in cases of abortion," by G. Castellari, et al.
MINERVA GINECOLOGIA 27(9):717-721, September,
1975.

"Repeated abortion. pp. 213-218," by C. Serrao. In:
Marchesi F, Cittadini E, ed. Fertilità e sterilità.
Taormina, Minerva medica, 1974. WP 570 S679f
1973.

"Significance of placenta lactogen and placenta isoenzyme of alkaline phosphatase in the diagnosis of
threatened gravidity," by J. Sedlak, et al. CASOPIS
LEKARU CESKYCH 115(2-3):79-81, January 23, 1976.

"Sonar in the diagnosis of threatened abortion," by P. L.
Ceccarello, et al. MINERVA GINECOLOGIA 27(12):
983-987, December, 1975.

"Sonar in early abnormal pregnancy. pp. 273-279," by
P. L. Ceccarello, et al. In: Kazner E, et al., ed.
Ultrasonics in medicine. Amsterdam, Excerpta
Medica, 1975. W3 EX89 no.363 1975.

"Sudden infant death syndrome and subsequent pregnancy,"
by F. Mandell, et al. PEDIATRICS 56:774-776,

THREATENED ABORTION

November, 1975.

"Surgical treatment of the abortion at the Gynecologic-
Obstetrical Department of the General Hospital in
Zrenjanin in the period 1967-1974," by B. Nedejković,
et al. MEDICINSKI PREGLED 29(5-6):231-235, 1976.

"Treatment of threatened early abortion (6th-16th week
of pregnancy) of Th 1165a (Partusisten)," by H.
Bärmig, et al. ZENTRALBLATT FUR GYNAEKOL-
OGIE 98(13):792-794, 1976.

"Threatened or protected risky gravidity," by V. Kliment,
et al. CESKOSLOVENSKI GYNEKOLOGIE 41(1):30-31,
March, 1976.

"Treatment of threatened abortion in a serotonin antagonist. Clinico-statistical data," by M. Goisis, et al.
MINERVA GINECOLOGIA 27(9):773-778, September,
1975.

"Treatment of threatened and habitual abortions with
Turinal preparations," by H. Szucka-May, et al.
GINEKOLOGIA POLASKA 46(12):1265-1269, Decem-
ber, 1975.

"Use of E-aminocaproic acid for blocking uterine contractions in threatened, premature labor and late abortion,"
by A. Donchev. AKUSHERSTVO I GINEKOLOGIIA
(Sofia) 14(5):368-371, 1975.

"Value of intradermal hormone tests in the diagnosis of
causes of threatened abortion," by L. P. Peshev.
VOPROSY OKHRANY MATERINSTVA I DETSTVA
20(9):67-70, September, 1975.

TOXOPLASMAS
see: Complications

TRANSPLACENTAL HEMORRHAGE
 see: Complications

TRIPLOIDY
 "Pathomorphological changes in an early spontaneous
 abortus with triploidy," by V. P. Kulazenko, et al.
 HUMAN GENETICS 32(2):211-215, 1976. (Bio.
 Abstrs. 1976, 60586)

TURINAL
 "Treatment of threatened and habitual abortion with
 Turinal preparations," by H. Szucka-May, et al.
 GINEKOLOGIA POLASKA 46(12):1265-1269,
 December, 1975.

VETERINARY ABORTIONS
 see: Research

YOUTH
 see also: Laws and Legislation

 "Abortion attitudes among Catholic college students," by
 P. D. Bardis. ADOLESCENCE 10(39):433-441, Fall,
 1975.

 "Abortion in 1975: the psychiatric perspective and contra-
 ception in adolescence," by P. D. Barglow. JOGN;
 JOURNAL OF OBSTETRIC, GYNECOLOGIC AND
 NEONATAL NURSING 5:41-47, January-February, 1976.

 "Abortion in 1975: the psychiatric perspective, with a
 discussion of abortion and contraception in adolescence," by P. D. Barglow. JOGN; JOURNAL OF
 OBSTETRIC, GYNECOLOGIC AND NEONATAL
 NURSING 5(1):41-48, January-February, 1976.

 "Adolescent pregnancy and abortion," by D. D. Youngs,
 et al. MEDICAL CLINICS OF NORTH AMERICA
 59(6):1419-1427, November, 1975.

"Availability of abortion, sterilization, and other medical treatment for minor patients," by L. J. Dunn, Jr. UNIVERSITY OF MISSOURI AT KANSAS CITY LAW REVIEW 44:1-22, Fall, 1975.

"City setting and tolerance toward abortion: an exploratory study of attitudes of coeds," by J. P. Reed, et al. INTERNATIONAL JOURNAL OF SOCIOLOGY OF THE FAMILY 5, 1:103-110, Spring, 1975. (Socio. Abstrs. 1976, 76I2582)

"Domestic relations: minors and abortions--the requirements of parental consent." OKLAHOMA LAW REVIEW 29:145-155, Winter, 1976.

"Induced legal abortions of juveniles," by M. Farkas, et al. DEMOGRAFIA 17, 1:236-243, 1974. (Socio. Abstrs. 1976, 76I1399)

"Legal rights of minors to sex-related medical care," by E. W. Paul. COLUMBIA HUMAN RIGHTS LAW REVIEW 6:357-377, Fall-Winter, 1974-1975.

"Pregnancy and abortion in adolescence: a comparative legal survey and proposals for reform," by L. T. Lee, et al. COLUMBIA HUMAN RIGHTS LAW REVIEW 6:307-355, Fall-Winter, 1974-1975.

"Pregnancy and abortion in adolescence. Report of a WHO meeting." WORLD HEALTH ORGANIZATION TECHNICAL REPORT SERIES (583):1-27, 1975.

"Premarital sexual permissiveness and abortion: standards of college women," by A. M. Mirande, et al. PACIFIC SOCIOLOGICAL REVIEW 17, 4:485-503, October, 1974. (Socio. Abstrs. 1976, 76H8170)

"Teen-age Abortions Without Family Consent Hang in the Balance," by G. Dullea. THE NEW YORK TIMES

(M) June 22, 40:1, 1976.

"Teenagers: fertility control behavior and attitudes before and after abortion, childbearing or negative pregnancy test," by J. R. Evans, et al. FAMILY PLANNING PERSPECTIVES 8(4):192-200, July-August, 1976.

"Understanding adolescent pregnancy and abortion," by S. L. Hatcher. PRIMARY CARE; CLINICS IN OFFICE PRACTICE 3(3):407-425, September, 1976.

AUTHOR INDEX

Abse, L. , 99
Adamkiewicz, V. , 124
Adams, G. K. , 87
Adams, R. , 43
Agostini, R. , 54-55
Ahmad, A. J. , 123
Ahmad-Zadeh, C. , 119
Akhtae, H. , 86
Akkermans, J. P. , 51
Alberman, E. , 75
Allan, T. R. , 91
Alleva, F. R. , 43
Alumna, R. , 16
Alves, J. E. , 93
Amamo, Y. , 62
Amundson, M. , 59
Andersen, K. W. , 61
Anderson, G. G. , 29
Anderson, J. , 19
Andersson, K. E. , 114
Andorka, R. , 77
Andreev, D. , 90-91
Andress, C. E. , 109
Andriesse, R. , 93
Andriishin, Iu. T. , 87
Angelov, A. , 80
Anisimova, M. I. , 27
Annas, G. J. , 70
Arkes, H. , 38
Armstrong, J. , 90
Armstrong, P. J. , 117
Arnesen, E. , 109

Arney, W. R. , 108, 118
Asbury, E. E. , 111
Ashdawn-Sharp, P. , 9
Aso, T. , 51
Asplund, J. , 85
Atanasov, A. , 20-21
Augustin, J. , 27
Axe, K , 73

Bagley, C. , 84
Baird, D. , 61
Baird, M. A. , 79
Bajema, C. E. , 1
Baker, R. , 73
Balfour, R. P. , 51
Barclay, W. R. , 5
Bardis, P. D. , 7
Barglow, P. D. , 9
Bärmig, H. , 118
Basler, A. , 46
Bauman, K. E. , 101
Beckman, G. , 88
Becker, L. C. , 58
Bekker, S. M. , 27
Beckwith, B. , 45
Bendel, R. P. , 46
Bennett, M. J. , 91
Berger, G. S. , 71
Bergsjö, P. , 109
Bergström, S. , 1, 66
Bernardin, J. L. , 12, 22
Berstein, A. H. , 11

Berta, I., 39
Beyth, Y., 17
Black, M. M., 27
Block, S. K., 83
Blockwood, R., 124
Blair, M., 36
Blake, D. A., 88
Blasi, A. J., 101
Blum, M., 61, 63
Bodrova, V. V., 94
Bognar, Z., 79
Bokiniec, M., 16
Bolognese, R. J., 115
Bompiani, A., 124
Borko, E., 52
Borovik, R. V., 67
Bottini, E., 9
Boué, A., 28, 103, 113
Boué, J., 20, 88
Bourg, R., 100
Bourgeois, M., 62, 78, 123
Bowden, A., 100
Bowman, E., 24
Bracken, M. B., 52, 97
Brand, A., 62
Brandmeyer, G., 90
Brandt, M., 104
Brekke, B., 55
Brenner, W. E., 37, 45, 103
Briggs, K. A., 22, 25
Brody, B., 7
Brook, C., 6
Brown, J., 48
Brown, L. R., 11, 20
Bryant, M. D., Jr. 110
Bryner, J. H., 69
Bryn, R. M., 81
Buckley, J., 26
Bulic, M., 94
Bunson, M., 41, 51, 58, 76, 116, 120

Burckhardt-Tamm, E., 52
Burek, J. D., 123
Burkman, R. T., 65
Burnhill, M. S., 58
Butt, R., 11, 13
Bygdeman, M., 42, 62, 85-86, 96
Byrn, R., 33

Caffaratto, T. M., 57
Calder, A. A., 66
Camenisch, P. F., 9, 38
Cammelli, S., 102
Campana, A., 53
Caprile, G., 50
Carlson, J., 117
Carlton, L., 106
Carr, D. H., 52
Carrier, L. S., 7
Carruthers, G., 80
Carter, J. L., 107
Casey, R., 23, 110, 125
Caspi, E., 103
Castellari, G., 100
Castelli, J., 18, 68, 96, 120
Castro, A., 39
Castro, M. J., 120
Cates, W., Jr. 59
Cavadino, P., 59
Cavallaro, N. S., 39, 59, 99, 110-111
Ceccarello, P. L., 109, 110
Chalmers, G. A., 86
Chandy, T., 76
Charlton, L., 25
Chaudhury, R. H., 21
Chef, R., 18
Chernukha, E. A., 115, 121
Chi, I. C., 60-61
Cianci, S., 92

Cilensek, M., 22
Cittandini, E., 3
Clarity, J. F., 53
Clarke, C., 110
Clarke, P., 99
Clements, R. V., 79
Cobliner, W., 87
Cocks, D. P., 110
Coco, R., 26
Coffey, P. G., 24, 124
Cohen, M., 24
Coles, R. E., 44, 103-104
Colombo, Card. G., 60
Connolly, T. L., 26
Cook, J., 52
Cooke, T. Card., 24-25, 86
Cooper, R. M., 12
Coopland, A. T., 15
Corbett, T. H., 64
Corenblum, B., 50
Cormier, R., 117
Corson, S. L., 88
Craft, I., 30
Crandall, B. F., 93
Crawford, J. M. B., 10, 11
Creasman, W. T., 53
Creasy, M. R., 33, 37
Creighton, H., 71
Crisnic, I., 107
Croce, C., 48
Crowther, R. W., 10
Csapo, A. I., 77, 115
Cummings, J., 54
Curbelo, A. A., 32
Curtin, I., 83
Cutright, P., 110

Dakov, L., 99
Danon, A., 11
da Paz, A. C., 1
Darbois, Y., 88

Darwish, D. H., 74
Davidsen, P. C., 72
Davis, C. D., 33
Dawn, C. S., 77
Deedy, J., 28
De George, R., 72
De Giacomo, J., 1-2
Dellapenna, J. W., 82
de Leo, S., 55
Denes, M., 1, 87
Dennis 1
Dérobert, L., 101
Deskmukh, M. A., 49
Destro, R. A., 6
Devereux, G., 1
de Watteville, H., 57
Dewhurst, J. E., 83
Deyak, T. A., 43
Diamond, E., 41, 101
Dickens, B. M., 47
Diederick, P., 71
Dijkstra, R. G., 46-47
di Leo, S., 118
Dillon, T. F., 45
Dilovski, M., 67
Dingfelder, J. R., 65
Dix, C., 23
Dixon, G., 44
Doenicke, A., 15
Doerr, E., 7
Dolan, W. V., 13
Donaldson, F., 104
Donchev, A., 121
Donev, A., 111
Donovan, C. M. 91, 98
dos Santos Alves, J. E., 34
Dossland, S., 122
Dourlen-Rollier, A. M., 72
Dreger, M. D., 79
Driscoll, P. G., 57
Drogendijk, A. C., Jr. 19

Dubec, P., 10

Dudenhausen, R., 58

Duenhoelter, J. H., 32, 52

Duff, G. B., 95

Dugan, G., 24, 26, 35

Dullea, G., 114

Dunn, L. J., Jr. 21

Duranov, V. S., 96

Durham, P. J., 63

Durveniashki, Kh., 111

Dutta, R., 6

Duva Palacios, J., 106

Edleman, D. A., 31

Edstrom, K. G. B., 42, 101

Einarsson, S., 50

Eisinger, S. H., 105

El-Azzabi, S. S., 44

Ellis, W. A., 7

Emmanoulel, D. S., 101

Endre, N., 72

Engelhardt, H. T., Jr. 84

English, J., 6

Erb, R. E., 40

Eskes, T. A., 20

Evans, J. R., 114

Evans, T. N., 3

Everingham, D., 98

Exalto, N., 122

Faden, A., 45

Fallaci, O., 2

Farak, L. M., 21-22

Faris, B., 39

Farkas, M., 62

Farr, L., 59

Farza, B., 16

Fedrick, J., 19

Feichter, G. E., 32

Feishart, K., 10

Ferretti, F., 74

Ferris, P., 99

Fink, J., 69

Floyd, M. K., 2

Fogarty, J., 101-102

Fonty, B., 91

Foster, C., 116-117

Fraker, S., 79

Francesoni, D., 119

Francis, R. C., 113

Francke, U., 93

Fraser, I. S., 45

Frech, F., 104

Freda, V. J., 94

Freund, M. M., 54

Fritsche, U., 109

Fukalová, D., 21, 95

Funderburk, S. J., 112

Galan, G., 21

Galliani, G., 92-93

Ganes, T., 13

Gannon, F., 67

Gardner, H. A., 89

Gardner, R. F., 81

Garofalo, S., 93

Garrett, J. H., 51

Gasic, G. J., 5

Gaylor, A. N., 2

Gayton, W. F., 31

Geary, P. F., 113

Gebhard, P. H., 2

Gedan, S., 97

Gelev, I., 18, 21

Georgian, M., 35

Georgiev, S., 111

Gergely, G., 92

Geshev, G., 65, 110

Ghosh, R. N., 60

Gillon, R., 108

Giniger, H., 99

Gitlow, H. S., 78
Glenn, G. D., 6
Glenn, H. P., 35
Goisis, M., 118
Golbus, M. S., 49
Golditch, I. M., 63
Goldstein, T., 13
Gonzalez, A. F., Jr. 108
Goodhart, C. B., 6
Goodman, G., Jr. 46
Goraya, R., 88
Gorby, J. D., 123-124
Goujard, J., 109
Gould, D., 82
Green, K., 69, 89
Greendyke, R. M., 39
Greenfield, M., 11
Greenglass, E. R., 116
Greenhouse, L., 82
Greer, H.S., 98
Grigorov, S., 57
Gruber, W., 48
Guastella, G., 60
Gudakova, N. T., 118
Guerresi, E., 95
Gupta, I., 111
Gurtovoi, B. L., 106
Gustafson, D., 109
Gustavii, B., 41
Gutknecht, G. D., 114
Guzzetti, G., 37

Hafter, R., 79
Hall, G. A., 49
Halle, H., 69
Hamer, J., 38
Hardt, W., 120
Harlop, S., 27
Harrison, C. P., 2
Harrison, J. R., 31-32
Harrison, P., 14

Hatcher, S. L., 119
Hayashi, R. H., 121
Hechtermans, R., 19, 100
Hefnawi, F., 2
Hendricks, C. H., 29
Hennesee, J., 74
Henrion, J., 94
Henry-Suchet, J., 85
Herbenick, R. M., 102
Hern, W. M., 70
Herrera, M., 106
Herva, R., 70
Hewitt, J., 11
Hipkiss, R. A., 10
Hisanaga, S., 29
Hochman, M., 78
Hogan, J. E., 33
Hogue, C. J., 70, 73
Holzl, M., 80
Honore, L. H., 78
Houmont, M., 83
Howard-Jones, N., 55
Howe, M., 14
Hrabak, R., 37
Hsu, C., 46
Hughes, B. R., 11-12
Humber, J. M., 7
Hung, N. S., 14
Huntingford, P. J., 40

Iachello, L., 55
Iatsyshin, A. I., 87
Idahl, U., 126
Illsley, R., 98
Inderbiev, M. T., 109
Ingham, C., 18
Irani, K. R., 77
Irwin, C. F., 42

Jacobsson, L., 102, 126
Jadoul, P., 97

353

Jagtap, P., 53
James, J. D., 69-70
Jameson, S., 126
Jeffcott, L. B., 92
Jegede, S. A., 96
Jewelewicz, R., 83
Jewett, J. F., 50, 104
Johnstone, F. D., 27
Jones, D. E., 54
Jones, G. S., 73
Jouppila, P., 88-89
Jiménea-Vargas, J., 7
Ju, K. S., 36-37

Kahn, R. H., 2
Kahoe, R. D., 97
Kaplan, B. A., 2
Karavaev, Iu. D., 28
Karoly, M., 59
Karvounaris, P. A., 29
Kazeev, R. V., 86
Kazner, E., 2
Keele, A. F., 47
Kellett, J., 98
Kelly, S., 2
Kendrick, J. W., 23, 46, 118-119
Kettle, J., 90
Khamadaw, R. Kh., 83
Kihss, P., 114
Kim, H. J., 37
King, S. S., 13
Kirkbride, C. A., 63, 80
Kirsch, E. J., 84
Kirkwood, B. J., 99
Kiseleva, L. F., 106
Kivikoski, A., 107
Kleinebrecht, J., 28, 56
Kleinman, R. L., 2
Kliment, V., 117
Kluge, E. H. W., 3

Knorre, P., 63, 64
Knudtson, W. U., 23, 89
Koetsawany, S., 31
Kohler, H. G., 28
Kohn, G., 112
Kong, Y. C., 91
Kooistra, L. K., 115
Koren, Z., 95
Kosowski, 117-118
Koslowsky, M., 18-19
Kotásek, A., 20
Kress, R., 18
Krzysiek, J., 54
Kulazenko, V. P., 87
Kullander, S., 96
Kundsin, R. B., 80
Kunitz, G. J., 121
Kunz, J., 56
Kushnick, T., 59
Kuznetsova, V. I., 29

Lader, L., 14
Lahmann, H., 103
Lajos, K., 74
Lands, W. E., 2
Lang, R., 23
Lange, A. P., 115
Lanman, J. T., 45
Lanoy, A. M., 117
Laros, R. K., Jr. 87
Larrieu, H., 50
Larsson-Cohn, U., 14
Lau, I. F., 114
Laube, J., 25
Lauersen, N. H., 57, 63, 73-74, 74, 78, 107, 115
Lauritsen, J. G., 16, 39, 84, 108
Lazar, P., 45
Lazarini, H. J., 50
Leader, A., 61-62, 96

Lee, F., 26
Lee, L. T., 72, 92
Leeton, J., 90
Leon, J. J., 26
Levi, S., 47, 76
Lewis, A., 82
Lewis, R. A., 95
Linklater, J., 69
Lio, E., 81, 101
Llusia, J. B., 123
Lord, C., 8
Loshak, D., 22
Luker, K., 3
Lundvall, F., 71
Lure, I.V., 54
Lusvarghi, E., 52
Lüthje, D., 69
Lynch, R. N., 7
Lynn, F., 73, 84
Lyons, R. D., 33
Lysican, J., 109

Macaluso, C., 122
Mac Dougal, D., 8
Mace 3
Mahdwa, R. H. G., 45
Machol, L., 11
Mackenzie, I. Z., 30, 38, 49, 108
Maeda, T., 119
Maher, J., 82-83
Makkaveeva, M., 66
Mancari, C. R., 3
Mandell, F., 112
Mangiameli, S., 40
Manning, Card. T., 123
Manocha, S. L., 6
March, C. M., 65
Marchesi, F., 3
Marchin, J. R., 88
Margolis, J., 5

Marotta, N., 53
Marshall, W. C., 86
Martin, J. N., 122
Masiello, R., 83
Massouras, H. G., 20
Máthi, I., 27
Matthiessen, P. C., 9
Mayer, H.G., 118
Maynard, J., 55
McCann, J., 112
McHardy, A., 89
McIntyre, R., 96
McLachian, H. V., 79
McLaren, A., 8
McLaren, H. C., 105
McQueen, A., 115
Mead, P. B., 60
Medeiros, Card. H., 74
Mehta, A. C., 17
Melamed, L., 116
Metcalfe, J. B., 6
Meyer, A., 26
Miklos, M., 43-44, 84
Miller, E. R., 42
Mims, F. H., 64
Mirande, A. M., 93
Mishev, D., 64
Misinger, I., 36
Mizejewski, G. L., 15
Modly, T., 96
Moe, N., 66
Moghadam, S. S., 31
Moghissi, K. S., 3
Mohan, R. P., 9
Mohr, C., 13
Mokrousova, A., 25-26
Moller, B. R., 72
Mollica, F., 54
Molne, K., 109
Monnier, J. C., 76
Monrozies, M., 49

Monteiro, G., 14
Montoneri, C., 46
Moody, H., 13, 122
Moore, E. N., 79
Morin, P., 15
Moult, E., 73
Mowery, E., 25
Mukherjer, J. B., 77
Mulder, M., 70
Murstein, M.C., 3-4
Musso, G., 108
Musso, S., 107
Murphy, M., 98
Myrna, F., 12

Naftolin, F., 97
Narvaez, A. A., 82, 94
Naughton, J. M., 52
Nedejković, B., 113
Nesheim, B. I., 121
Newman, C., 91
Ng, K. H., 75
Nicora, G., 55
Niebyl, J. R., 64
Nielsen, F. H., 71
Nikberg, I. I., 43
Nishi, N., 115
Niswander, K. R., 79
Noonan, J., 120
Nowlan, A., 73
Nwaepke, C. C., 83
Nwoser, U. C., 81
Nygren, K. G., 91

Oakley, G. P., 121
Obel, E., 16, 70
O'Brien, J. R., 30
Oelsner, L., 46, 56, 68
O'Hare, J. A., 8, 84
Ohmura, G., 100
Olsen, P. P., 17

Omarov, M. A., 27
Orcel, L., 122
Orlova, V. G., 47
Ornoy, A., 20, 87
Osofsky, J., 3, 98
Osterhaven, M., 14
Ough, R. N., 116

Padawer, M. J., 48
Pakrashi, A., 5, 43, 104
Paker, J., 71
Panella, I., 47
Parmley, T. H., 90
Pasanku, T., 75, 122-123
Paul, E. W., 72-73
Payne, E. C., 85
Pelosi, M. A., 114
Perry, M. J., 12
Persianinov, L. S., 65, 76
Pescetto, G., 22
Peshev, L. P., 122
Peterson, I., 18
Phillip, J. I., 47, 53
Picha, E., 94
Pigarevskii, V. E., 43
Pilpel, H. F., 8
Pion, R. J., 48
Poletti, U., 82
Polgar, S., 21
Poradovský, K., 40
Potter, R. G., 32, 102
Pratt, L., 33
Prest, J., 85
Preston, E. J., 106-107
Prywes, R., 81
Puri, C. P., 107
Puri, S., 57
Pyle, N., 124

Quereux, C., 111-112

Rabineau, D., 68
Radzuweit, H., 51
Ragab, M. I., 42
Ramos Netto, M. D., 31
Reches, A., 104
Reed, G. E., 112
Reed, J. P., 29
Reed, R., 123
Rehzi, M., 59
Reinhold, R., 75
Remsberg, C., 105
Renaud, R., 102
Resta, G., 103
Rewell, R. E., 46
Rice, D., 13
Richardson, B., 80
Richardson, J. A., 44
Richardson, J. T., 101
Rider, R. V., 31
Roberts, C. J., 124-125
Roberts, C. S., 73
Roberts, S. V., 89
Robins, J., 70, 78, 105, 121
Robinson, M., 76
Robinson, P., 39
Rocha, F., 118
Rockefeller, J. D., III 82
Rodriguez, N., 95
Roht, L. H., 62
Roopnarinesingh, S., 114
Rosal, T. P., 19
Rosenbaum, D. E., 32, 33, 105-106
Rosner, F., 62
Rosoff, J. I., 92
Rozovsky, L. E., 72
Rozynkowa, D., 101
Rudd, N. L., 40
Ruppersberg, A., Jr. 13

Rushton, D. I., 17
Ryan, Arbp. D., 79

Safire, W., 113
Sainz, S. G., 12
Saito, N., 40-41
Salm, R., 99
Samochowiec, E., 48
Sanders, R. C., 119
Scanlan, A., 100
Schmidt, R., 37
Schneider, S. M., 102
Scheidler, J., 105
Scholten, P., 93
Schoysman, R., 90
Schrank, J., 116
Schulte, E. J., 33
Schwarz, R. H., 106
Schwinger, E., 8
Sedlák, J., 108
Segal, S. J., 2, 3
Segers, M. C., 10
Seibert, M. A., 58
Sele, V., 54, 72
Seller, M. J., 33
Selzer, R., 124
Serrao, C., 102
Servan-Schreiber, C., 108
Seski, J. C., 15
Sevyhart, B. A. D., 3
Shabecoff, P., 93-94
Shanahan, E., 52
Shane, F., 116
Shannon, W. V., 68
Shapiro, A. G., 66
Sharma, S. D., 65
Shaw, W. B., 24
Shepard, T. H., 3
Sher, G., 116
Shulman, J. J., 91
Shuster, A., 67, 68, 89

Siegel, M. H., 120
Sielicka, B., 9
Sievers, V. S., 35, 95
Simms, M., 13, 75
Singer, K., 97
Singh, N. P., 71
Singh, U., 44
Singh-Kahlon, D., 50
Sklar, J., 17
Skouby, S. O., 68
Slesinski, R., 36
Sloan, C. A., 31
Slozina, N. M., 68-69
Slunsky, R., 56-57, 71
Smith, A. M., 7
Smith, J. C., 32
Smith, R. E., 36, 73
Smith, R. G., 77
Smith, T., 35
Smothers, R., 17, 20,
   22, 75
Smythe, A. R., 43
Snegroff, S., 39
Sobran, M. J., Jr. 8
Solheim, F., 122
Solomon, K., 100
Solyn, R. J., 29
Somers, R. L., 60
Sönnichsen, N., 61
Sonsmith, M., 100
Southern, E. M., 74, 93
Southwick, T. P., 32
Soveri, P., 89
Spanio, P., 94
Spiegel, I., 85
Spilman, C. H., 48
Stalheim, O. H., 49
Staurousky, L. G., 44
Steel, D., 117
Stein, W. W., 44
Stein, Z., 110

Stencel, S., 12
Sternberger, R. S., 22
Stith, R., 126
Stoll, P., 96
Stone, M., 116
Stroh, G., 87-88, 103
Stubblefield, P. G., 30, 70
Stucki, D., 76
Su, I. H., 61
Sullivan, D., 10
Sullivan, J. F., 82
Sullivan, J. M., 64
Sundström, K., 6, 10
Susemihl, D., 65
Swan, G. S., 32
Swartz, D. P., 60
Swigar, M. E., 54
Swinhoe, J., 15
Szablya, H., 47
Szabo, E., 107
Szueka-May, H., 118

Taché, Y., 117
Talchin, M., 100
Taillemite, J. L., 28
Tanimura, T., 66-67
Targaszewska, A., 51
Tatic, C., 95
ten Cate, J. W., 30
Teo, W. D. H., 9
Thambu, J. A., 14
Thomas, A. K., 106
Thomascheci, G., 80
Thorman, D., 111
Tietze, C., 3-4, 38-39, 62,
   92, 119
Tomalin, C., 38
Tomassini, A., 64
Topciu, V., 15
Toppozada, M., 113-114,
Trammell, R. L., 117

Trichopoulos, D., 61
Trlin, A. D., 9
Trojan, A., 77
Trube-Becker, E., 69
Trumbull, R., 15, 103
Tsenghi, C., 28
Turcas, A., 51
Turner, J., 22, 25, 36,
  38, 125
Turpin, J. A., 75
Tykal, P., 48-49

Valder, W. A., 44
van Bogaert, E., 57
Vandelli, I., 35
Vandeplassche, M., 42
Van De Veer, D., 68
van Dreumel, A. A., 7
Vaughan, M. K., 51
Vecsey, G., 18
Venev, S., 14, 49
Vermouth, N. T., 64
Vernaschi, A., 38
Veropotuelian, P. M., 25
Visentin, C., 4
Voigt, R., 94
Vokaer, R., 4
von Mühlenfels, W., 72
Vujaković, N., 113
Vulkova, G., 37

Wade, F. C., 91
Waggoner, W.E., 76
Wahlberg, R. C., 126
Waldron, M., 47, 52, 82
Wall, J. M., 84
Walley, R., 99
Wallner, H. J., 50
Walsh, D., 92
Waltman, R., 43
Ward, R. H., 17

Warnock, D. H., 95
Waters, E. G., 20
Watkin, B., 99
Watt, M., 74
Weber, P. J., 23
Wehr, K., 36
Weinstein, L., 113
Weinstock, E., 11
Weir, E. K., 24
Weisheit, E., 4
Weiss, D. B., 18
Wenderlein, J. M., 98
Werdin, R. E., 90
Werner, R., 55
Wery, A., 94
Westley, R. J., 8
White, J., 11, 68
White, M., 124
Whitehead, S., 12
Wicker, T., 10
Wildschut, J., 19
Will, G. F., 40
Willdeck-Lund, G., 86
Williams, P., 106
Willoughby, W. F., 26
Wilken, H., 39-40
Wilson, R. W., 55
Winikoff, D., 92
Wiqvist, N., 96-97
Wisniewski, L., 69
Witherspoon, J. P., 59, 81
Wolters, G., 32
Woolf, L. A., 120
Wooten, J. T., 20
Wynn, R., 16
Wynnyczukova, H., 63, 115-
  116
Wyss, R., 70

Yamamoto, M., 28, 53
Yeager, H., 54

Ylikorkala, O., 5, 63, 66
Youngs, D. D., 16

Zakharov, A. M., 112
Zasowska, M. A. A., 55
Zdebski, Z., 111
Zilliacus, R., 75
Zrubek, H., 61
Zuspan, F. P., 105
Zwinger, A., 28